AMERICAN LIBRARY HISTORY

A Bibliography of Dissertations and Theses

Third revised edition

ARTHUR P. YOUNG

The Scarecrow Press, Inc.
Metuchen, N.J., & London
1988

This third, revised edition is based on Michael H. Harris' *A Guide to Research in American Library History* (Scarecrow, 1968; 2d edition, 1974).

Library of Congress Cataloging-in-Publication Data

Young, Arthur P.
  American library history: a bibliography of dissertations and theses / Arthur P. Young.
      p.   cm.
  Includes indexes.
  ISBN 0-8108-2138-9
  1. Library Science—Bibliography. 2. Libraries—United States—History—Bibliography. 3. Dissertations, Academic—United States—Bibliography. I. Title.
Z666.Y68 1988
016.02—dc19   88-10072

Copyright © 1988 by Arthur P. Young
Manufactured in the United States of America

To
Michael H. Harris
Seeker and Friend

TABLE OF CONTENTS

Preface ix

PART ONE - Guide to the Sources 1

PART TWO - Dissertations and Theses

I. Predecessors of the Public Library

    A. Private Libraries and Reading Tastes in Early America   19
    B. Thomas Bray and American Libraries   27
    C. Circulating, Social, Mercantile, and School District Libraries   30

II. Public Libraries

    A. General Studies   45
    B. Studies Arranged by State   63

III. College and University Libraries

    A. General Studies   151
    B. Studies Arranged by State   165

IV. Special Libraries

    A. Business and Industrial Libraries — 217
    B. Correctional Institution Libraries — 219
    C. Medical, Dental, Hospital Libraries — 220
    D. Museum and Historical Society Libraries — 224
    E. Governmental Libraries and Programs — 228
    F. Other Special Libraries — 236

V. School Libraries

    A. General Studies — 243
    B. Studies Arranged by State — 248

VI. State Libraries — 263

VII. Types of Library Service

    A. Cataloging and Classification — 275
    B. Reference — 283

VIII. Library Education

    A. General Studies — 287
    B. Studies Arranged by State — 291

IX. Library Associations — 297

X. Biographical Studies — 315

XI. Studies of the Literature — 353

XII. Censorship and Freedom of Information — 369

XIII. American Influence Abroad — 373

XIV. Miscellaneous Studies — 377

PART THREE - Papers and Reports

XV.	Public Libraries		
	A. General Studies		385
	B. Studies Arranged by State		386
XVI.	College and University Libraries		
	A. General Studies		399
	B. Studies Arranged by State		399
XVII.	Special Libraries		
	A. General Studies		401
	B. Studies Arranged by State		401
XVIII.	Library Associations, Commissions, Consortia		405
XIX.	Biographical Studies		409
XX.	Miscellaneous Studies		413

Author Index — 415

Subject Index — 431

PREFACE

THESES and dissertations record the culminating experience for students engaged in graduate education at the master's and doctoral level. Candidates for the doctoral degree, in particular, are expected to make an original contribution in their field. This subset of the scholarly communication system is often difficult to locate, especially master's theses, and frequently underutilized. The substantial body of thesis and dissertation literature on the subject of American library history produced over the past six decades is identified, organized and annotated. The present work extends and updates Michael H. Harris' pioneering bibliography, *A Guide to Research in American Library History*, published by Scarecrow Press in 1968 and 1974. Between 1974 and late 1986, the number of entries has grown from 653 to 1,174, an increase of 80 percent. Some 150 master's theses issued before 1974, many completed in academic departments other than library science, are now added to the corpus of accessible titles.

Like Gaul, this bibliography is divided into three sections. Part One is a selective introduction to the bibliographic sources which provide access to all types of literature relevant to the study of American library history. Part Two, the core section, is an annotated bibliography of 964 master's theses and doctoral dissertations. The final section, Part Three, contains a list of 210 unannotated citations to papers and reports. All theses, dissertations, papers and reports are indexed by author and subject. In addition to the expected topical categories, the subject index treats personal and institutional names found in the annotations and collates all items by state.

Research on American library history appearing in thesis and dissertation form constitutes a small proportion of all graduate-level studies in library science. Although the annual output in library history remains steady at

10-15 studies, some of the theses and dissertations are regularly published in journal or monographic form. Recent activity has shifted from biographical and single library studies to works on library associations at the state and national levels, thematic explorations such as censorship and the role of women, and bibliometric studies. For example, there are now 21 studies on the American Library Association, a solid foundation for a future interpretive history. Methodologies from the social sciences and the extensive use of archival sources are increasingly reflected in the research studies on library history.

Many individuals, some directly and others by example or encouragement, contributed to this project: Phyllis Dain, Donald G. Davis, Jr., Edward G. Holley, David Kaser, D.W. Krummel, and Wayne Wiegand. I am especially indebted to Boyd Rayward for facilitating access to material from the Graduate Library School, University of Chicago. Numerous citations would not be included without the magnificent resources in higher education held by the University of Illinois Library. Creative pursuit of titles by the interlibrary loan office, University of Rhode Island Library, was an indispensible asset. Special appreciation is extended to Vicki Burnett, Marie Rudd and Roberta Doran. Excellent secretarial service was rendered by Barbara George and Sheila Felice. Patricia Young assisted at many critical points along the way. The wonders of desktop publishing and sundry typographical fantasies were choreographed by Robert M. Gutchen.

Arthur P. Young
Kingston, Rhode Island

PART ONE

AMERICAN LIBRARY HISTORY: A GUIDE TO THE SOURCES

The literature of American library history is vast, scattered, and only partially recorded in the bibliographic sources. Although the challenge of locating sufficient and relevant material may intimidate the novice historian, there are a growing number of helpful guides and indexes to the primary and secondary literature which facilitate research. Items noted in this section cover general access tools as well as specific sources for the study of American librarianship. Many research projects will require the consultation of additional bibliographic sources related to the subject under review and the mining of unique archival resources. Comprehensiveness, invariably an elusive goal, is not claimed for the listing which follows.

Note: References to the *Journal of Library History* are abbreviated as *JLH*.

I. General Works

A. Guides

> Downs, Robert B. *American Library Resources: A Bibliographical Guide.* Chicago: American Library Association, 1951. *Supplement, 1950-1961; Supplement, 1961-1970; Supplement, 1971-1980.* For a cumulative index for 1870-1970, see Keller, Clara D. *American Library Resources: Cumulative Index, 1870-1970.* Chicago: American Library Association, 1981.

The main volume and supplements contain about 16,000 entries to bibliographical works which facilitate access to the nation's library holdings. Catalogs, checklists, surveys, and union catalogs are representative forms which are included. Basic arrangement is by subject, followed by author and topical index entries.

Lilley, Dorothy B. and Badough, Rose M. *Library and Information Science: A Guide to Information Sources.* Detroit: Gale, 1982.

Focuses on bibliographic sources in library and information science and relevant general works which cover the field. Entries are annotated. Access by author, title, and subject is furnished.

Ollé, James G. *Library History.* London and NY: K.G. Saur, 1979.

A solid handbook on the literature of library history with a distinctly British orientation.

Purcell, Gary R. and Schlachter, Gail A. *Reference Sources in Library and Information Services: A Guide to the Literature.* Santa Barbara, CA: ABC-Clio, 1984.

International coverage of 1,200 reference works by type of source in Part One, and subject-related titles in Part Two. Systematic cross-references. All entries are annotated. Author, title, and geographical indexes.

B. Encyclopedias and Handbooks

ALA World Encyclopedia of Library and Information Services. 2d ed. Robert Wedgeworth, ed. Chicago: American Library Association, 1986.

Second edition of a single-volume compendium of articles on all facets of library work. Several hundred biographical sketches are included.

Encyclopedia of Library and Information Sciences. Allen Kent, Harold Lancour and Jay E. Daily, eds. NY: Marcel Dekker, [1968-86]. v.1-41 (continuing).

Signed articles in an alphabetical arrangement which covers all aspects of librarianship. Articles vary in length and quality. Biographies of deceased librarians are valuable.

Stone, Elizabeth W. *American Library Development, 1600-1899.* NY: H.W. Wilson, 1977.

Chronological treatment of dates, events, and people significant in the development of American librarianship.

C. Critical Essays and Historiography

Colson, John C. "The Writing of American Library History, 1876-1976," *Library Trends* 25 (July 1976): 7-21.

Historiographical essay on the writings of American library history since Jesse Shera's seminal paper in 1945. Covers methodological approaches and assesses the quality of individual contributors.

Harris, Michael H. "Antiquarianism, Professional Piety, and Critical Scholarship in Recent American Library Historiography," *JLH* 13 (Winter 1978): 37-43.

Explores recent library historiography from three vantage points: methodological concerns; perspective; and professional issues. Passionate argument for the contributions of revisionist history.

Holley, Edward G. "The Past as Prologue: The Work of the Library Historian," *JLH* 12 (Spring 1977): 110-27.

Reflections on the Michael Harris-Phyllis Dain debate on the nature of public library development serve as the springboard for the author's skepticism regarding revisionist trends.

Kaser, David. "Advances in American Library History," *Advances in Librarianship* 8 (1978): 181-99. NY: Academic Press, 1978.

Concise, insightful exposition of research trends and historiographical issues.

Krzys, Richard. "Library Historiography," *Encyclopedia of Library and Information Science* 15: 294- 330. NY: Marcel Dekker, 1975.

A useful, if somewhat unbalanced, review of library historiography from earliest times to the 1930s.

Miksa, Francis L. "The Interpretation of American Public Library History." In Robbins-Carter, Jane, ed., *Public Librarianship: A Reader* (Littleton, CO: Libraries Unlimited, 1982): 73-90.

Examines the writings of four seminal authors who have shaped the historiography of public library development: Jesse Shera, Sidney Ditzion, Michael Harris, and Dee Garrison.

Shera, Jesse H. "The Literature of American Library History." In his *Knowing Books and Men; Knowing Computers Too* (Littleton, CO: Libraries Unlimited, 1973): 124-61.

Revised and expanded version of Shera's classic 1945 paper on the literature of American library history. In this essay, Shera evaluates the literature from 1850 to the present; traces the development of the research and writing of library history during the same period; discusses the obstacles which confront the library historian; and pinpoints research needs.

Shiflet, Orvin L. "Clio's Claim: The Role of Historical Research in Library and Information Research." *Library Trends* 32 (Spring 1984): 385-406.

Examines the purpose of library history research and its relationship to the broader research context of library and information science.

Stevens, Rolland E., ed. *Research Methods in Librarianship: Historical and Bibliographical Methods in Library Research.* Urbana, IL: Graduate School of Library Science, University of Illinois, 1971.

Eleven essays on the research methodology of bibliographical and historical studies are collected in this volume. See especially the essays by Haynes McMullen on primary sources, Edward G. Holley on textual criticism, and Ronald Hagler on research needs.

Winger, Howard W., ed. "American Library History: 1876-1976," *Library Trends* 25 (July 1976): 3-416.

A collection of papers on American library history subdivided into four sections: 1) context and historiography; 2) library profession; 3) bibliographic organization; and 4) user categories.

D. Reviews of the Current Literature

For two decades the *Journal of Library History*, published by the University of Texas Press, has printed invaluable reviews of the literature related to American library history.

Harris, Michael H. "The Year's Work in American Library History, 1967," *JLH* 3 (October 1968): 342-52; Harris, Michael H. "The Year's Work ...1968," *JLH* 5 (April 1970): 133-45; Harris, Michael H. "The Year's Work...1969-70," *JLH* 7 (January 1972): 33-49; Davis, Donald G., Jr. and Harris, Michael H. "Three Years' Work 1971-1973," *JLH* 9 (October 1974): 296-317; Davis, Donald G., Jr. and Michael H. Harris. "Two Years' Work...1974-1975," *JLH* 11 (October 1976): 276-96; Davis, Donald G., Jr. "The Year's Work...1976," *JLH* 13 (Spring 1978): 187-203; Wiegand, Wayne A. "The Literature of American Library History, 1977-1978," *JLH* 14 (Summer 1979): 319-48; Wiegand, Wayne A. "The Literature...1979-1980," *JLH* 17 (Summer 1982): 291-327; Wiegand, Wayne A. "The Literature ...1981-1982," *JLH* 19 (Summer 1984): 390-425; Wiegand, Wayne A. "The Literature of...1983-1984," *JLH* 21 (Fall 1986): 723-63.

E. Biography

Biography Index. NY: H.W. Wilson, 1947-. Quarterly and annual volumes.

Coverage extends to librarians, most easily accessed through the "Index to Professions and Occupations" which appears in each volume.

Dictionary of American Biography. NY: Scribner, 1928-37. 20v. and Index. Supplements 1-7. NY: Scribner, 1944-81.

Scholarly biographical portraits of more than 13,600 individuals in the basic set, including many librarians. Signed articles and references for further study.

Dictionary of American Library Biography. Bohdan S. Wynar, ed. Littleton, CO: Libraries Unlimited, 1978.

Biographical essays, ranging in length from 1,000 to 5,000 words, about 301 prominent librarians who died prior to June 30, 1976. Entries are scholarly and include references for further study.

Engelbarts, Rudolf. *Librarian Authors: A Bibliography.* Jefferson, NC: McFarland, 1981.

Short biographical vignettes of 108 European and American librarians from the 1600s to the present. Bibliographical sources are appended.

Harris, Michael H. "American Librarians as Authors: A Bibliography of Bibliographies," *Bulletin of Bibliography* 30 (October-December 1973): 143-46.

Furnishes citations to bibliographies of the works of more than 50 librarians.

Who's Who in Library and Information Services. Joel M. Lee, ed. Chicago: American Library Association, 1982.

Sixth edition of the most comprehensive biographical directory of American and Canadian librarians. Earlier editions were published in 1933, 1943, 1955, 1966, and 1970.

Wiegand, Wayne A., ed. *Leaders in American Academic Librarianship: 1925-1975.* Pittsburgh, PA: Beta Phi Mu, 1983.

Substantial, archival-based essays on fifteen prominent academic library leaders, including Charles Harvey Brown, Robert B. Downs, Blanche McCrum, Lawrence Clark Powell, Ralph Shaw, and Louis Round Wilson.

II. Indexes

A. General

America, History and Life: A Guide to Periodical Literature. Santa Barbara, CA: Clio Press, 1964-. Quarterly. Cumulated indexes, 1964-1983.

Commencing in 1974, issued in four parts: A) article abstracts and citations; B) book reviews; C) American history bibliography (articles, books, dissertations); D) annual index. Surveys more than 2,000 serial publications.

Arts & Humanities Citation Index. Philadelphia, PA: Institute for Scientific Information, 1978-. Two softcover issues (Jan./Apr., May/Aug.) and annual hardbound cumulative volume.

More than 1,300 scholarly journals are indexed in the citation linking format. Each issue contains journals list, citation index, permuterm (subject) index, source index, and institutional index.

Humanities Index. NY: H.W. Wilson, 1974-. Quarterly. Continues, in part, *Social Sciences and Humanities Index.* NY: H.W. Wilson, 1916-74.

Coverage of 300 English language titles in such fields as archaeology, area studies, history, language, literature, philosophy, and religion. Author and subject entries.

Readers' Guide to Periodical Literature. NY: H.W. Wilson, 1905-. Semi-monthly, annual cumulation.

The best known index to popular American periodicals. Approximately 200 periodicals are indexed in a dictionary arrangement with author and subject entries. For nineteenth century citations, one must consult *Poole's Index to Periodical Literature,* (Boston: Houghton Mifflin, 1891, 1887-1908) which encompasses the years 1802-1906. Author access is facilitated by C. Edward Wall, *Cumulative Author Index for Poole's Index to Periodical Literature, 1802-1906.* Ann Arbor, MI: Pierian Press, 1971.

Social Sciences Citation Index. Philadelphia: Institute for Scientific Information, 1973-. Two softcover issues (Jan./Apr., May/Aug.) and annual hardbound cumulative volume.

Covers approximately 2,000 scholarly journals in the social sciences and indexes citations listed in article references. Separate sections for citations, source, permuterm (subject) index, and institutional index.

Social Sciences Index. NY: H.W. Wilson, 1974-. Quarterly. Continues, in part, *Social Sciences and Humanities Index.* NY: H.W. Wilson, 1916-1974.

More than 300 English language journals in the areas of anthropology, area studies, economics, environmental science, psychology, public administration, and sociology are covered. Access is by author and subject entries.

Writings on American History. Washington, DC: American Historical Associations; Milwood, NY: Kraus-Thomson, 1904-. No volumes for 1904-05, 1941-47 issued.

Until 1961 covered articles and books pertaining to all facets of American history. The index volume covering the years 1902-40 provides excellent, expanded access to the items in the individual volumes. Beginning in 1962, *Writings* included only articles. Books are enumerated in *Writings on American History 1962-73, A Subject Bibliography of Books and Monographs.* White Plains, NY: Kraus International, 1985. 10v.

B. Librarianship

ABHA: Annual Bibliography of the History of the Printed Book and Libraries. Ed. by Hendrik D.L. Vervliet. The Hague: Martinus Nijhoff, 1970-. Annual.

Each volume contains about 3,000 entries selected from 2,000 international periodicals. Also includes monographs, dissertations, catalogs and other relevant items. One section deals with the history of libraries. Arranged by topic, with author and geographical indexes.

Barr, Larry, Jr., McMullen, Haynes, and Leach, Steven G. *Libraries in American Periodicals Before 1876: A Bibliography with Abstracts and an Index.* Jefferson, NC: McFarland, 1983.

Extends coverage to material appearing before Cannons' bibliography. The compilers identified 1,500 articles and reviews from 153 periodicals. Short articles are printed; longer articles are abstracted. Arrangement is by geographic area. A comprehensive index of authors, types of libraries, cities, librarians, and donors rounds out the volume.

Burton, Margaret and Vosburgh, Marion E. *A Bibliography of Librarianship.* London: The Library Association, 1934.

This volume is world-wide in coverage, and contains many items on American library history. Entries are briefly annotated, and author and subject indexes are provided.

Cannons, H.G.T. *Bibliography of Library Economy; A Classified Index to the Professional Periodical Literature in the English Language Relating to Library Economy, Printing, Methods of Publishing, Copyright, Bibliography, etc., from 1876 to 1920.* Chicago: American Library Association, 1927. For author access, consult Jordan, Anne H. and Jordan, Melbourne. *Cannons' Bibliography of Library Economy, 1876-1920: An Author Index.* Metuchen, NJ: Scarecrow Press, 1976.

Coverage of more than 60 American and British library periodicals, including those relevant to library history. Classified arrangement with no author index. Continued by *Library Literature*.

Danton, J. Periam. *Index to Festschriften in Librarianship.* With the assistance of Ottilia C. Anderson. New York: R.R. Bowker, 1970. Supplement (with Jane F. Pulis) for years 1967-75 published by K.G. Saur, 1979.

An index to approximately 4,800 articles in 426 festschriften published between 1864 and 1975. Authors, editors, and subjects are arranged in alphabetical sequence.

Dictionary Catalog of the Library of the School of Library Service, Columbia University. Boston: G.K. Hall, 1962. 7v. *First Supplement,* 1976. 4v.

This printed catalog is the most comprehensive retrospective bibliography of works pertaining to libraries and librarianship. Reproduces approximately 127,000 cards in the main set, and another 62,000 cards in the supplement. All types of material are included. Author, title and subject entries are arranged in a dictionary sequence.

Harris, Michael H. and Davis, Donald G., Jr. *American Library History: A Bibliography.* Austin: University of Texas Press, 1978.

A comprehensive, landmark bibliography of 3,260 items which includes monographs, articles, dissertations, and master's theses. All aspects of American library history are treated.

Library and Information Science Abstracts. London: The Library Association, 1950-. Bimonthly. Online as LISA.

Items are abstracted from more than 300 serials, with emphasis on British and European journals. Main arrangement is classified according to the Classification Research Group System, supplemented by author and subject indexes.

Library Literature. NY: H.W. Wilson, 1934-. Bimonthly. Online as a Wilsonline service.

Basic index to the literature of librarianship which includes books, periodicals, theses, and microforms. More than 200 journals are covered. Book review citations are furnished in a separate section.

III. Bibliographies

A. States

Alaska

Drazan, Joseph. "Alaskan Libraries in Print, 1905-1971," *JLH* 7 (January 1972): 50-60.

California

Kunkle, Hannah J. *Bibliography of the History of Libraries in California.* Tallahassee: Journal of Library History and School of Library Science, Florida State University, 1976.

Connecticut

Hart, Mary L. "A Bibliography of Connecticut Library History," *JLH* 7 (July 1972): 251-74.

Florida

Bergquist, Constance C. "A Bibliography of Florida Library History," *JLH* 5 (January 1970): 48-65.

Hawaii

Kittleson, David. "A Bibliography of Hawaii Library History," *JLH* 5 (October 1970): 341-55.

New York

Lopez, Manuel D. *Bibliography of the History of Libraries in New York State.* Tallahassee: Journal of Library History and School of Library Science, Florida State University, 1971.

Illinois

Dale, Doris C. *Bibliography of Illinois Library History.* Tallahassee: Journal of Library History and School of Library Science, Florida State University, 1976.

Minnesota

See South Carolina entry.

Mississippi

See South Carolina entry.

North Carolina

Carpenter, Ray; Bruce, Bea; and Oliver, Michele. "A Bibliography of North Carolina Library History," *JLH* 6 (July 1971): 212-64.

Ohio

Agriesti, Paul A. "A Bibliography of Ohio Library History," *JLH* 7 (April 1972): 157-88.

Pennsylvania

Harris, Michael H. "Pennsylvania Library History: A Bibliography," *Pennsylvania Library Association Bulletin* 25 (1970): 19-28.

South Carolina

Wilkins, Barratt. *A Bibliography of South Carolina Library History*; Halsell, Willie. *A Bibliography of Mississippi Library History*; Kellen, James D. *A Bibliography of Minnesota Library History.* Combined issue. Tallahassee: Journal of Library History and School of Library Science, Florida State University, 1976.

Texas

Skinner, Aubrey E., ed. *Texas Library History.* Phoenix, AZ: Oryx Press, 1983.

Virginia

Gillespie, David and Harris, Michael H. "A Bibliography of Virginia Library History," *JLH* 6 (January 1971): 72-90.

Wisconsin

Schwartz, Philip J. "A Bibliography of Wisconsin Library History," *JLH* 11 (April 1976): 87-166.

B. Special Topics

Bach, Harry. *Bibliographical Essay on the History of Scholarly Libraries in the United States, 1800 to the Present.* University of Illinois Graduate School of Library Science, *Occasional Paper,* No. 54, 1959. 24p.

Critical evaluation of 134 studies dealing with college and university libraries which appeared prior to 1959.

Correll, Laraine. "American Theatre Libraries: Sources of Information," *JLH* 7 (July 1972): 197-207.

Outlines the development of theatre libraries, and concludes with a four-part bibliography on the literature of theatre libraries.

Gormley, Dennis M. "A Bibliographic Essay of Western Library Architecture to the Mid-Twentieth Century," *JLH* 9 (January 1974): 4-24.

Evaluative essay on the western library architectural tradition, with a brief mention of the American scene.

Jackson, Sidney L. "Materials for Teaching Library History in the U.S.A.," *Journal of Education for Librarianship* 12 (Winter 1972): 178-92.

Special emphasis on materials useful to the teacher of library history.

Oehlerts, Donald E. "Sources for the Study of American Library Architecture," *JLH* 11 (January 1976): 68-78.

Identifies archival collections and secondary literature relevant to the history of American library architecture.

Stewart, Nathaniel. "Sources for the Study of American College Library History, 1800-1876," *Library Quarterly* 13 (July 1943): 227-31.

Lists primary and secondary sources of information on the development of college libraries from 1800 to 1876, and describes various research approaches.

Thompson, Donald E. "A History of Library Architecture: A Bibliographical Essay," *JLH* 4 (April 1969): 133-41.

One section of this critical essay deals with American libraries.

Tucker, John M. *Articles on Library Instruction in Colleges and Universities, 1876-1932.* University of Illinois, Graduate School of Library Science, *Occasional Paper*, No. 143, 1980. 45p.

An annotated bibliography of 121 articles culled from three sources. Author and institutional indexes are furnished.

Williams, Robert V. "Document Sources for the History of Federal Government Libraries." In Marshall, John D., *Approaches to Library History* (Tallahassee: Journal of Library History and School of Library Science, Florida State University, 1966): 61-80.

Reviews approaches to historical research on federal libraries, and includes an extensive bibliography of sources.

Winans, Robert B. *A Descriptive Checklist of Book Catalogues Separately Printed in America, 1693-1800.* Worcester, MA: American Antiquarian Society, 1981.

Comprehensive list of catalogues issued by booksellers, social libraries, auction houses, circulating libraries, college libraries, and publishers during the late seventeenth and eighteenth centuries.

Zubatsky, David S. *The History of American Colleges and Their Libraries in the Seventeenth and Eighteenth Centuries: A Bibliographical Essay.* University of Illinois, Graduate School of Library Science, *Occasional Paper,* No. 140, 1979. 66p.

Discusses the general literature on colonial higher education, and then follows with sections on Harvard, William and Mary, Yale, Princeton, Pennsylvania, Columbia, Brown, Rutgers and Dartmouth.

IV. Dissertations and Theses

Comprehensive Dissertation Index, 1861-1972. Ann Arbor, MI: Xerox University Microfilms, 1973. 37v. Ten-year cumulation, 1973-1982, published in 1984.

All U.S. dissertations arranged by key-word generated indexes of titles and an author index.

Dissertation Abstracts International. Ann Arbor, MI: Xerox University Microfilms, 1938-. Monthly.

Collection of abstracts of doctoral dissertations completed at 375 cooperating universities. Appears in two separate sections: (A) Humanities and Social Sciences; and (B) Sciences and Engineering.

Magnotti, Shirley. *Master's Theses in Library Science, 1960-1969.* Troy, NY: Whitson, 1975. Supplements for 1970-1974 and 1974-1979 published in 1976 and 1982, respectively.

These volumes list approximately 4,000 master's theses and research reports from about 30 accredited library schools. Author and subject access.

Schlachter, Gail A. and Thomison, Dennis. *Library Science Dissertations, 1925-1972: An Annotated Bibliography.* Littleton, CO: Libraries Unlimited, 1974. Supplement for the period 1973-1981 published in 1982.

A chronologically arranged, annotated listing of approximately 1,600 dissertations related to the field of library science. Access to the main section is by author and subject.

V. Statistical Sources

Statistical data, often essential to library research, may be found in such sources as annual and special reports of libraries, the publications of various government agencies, and the research literature. To sample the possibilities, consult Purcell and Schlachter, *Reference Sources in Library and Information Services*; and Sheehy, Eugene P., ed. *Guide to Reference Books*. Chicago: American Library Association, 1986.

VI. Manuscript Resources

Brichford, Maynard. "Original Source Materials for the History of Librarianship," *JLH* 5 (April 1970): 177-81.

Analyzes the substantial amount of primary source materials relating to library history held by the archives at the University of Illinois Library.

Dale, Doris C., compiler. *A Directory of Oral History Tapes of Librarians in the United States and Canada*. Chicago: Library History Roundtable and American Library Association, 1986.

A detailed list of 205 oral history tapes available for research. Personal name and subject indexes are appended.

Guide to the American Library Association Archives, 2d ed. Maynard Brichford and Anne Gilliland, compilers. Chicago: American Library Association, 1987. 11p. 3 microfiche.

Comprehensive record series description and subject index to the archives of the American Library Association, located at the University of Illinois Library.

National Catalog of Sources for the History of Librarianship. [Maynard Brichford, compiler]. Chicago: American Library Association, 1982. 7p., 3 microfiche.

Extensive listing of archival collections throughout the nation relevant to the study of library history. Useful introductory essay by Marion Casey.

National Union Catalog of Manuscript Collections. 1959/61-. Hamden, CT: Shoe String Press, 1962-. Annual.

Furnishes description and location of manuscript collections throughout the nation reported to the Library of Congress. Includes oral history transcripts and sound recordings.

Woods, Bill M. "Library Association Archives and Library History." In *Approaches to Library History,* p. 49-60.

Indicates the types of library association records which are useful to the historian, and provides location and details on the archives of 13 major American library associations.

Yates, Barbara. "The Joseph L. Wheeler Papers." *JLH* 8 (April 1973): 96-98.

Describes the Wheeler papers and assesses their significance to library historians. Wheeler, a long-time director of the Enoch Pratt Library, Baltimore, was also a major library consultant. His papers reside at the School of Library Science, Florida State University.

VII. Research in Progress

"Research Record," *Journal of Education for Library and Information Science.*

Quarterly list of doctoral dissertation research in progress.

PART TWO

BIBLIOGRAPHY OF DISSERTATIONS AND THESES

I. PREDECESSORS OF THE PUBLIC LIBRARY

A. Private Libraries and Reading Tastes in Early America

1   Anderson, Maurine T. "History of Colonial American Libraries, 1607-1776." Master's thesis, University of Missouri, 1966. 67p.

   A general history of colonial libraries with an emphasis on large private collections and the libraries of the colonial colleges.

2   Baer, Eleanor A. "Books, Newspapers, and Libraries, in Pioneer St. Louis (1808-1842)." Master's thesis, University of Wisconsin, 1961. Published: University of Kentucky Press, Kentucky Microcard Series B, Number 50. Summary published: *Missouri Historical Review* 56 (1961-62): 347-60.

   The author provides a historical overview of the availability of books and the nature of book ownership in St. Louis, 1808-1842. One of four chapters is devoted to a discussion of libraries in early St. Louis, and Appendix C lists the names of the persons who owned private libraries in early St. Louis and gives the size of each library.

3   Bradley, Ruth. "Books in the California Missions." Master's thesis, Columbia University, 1950. 42p.

The author traces the history of the book collections located in California Catholic missions beginning in 1769. The study begins with a brief survey of a number of mission libraries in California in 1950, and then examines the historical references to books in the missions.

4   Cantrell, Clyde H. "The Reading Habits of Antebellum Southerners." Doctoral dissertation, University of Illinois, 1960. 419p. UMI# 60-3886.

This study of the reading of thirteen antebellum southerners from Alabama, Georgia, North and South Carolina, and Mississippi is based upon diaries, journals, autobiographies, and letters. Contrary to the claims of earlier scholars, the author found that the subjects of this study were quite well read. Of the 1,157 titles identified, 741 were classed in the humanities, 300 in the social sciences, 65 in the sciences, and 51 miscellaneous. Few books written by New England literary figures were read—only about 11 percent of the total. This dissertation includes representative lists of books advertised in contemporary papers.

5   Coghlan, Jill M. "The Library of St. George Tucker." Master's thesis, College of William and Mary, 1973. 211p.

Bermuda-born St. George Tucker (1752-1827), prominent Virginia lawyer and judge, amassed a considerable personal library. Of the 1,564 items known to be in his collection, 488 survive which can be positively identified. His correspondence with printers and publishers documents how many volumes were acquired. Law books constitute one-third of the collection, with lesser holdings recorded in American history, geography, and poetry. A brief comparison of Tucker's library with the great collection acquired by Thomas Jefferson reveals that Jefferson was more eclectic and ambitious. Volumes owned by Tucker are listed in full bibliographic detail.

6   Crook, Miriam R. "Collections of Books and the Beginnings of Libraries in the Oregon Territory from the Great Migration to the End of the Frontier Period." Master's thesis, University of Washington, 1960. 174p.

The study covers library history in the Oregon Territory from 1842 to 1900 and describes the many types of libraries available on the frontier—circulating libraries, social libraries, private libraries, religious and academic libraries, and the territorial libraries of Oregon and Washington. Brief histories of over 25 libraries are included. The author found a wide assortment of materials available to people from every walk of life, from the mountain man to the university professor. The appendix contains numerous catalogs of libraries in the Territory.

7   Dugger, Harold H. "Reading Interests in Eastern and Central Missouri Prior to the Civil War." Master's thesis, University of Missouri, 1948.

See next entry.

8   Dugger, Harold H. "Reading Interests and the Book Trade in Frontier Missouri." Doctoral dissertation, University of Missouri, 1951. 395p. UMI# 1877.

The author found that books were widely available through general stores, book stores, auctions, and subscription agents. He determined that approximately one-third of the 400 estates studied (by means of selected probate records) contained books. The author concludes that reading interests in frontier Missouri (during the first half of the nineteenth century) differed little from those evidenced in the East.

9   Edgar, Walter B. "The Libraries of Colonial South Carolina." Doctoral dissertation, University of South Carolina, 1969. UMI# 72-12,032. Summary published: *South Carolina Historical Magazine* 72 (1971): 105-10, 174-78.

This study of the availability of books and the nature of book ownership in colonial South Carolina, 1670-1776, is based on an analysis of various records, especially county probate records. The author describes some 2,000 private libraries owned by South Carolinians. The libraries of Thomas Bray in South Carolina are also analyzed.

10 Evtushenko, Tatiana B. "The Library in Colonial Connecticut." Master's thesis, Trinity College, 1968. 208p.

Not examined.

11 Goudeau, John M. "Early Libraries in Louisiana: A Study of Creole Influence." Doctoral dissertation, Western Reserve University, 1965. 2 vols. UMI# 66-8005. Summary published: *Journal of Library History* 5 (1970): 5-19.

This study deals with the evolution of Creole culture and its influence on library development in early Louisiana. Six sections make up the work: 1) historical and cultural background; 2) private libraries in New Orleans; 3) plantation libraries; 4) public and semi-public libraries; 5) booksellers and printers in New Orleans; and 6) summary. A good deal of the information on private libraries was drawn from will inventories and a number of the more important lists are found in an appendix to Volume I. Volume II is devoted to source materials.

12 Harris, Michael H. "The Availability of Books and the Nature of Book Ownership on the Southern Indiana Frontier, 1800-1850." Doctoral dissertation, Indiana University, 1971. 307p. UMI# 71-25,345. Portions published: *American Journal of Legal History* 16 (1972): 239-51; *Proceedings* of the Fourth Library History Seminar. Tallahassee: Florida State University, 1972; *Library Quarterly* 42 (1972): 416-30; *Journal of Library History* 8 (1973): 124-32.

The first part of this study treats the outlets for books on the southern Indiana frontier; that is, bookstores, general stores, auctions, the church, etc. The second part describes some 500 private libraries owned by early Indiana residents. An analysis of these libraries shows that the pattern of book ownership was not startlingly different from that revealed by similar studies of book ownership on the earlier frontiers. Clearly, books were available in large numbers in early Indiana, and a sizeable portion of the estates inventoried in the southern part of the state contained books.

13 Hedbavny, Leopold, Jr. "Some Leisure-Time Organizations in New York City, 1830-1870: Clubs, Lyceums, and Libraries." Master's thesis, New York University, 1952. 76p.

Clubs, lyceums, and libraries flourished in New York City from 1830-1870. Cultural opportunities and leisure time all contributed to the growth of these social organizations. The transmission of foreign culture to American society and the benefit of personal contact with those of similar interests also influenced the spread of clubs and libraries. Large sums of money were invested in clubs and libraries, and membership often enhanced social standing. The informal atmosphere of the early period gave way to a more formal, impersonal organization following the Civil War.

14 Houlette, William D. "Plantation and Parish Libraries in the Old South." Doctoral dissertation, University of Iowa, 1933. 2 vols. Summary published: *Library Quarterly* 4 (1934): 588-609; *Ibid.* 24 (1954): 226-39.

An analysis of book ownership in the Old South with an emphasis on the larger libraries such as those of Jefferson, Madison, Byrd and other "first gentlemen." Volume two contains many of the sources upon which the study is based. It includes dozens of inventories of early book collections, lists of books for sale in the Old South, and library catalogs.

15 Keys, Thomas E. "Private and Semi-Private Libraries of the American Colonies." Master's thesis, University of Chicago,

1934. 89p. Summary published: *Library Quarterly* 7 (1938): 373-90.

This study is based on an analysis of data relating to book ownership found in early catalogs and inventories of early libraries as recorded in wills. Concludes that in New England the best libraries were owned by the clergy and government officials, while Virginia's libraries were owned largely by the cavalier planters. Notes the difference in reading interests between the groups—the Virginia planter was far more interested in secular reading than in the theological books favored in New England. The author also presents ideas on specific reading interests of the day, based on catalogs and will inventories.

16 Manning, James W. "Books in Early Oregon: 1821-1883." Master's thesis, University of Oregon, 1940. 187p.

The author finds that books were present in Oregon from its first settlement by trappers and traders in the early 19th century. Books were difficult to come by and the settlers selected only those that might help them in their frontier struggles—guidebooks, and books on medicine, law, agriculture, and religion. Manning discusses the private collections of early settlers and the early subscription and church library collections. A separate chapter is devoted to the history of the Oregon State Library from 1843 to 1883, and another deals with the Library Association of Portland.

17 Mayfield, Selby N. "Reading Interests in New Orleans, 1848-1942." Master's thesis, Tulane University, 1942. 93p.

The reading interests of New Orleans residents are analyzed by an evaluation of library catalogs produced in 1848 and 1942. Early plantation inventories, periodical literature, and libraries are treated. Between 1848 and 1942 reading interests shifted toward more local subjects, books on practical topics, and the fine arts. Declining interest was reported in religion, ancient history, law, and poetry.

18   Molnar, John E. "Publication and Retail Book Advertisements in the *Virginia Gazette*, 1736-1780." Doctoral dissertation, University of Michigan, 1978. 853p. UMI# 7822969.

Advertisements for Virigina imprints and imported retail titles which appeared in the middle eighteenth century are analyzed for subject, frequency, and periodicity. Virginia imprints were primarily utilitarian; the retail titles cover the entire range of subjects. Classical, contemporary, and controversial titles were available. Literate Virginians in colonial America were probably as well read as the English landed gentry.

19   Patrick, Walton R. "Literature in the Louisiana Plantation Home Prior to 1861: A Study in Literary Culture." Doctoral dissertation, Louisiana State University, 1937. 197p. Portions published: *Louisiana Historical Quarterly* 23 (1940): 131-40; *French-American Review* 1 (1948): 47-67.

The author's goal is to demonstrate the nature of the cultural life on Louisiana plantations. First, he examines the reading tastes of the Louisiana planters as they are reflected by booksellers' advertisements appearing in Louisiana newspapers and periodicals during the period covered. Second, he examines the contents of a number of plantation libraries. From this combined evidence the author draws conclusions relative to the literary culture of the plantation class.

20   Patterson, John M. "Private Libraries in Virginia in the Eighteenth Century." Master's thesis, University of Virginia, 1936. 97, [20]p.

This study examines 46 inventories of private libraries in four Virginia counties during the period 1715 to 1795. These inventories contain 3,879 volumes and 696 titles. Collections are evaluated in terms of size, categories of literature, and trends over time. A list of titles is included.

21   Read, Katherine T. "The Library of Robert Carter of Nomini Hall." Master's thesis, College of William and Mary, 1970. 132p.

This study examines the personal library of a Virginia aristocrat, Robert Carter (1728-1804) of Nomini Hall. A wealthy planter and member of Virginia legislature, Carter amassed a library of 1,500 volumes which contained the standard classics along with contemporary works of literature, religion, history, and law. An analysis of the library demonstrates that wealthy colonists emulated the reading patterns of their European counterparts. Carter's library, concludes the author, is a "valuable social document of the cultural state of the Virginia colony just prior to the Revolution." A catalog of titles in the library is appended.

22 Ribbens, Dennis N. "The Reading Interests of Thoreau, Hawthorne, and Lanier." Doctoral dissertation, University of Wisconsin, 1969. 527p. UMI# 70-3677.

The author prepared case studies of the reading of Thoreau, Hawthorne, and Lanier. The subject content of the books read by the three men were identified and categorized by dominant subject content and then evaluated. Each of the author's borrowings from these sources was also analyzed in the same way.

23 Shaw, Ralph R. "Engineering Books Available in America Prior to 1830." Master's thesis, Columbia University, 1931. 140p. Reprinted: New York Public Library, 1933.

Dozens of library catalogs and bibliographies were consulted to ascertain the availability of engineering books in America before 1830. The result is a list of 692 titles. Introductory sections elaborate on publishers, language, location of copies, and similarities to other types of literature.

24 Smith, Loren E. "The Library List of 1783: Being a Catalogue of Books, Composed and Arranged by James Madison, and others, and Recommended for the Use of Congress on January 24, 1783, with Notes and an Introduction." Doctoral dissertation, Claremont Graduate School and University Center, 1969. 258p. UMI# 69-14, 606.

On January 24, 1783, a committee of the Continental Congress, consisting of James Madison, Hugh Williamson, and Thomas Mitelin, recommended creation of a Congressional library. Although the list of 309 titles did not become the nucleus of a proposed library, the document deserves study as an intellectual statement. Madison, the principal compiler, selected works of reference and titles on history and political science. Collectively, these volumes offer insight into Madison the politician, the intellectual climate of the period, and the formative quest for a Congressional library.

25 Stanley, Clyde V. "The Library of William Byrd II of Westover." Master's thesis, University of Chicago, 1984. 161p.

William Byrd II (1674-1744) of Westover was an author, government official, and member of landed aristocracy in the Virginia colony. He amassed one of the largest private libraries in America, a collection of more than 3,500 volumes. The library's subject content, his references to the library, and Byrd's reading habits are analyzed. Byrd's library is compared to the collections of James Logan and Cotton Mather.

26 Wheeler, Joseph T. "Literary Culture in Colonial Maryland, 1700-1776." Doctoral dissertation, Brown University, 1938. Published: *Maryland Historical Magazine* 34 (1939): 111-37, 246-65; 35 (1940): 60-73, 337-58; 36 (1941): 184-201, 281-301; 37 (1942): 26-41, 291-310; 38 (1943): 37-55, 167-80, 273-76.

Chapters deal with books owned by colonial Marylanders, the development of reading tastes in Maryland, book sellers and circulating libraries, and the libraries of Thomas Bray in Maryland.

B. Thomas Bray and American Libraries

27 Gordon, Norma S. "Thomas Bray: A Study in Early Eighteenth-

Century Librarianship." Master's thesis, Catholic University of America, 1961. 105p.

This paper, which examines Bray as a bookman extraordinary, attempts to determine the background and source of his attitudes, the nature of his ideas on libraries and books, his choice of books, and his ideas about their classification. It briefly assesses the influence of the Bray libraries upon the American library movement. Appendices include: 1) a general catalog for a provincial library (Boston); 2) secular works included in a parochial library sent to Pamplico, New Jersey, in 1700; and 3) a catalog of a typical layman's library.

28 Laugher, Charles T. "The Beginnings of the Library in Colonial America: Dr. Thomas Bray and the Religious Societies, 1695-1795." Doctoral dissertation, Western Reserve University, 1963. 289p. Published: American Library Association, 1973.

This study is a history of the American libraries organized in the 17th and 18th centuries by Thomas Bray, the Society for the Propagation of the Gospel in Foreign Parts, and Dr. Bray's Associates. Bray was offered the Commissary to Maryland in 1695, but refused unless he could win support for his plan to establish libraries in each of the parishes in Maryland. Bray was responsible for the establishment of over 70 general, parochial, or layman's libraries. Bray's ideas were remarkably modern—he planned for public support and protection, he foresaw a subscription plan as the best method for making additions, and he stressed the principle of free access.

29 Livingston, Helen E. "Early American Schoolbooks and Libraries as Revealed in the Records of Thomas Bray and the Society for the Propagation of the Gospel in Foreign Parts." Master's thesis, University of California at Los Angeles, 1945. 128p.

The Reverend Thomas Bray (1656-1730), Anglican cleric, was America's first organizer of libraries on a broad scale. As part of his missionary work in the colonies, Bray dispatched 39 libraries to America. Several types were created. Parish libraries served the needs of religious instruction and lay man's libraries were prototypes of the public library. Special materials supported schools, Negroes, and Indians. Although primarily theological, Bray's benefaction ensured the transmission of European culture and affirmed the value of literacy for the general population.

30 Molz, Jean B. "The Reverend Thomas Bray, Planner of Libraries: A Study of an Early Benefactor of Maryland Libraries." Master's thesis, Drexel Institute of Technology, 1950. 41p.

The author traces the work of Bray in establishing in Maryland 29 parochial libraries for the clergy, one provincial library, and 11 lending libraries. These libraries, intended for the religious instruction of the clergy and laity, lasted only a few years after their founder's death in 1730. Three reasons are cited for their failure: 1) the specialized nature of the collections was of little interest to most of the colonists; 2) there was inadequate provision for continuing and strengthening the collections; and 3) the people had little interest in supporting the libraries.

31 Sahli, Marilyn S. "Thomas Bray and the Founding of Libraries in Maryland." Master's thesis, Western Reserve University, 1952. 35p.

This study traces the history of Thomas Bray's efforts to establish libraries in Maryland after 1698. Bray established nearly 30 libraries in Maryland. It is estimated that Bray sent over 34,000 books and tracts to America. The author describes many of the collections and indicates their use. She says the libraries failed for two basic reasons: 1) little provision was made to found new libraries, or to augment the collections after Bray's death; and 2) the collections were forced on the colony from without.

32 Searcy, Herbert L. "Parochial Libraries in the American Colonies." Doctoral dissertation, University of Illinois, 1963. 234p. UMI# 64-6146.

This study deals mainly with the library work of the Reverend Thomas Bray in the American colonies. Bray was concerned about the lack of capable men to serve as Anglican priests in the colonies. He felt that the establishment of libraries would help attract new recruits in addition to aiding the less qualified priests in their religious duties. In the years 1695-1699, Bray met extensive difficulties, the most serious of which were financial, but he persevered in his efforts until he had established nearly 40 parochial libraries containing 35,000 items. Bray envisioned his libraries as open to all readers, and the books he chose were theological and practical in nature. The libraries were not supported by the local authorities and finally disappeared.

33 Van Horne, John C. "'Pious Design': The American Correspondence of the Associates of Dr. Bray, 1731-1775." Doctoral dissertation, University of Virginia, 1979. UMI# 8002511.

The Associates of Dr. Bray, an Anglican philanthropic organization based in London, was founded by the Reverend Thomas Bray (1658-1730) in 1723. The Associates was concerned with the conversion and education of blacks in the American colonies; with the establishment of libraries in the colonies and in the British Isles; and with the founding of the colony of Georgia. Accompanying an extensive narrative are annotated descriptions of 200 previously unpublished documents.

C. Circulating, Social, Mercantile, and School District Libraries

34 Backus, Joyce. "A History of the San Francisco Mercantile Library Association." Master's thesis, University of California, 1931. 191p.

This study covers the history of the San Francisco Mercantile Library from its origination in 1853 to 1905, when it was merged with the Mechanics Institute. Regrettably, the collections of both libraries were destroyed by fire in 1906, before they could be combined. Started by a group of education-minded Californians, the Mercantile Library reached its high point in 1876, when it was adding some 2,000 volumes a year and had an annual circulation of 80,000. Cramped quarters, the depression of the latter 1870s, and competition from other libraries are some of the reasons cited for the library's rapid decline after 1876.

35 Boyd, William D., Jr. "Books for Young Businessmen: Mercantile Libraries in the United States, 1820-1865." Doctoral dissertation, Indiana University, 1975. 233p. UMI# 76-11, 358.

Mercantile libraries, established by young merchants' clerks for self-improvement, began in the 1820s. The catalogs of 26 mercantile libraries were examined to determine subject breadth of the collections and to ascertain the degree of similarity between collections. Typically, the libraries held general collections and only two percent of the holdings represented trade-related literature. The non-specialized nature of these libraries is discussed in terms of the founders' goals, educational ideas, and the cognate institution known as social libraries.

36 Brophy, Elaine D. "The History of the Libraries of Windsor, Connecticut." Master's thesis, Southern Connecticut State College, 1975. 117p.

A brief history of library development in small New England towns and the growth of Windsor, Connecticut introduce this study of the Windsor Public Library. Five libraries predated formation of the Windsor Library Association (1888): Union Library Company in Windsor (1774-1846); Poquonock Social Library (1828-1841); Library of the Sixth District School (1841); Windsor Book Club (1862-1864); and Library of the Windsor Congregational Church (1819-1900). Private control of the library retarded adequate support until 1971 when the town assumed fiscal responsibility. By that time the library held 54,509 volumes.

37 Burke, Betty L. "The Development of Libraries in Guilford,

Connecticut." Master's thesis, Southern Connecticut State College, 1959. 60p.

The author presents a brief history of Guilford and traces the development of libraries there dating from 1737, when the cities of Guilford, Killingworth, Saybrook and Lyme pooled their book resources and started the Four-Town Library, to 1959. She then examines six basic factors that seemed to influence library development in Guilford: 1) the librarian's concept; 2) the role of women; 3) changes in financial conditions; 4) the importance of local history materials; 5) concern with school libraries; and 6) changes in book selection policy.

38   Byrnes, Hazel W. "The Library Movement in the United States." Master's thesis, Columbia University, 1935. Published: *Franklin Lectures*, 1 (1935): 48-68.

This study is an episodic treatment of American library development from the colonial period to the 1930s. European antecedents, precursors of the public library, state libraries, school libraries, public libraries, and federal influences are briefly treated in the narrative. The library, which has served as a bastion of adult learning and free inquiry, will flourish and adapt to the future.

39   Carter, Merle. "The Young Men's Mercantile Library Association of Cincinnati." Master's thesis, Western Reserve University, 1951. 71p.

When this paper was written, the Young Men's Mercantile Library Association was 115 years old, one of the few mercantile libraries still in existence. The author first surveys the history of the mercantile library movement in America and then chronologically traces the library's history from its inception in 1835 to 1950. From an original 45 members and 700 books, it grew to over 800 members and 20,000 volumes in 1944. Numerous gifts and a relatively steady membership enabled the library to maintain its high standards.

40 Cross, Wilford O. "Ralph Waldo Emerson's Reading in the Boston Athenaeum." Master's thesis, Columbia University, 1930. 111p.

The author analyzes Emerson's reading and assesses the impact of reading on his intellectual development. Emphasis is on the books that Emerson checked out of the Boston Athenaeum from 1830 to 1840. During this time Emerson checked out over two books per month, and from 1840 to 1860 he charged out at least one book a month.

41 Davis, Elizabeth G. "John Bradford's Contributions to Printing and Libraries in Lexington, Kentucky, 1787-1800." Master's thesis, University of Kentucky, 1951. 89p.

This study deals with Bradford's efforts on behalf of publishing and education in Kentucky. A final chapter deals with his significant contributions to libraries in Lexington. Under his leadership, the Transylvania Seminary Library, established in 1784, gained considerable stature after near failure due to disinterest of the original directors. Out of this library grew the library of Translyvania University, which was for many years the largest and most famous library in the West. Bradford was also the initial force behind the establishment of the Lexington Library in 1795, one of the earliest social libraries in the western United States.

42 Day, Nancy J. "History and Administration of the Social Library of Bedford, New Hampshire." Master's thesis, University of Michigan, 1943.

Reported missing.

43 Dodge, Alice C. "Origins of the School District Library Movement in New York State." Master's thesis, University of Chicago, 1944. 101p.

The New York school district library law of 1835 incorporated the then forward-looking principle of tax support. The movement gained impetus from the new belief in education as a safeguard of democracy, the example of already existing social libraries, and the influence of a number of public-spirited leaders. James Wadsworth originated the idea of school district libraries, Dr. Jesse Torrey, Jr., gave it support, and Governor DeWitt Clinton presented the idea to the state legislature in 1825 and again in 1827. Once the libraries were established, most of them finally agreed on buying books from a series of 295 titles known as the *Harper's School District Library*. By 1850 there were nearly 1,500,000 volumes in the school district libraries of New York.

44 Fedder, Maxine B. "The Origin and Development of the Sunday School Library in America." Master's thesis, University of Chicago, 1951. 139p.

The 19th century saw a rebirth of religious fervor and an attempt at re-establishing the church in America. The author surveys the development of Sunday school libraries during this period, with special emphasis on the influence of the American Sunday School Union. Largely due to the Union's efforts, the Sunday school library was well established in America by 1830. By 1880 most Protestant churches in America had a library; after this high point, the Sunday school library met with a serious decline and by 1900 had faded from the picture. The author cites the following causes of its demise: 1) the growth of children's reading rooms in public libraries; 2) the poor administration of Sunday school libraries; and 3) a growing trend toward the secularization of Sunday school collections.

45 Flener, Jane G. "A History of Libraries in Tennessee Before the Civil War." Doctoral dissertation, Indiana University, 1963. 169p. UMI# 64-5126.

The author divides her paper into five major sections: 1) a brief history of Tennessee before the Civil War; 2) a history of over 25 social libraries in Tennessee before the Civil War; 3) history of over a dozen college libraries in Tennessee before 1860; 4) the Tennessee Historical Society Library and the Tennessee State

Library; and 5) a comparison of Tennessee libraries before the Civil War with libraries in other states (Kentucky, South Carolina, Ohio, Indiana, and Illinois). The author finds that for a state which had many sections not far removed from the frontier stage of development, libraries had a firm footing. Appendix A is a chronological list of social and special libraries in Tennessee before the Civil War.

46 Gaskill, Gordon A. "The Cultural Significance of the Mercantile Library Association of Boston." Master's thesis, Brown University, 1949. 136p.

The Mercantile Library Association of Boston was established by a group of young mercantile clerks in 1820, a time which exalted the common man and the diffusion of knowledge. Soon the merchants and other wealthy men supported the Association and its educational program of lectures and library service. Standard and classical works were acquired in greater numbers than utilitarian titles. Competition from the Boston Public Library sent the Association into an irreversible decline beginning in the 1850s. A separate chapter is devoted to the library and a list of lectures is appended.

47 Gray, Garland. "A History of the Franklin Society and Library Company of Lexington, Virginia." Master's thesis, Washington and Lee University, 1922. 50p.

The Franklin Society and Library Company was founded in 1800 by leading citizens of the Scottish-Irish community of Lexington, Virginia. Dedicated to intellectual improvement, the Franklin Society flourished for almost a century. Community support from neighboring schools, Washington College and the Virginia Military Institute, helped to ensure steady growth. John W. Davis served as librarian from 1830 to 1870. Dissolved in 1891, the library collection was deeded to Washington and Lee University that year.

48 Grimm, Dorothy F. "A History of the Library Company of

Philadelphia, 1731-1835." Doctoral dissertation, University of Pennsylvania, 1955. 367p. UMI# 55-1076.

Benjamin Franklin organized the first subscription library in America in 1731, and the Library Company of Philadelphia proved more durable than any of its followers. Nearly a thousand other subscription libraries rose and fell during the period covered, but the Library Company of Philadelphia endured through the Revolution and numerous other difficulties. The author discusses the development of the library's collections, its extensive influence on Philadelphia, and its evolution from a rather specific research library to what approximated a public library.

49 Gustafson, Richard E. "The Average Man's Library, 1830-1860." Master's thesis, Drake University, 1941. 126p.

A hypothetical average-man's library is constructed from the types of literature most frequently published to investigate social attitudes of the period 1830-1860. Observations are derived from a random sample of 1,560 titles drawn from Orville Roorbach's *Bibliotheca Americana*. Eleven categories, including religion, fiction, medicine, travel, and poetry, are examined. The books reveal themes of idealism, belief in man's perfectability, and pragmatic romanticism.

50 Hamner, Phyllis N. "The Ladies' Library Association of Michigan: A Curious Byway in Library History." Master's thesis, Western Reserve University, 1954. 43p.

This study, not intended as a history of individual libraries, traces the development and achievements of the Ladies' Library Association, 1851-1880. Over 44 libraries were established by the ladies during the 30 years. Organized by groups of local women, they were usually subscription libraries open to the public for a small fee. Appendix II contains excerpts illustrating the philosophy of service held by each of 26 of the Michigan Ladies' Library Associations. This study also contains a chronological list of the 44 libraries according to their dates of establishment.

51 Hatch, Orin W. "Lyceum to Library: A Chapter in the Cultural History of Houston." Master's thesis, University of Houston, 1964. Published: Texas Gulf Coast Historical Association, 1965.

The published volume traces the history of library development in Houston from 1837 to 1965. Most of the book is devoted to a history (1854-1904) of the Houston Lyceum, predecessor of the Houston Public Library.

52 Keep, Austin B. "The Library in Colonial New York." Doctoral dissertation, Columbia University, 1909. Published: *History of the New York Society Library, with an Introductory Chapter on Libraries in Colonial New York.* New York, Devinne Press, 1908. Reprinted: Burt Franklin, 1970. Reprinted: Gregg Press, 1972.

The published volume deals with the following subjects: 1) Bray Foundation Library at Trinity Parish; 2) the Sharpe Collection; 3) the Corporation Library, 1730-1776; 4) New York Society Library, 1754-1776; 5) Library of Kings College, 1757-1776; 6) Booksellers' circulating libraries, 1763-1776; and 7) the Union Library Society, 1771-1776.

53 Maestri, Helen L. "A History of the New Orleans Commercial Library Society, 1831-1842." Master's thesis, Tulane University, 1943. 81p.

After an initial chapter which presents brief histories of over a dozen nineteenth century New Orleans libraries, the author details the origins and development of the New Orleans Commercial Library Society, which was a social library founded in 1831. In 1842, the library was disbanded and its collection auctioned off, later to form a part of the first collection of the New Orleans Public Library founded in 1854. An analysis of the collection in 1838, based on a catalog published that year, is included.

54 Martin, Dorothy V. "A History of the Library Movement in Ohio

to 1850 with a Special Study of Cincinnati's Library Development." Master's thesis, Ohio State University, 1935. 83p.

The author traces library development in Ohio from its earliest beginnings in the latter part of the 18th century through 1950. This study is concerned mainly with social libraries and deals with private collections only when they evolved into social libraries. Library development in Cincinnati is described, beginning with the first efforts to establish a social library in 1802 through 1850. Appendices list the libraries incorporated by the Ohio legislature through 1850.

55 Moore, Mary V. "Circulating Libraries in the Southeastern United States, 1762-1842: A Selected Study." Master's thesis, University of North Carolina, 1958. Published: University of Kentucky Press, Microcard Publications, Series B, Number 22.

The major portion of the paper is devoted to a history of circulating libraries in five major southeastern cities: Annapolis, Baltimore, Fredericksburg, Charleston, and Savannah. Most of the libraries were established by businessmen, mainly stationers, booksellers and printers, and were aimed at attracting additional business to their stores. They proved to be relatively successful ventures but were nearly always subsidiary to the owners' main business. The growing popularity of the novel in America is cited as a major reason for the growth of the circulating library, and the author links the circulating library with the development of the public library.

56 Musmann, Victoria K. "Women and the Founding of Social Libraries in California, 1859-1910." Doctoral dissertation, University of Southern California, 1982. 235p.

The role of women in the establishment of California social libraries was more significant than prior research has indicated. Women founded 59 out of the 93 social libraries (63 percent) which preceded the first public libraries during the period 1878 to 1910. In 18 California cities, the antecedent social library was established by the Women's Christian Temperance Union

(WCTU). Women sought to control and influence behavior by supporting libraries. The social ideology of clubwomen and WCTU members was similar to the disestablished ministers who attempted to exert conpensatory control by influencing mass reading tastes. Early female library founders shared the same goals as the pioneer library leaders.

57 O'Connor, Sister Mary V. "History of the Redwood Library and Athenaeum of Newport, Rhode Island." Master's thesis, Catholic University of America, 1956. 74p.

This paper traces the history of the Redwood Library from 1747 to 1950. It was founded with a £5,000 donation from Abraham Redwood, followed by a gift from Henry Collins of a piece of property on which to erect a building. The author describes the economic difficulties the Redwood Library faced and the impact of the Revolutionary and Civil wars on its development. After 1865, the library made consistent progress.

58 O'Rourke, Margherita M. "A History of the Cathedral Library." Master's thesis, Catholic University of America, 1952. 82p.

Traces the history of the Cathedral Free Circulating Library of New York City from its inception in 1887 to the date of its consolidation with the New York Public Library in 1904. By the time of consolidation, the library had amassed 50,000 volumes, circulated 300,000 items annually, established five branches, and qualified for state aid. The Cathedral Library Association, a support group and distributor of Catholic literature, is also examined. The consolidation was not supported by the church hierarchy.

59 Reilly, Pamela G. "Some Nineteenth-Century Predecessors of the Free Library of Philadelphia." Master's thesis, Drexel Institute of Technology, 1951. 53p.

After first describing library facilities in Philadelphia to 1800, the author analyzes six libraries considered predecessors of the

Free Library. They are the Athenaeum, the German Society Library, the Apprentices' Library, the Mercantile Library, the Library Company, and the Philadelphia City Institute Library. The aims of the libraries, their book collections, types of clientele, and special services are covered.

60 Richie, Joan F. "Railroad Reading Rooms and Libraries in Ohio, 1865-1900." Master's thesis, Kent State University, 1965. Published: Association of College and Research Libraries Microcard Number 149.

Examines the development and expansion of Ohio's railroad reading rooms and libraries from 1865 to 1900. The author discusses the origins, purposes, locations, longevity, and services of the railroad reading rooms, with special attention to the efforts of the YMCA and the vigorous activities of temperance groups in Ohio from 1865-1900. The considerable influence of John Henry Devereaux, railroad executive and financier, on the development of railroad reading rooms and libraries in Ohio is also discussed.

61 Robinson, Ruth W. "Four Community Subscription Libraries in Colonial Pennsylvania: Darby, Hatboro, Lancaster, and Newtown, 1743-1790." Doctoral dissertation, University of Pennsylvania, 1952. 291p. UMI# 12,159.

Traces the history of the four community subscription libraries in eighteenth-century Pennsylvania from the establishment of the Darby Library Company in 1743 until 1790. The study begins with a general discussion of the development of subscription libraries in America and the colonial background of the four communities, with a consideration of the people and events influential in the founding of libraries. The history of the four libraries is presented in chronological order: Darby, founded 1743; Union Library Company, founded 1755; Newtown Library Company, founded 1760; and Lancaster Library Company, founded 1769. The author finds that literature was the most popular reading material in the four libraries, modifying the concept of the utilitarian reading interests of the colonials.

62 Sabine, Julia E. "Antecedents of the Newark Public Library." Doctoral dissertation, University of Chicago, 1946. 169p.

The author is concerned with the factors that led to the establishment of the Newark Public Library in 1888. She analyzes the social and intellectual background of the Middle Atlantic States, with emphasis on New Jersey. The influence of the Newark Library Association from 1845 to 1888 is carefully traced. The author finds the following factors influential in the founding of the Newark Public Library: the precedent of subscription libraries; the urge for self-improvement; a demand for wholesome literature for young people; enabling legislation; and an expanding economy.

63 Shera, Jesse H. "Foundations of the Public Library: The Origins of the Public Library Movement in New England, 1629-1855." Doctoral dissertation, University of Chicago, 1944. Published: University of Chicago, 1949. Reprinted: Shoe String Press, 1965.

Traces the history of library development in New England to the establishment of the Boston Public Library and discusses the social, economic, and cultural factors that influenced this development. Extensive treatment is given to the development of social and circulating libraries in New England. A careful analysis is made of the causal factors responsible for public library development: national and local pride; historical scholarship and the urge for preservation; increasing concern with vocational problems; and the contribution of religion.

64 Spain, Frances L. "Libraries of South Carolina: Their Origins and Early History, 1700-1830." Doctoral dissertation, University of Chicago, 1944. 179p. Summary published: *Library Quarterly* 16 (1947): 28-42.

The author traces library development in South Carolina from 1700, when the state legislature passed its first library law, to 1830. The library societies of Charleston (1748), Georgetown (1800), and Beaufort (c. 1802) are among those extensively discussed. The author finds that these libraries served only limited groups; that they were established only in stable urbanized areas with refined societies and ample economic resources; and that there was a very close relationship between church, school, and library. An appendix includes a chronological table of library societies in South Carolina from 1700 to 1837.

65　Stark, Bruce. "Libraries, Education and Culture in Eighteenth Century Lebanon, Connecticut." Master's thesis, Southern Connecticut State College, 1977. 114p.

The educational and cultural milieu of eighteenth century Lebanon, Connecticut is examined in the first three chapters. Although Lebanon was a rural community, the town's elite formed the Philagrammatican Library in 1739, the third oldest proprietary library in New England. It fourished until 1792. Several chapters are devoted to an examination of personal libraries as revealed in the estate inventories of 432 men and 39 women. The average library contained 10.5 volumes and 74% of titles were religious. Larger libraries were owned by males and the college educated. Findings from this investigation are carefully related to other studies of larger, urban personal libraries.

66　Stiffler, Stuart A. "The Antecedents of the Public Library in the Western Reserve, 1800-1860." Master's thesis, Western Reserve University, 1957. 53p.

The author surveys library development in the Reserve in terms of the socio-economic environment and popular beliefs of the nineteenth century and their expression in reading and other literary activities. The first Cleveland library was organized in 1811, when 17 of the 45 residents of that city established a Library Association, and after that time many libraries rose and fell in the Reserve. The lack of organization structure, the increasing democratization of the social order, and recurrent financial crises are cited as factors in the demise of the social library. Appendix I is a list of libraries organized and incorporated in the Western Reserve, 1819-1850.

67 Tietjen, Louise M. "A History of the Libraries in Old Saybrook." Master's thesis, Southern Connecticut State College, 1975. 260p.

This study opens with an extended survey of the colonial context and history of Old Saybrook, Connecticut. Old Saybrook is considered by some historians to be the earliest Connecticut settlement. Saybrook's distinction as the first home of Yale University (1702-1716) occasioned the first library. In 1737 the Four Town Library (Old Lyme, Old Saybrook, Guilford, Killingsworth) was formed as a subscription library. The theological orientation and large geographical area of Four Town Library limited its usefulness to the point of extinction in the 1790s. By contrast, The Ladies Circulating Library, funded in 1852 by a voluntary organization, flourished with a recreational collection. This private library, in turn, became the Acton Library in 1874 and served Old Saybrook until 1965 when it became a publicly supported library.

68 Van Beynum, William J. "United to Buy Books, a History of the Book-Company of Durham; A Public Library, 1733-1865." Master's thesis, Southern Connecticut State College, 1961. 79p. Summary published: *Library History Seminar* No. 3. Edited by Martha Jane Zachert (Tallahassee: Journal of Library History, 1968): 73-97.

Founded on the 30th of October, 1733, the Book-Company of Durham is generally recognized as the first proprietary library established in New England. The author is unable to ascertain exactly what inspired the founding of the library, whether Franklin's example was responsible, whether an English model provided an influence, or whether it was simply a spontaneous growth. The author assesses the value of the library in the education climate of the community, and then discusses the book purchases made by the library over the 123 years of its existence. Catalogs of the library's holdings and the articles of the Book-Company are included in the Appendix. The author also includes a list of books sent by the Rev. Thomas Bray to the Rev. Ichabod Camp of Middleton, New England.

69 Welborn, Elizabeth C. "The Development of Libraries in South Carolina, 1830-1860." Master's thesis, George Peabody College for Teachers, 1956. 163p.

This study encompasses all types of libraries, both social and academic. The author devotes about one-third of her paper to a history of libraries in Charleston and then presents brief histories of some 30 libraries established outside of Charleston from 1830 to 1860. The author finds that the great majority of the 36 libraries in existence between 1830 and 1860 were social libraries. The next largest group were the academic libraries. Appendices include a "Chronological Table of Library Societies in South Carolina, 1700-1837," and "Libraries Founded Between 1830-1860."

70 Wilcox, Helen M. "School District Public Libraries - A Step in Popular Education in the Nineteenth Century with Emphasis on the Period from 1820-1850." Master's thesis, Drexel Institute of Technology, 1953. 56p.

The author divides her paper into five major sections: 1) cultural, economic, and social conditions; 2) development of the publishing industry from 1820 to 1850; 3) description of libraries already existing at that time; 4) analysis of the origin and evolution of school district libraries from 1820 to 1850; and 5) reasons for the final demise of the school district libraries. School district libraries were forced upon the populace rather than being a response to public demand. They failed for several reasons: the governmental unit was too small (over 11,000 districts in New York); there was a distinct lack of sound administration; and the financial base was too small. *Harper's School District Libraries Catalog*, 1853, is included as an appendix.

II. PUBLIC LIBRARIES

A. General Studies

71 Anders, Mary E. "The Contributions of the Carnegie Corporation and the General Education Board to Library Development in the Southeast." Master's thesis, University of North Carolina, 1950. 134p.

The southeastern states did not join the modern library movement until the beginning of the twentieth century due to the Civil War, low per capita income, and widespread illiteracy. Beginning in the 1890s, the Carnegie Corporation financed the erection of 174 academic and public library buildings, and supported library education, outreach programs, and consolidation projects. Another philanthropy, the General Education Board, awarded grants for library training, cooperative agreements such as the Joint University Libraries and the Atlanta University Center, collections, and buildings. The two foundations each bestowed about $6,000,000 to the area.

72 Anders, Mary E. "The Development of Public Library Services in the Southeastern States, 1895-1950." Doctoral dissertation, Columbia University, 1958. 290p. UMI# 58-2670.

The public library movement was slow in developing in the southeastern states. It was not until the last decade of the nineteenth century that any significant progress was made. During this period, the interest of women's clubs and professional leaders, along with generous Carnegie grants, led to the establishment of numerous free libraries in the Southeast. The author finds that the Southeast adopted county and regional libraries more readily than did the rest of the nation and that the greatest growth in library facilities took place after 1935. Financial capability was found to be the overriding factor in library development in the area.

73 Atkins, Eliza. "The Government and Administration of Public Library Service to Negroes in the South." Doctoral dissertation, University of Chicago, 1940. 173p.

This study is primarily concerned with an appraisal (1940) of the southern Negro in relation to public libraries. However, the author traces the history of library service to Negroes in the South. Almost no service was offered before 1900. After that time, the Negro was given limited privileges at the main library or a special Negro branch library was established. Louisville, Kentucky was a leader in early attempts at providing extensive service to Negro patrons.

74 Bell, Bernice L. "Integration in Public Library Service in Thirteen Southern States, 1954-1962." Master's thesis, Atlanta University, 1963. 134p.

Although this paper concerns itself mainly with the present status (1962) of library service to Negroes in the South, it also presents brief digests of the historical development of this service in the following states: Alabama, Arkansas, Florida, Georgia, Kentucky, Louisiana, Mississippi, North and South Carolina, Oklahoma, Tennessee, Texas, and Virginia.

75 Black, Dorothy M. "The Influence of Public Libraries as Revealed Through Biography and Autobiography." Master's thesis, University of Illinois, 1928. 150p.

The author surveyed 350 biographies and autobiographies to ascertain the influence of public libraries on the lives of individuals drawn from many vocations. American and British luminaries are included. Ninety-three cases are cited in detail. Libraries, concluded the author, had an "intimate relation to the mature individual's productiveness in his chosen field." An extensive bibliography of sources consulted is furnished.

76 Bobinski, George S. "Andrew Carnegie's Role in American Public Library Development." Doctoral dissertation, University of Michigan, 1966. UMI# 66-14492. Published: American Library Association, 1969.

Andrew Carnegie donated over $40,000,000 for the construction of some 1,600 public library buildings in the United States. Bobinski traces the history of the Carnegie philanthropy and assesses the impact of his gifts on the development of public libraries in the United States. Discusses grant applications, library architecture, reaction to the donations, and libraries which never materialized. Provides a list of communities which received Carnegie building grants.

77 Boyd, Maurice R. "The Effect of Censorship Attempts by Private Pressure Groups on Public Libraries, 1945-1957." Master's thesis, Kent State University, 1959. 69p.

The first two chapters briefly chronicle private pressure groups such as Boston's Watch and Ward Society and the New York Society for the Suppression of Vice. Variant forms of censorship are examined in three episodes during the early 1950s: 1) the unsuccessful attempt to label books on communism purchased by the San Antonio Public Library; 2) the successful attack on the Bartlesville (Oklahoma) Public Library for holding subversive literature, a case which resulted in the dismissal of a courageous librarian; and 3) the failed attempt by the *Boston Post* to force the Boston Public Library to label communist literature. Concludes with the various arguments for defending freedom of speech and press.

78 Braverman, Miriam R. "Public Library and the Young Adult: The Development of the Service and Its Philosphy in the New York Public Library, Cleveland Public Library, and Enoch Pratt Free

Library." Doctoral dissertation, Columbia University, 1974. 444p. UMI# 77-27850. Published: American Library Association, 1979.

The focus of this study is the development of young adult service in three large urban libraries during the period 1920-1960. Significant factors affecting service to young adults include the disjunction between social values and social reality, the inconsistency between librarians' humanistic approach and large numbers of minorities, the general hostility of adults toward young people, the amorphous character of the young adult population, and the failure to integrate non-print and print forms of communication. Two basic approaches, the cultural preoccupation with literature and the social emphasis on the environment, were identified in the three libraries.

79 Breish, Kenneth A. "Small Public Libraries in America, 1850-1890: The Invention and Evolution of a Building Type." (Vols. I, II). Doctoral dissertation, University of Michigan, 1982. 680p. UMI# 8304450.

Small public libraries constructed between 1850 and 1890 are evaluated in this historical study. A majority of the 400 libraries erected during this period were built in Massachusetts. The architects' quest for iconographic form tended to overshadow the librarians' concern for functional planning. This tension precipitated a series of intense debates between librarians and architects in the 1870s and 1880s. Ironically, the architecturally admired buildings of Henry Hobson Richardson fueled the controversy.

80 Carrier, Esther J. "Fiction in Public Libraries of the United States, 1896-1900." Doctoral dissertation, University of Michigan, 1960. UMI# 60-02513. Published: Scarecrow Press, 1965.

The author presents an analysis of the philosophy and policies American librarians held regarding fiction during the last quarter of the nineteenth century. Through the use of materials from the *Library Journal* and *Public Libraries*, plus contemporary reviews from a number of other magazines, the author is able to isolate points of contention and agreement. Carrier finds that no solution to the problem of fiction's place in the public library was arrived at during the period covered. Two points evoked consensus: that no immoral books should be presented and that libraries should make a serious attempt to raise the level of reading sophistication.

81 Clopine, John. "A History of Library Unions in the United States." Master's thesis, Catholic University of America, 1951. 183p. Published: Association of College and Research Libraries Microcard, Number 43.

Studies the history of library unions in the United States from the establishment of the first union in the Library of Congress in 1916 to 1955. The author finds that the library unions have existed only in limited geographical areas. No locals had appeared in the far West by 1955, while only one local (Atlanta) had appeared in the South. Most unions were established in the Great Lakes or Middle Atlantic states areas, and all but three of the unions developed in cities of 250,000 or more residents. The mortality rate among library unions was found to be very high.

82 Collier, Francis G. "A History of the American Public Library Movement Through 1880." Doctoral dissertation, Harvard University, 1953.

Traces public library history from the social library to state, county and school district libraries and, finally, to the local tax-supported public library. By 1880 over 200 public libraries had been established; Massachusetts had the largest number, followed by Illinois and Ohio. The author discusses the influence of three events in 1876: the founding of the American Library Association; the founding of the *American Library Journal*; and the publication of the influential report *Public Libraries in the United States of America: Their History, Condition, and Management*.

83 Davis, Faye C. "The Development of the Traveling Library." Master's thesis, East Texas State College, 1959. 68p.

The author devotes about a third of this study to a survey of the history of the traveling libraries, from their beginnings in Scotland in 1730 to 1959. As early as 1831, under the stimulus of the lyceum movement, the first "itinerating libraries" were proposed. These were followed by libraries housed on American ships, in hospitals and in lighthouses. In 1892, the first general American traveling libraries supported by public funds were authorized by the New York State Legislature. Subsequently, every state instituted traveling library systems. Federal support, through such programs as the Civilian Conservation Corps, the Works Progress Administration, and the Library Services Act was a major factor in this development.

84 Ditzion, Sidney H. "Arsenals of a Democratic Culture: A Social History of the American Public Library Movement in New England and the Middle Atlantic States from 1850 to 1900." Doctoral dissertation, Columbia University, 1945. Published: American Library Association, 1947.

Traces the growth of the public library in the East in relation to social, economic and political factors. Ditzion discusses the transition from social library pioneers, the influence of ideas such as democracy and humanitarianism, philanthropy, and the services offered by early public libraries.

85 Ditzion, Sidney H. "The Public Library Movement in the United States as It Was Influenced by the Needs of the Wage Earner; 1850-1900." Master's thesis, College of the City of New York, 1938. 155p.

The author discusses the development of public library services to readers of all kinds with special emphasis on the wage earner. He begins with an examination of the predecessors of the tax-supported free library, follows with a discussion of the origins of the tax-supported library, and concludes with the expansion of public library services as they related to the wage earners' interests. Ditzion cites five factors which were major influences in the development of the public library: philanthropy; the labor movement; the organized library profession; the expansion of the educational system resulting in an increased demand for books; and humanitarianism.

86 DuMont, Rosemary R. "The Large Urban Public Library As An Agency of Social Reform, 1890-1915." Doctoral dissertation, University of Pittsburgh, 1975. 201p. UMI# 76-5430. Published: Greenwood Press, 1977.

Beginning in the 1890s, the American urban public library faced new challenges. Industrialization accelerated, immigrants from Europe filled the cities, and social problems erupted. This study examines the extent to which urban public libraries promoted social control in the guise of community reform. Various programs and services which developed in response to new clientele are reviewed: branch libraries, adult services, work with children, and open-shelf collections. Education of the individual to achieve happiness and security was preferred over group action. Librarians' conservative approach was not fully successful due to the library's organizational marginality.

87 Eberhart, Lyle. "Concepts of the (American) Library's Role in Adult Education, 1926-1951." Master's thesis, University of Wisconsin, 1951. 45p.

The author finds that the 1920s gave birth to three basic functions of adult education in the library: direct service to individuals; clearing house for community adult education activities; and organized adult education classes. Despite this threefold purpose, the emphasis was on planned reading courses guided by readers' advisors. During the war years, librarians evidenced a new idealism in relation to adult education, a feeling that the public library could take the lead in guarding America's freedom. After the war, more emphasis was placed on the professional staff working with groups.

88 Garrison, Lora D. "Cultural Missionaries: A Study of American Public Library Leaders, 1876-1910." Doctoral dissertation, University of California-Irvine, 1973. 375p. UMI# 73-31432. Published: Free Press, 1979.

The socio-economic background and social ideals of 36 public library leaders are evaluated for the period 1876-1910. Special emphasis is devoted to the search for professionalization, the changing social objectives of the library, the role of librarians as educational reformers, and the effects of feminization upon librarianship. The controversy over "immoral" fiction is also examined. Female dominance of the library profession perpetuated the servile status of women and crippled the development of the library as a significant cultural institution.

89 Geller, Evelyn G. "Ideas and Ideology: The Freedom to Read in American Public Libraries, 1876-1939." Doctoral dissertation, Columbia University, 1980. 674p. UMI# 3222389. Published: Greenwood Press, 1984.

Freedom to read is explored from the perspective of the sociology of knowledge and the sociology of the professions. Censorship and freedom are viewed as components of professional culture, especially the assertion of autonomy. The study is divided into four major sections. Part I describes the movement for free libraries. Part II, "Missionaries of the Book: 1876-1900," examines early library development and the emergence of professional culture. Part III, "Structures of Ambivalence, 1900-1922," covers censorship as a professional ethic. Part IV, "From Secular to Sacred: 1923-1939," documents the rise of an ideology of freedom as a central tenet of libraries.

90 Green, Carolyn S. "Library Service to the Blind in the United States: Origins and Development to 1931." Master's thesis, University of Chicago, 1967. 106p.

The author traces the origins and development of library service to the blind from the initiation of the idea of embossed books to the establishment of national library service to the blind in 1931, when the Pratt-Smoot Bill was passed by Congress—a bill which authorized the manufacture and distribution of books for the blind.

91   Guyton, Theodore L. "Unionization of Public Librarians: A Theoretical Interpretation." Doctoral dissertation, University of California, Los Angeles, 1972. 332p. UMI# 73-10426. Published: American Library Association, 1975.

This study provides a theoretical interpretation of the development of library unionism in the public library sector from 1917 to the present. The pattern which emerges is summarized: 1) the degree of unionization among public librarians is relatively low; 2) unions predominate in large libraries and specific geographic regions; 3) economic and non-economic issues have been pursued by unions; and 4) there has not been a systematic national effort to organize librarians. Three environmental factors led to the promotion of unions: libraries with a high degree of employment concentration; favorable legislation; and local labor traditions.

92   Herdman, Margaret M. "The Public Library in Depression." Doctoral dissertation, University of Chicago, 1941. 116p. Summary published: *Library Quarterly* 13 (1943): 310-34.

This study, covering the period 1930-1935, provides a picture of how the public libraries weathered a great economic depression. Based on statistics gathered from some 150 American public libraries, this study points out the courses of action taken by libraries when they had to cut back their budgets in the face of increased work loads.

93   Hurwitz, Jack D. "The Public Library as 'People's University': An Analytical History of the Concept as a Part of the American Public Library Movement in the Late Nineteenth and Early Twentieth Centuries." Master's thesis, University of Chicago, 1974. 79p.

The concept of the public library as the "People's University" was the grand vision of the American public library movement from 1875 to 1920. Implicit in the concept was the notion that the tax-supported public library was the agency for "higher education." The concept was a powerful metaphor which energized the public library movement. By the 1920s, the public library realigned goals and the "People's University" disappeared from the pantheon of rationales.

94 James, Stephen E. "An Investigation of the Relationship Between Public Library Use Patterns and Local Economic Conditions in Twenty Urban Areas: 1960-1979." Doctoral dissertation, University of Wisconsin, 1983. 270p. UMI# 832175. Summary published: *Library Quarterly* 55 (July 1985): 255-72.

This study tests an axiom that libraries are used more heavily whenever citizens experience economic hardship. Data for the 20 cities found on the 1960 Consumer Price Index were used for the period 1960-1979. Three dependent variables (circulation, library cards in force, annual registrations), three independent variables (unemployment rate, inflation rate, discomfort index), and four extraneous variables (book collection size, total volumes added yearly, library personnel, total expenditures) were examined. No significant correlation was identified between the measures of library use and the measures of economic stringency.

95 Kittle, Arthur T. "Management Theories in Public Library Administration in the United States, 1925-1955." Doctoral dissertation, Columbia University, 1961. 289p. UMI# 613446.

The author analyzes the interrelationships between library administrative policy and the "human aspects" of management, and demonstrates the ways in which public library management has been influenced by general developments in management theory.

96 Klopfenstein, Martha J. "The American Library and Some of Its

Benefactors." Master's thesis, Western Reserve University, 1955. 83p.

The author examines the factors that stimulated individuals to give money for the establishment of libraries in America. Twenty philanthropists are discussed and motives such as patriotism, local pride, practicality, genuine interest, egotism, charity, religion, democracy, and humanitarianism are delineated. The study is chronological and deals with the following men: Robert Keayne, Ben Franklin, John Jacob Astor, Henry Barnard, Joshua Bates, Edward Everett, Abbott Lawrence, George Peabody, George Ticknor, Francis Wayland, Daniel Fiske, James Lenox, Enoch Pratt, John Crerar, Walter Newberry, Andrew Carnegie, John D. Rockefeller, John Sterling and Henry Folger.

97 Kramp, Robert S. "The Great Depression: Its Impact in Forty-Six Large American Public Libraries, An Inquiry Based on a Content Analysis of Published Writings of Their Directors." Doctoral dissertation, University of Michigan, 1975. 227p. UMI# 752966.

Content analysis was employed to determine the impact of the great depression on American public libraries from 1930 to 1940. Journal articles and annual reports constituted the major sources for study. Directors were more concerned with internal operations than services, discussed policy matters infrequently, and revealed few changes in attitudes.

98 Lee, Robert E. "The Educational Commitment of the American Public Library: 1833-1956." Doctoral dissertation, University of Chicago, 1963. Published: American Library Association, 1966.

Describes the evolution of the adult education commitment of the American public library with particular attention to the most prevalent interpretation of the library's educational services provided in each period discussed.

99 McCauley, Elfrieda B. "The New England Mill Girls: Feminine Influence in the Development of Public Libraries in New Eng-

land." Doctoral dissertation, Columbia University, 1971. 371p. UMI# 7417883. Portion published: *Wilson Library Bulletin* 51 (1977): 648-55.

The author analyzes the relationship between the rise of the New England textile industry and the establishment of libraries in New England. Focuses on this relationship as evidenced in ten New England towns from 1820-1860, and discusses at length the evolution of public libraries in each community.

100 Monroe, Margaret E. "The Evolving Conception of Adult Education in Three Public Libraries: 1920-1955." Doctoral dissertation, Columbia University, 1962. UMI# 65-07384. Published: Scarecrow Press, 1963.

After tracing the general history of adult education in American libraries 1920-1950, the author presents a historical analysis of the development of adult education activities in three particular libraries: the Kern County Free Library, the Enoch Pratt Free Library, and the New York Public Library.

101 Moss, James R. "A Historical Survey of Ultra-Right Pressure Groups: Their Effect on Public Library Policy, 1950-1967." Master's thesis, East Texas State University, 1968. 64p.

The purposes of this study are to: 1) show the existence of ultra-right pressure groups; 2) demonstrate how these groups affect public library policy in regard to "subversive literature"; and 3) inform the public librarian how to defeat censorship attacks by these groups. Groups considered are from the national and local levels. Only histories of the national groups are given, but individual incidents of censorship activities are provided from both levels.

102 Newell, Mary M. "The Development of Library Services to the Blind in the United States." Master's thesis, Southern Connecticut State College, 1966. 82p.

The first part of this study traces the development of service to the blind in American libraries with an emphasis on the public library.

103 Newman, William A. "Congress and the Public Library: Legislative Proposals and Action for Federal Assistance 1938-1956." Doctoral dissertation, Case Western Reserve University, 1980. 314p. UMI# 8021707.

This study of the U.S. Congress and its actions on federal library legislation is written from the viewpoint of Congressional motivations and perceptions. There were many reasons why federal aid to rural libraries did not pass Congress until 1956: concern over federal control; opposition to national funding of a local matter; doubt over public support; fear of a permanent program; concern that states would reduce tax support for libraries; and objection on economic grounds. Resolution of these concerns and evolution of a conception that the federal government should foster social change ensured passage in 1956.

104 Nourse, Louis M. "A Comparison of the Establishment and Growth of County Libraries in California and New Jersey As Influenced by Their Respective Legal, Geographical, and Administrative Differences." Master's thesis, Columbia University, 1931. 110p.

Studies factors in the development of the individual features of each system. The development of California's county library system is traced from the establishment of the State Library in 1850. New Jersey's county system is discussed from the founding of the New Jersey Library Commission in 1900. The author finds that in both states one or two individuals were responsible for the successful introduction of the county library system. In both systems there was great variation among state and county laws.

105 Oehlerts, Donald E. "The Development of American Public Library Architecture from 1850 to 1940." Doctoral dissertation, Indiana University, 1975. 250p. UMI# 7517029.

Examines the changes which occurred in the planning of large public library buildings between 1850 and 1940. Changes resulted from the enhanced place of the public library in American society, the advances in the architectural and library professions, the proliferation of library services, and the increased amount of public funds for construction. Certain principles evolved during this period: modular interiors; open shelves; rooms for special types and forms of materials. Concludes that New York architects Edward L. Tilton and Alfred M. Githens and librarian Joseph L. Wheeler made the seminal impact of the era, especially in their collaboration on the Enoch Pratt Free Library.

106   Olech, Jadwiga. "Public Library Service to Business, 1904-1964." Master's thesis, Southern Connecticut State College, 1967. 70p.

A history of service to business from 1904, when the Newark (New Jersey) Public Library introduced its services to business, to 1964. The author focuses on trends and developments as they are reflected in library literature from 1904-1964, and considers only service given to business by public libraries through their special business branches or departments.

107   Poll, Bernard. "Working People and Their Relationship to the American Public Library: History and Analysis." Master's thesis, University of Washington, 1953. 42p.

Evaluates the various theories of worker origins of the public library movement and reviews worker behavior toward use of the public library through the lens of three surveys. Rival hypotheses regarding the establishment of public libraries—social control imposed by philanthropists versus a grass roots "common will"—are identified. The writings of James Welland, Lowell Martin, Jesse Shera, Sidney Ditzion, Gwladys Spenser, and Lewis Steig are highlighted. Concludes that the working class did not participate significantly in the development of public libraries.

108   Purdy, Betsy A. "Famous Children's Libraries: A Survey of Five

Libraries Devoted Exclusively to Work with Children." Master's thesis, Pratt Institute, 1952. 51p.

This study is a history and survey of five children's libraries, only three of which are American— the Brownsville Children's Library, a branch of the Brooklyn Public Library; the Fitchburg Youth Library of Fitchburg, Massachusetts; and the Robert Bacon Memorial Library of Westbury, Long Island, New York.

109 Rouzer, Steven M. "The Great Books Movement in the American Public Library." Master's thesis, University of Chicago, 1984. 78p.

The Great Books program and its influence on the American public library from 1947 to 1967 is written from an historical and philosophical perspective. The program's loss of appeal and decline in the 1960s is discussed.

110 Savage, Alice L. "Access to Information: The Development of the American Public Library as a Social Institution." Doctoral dissertation, State University of New York at Buffalo, 1978. 216p. UMI# 7905315.

Traces the historical development of the American public library from colonial times to the present in order to assess changing methods of providing and disseminating information as they are influenced by social conditions. Discusses methods for facilitating and impeding access to information. Elitist and liberal approaches to dissemination are analyzed. Despite a largely popular approach, the public library has evolved into a minority institution used by opinion leaders.

111 Sloan, Roberta M. "The History of the Phonograph Record in the American Public Library, Its Origins and Growth Through 1949." Master's thesis, Western Reserve University, 1950. 53p.

The author has divided this study into four parts: 1) a survey of phonograph record history; 2) a short history of the development of music collections in the public library; 3) an analysis of the forces that brought the record into the library— such as women's clubs, music groups, and school teachers; and 4) a history of the phonograph record in libraries as illustrated by early record collections and their growth to 1949.

112 Speirs, Charles H. "The Effects of Political Censorship in the United States on Public Libraries and Librarians from 1945 to 1955." Master's thesis, Western Reserve University, 1957. 55p.

This study describes a crucial period in American history—the postwar years when the library faced a serious attack of political censorship. After the end of World War II, groups throughout the United States campaigned to remove and exclude all material that might be considered anti-American from public and school libraries. The author discusses those attempts and shows how librarians and organizations tried to deal with the situation.

113 Stevenson, Gerald M. "The Changing Concepts in Public Library Service as Evidenced by the Three Major Surveys: 1876, 1926, and 1950." Master's thesis, Kent State University, 1950. 87p.

Explores three seminal reports in the history of American librarianship: the 1876 report issued by the Bureau of Education; the 1926 report sponsored by the American Library Association; and the report of the Social Science Research Council/Carnegie Corporation released in 1950. The 1876 report, *Public Libraries in the United States of America*, compiled important statistical data and included chapters on library history and procedural matters. In contrast, the *Survey of Libraries in the United States* (1926) concentrated on techniques and administrative practices. The multivolume "Public Library Inquiry" (1950) reappraised the social objectives and services of public libraries.

114 Stibitz, Mildred T. "Relation of the Public Library to Workers' Education, 1918 to 1939." Master's thesis, Columbia University, 1949. 142p.

The author selected the period between the first and second

World Wars because that was the time when workers' education expanded rapidly and won the attention of adult educators and librarians. The major themes presented are: 1) the extent to which libraries attempted to serve the special needs of labor unions and workers' education classes; and 2) the specific programs and procedures developed by libraries to implement these services.

115   Thompson, Leone B. "Book Selection Policies and Practices in Public Libraries, 1876-1900." Master's thesis, Catholic University of America, 1953. 136p.

The literature of book selection in public libraries is recorded and summarized in this study of the formative years of American library development. Separate chapters address the issues of theory and philosophy, fiction, and the relation of the public library to the public schools. During this period, librarians espoused a variety of theories which centered on the value and demand approaches to selection. Differences were apparent over the relative emphasis placed upon the objectives of education, information, and recreation. No consensus was identified by the author.

116   Tracy, Warren F. "The Public Library and the Courts." Doctoral dissertation, University of Chicago, 1958. 203p.

Public library legislation and court decisions which interpret the legal aspects of the library as a public institution are the focus of this study. Chapters deal with the state, trusts, boards, funding, contracts, property, and statutes. Relevant court decisions are cited throughout the text.

117   Unger, Carol P. "The School-Housed Public Library, Revisited." Master's thesis, University of Chicago, 1975.

Not examined.

118 Wadsworth, Robert W. "Notes on the Development of Music Collections in American Public Libraries." Master's thesis, University of Chicago, 1943. 140p.

The first chapter offers a brief summary of the development of music collections in the United States. Subsequent chapters deal with the acquisition, preparation, and servicing of music materials.

119 Wannarka, Marjorie B. "Medical Collections in Public Libraries of the United States: A Historical Study." Master's thesis, University of Minnesota, 1967. 107p. Portion published: *Bulletin of the Medical Library Association* 56 (1968): 1-14.

Although medical libraries in public libraries represented a small percentage of the total number of medical collections, they played a significant role in the preservation of medical literature. The earliest medical collection was housed in the Boston Public Library (1852). By 1926, the number of medical libraries in public libraries reached a high of 28. The contributions of John Cotton Dana in Denver and George M. Gould, founder of the Medical Library Association (1898), are reviewed. Medical libraries in public libraries declined due to difficulties of administration, under utilization by the medical profession, and the expansion of hospital libraries.

120 Williams, Robert V. "Sources of the Variability in the Level of Public Library Development in the United States: A Comparative Analysis." Doctoral dissertation, University of Wisconsin, 1978. 251p. UMI# 7919832. Summary published: *Library Research* 2 (1980): 157-76.

The influence of nine characteristics (e.g. education, economic ability, industrial status, age composition) on public library development (e.g. staff, size of collection) were examined to determine the variables with the most explanatory power. All nine characteristics were significantly associated with public library development, with the median level of formal education of adults accounting for 56 percent of the explained variance.

Education, economic ability, and occupational prestige predicted 60 percent of the library development in the nation, four selected regions, and three size groupings.

B. Studies Arranged by State

ALABAMA

121   Fonville, Emma R. "A History of Public Library Service to Negroes in Bessemer, Alabama." Master's thesis, Atlanta University, 1962. 47p.

This paper presents a history of the development of library services to Negroes in Bessemer, Alabama, from its beginnings in 1950 to 1962. The author emphasizes the legal provisions for library service to Negroes. The Bessemer Public Library was established in 1907, but it was not until 1950 that service was extended to Negroes, and then only in a token fashion. In 1961, the Negro branch had only 3,774 volumes and was open only 20 hours per week. There were 18,982 Negroes living in Bessemer at that time.

122   Grayson, Bessie R. "The History of Public Library Service for Negroes in Montgomery, Alabama." Master's thesis, Atlanta University, 1965.

The first library in Montgomery was founded in 1899. It evolved into a public library that until 1948 served only the white population of the city. The first formal library service for Negroes was provided in 1942 by the Rev. Ralph O. Daly, a Negro who set up a very limited service in his church. This small library grew slowly into the Union Street Branch Library of the Montgomery Public Library, and it served the Negro population of Montgomery until 1960. In 1960 the collection contained 4,000 books and the number of registered borrowers numbered 4,283. In 1962 the Montgomery Public Library System was forced to integrate by a court order.

123 Levy, Roland G. "Certain Aspects of the Library Movement in the Southern Association of Colleges and Secondary Schools from 1929 to 1941." Master's thesis, University of Alabama, 1941. 66p.

Describes the cultural background of the library movement in Alabama including economic, religious and industrial factors. Documents growth patterns of library schools and high school libraries. High school libraries are examined in terms of regional standards for collections, staff, and services.

ALASKA

124 Mauseth, Barbara J. "A Brief History of the Ketchikan, Alaska Public Library, 1901-1956." Master's thesis, University of Washington, 1956. 34p.

The first library in Ketchikan, a town incorporated in 1900 with 500 residents, was the Ladies Library Club founded in 1901. This club was in essence a subscription library supported by the dues of 25 cents per month from each member. The Ladies slowly relinquished control and responsibility for the support of the library to the city fathers. By 1909 the city was financing a public reading room in conjunction with the Ladies' private-circulating library. In 1943 total municipal support was initiated.

125 Phelps, Dorothy J. "Organization and Development of the Alaska Department of Library Service, 1955-1959." Master's thesis, University of Utah, 1960. 191p.

This paper deals with four major problems: 1) a history of the libraries and library services before the organization of the Department of Library Service in Territorial Alaska in 1955; 2) an analysis of the Department of Library Services under the new department to 1959; 3) a brief history of each of 32 public libraries in Alaska, 1929-1959; and 4) a description of the impact of Public Law 597, Library Services Act of 1956, on public library development in Alaska. The author was the first head of the Department of Library Service.

126 Stewart, Jeannette. "Library Service in Alaska: A Historical Study." Master's thesis, University of Washington, 1957. 141p.

Presents an outline of library service in Alaska from the days of Russian occupation to 1957. The history of libraries in Alaska from 1900-1957 is described in terms of the type of library: territorial, community, college and university, school, government, and special. The author finds that libraries were established and withstood long periods of economic instability. The organization of the Department of Library Services (1955) is seen as a vital development in an area that has suffered from a lack of professional guidance.

ARKANSAS

127 Gates, Jean K. "Library Progress in Tax-Supported Institutions in Arkansas, 1924-1949." Master's thesis, Catholic University of America, 1951. 65p.

This study traces the history of tax-supported libraries in Arkansas from 1924, when the first free library service began, to 1949. The author uses a number of statistical tables to illustrate this development. Four major sections deal with the state library system, city and community libraries, public school libraries, and college and university libraries. The author finds that all phases of library development for the 25 years lagged behind average development in the rest of the nation.

128 McNeil, Gladys. "History of the Library in Arkansas." Master's thesis, University of Mississippi, 1957. 60p.

This paper traces the history of Arkansas libraries from the establishment of William Woodruff's lending library in Little Rock in 1843 to 1957. The first library law in Arkansas was passed in 1901, and in 1927 a county library bill was passed. The author lists and briefly describes the 19 county libraries established in Arkansas by 1941. The development of the State Library and the contents of the collections of various Arkansas libraries are treated. A directory of county and regional libraries is furnished.

129 Tillman, Rosebud H. "The History of Public Library Service to Negroes in Little Rock, Arkansas, 1917-1951." Master's thesis, Atlanta University, 1953. 49p.

This study traces the development of public library service to Negroes in Little Rock, isolates the factors leading to integrated service, and recommends certain improvements for the provision of library service to Negroes. The Little Rock Public Library was founded in 1867 as a mercantile library. In 1917 a separate branch was established for Negro clientele and by the 1950s it held a collection of 6,000 volumes. The main library was opened to all races in 1951. The transition was effected without prior public debate or subsequent rancor.

CALIFORNIA

130 Benedetti, Lucile S. "A History of Public Library Service in Menlo Park, California, 1889-1969." Master's thesis, San Jose State College, 1970. 190p.

The Menlo Park branch of the San Mateo County Library was established in 1916 following several decades of library service by literary clubs. Although Menlo Park was an affluent community, library progress was modest until the remarkable population increase of the 1950s. Reacting to public pressure for improved library service, the city council withdrew from San Mateo and authorized a municipal library. A new building was dedicated in 1968. Photographs and charts enhance the text.

131 Cao, Jerry F. "The Los Angeles Public Library: Origins and Development, 1872-1910." Doctoral dissertation, University of Southern California, 1977.

The Los Angeles Public Library and three predecessor libraries were studied to determine the motivational influence of self-improvement and moral uplift. All the early institutions displayed motives of recreation and self-benefit, all components of self-improvement. Local pride was also present and considered a major factor behind the public library movement in southern California.

132 James, Betty L. "History of the Redwood City Public Library, Redwood City, California, 1865-1939." Master's thesis, San Jose State College, 1971. 83p.

The Redwood City Public Library traces its origins to the Franklin Library Association (1865-1878) and the Redwood City Library Association (1889-1900). The city assumed responsibility for the library in 1900 and a Carnegie building grant was secured in 1905. After failing to pass a bond issue in 1932 for a new building, another bond issue was attempted and approved in 1938. Wilhelmina Harper guided the library with considerable success from 1930 to 1954. Study emphasizes services and personnel.

133 Mahoney, Barbara L. "The History of the Marin County Free Library System." Master's thesis, San Jose State College, 1972. 120p.

Marin County, situated north of San Francisco, established a county library in 1926. This study traces the development of the county library and its two regional branches and eleven stations, from that date until 1972. Two chapters are devoted to the early history of California libraries and Marin County. Collections, special services, facilities, and staff are treated in detail. Capsule histories of each branch are rendered.

134 Sigler, Ronald F. "The Film Censorship Controversy at Los Angeles Public Library-1971: A Case Study." Doctoral dissertation, Florida State University, 1977. 332p. UMI# 7726990.

A library-sponsored Young Adult Film Discussion erupted into a censorship episode in 1971 which lasted for nine months. The dispute led to the temporary impoundment of the entire library film collection and to the withdrawal from circulation of 19 films.

Documents and interviews are used to reconstruct events. Findings reveal that the origin of some films from communist-bloc countries, lack of film literacy, and literal interpretation contributed to the escalation of criticism.

135   Souza, Margaret A. "The History of the Santa Cruz Public Library System." Master's thesis, San Jose State College, 1970. 169p.

The Santa Cruz Public Library, founded in 1881, was preceded by the Library Association which was formed in 1868. Minerva Waterman, appointed librarian in 1890, served in that post until 1941. A Carnegie building was erected in 1904 and four branches were established by the 1920s. In 1916 the library contracted to serve the county and supported 12 county branches as of 1970. The Santa Cruz Public Library was a pioneer in the adoption of open shelves.

COLORADO

136   Minnick, Nelle F. "A Cultural History of Central City, Colorado, from 1859 to 1880, in Terms of Books and Libraries." Master's thesis, University of Chicago, 1946. 121p.

Central City was settled in 1859, during the gold rush, and developed rapidly until 1879, when the discovery of silver in Leadville drew people away. The author outlines the social, economic, and political nature of the times and then traces the history of local library movements. Provides an analysis of local reading interests based mainly on the *Catalogue of the Public Library of Central City* (1878) and a list of 51 leaders of library movements in Central City 1860-1880, classified by occupation.

CONNECTICUT

137   Agard, Robert M. "The Development of Public Libraries in

Connecticut, 1875-1900." Master's thesis, Brown University, 1944. 126p.

Describes the development of public libraries in Connecticut during the last quarter of the nineteenth century. Following a general history of public libraries in America, the study examines the adoption of library legislation in Connecticut, the transformation of social libraries into public libraries, and the evolution of various services. Tax levies were permitted for public libraries in 1869, and the library law of 1893 provided for state aid to libraries supported by towns. By 1900, there were 112 public and 39 subscription libraries with an aggregate circulation of 1,894,511. The geographic distribution, financial condition, collections, and circulating patterns of public and social libraries are examined.

138 Bergen, Eleanor. "History of the Bridgeport Public Library and Reading Room." Master's thesis, Southern Connecticut State College, 1969. 143p.

This thesis chronicles the history of library service to Bridgeport, Connecticut, the socio-economic development of the city, and the significant factors in the formation of the unique type of library service offered in Bridgeport. Special consideration is given to the war periods and the depression years as related to library service and use.

139 Bryan, Barbara D. "Fairfield Public Library: Antecedents and Development." Master's thesis, Southern Connecticut State College, 1964. 115p.

The Fairfield Memorial Library had been preceded by at least eight local social libraries when it was founded in 1876 as an incorporated subscription library. In 1898 it was opened to the public on a no-fee basis supported mainly by private funds. In 1950 it was renamed the Fairfield Public Library and became a city-supported agency. The author states that after World War II, the old library, with an increasing population to serve and faced with changing concepts of library service, was not able to meet reader needs and was reorganized as a publicly supported library.

140   Castegnetti, Nancy R. "The History of Russell Library Company, Middletown, Connecticut." Master's thesis, Southern Connecticut State College, 1966. 100p.

This historical study of the Russell Library Company looks at: 1) the social, cultural, education, economic, and political outline of the town of Middletown; 2) a history of the forerunners of the public library in Middletown; and 3) the history of the Russell Library from its founding to 1966. Also discussed are the various services that have been offered by the library and the persons involved in the library's operation.

141   DeAngelis, Patrick. "A History of Library Service in Kensington, Connecticut." Master's thesis, Southern Connecticut State College, 1967. 153p.

The author traces the history of library development in Kensington, Connecticut from the eighteenth century. Using Jesse Shera's *Foundations of The Public Library* as a model, the author analyzes the economic, political, and intellectual factors which influenced library development in the small Connecticut town of Berlin of which Kensington is a part.

142   Early, Susan E. "The History of Public Library Service in Milford, Connecticut, 1639-1970." Master's thesis, Southern Connecticut State College, 1971. 181p.

The development of public libraries in Milford, Connecticut corresponded to the national pattern with the formation of two social libraries in the eighteenth century and a lyceum library in the nineteenth. Henry A. Taylor, a railroad man of considerable wealth, donated the building which became the Taylor Library in 1895. For years the library was inadequate to serve the town's growing population. In a survey conducted by Joseph L. Wheeler in 1947, he concluded: "I have never seen a public library in such a state of confusion and disorder...." Reasons for this poor showing include the absence of a professional until 1950 and the private nature of the board which was not assimilated by the city until 1969.

143   Gates, Elizabeth S. "The Library-School Council of Wethersfield, Connecticut." Master's thesis, Southern Connecticut State College, 1964. 87p.

The first 20 pages of this paper are devoted to a survey of library development in Wethersfield from 1783, when the first subscription library was established, to 1960. All types of libraries are treated in this section—private, school, public, and academic.

144   Giddings, Ruth L. "The West Hartford Public Library: Its History and Present Status." Master's thesis, Southern Connecticut State College, 1965. 172p.

The West Hartford Public Library, founded in 1897, traces its early history to the West Division Book Society (1753), the West Hartford Library Association (1837), and the Free Circulating Library of the First Congregational Church (1883). Following the appointment of Margery Burditt as the first professionally trained librarian in 1926, the library dramatically expanded its services and collections. The library is named for Noah Webster, native son and renowned lexicographer. Throughout its history the town generally supported the library and the library responded constructively to changing social and professional trends.

145   Hausmann, Albert F. "Origin and Development of the New Haven Free Public Library, 1886-1911." Master's thesis, Southern Connecticut State College, 1968. 238p.

The author analyzes the origin of the New Haven Free Public Library in relation to the public library movement as a whole and describes the development of the library during the first twenty-five years of its existence. The paper also includes details of the personal life and professional contributions of Willis K. Stetson, first City Librarian of the New Haven Library.

146 Lowrey, Silvia G.R. "A History of Libraries in Madison (East Guilford), Connecticut." Master's thesis, Southern Connecticut State College, 1963. 201p.

This paper treats the history of the libraries in the town of Madison, Connecticut beginning from the time that Madison was still part of Guilford and continuing to 1963. The libraries discussed are the Four-Town Library serving colonial Lyme, Saybrook, Dillingworth, and Guilford from 1737-1787; the Farmer's Library serving East Guilford, and later Madison from 1793 to about 1852; the People's Library serving Madison from 1852 to approximately 1857; the North Bristol Library in Madison in 1824; the East River Library Company in existence from 1874 to the 1930s; and the Madison Library Association Library which served Madison from 1878 until it was merged with the E.C. Scranton Memorial Library which serves the town to this very day. The catalogs of several of these libraries appear in the appendices.

147 Mitchell, Minnie W. "An Historical Study of the Silas Bronson Library of Waterbury, Connecticut." Master's thesis, Southern Connecticut State College, 1966. 127p.

The purpose of this thesis is to present a chronological history of the Silas Bronson Library, especially its changing environment, its endowment, and the contributions of its outstanding librarians. The study covers the original reference library through its expansion and establishment of various branch libraries and departments. Also included is coverage of the overall development of libraries in New England.

148 Semmler, Elizabeth A. "A History of the Public Library in Plainville, Connecticut, 1785-1973." Master's thesis, Southern Connecticut State College, 1973. 148p.

The threefold purpose of this paper is to organize the history of the public library in Plainville; compare the library's pattern of growth with others in the state and region; and relate the development of the Plainville Public Library to the educational and socio-economic growth of the community which it serves. Three social libraries preceded the public library: West Plain Library (1785-1823); Farmington Plain Library (1823-1855); and White Oak District Library (1823-1862). Agitation for a public library secured a tax-supported library in 1894. Throughout the twentieth century the Plainville Public Library emphasized the educational role of the library in community affairs.

149 Via, Nancy S. "The History, Development, and Growth of the Clark Memorial Library, Bethany, Connecticut." Master's thesis, Southern Connecticut State College, 1973. 129p.

Introductory chapters trace the history of the American public library, summarize the development of Connecticut public libraries, and review the history of Bethany, Connecticut. Although a proprietary library existed for a short time in 1798, Bethany did not have another library until 1930 when the Bethany Library Association was created. Bethany's library was named the Clark Memorial Library in honor of benefactor Noyes Dwight Clark. The Clark Memorial is maintained as a private endowed library with a collection of 11,060 volumes as of 1970.

150 Waggoner, Lois B. "The Development of the Cheshire Public Library." Master's thesis, Southern Connecticut State College, 1965. 128p.

The author briefly discusses the antecedents of the Cheshire Public Library, and then describes its development from 1892 to 1965. In 1894 the town received a gift from Mrs. Julia Tompkins, and the Library Association of Cheshire was founded that same year. In 1903 subscription fees were abolished and the library developed very slowly until after World War II due to the lack of financial support. The greatest growth has taken place since 1957.

DELAWARE

151 Richards, Emma S. "Fifty Years with the Library Commission for the State of Delaware." Master's thesis, Drexel Institute of Technology, 1951. 39p.

In 1951 the Library Commission of Delaware completed its 50th year. The Library Commission, which now serves only Kent and Sussex counties, formerly included New Castle County as well. The Library Commission was founded by some Delaware women's clubs that wanted to institute traveling libraries and later bookmobiles in the state.

DISTRICT OF COLUMBIA

152 Cook, Verla R. "A History and Evaluation of the Music Division of the District of Columbia Public Library." Master's thesis, Catholic University of America, 1952. 87p.

This paper begins with a brief history of music departments in public libraries in the United States and traces the origins of the Music Division of the District of Columbia Public Library. A final section is devoted to a topical history of the various departments, i.e. cataloging, staff, quarters. In 1933 the Civil Works Administration assigned two people to prepare the collection for public use. In 1934 a plea for financial aid from private sources to open the collection to the public was successful and the Division became a reality. Starting with a small collection of sheet music, the Division's holdings had grown to over 15,000 compositions by 1951.

153 King, Margaret L. "Beginnings and Early History of the Public Library of the District of Columbia, 1896-1904." Master's thesis, Catholic University of America, 1953. 86p.

The author briefly discusses the predecessors of the Public Library of the District of Columbia from the founding of the

District in 1800 to the establishment of the Public Library in 1896. Traces the history of the Public Library to the retirement in 1904 of its first administrator, Weston Flint.

154 Maples, Houston L. "The Peabody Library of Georgetown, District of Columbia: A History and Evaluation." Master's thesis, Drexel Institute of Technology, 1952. 84p.

Presents a history of the Peabody Library of Georgetown from its inception in 1876 as a privately endowed library until 1935, when it was disbanded. The author illustrates both the limitations and advantages of a library functioning without public funds, and evaluates the library's performance over the 60-year period covered.

FLORIDA

155 Barfield, Isaac R. "A History of the Miami Public Library, Miami, Florida." Master's thesis, Atlanta University, 1958. 43p.

The beginnings of library service in Miami date from 1897 when club women established a small library to serve the community. By 1924 the city appropriated tax revenues to support library operations. A Negro branch, the Dunbar Branch, was opened in 1938. Between 1938 and 1951, the Miami Public Library fell below comparable cities in the provision of volumes per capita. Integrated library service was introduced in 1951. Summarizes the growth of branches, administrative reorganizations, circulation, and expenditures.

156 Curry, John L. "A History of Public Library Service to Negroes in Jacksonville, Florida." Master's thesis, Atlanta University, 1957. 45p.

The Jacksonville Public Library (1905) was the first tax-supported library established in the state of Florida. A library for Negroes, the Wilder Park Branch, was opened in 1927. Negroes were allowed to use the main library only when the branch was closed. An overview of the branch's collections, staff, services, and patterns of circulation is furnished.

157 Gill, Sylvia. "The History of the Miami Public Library System, Miami, Florida." Master's thesis, Western Reserve University, 1954. 131p.

In 1902 a Miami women's club voted to circulate its books for $1.50 per year to non-members. In 1912 railroad magnate Henry M. Flagler donated a parcel of land worth around $20,000 so that the women's club could build a meeting house and library. In 1923, due to the land boom, the women were able to sell their $13,000 building and the property for nearly $400,000 which was promptly spent on a beautiful new home for the club and library. In 1924 the city began supporting the library, and in 1936 a central library was established to serve the entire city. The author traces the development of the main library and branches to 1950.

158 Mason, Pamela R. "A History of Public Library Development in Florida." Master's thesis, University of Chicago, 1968. 79p.

Public library development in Florida has been slow due to lack of communication between the various media, duplication of resources, and insufficient financial support. The library must work with the community and join the cultural revolution to advance its cause.

159 Perres, Myrtle J. "History and Development of Public Library Service for Negroes in Pensacola, Florida, 1947-1961." Master's thesis, Atlanta University, 1963. 42p.

The Pensacola Free Public Library began as a small subscription library in 1855 and it was not until 1937 that the city council authorized tax support. A separate library for Negroes, the Alice S. Williams Branch Library, was opened in 1952. Following a rather brief history of library development in Pensacola, the author describes the collections, staff, and services of the branch library. Little outreach activity is evident.

GEORGIA

160 Adkins, Barbara M. "A History of Public Library Service to Negroes in Atlanta, Georgia." Master's thesis, Atlanta University, 1951. 44p.

The author traces the development of library services to Negroes in Atlanta to 1950. Initially there were no real library services for Negroes in Atlanta. In 1921, the Auburn Branch Library of the Atlanta Public Library was opened to serve Negroes. Since that time to 1950 services increased to the point that Negroes had fair library service.

161 Cooper, Neloweze W. "The History of Public Library Service to Negroes in Savannah, Georgia." Master's thesis, Atlanta University, 1960. 41p.

The introductory chapter delineates the history and socio-economic fabric of Savannah. Public service for whites was inaugurated in 1903. A Negro branch, funded by a Carnegie grant, was opened in 1906. Two branches were subsequently established. Brief comments are provided on the collection, quarters, staff, and administration. The author concludes with a call for integrated library service.

162 Crittenden, Juanita L. "A History of Public Library Service to Negroes in Columbus, Georgia, 1831-1959." Master's thesis, Atlanta University, 1960. 43p.

When the new library of Columbus, Georgia opened in 1907 it was closed to Negroes. In 1950 it was still closed to Negroes. By 1944 the Negro population was allowed to use the Spencer High School Library and in 1945 a small Negro branch library was established. This small library proved totally inadequate and in

1952 a new Negro branch library was established. By 1959 this collection contained only 15,000 volumes and had little success in acquiring books from the main library for the use of Negro patrons. In 1959 the librarian had no formal book budget. Negroes, who made up 32.2 percent of the population of Columbus, were receiving an infinitesimal amount of the main library's total services.

163 Howard, Lucille. "The Statesboro Regional Library: History, Development and Services." Master's thesis, Florida State University, 1964. 63p.

The author devotes about one-third of this paper to a historical consideration of the Statesboro, Georgia, Regional Library. Agitation for the establishment of regional libraries, which are economical and efficient, first began in 1922. In 1935 the state of Georgia found that over 70 percent of its population was without library service. This led to the establishment of a number of regional libraries, the first of which was in Athens. The Statesboro Regional Library, the third founded in Georgia, began operation in 1944. The author traces the antecedents of the system and its growth to 1954.

164 Hutzler, Helen C. "History of the Rome, Georgia, Carnegie Library (1911-1961)." Master's thesis, Catholic University of America, 1963. 108p.

Presents a chronological history of library development in Rome, Georgia, from the establishment of the first subscription library in 1879 to 1961. In 1911 the town received a Carnegie grant to build a public library building, but the library grew slowly until 1919 due to a lack of funds. In the 1930s, extensive WPA help enabled the library to extend its hours, services, and book collection. By 1962 the library was circulating 200,000 volumes per year. The library was integrated in 1963.

165 Redd, Gwendolyn L. "A History of Public Library Service to

Negroes in Macon, Georgia." Master's thesis, Atlanta University, 1961. 50p.

Traces the history of the community, and then presents a history of library service to Negroes in Macon from 1928 to 1960. The first library service to Negroes was provided by a Negro branch established in 1928. Services, facilities, and the collections were very weak and in 1949 the library was discontinued. It was reopened in 1953 in a permanent location as the Amelia Hutchings Memorial Library. The author describes the development of this library to 1960 including the organization, staff, services, collection, and physical plant.

166 Williams, Barbara C. "A History of the Cairo, Georgia, Public Library." Master's thesis, Florida State University, 1961. 104p.

This study traces the organization and development of the Cairo, Georgia Public Library from its founding in 1939 to 1960. Established during the Depression under the auspices of the WPA, the library obtained permanent county support within four years. Children's services were emphasized for a decade and then a variety of special outreach programs were initiated. Strong community backing and the able leadership of Librarian Wessie Connell produced four John Cotton Dana Publicity Awards during this period. Draws upon secondary literature, correspondence, and interviews to reconstruct the library's history.

GUAM

167 Caldwell, Mary S. "A History of the Guam Public Library System, 1947-1975." Doctoral dissertation, Western Michigan University, 1977. 265p. UMI# 7804237.

This historical treatment of the Guam Public Library System analyzes the multiple factors which contributed to the growth of a coordinated library system. The library in Guam was imposed by U.S. citizens and did not evolve as a local institution. Growth of the system was influenced by fiscal appropriations, geographic isolation, promotion activites, and contributions of such organizations as the Los Angeles Times Charities, the Assistance League of Southern California, and the U.S. Navy. Currently, the Guam Public Library System operates five permanent facilities and a bookmobile.

HAWAII

168   Tachihata, Chieko. "The History and Development of Hawaii Public Libraries: The Library of Hawaii and the Hawaii State Library, 1913-1971." Doctoral dissertation, University of Southern California, 1981. 373p. Portion published: *Hawaii Library Association Journal* 38 (1981): 47-54.

This study traces the history of public libraries from early reading rooms to the founding of the Library of Hawaii (1913), county libraries (1921), and the statewide system (1964). Library development is considered in the context of features unique to Hawaii such as geographic isolation, centralized form of government, and multicultural populations. Coverage of the Library of Hawaii includes collection development, service to children and young adults, extension work, and censorship episodes.

ILLINOIS

169   Berg, Virginia A. "History of the Urbana Free Library, 1874-1894." Master's thesis, University of Illinois, 1948. 82p.

The author traces the development of the Urbana, Illinois, Free Library during its first two decades of growth. The predecessor of the Free Library was the Urbana Library Association founded by forty men in 1872. Due to financial restraints, the Library Association transferred its property to the Urbana Free Library in 1874. The author deals with the Free Library's struggling years in a topical fashion—staff, facilities, collections.

170 Bullock, Esther V. "A History of the Geneva Public Library." Master's thesis, Northern Illinois University, 1965. 110p.

The first attempt at establishing a public library in Geneva was made in 1874, but due to lack of funds it quickly failed. Started again in 1894 with about 800 books, the library soon became too large for its rented quarters. However, it was not until 1908 that a new building, financed by a $7,500 grant from Andrew Carnegie, was finished. The first children's room was established in 1938 and the first professional librarian, Ruth Sibley, was hired in 1953. As far back as 1897 the library had instituted a loan service to the prisoners in the county jail; over the years it has served schools, businesses, and churches.

171 Clayton, Sheryl A.H. "A Public Library's History and Development; East Saint Louis, Illinois' Public Library." Doctoral dissertation, Southern Illinois University at Carbondale, 1981. 305p. UMI# 8122626.

Historical coverage of the East Saint Louis Public Library encompasses the appointment and contributions of board members, the city's role in financing the library, and the impact of various mayors and librarians on library development. The library is described as a quiet, conservative institution functioning at the periphery of city life. Future options include intensified programs in the areas of continuing education and service to minorities.

172 Kram, Regina I. "The Foreign Language Collections of the Chicago Public Library, 1872-1947." Master's thesis, University of Chicago, 1970. 118p.

Foreign language collections and facilities of the Chicago Public Library and their contribution to Americanization are the focus of this study. Heavily used collections included those foreign language titles in Italian, Polish, Yiddish, Greek, and German. In general, the foreign language collection mirrored population trends in Chicago. Circulation climbed from the 1870s to the 1930s.

173 Prichard, Louise G. "A History of the Chicago Public Library." Master's thesis, University of Illinois, 1928. 128p.

After briefly surveying the predecessors of the Chicago Public Library, the author traces its development, with emphasis on the contributions of its four librarians to 1928: William Frederick Poole, 1873-1887; Frederick H. Hild, 1887-1909; Henry E. Legler, 1909-1917; and Carl B. Roden, 1917-1928.

174 Spencer, Gwladys S. "The Chicago Public Library: Origins and Backgrounds." Doctoral dissertation, University of Chicago, 1939. Published: University of Chicago, 1943. Reprinted: Gregg Press, 1972.

Examines the many social forces that influenced the development of the Chicago Public Library in 1872. Documents the public library's dependence on the whims of local government, presents a history of other libraries in Chicago, describes early leaders in the Illinois library movement, and outlines library legislation in Illinois.

INDIANA

175 Beamon, Mamie. "The Origin and Development of the School Services Department of the Indianapolis Public Library." Master's thesis, Indiana University, 1962. 80p.

The author traces the history of the school library services of the Indianapolis Public Library before 1917, when the School Services Department was established, and the development of the Department from 1917 to 1962. The author finds that the Department's policies were influenced and kept in a state of constant evolution by the ever-increasing demands placed on it. The main service of the Department is to elementary schools, but community organizations and county schools are served to a lesser extent.

176 Feaster, Doris M. "History of Story Telling in the Indianapolis Public Library." Master's thesis, Western Reserve University, 1951. 37p.

The author begins with an essay on the life of Carrie Emma Scott, children's librarian at Indianapolis (1917) and editor of an anthology of children's literature. She was in considerable demand as a teacher and taught at the University of Illinois and the University of Minnesota. The remainder of the paper is devoted to a history of story telling at the Indianapolis Public Library from 1917-1950, and the efforts there to interest children in reading.

177 Hull, Thomas V. "The Origin and Development of the Indianapolis Public Library, 1873-1899." Master's thesis, University of Kentucky, 1956. Published: University of Kentucky Press, Microcard Publications, Series B, Number 2.

The author begins with a survey of the cultural backgrounds of Indianapolis and then discusses some early predecessors, the first established in 1823, of the Indianapolis Public Library. Finally, the history of the public library from its opening in 1873 to the year 1899 is traced. The noted bibliographer Charles Evans served as the Indianapolis librarian from 1872-1878 and again from 1889-1892. His achievements included an enlightened book selection program and completion of the library's first printed catalog. An appendix includes the Rev. Hanford A. Edson's influential sermon, "A Plea for a Public Library," delivered in November of 1868.

178 Lewis, Dorothy F. "History of the Marion County, Indiana Library, 1844-1930." Master's thesis, Indiana University, 1954. 54p.

The Marion County Library, established in 1844, served the county's population for more than 86 years before it was replaced by state and city libraries. From the beginning the library developed slowly and the author traces this to the following causes: 1) the small population and the concomitant shortage of funds; 2) difficulties in transportation and communication; 3) defects in the political organization of the library; and 4) the lack of qualified professional librarians. Despite its many difficulties, the Marion County Library lasted longer than any other county library in the state of Indiana.

179 Taylor, Mary V. "The Public Library Commission of Indiana, 1899-1925." Master's thesis, University of Kentucky, 1953. 110p. Published: University of Kentucky Press, Microcard Publications, Series B, Number 3.

This study is divided into five sections: 1) a summary of library services in nineteenth-century Indiana; 2) the establishment and organization of the Public Library Commission, with emphasis on the law of 1899; 3) legislation which influenced the Commission's work; 4) the rise of public libraries in Indiana, 1899-1925; and 5) the Commission's role in the extension and improvement of public library service in Indiana, 1899-1925. In 1925, the Public Library Commission was absorbed by the Indiana Library and Historical Department. However, in the 26 years of its existence, the Commission was instrumental in fostering the library idea in Indiana.

180 Walther, La Vern A. "Legal and Governmental Aspects of Public Library Development in Indiana, 1816-1953." Doctoral dissertation, Indiana University, 1957. 113p. UMI# 584833.

Walther divides this study into four major sections: 1) a survey of the history of the Indiana State Library; 2) the development of library legislation in Indiana; 3) a comparison of public library service in Indiana and in the United States for the years 1945 and 1950; and 4) a consideration of the factors that influenced public library development in Indiana. Like other states, Indiana has found it difficult to provide library service for the rural population. An ever-increasing shift of population from rural to urban areas and the steady flow of people from the city centers to the suburbs have also posed serious problems for library planners in Indiana.

181 Zimmerman, Mary. "A History of the South Bend Public Library from 1888 to 1961." Master's thesis, Catholic University of America, 1962. 65p.

In this history of the South Bend Public Library, which covers the period from 1888, when the library was established, to 1961, emphasis is placed on the decade 1951 to 1961. Some attention is given to the contributions of outstanding staff members to the library's development and to the planning of a new building, opened in 1960.

IOWA

182 Blanks, Eleanor W. "The Public Library of Des Moines, Iowa: A History of the First Fifty Years, 1866-1916." Master's thesis, University of Texas, 1967. 188p.

The Des Moines Library Association, established as a subscription library in 1866, operated with modest success until the city agreed to permanent support in 1882. After several temporary quarters, the library occupied a new building in 1903. By 1916, the library staff numbered 17 and the collection boasted 90,000 volumes. Various controversies between the board of trustees and the city government are chronicled, together with detailed coverage of the collections, staff, technical routines, and services.

183 Coughlin, Betty. "History of the Davenport Public Library." Master's thesis, Western Reserve University, 1952. 57p.

The first library in Davenport was established in 1839 but soon failed. In 1854 the Young Men's Library Association was founded. In 1901 this library evolved into the Davenport Public Library and was housed in a new building built with $75,000 given by Andrew Carnegie. The collection then numbered slightly over 13,000 volumes; as of 1952, it numbered nearly 200,000. The author also includes a survey of Iowa library history in this study.

184 McGuire, Letha P. "A Study of the Public Library Movement in Iowa with Special Reference to Certain Outstanding and Typical Libraries." Master's thesis, University of Illinois, 1929. 147p. Summary published: *Iowa Journal of History and Politics* 35 (1937): 22-72.

Describes the development of the public library movement in Iowa from 1853, when the first social library was established in the state, to 1929. Overall development of public libraries in the state is briefly traced with emphasis on library legislation, library services, and library administration. Detailed treatment is given to four public libraries: Des Moines, Sioux City, Davenport, and Webster City.

185 Pease, Kenneth R. "Iowa Public Library Service in Recent History." Master's thesis, University of Chicago, 1968. 94p.

The author deals with three basic aspects of Iowa library history: 1) the factors which have been salient in the cultural history of Iowa; 2) the recent history of Iowa public libraries, 1930-1965; and 3) a survey of contemporary conditions. The period from 1930-1956 was found to be one of slow and frustrating development, and it was not until the passage of the Library Services Act that the situation improved.

186 Snyder, Esther B. "The History and Development of the Music Collection and Department of the Public Library of Des Moines." Master's thesis, Western Reserve University, 1958. 82p.

This study is concerned with the history of the music collection from 1900 to 1958. The collection was housed in an area of the library before it was developed as part of the Art and Music Department and finally evolved into a major department in its own right. The collection, staffing, and program are discussed.

KANSAS

187 Crumpacker, Grace F. "Library Legislation and the Library Movement in Kansas." Master's thesis, University of Illinois, 1932. 134p.

While emphasizing the legislative history of libraries in Kansas, this thesis also traces in some detail the history of libraries in Kansas to 1931. Chapters deal with the history of Kansas; libraries during the Territorial period, 1854-1861; public and school library development in Kansas, 1901-1931; and academic libraries.

188 Gaiser, Bessie F. "A History of the Public Library of Leavenworth, Kansas." Master's thesis, Kansas State Teachers College of Emporia, 1959. 70p.

Predecessors of the Leavenworth Public Library in the 1850s, a subscription library and a mercantile library, are reviewed in the early chapters. The Leavenworth Public Library was established in 1895 with the assistance of various women's literary clubs. A Carnegie-funded building was constructed in 1902. Development of the library's collections, services, and use is addressed. Brief biographical sketches of eight library directors are appended.

LOUISIANA

189 Manint, Helen R. "A History of the New Orleans Public Library and the Howard Memorial Library." Master's thesis, Tulane University, 1939.

This study traces the history of the New Orleans Public Library and the Howard Memorial Library from 1888 to 1939. Discusses departments, services, key leaders, successes, and failures. Concludes that New Orleans has a relatively efficient library system despite slow progress in support for public libraries.

190 Morse, Dorothea B. "The Historical Development and Foreclosure of a Public Library." Master's thesis, University of Mississippi, 1960. 59p.

This study is a history of the Alexandria (Louisiana) Public Library from its establishment in 1907 to its merger with the Rapids Parish Library in 1956. The author approached this study with these aims in mind: 1) to evaluate the organization of the public library with emphasis on its history; 2) to evaluate the administration of the library with emphasis upon relationships between the library board and the general public; and 3) to consider the failure of the library's services to the public. She concludes that the library failed due to lack of support.

191 Rush, Shirley C. "History of Public Library Service to Negroes in Ouachita Parish, Monroe, Louisiana, 1949-1965." Master's thesis, Atlanta University, 1967. 42p.

The women of the Monroe Civic League established the first public library in Monroe in 1916. No library service was available for black citizens until 1949, when a separate branch library was established. Collections, staff, and services are described. In the fall of 1964, the central library was integrated following several civil rights demonstrations.

192 Smith, Robert C. "A Historical Study of Selected Effects of Federal Funding Upon Public Libraries in Louisiana 1956-1973." Doctoral dissertation, Louisiana State University, 1975. 284p. UMI#7522226.

Identifies the impact of federal funding on Louisiana public libraries, library planning, and the State Library during the period 1956 to 1973. The Louisiana State Library used Library Service and Construction Act (LSCA) funds for demonstration projects, cooperative activities such as a processing center, and service to special clients. LSCA had no effect upon local public funding effort and a negative influence on state legislative support for public libraries. Planning did improve at the state level.

MAINE

193 Hemmer, Phyllis B. "History of the Lewiston Public Library, Lewiston, Maine." Master's thesis, Catholic University of America, 1965. 63p.

In the first chapter the author outlines the history of Lewiston, Maine, which grew from one of the state's smallest villages to its second largest city in 1965. The first libraries in Lewiston were the Manufacturers' and Mechanics' Library Association, formed in 1861, and the Daughters of the American Revolution Library. Both libraries served a limited clientele and had limited facilities. In 1901 the city created a Free Public Library Commission to expend a $60,000 gift from Andrew Carnegie on a new public library. From that time until 1965 the library suffered from low tax support but grew substantially.

194 Scott, Kenneth J. "The Origins of the Public Library in Portland, Maine." Master's thesis, University of Chicago, 1974. 215p.

A tax-supported public library was established in Portland, Maine in 1889. Predecessor libraries—social, athenaeum, and mercantile—are identified and examined in depth.

MARYLAND

195 Blinkhorn, Margaret E. "A History of the Bethesda, Maryland, Public Library." Master's thesis, Catholic University of America, 1963. 50p.

This paper presents a history of the Bethesda Public Library from its origin in 1925 to 1963. The first library consisted of a small collection of books known as the "public library shelf." Later this grew into a community library and finally it merged with the Montgomery County Library system in 1952. By 1961 the Bethesda Public Library was circulating over 500,000 volumes a year. The author traces the efforts of the Newcomb

Club, which established the public library that failed in 1936. In 1938 the tax-supported library was founded.

196 Darby, Mayzee R. "A History of the Prince George's County, Maryland, Memorial Library." Master's thesis, Catholic University of America, 1961. 99p.

The Prince George's County Memorial Library was created in 1946 as a tribute to World War II soldiers and in recognition of major deficiencies identified by a survey of library services. By 1960 the county system consisted of 11 branch libraries and a bookmobile service. Staffing, collections, services, and administrative arrangements are discussed. Despite significant gains through consolidation, the fast-growing population taxed space and staff to the limit.

197 Kalisch, Philip A. "The Social History of the Enoch Pratt Free Library." Doctoral dissertation, Pennsylvania State University, 1967. 413p. UMI# 683546. Published: Scarecrow Press, 1969.

This study explores the social relationships between the Enoch Pratt Free Library and Baltimore society from 1866 to 1966. Briefly treated are the history of the American public library movement and the rationale of library philanthropy in the Gilded Age. From its founding in 1886 to 1926, the library remained under the firm direction of Lewis Steiner and then his son, Bernard. Although an excellent collection of fine arts materials were acquired, the library did not reach out to the common man. Between 1926 and 1945, Joseph L. Wheeler effected a quiet revolution, introducing innovative services and a commitment to the community.

198 Koch, June V. "The Enoch Pratt Free Library, its History, Organization, and Service to Readers." Master's thesis, Western Reserve University, 1951. 60p.

This study presents a brief history (10 pages) of the Enoch Pratt Library from 1884 to 1950.

199 McMurty, Beulah B. "The County Public Library: With Special Reference to Maryland and to Prince George's County in Maryland." Master's thesis, Western Maryland College (Westminister), 1947. 109p.

The author treats her subject in four parts: 1) a comparison of library services for a defined rural area offered by a state library and a county library system serving the same region; 2) the interrelationship between the two systems; 3) a brief survey of the history of county libraries in the United States with special emphasis on Maryland and especially Prince George's County; and 4) a demonstration of the significance of the county library movement.

200 Powell, Nellie L. "A History of the Washington County, Maryland, Free Library 1952-65." Master's thesis, Catholic University of America, 1966. 84p.

This work is divided into three parts: 1) a brief history of Washington County; 2) the origins and history of the Washington County Free Library from its beginnings in 1901 to 1951; and 3) a detailed history of the library's development from 1952 to 1964. Here the author places emphasis on factors influencing the library's development such as the financial resources of the county, the inhabitants of the county, the library administration, and the organizational structure in the library.

201 Rice, Didrikke M. "A History of the Silver Springs, Maryland Public Library from 1931 to 1951." Master's thesis, Catholic University of America, 1961. 94p.

Describes the operation for 20 years of the Silver Springs, Maryland, Public Library which was founded in 1931. For the first ten years of its existence the library was supported almost totally by voluntary gifts. Its success is attributed to an industrious and dedicated board of trustees, to extensive community support, and to advisory aid received from the Maryland Public Library Commission.

202 Rubinstein, Stanley. "The Role of the Trustees and the Librarians in the Development of the Enoch Pratt Free Library and the Free Library of Philadelphia, 1880-1914." Doctoral dissertation, George Washington University, 1978. 296p. UMI# 7903796. Portion published: *Journal of Library History* 15 (1980): 445-53.

This study is a comparative historical assessment of two eastern urban libraries in their formative period of development. Special attention is devoted to branch library service for Russian Jewish immigrants. Differences of administration, city support, and sources of funding are examined. Both libraries prospered during a time of experimentation and great progress in free public library development.

MASSACHUSETTS

203 Baron, Michael S. "Evolution of the Springfield, Massachusetts, Public Library, 1796-1912." Master's thesis, Catholic University of America, 1966. 68p.

The author begins this work with an investigation of the precursors of the Springfield Public Library: the Springfield Library Company, founded in 1796; the Springfield Circulating Library; the Apprentice's Library; and the City Library Association. Then he traces the history of the Public Library from 1857 to 1912 when a new library building was constructed. Special attention is given to the contributions of Springfield's most prominent public librarian, John Cotton Dana, who served the city from 1898-1902.

204 Buchanan, Jean B. "Early Directions of the Boston Public Library and the Genesis of an American Public Library Psychology." Master's thesis, Southern Connecticut State College, 1962. 71p.

This thesis emphasizes the elements that combined to stimulate the establishment of the Boston Public Library in 1854, the first public library of any real significance in the United States. The author analyzes the contrasting philosophies of the two leading spirits in the library's early history—George Ticknor and Edward

Everett—and shows how Everett's philosophy not only won out in Boston but also proved highly influential all over America. The author also devotes some time to the forerunners of the Boston Public Library—parish libraries, early academic libraries, social libraries, town and school district libraries. Another chapter, on the Library of the British Museum, discusses the contrasts between the British Museum and American library philosophy.

205 Clark, Raymond B., Jr. "History of the Talbot County Free Library, Easton, Massachusetts, 1925-1962." Master's thesis, Catholic University of America, 1963. 94p.

This library, established in 1925, was a pioneer in the state of Massachusetts in the provision of bookmobile service, in establishing close relationships between library and school, and in children's work. At the beginning it was housed in one room of an office building. By 1962 it had much larger quarters but still faced serious space and staff problems. The author finds that the introduction of federal and state funds greatly aided the library during the period 1957-1962.

206 Fund, Claire K. "The Boston Public Library Building of 1895." Master's thesis, University of Chicago, 1973. 88p.

The Boston Public Library Building, opened in 1895, is evaluated as an architectural entity, a monumental public building in Copley Square, and a functioning library. The relationship between librarians and architect Charles F. McKim is given special emphasis.

207 McGowan, Owen T.P. "A Centennial History of the Fall River Public Library, 1861-1961." Master's thesis, Catholic University of America, 1964. 94p.

This study is divided into three parts: 1) the history of the Fall River, Massachusetts, Athenaeum (1835-1861), which evolved into the Fall River Public Library; 2) the early years of the library (1861-1891); and 3) the opening of the present library building and the history of the institution from 1899-1961. The library hit its peak in the 1920s when yearly circulation reached 600,000. After that time services were hampered by serious financial difficulties.

208   Salfas, Shirley G. "History of the Springfield City Library, 1912-1948." Master's thesis, Southern Connecticut State College, 1969. 104p.

This study covers one of the most prosperous eras in the history of the Springfield, Massachusetts, City Library. The year 1912 marked the opening of a new building, and 1948 was the year that Hiller C. Wellman retired as librarian after some 46 years of service.

MICHIGAN

209   Burich, Nancy J. "Years of Consolidation and Expansion: A History of the Lansing Public Library from 1930 to 1967." Master's thesis, Kent State University, 1968. 95p.

A history of the public library in the capital of Michigan, from its founding in the late nineteenth century to 1967, with emphasis on the last 30 years of that period.

210   Helms, Claxton E. "The Historical Foundations and Development of Library Services in Allegan County, Michigan." Master's thesis, Western Michigan University, 1961. 69p. Summary published in Thelma Eaton, ed. *Contributions to Mid-west Library History,* (Champaign, IL: Illini Union Bookstore, 1964): 106-29.

The author traces the development of libraries in Allegan County from their first establishment in the early years of the nineteenth century through 1950, with emphasis on the nineteenth century. Finds that the successful establishment of libraries in Allegan County was due in part to the cultural background of the first settlers. People from New England and

New York made up about two-thirds of the total population of Michigan in 1837. Most of these settlers had the Puritan respect for education. Churches, schools, and libraries developed rapidly under their influence.

211 Hoesch, Mary J. "A History of the Grosse Pointe Public Library." Master's thesis, Western Reserve University, 1955. 36p.

This study traces library development in Grosse Pointe from 1928 to 1955, stressing the influence of community action and interest on the development of library service. The author presents her account in three main sections: 1) the early history of the system; 2) the campaigns for a central library and their final success; and 3) the history of the main library which was opened in 1953.

MINNESOTA

212 Gibson, Frank E. "The Effects of the Activities of the Unions in the Minneapolis Public Library on Library Functions and Administrative Processes, and upon Union Members." Master's thesis, University of Minnesota, 1952. 84p.

This study treats the effects of unions upon library functions and administrative practices and upon salaries, working conditions, and morale of the union members. The first union influence was felt at the Minneapolis Public Library in 1935 when the janitors became associated with the AFL. By 1950 the professional librarians were members of a union. The author finds that although the union organizations were able to secure very substantial benefits for their members, union participation in management was unsatisfactory when it conflicted with the objectives and spirit of library service.

213 Lincoln, Sister Mary E. "Cultural Significance of the Minneapolis Public Library in its Origins and Development: A Study in the Relations of the Public Library and American Society." Doctoral

dissertation, University of Minnesota, 1958. 388p. UMI# 60974.

This study was undertaken to pinpoint the causal factors that influenced the development of the Minneapolis Public Library and to see whether they were similar to those which influenced the development of libraries in the East and Midwest. The author finds that, as in Boston and Chicago, the major factors in Minneapolis were economic ability, an interest in culture, local pride, and popular support for a free library. Traces the history of libraries in Minneapolis from the middle 1800s into the twentieth century and finds that the library leaders in Minneapolis seemed to be more pragmatic in approach than their philosophically inclined eastern counterparts.

214 Nylander, Enid P. "A History of the Duluth Public Library System." Master's thesis, University of Minnesota, 1962. 171p.

After briefly tracing the history of Duluth from 1853 to 1960, the author describes the evolution of the Duluth Public Library from the reading room founded in 1869 to its establishment as a public library in 1890. Seven chapters are devoted to the history of the public library, 1890-1960. A final chapter analyzes the development of the Duluth Public Library branches.

215 Ostendorf, Paul J. "The History of the Public Library Movement in Minnesota from 1849 to 1916." Doctoral dissertation, University of Minnesota, 1984. 599p. UMI# 8413812.

The author visited 46 Minnesota communities as part of his study of the early public library movement in Minnesota. Early Minnesota public libraries accepted the dual philosophy of educational and social service and the belief that patrons should be the primary source of library support. Growth was modest until 1899-1908, when several events converged: leadership by Gratia A. Countryman, Clara Baldwin, and the Minnesota Federation of Women's Clubs; the right of women to vote on library issues; receipt of Carnegie grants; and creation of the Minnesota Library Commission. The early history of Minnesota public libraries paralleled developments in other sections of the nation.

MISSISSIPPI

216   Dickey, Pennie W. "A History of Public Library Service for Negroes in Jackson, Mississippi, 1950-1957." Master's thesis, Atlanta University, 1960. 50p.

This study, details the efforts that led to the first public library in Jackson, Mississippi, in 1951. The author also describes the library quarters, services, and finances relating to library service to Negroes in Jackson.

217   Green, Elizabeth B. "The History and Growth of Lee County Library." Master's thesis, University of Mississippi, 1961. 53p.

This history traces the development of the Lee County Library, Tupelo, Mississippi from its earliest stirrings to 1960. Emma Edmonds, an English teacher at Tupelo High School, pushed for the establishment of a small public collection in the high school in 1915. She gained support from a number of club women in the city and the library flourished until it was crowded out of the school in 1917. For the next 15 years sporadic enthusiasm for the public library was evident, and in 1934 a WPA project began support of the library. The first professional librarian was hired in 1947.

218   Sparks, Eva C. "People with Books: The Services of Northeast Regional Library." Master's thesis, University of Mississippi, 1962. 85p.

The author devotes the first part of her paper to a brief analysis of the influences that led to the development of the Northeast Regional Library in northeastern Mississippi in 1951. She then traces the development of the system from 1951 to 1962. Brief accounts of the development of 13 branches are also included.

MISSOURI

219 Swartz, Roderick G. "The Ozark Regional Library: Its Background and Development, 1947-1965." Master's thesis, University of Chicago, 1968. 68p.

This study deals with the origins and development of the Ozark Regional Library. In 1947, four Missouri counties—Crawford, Iron, Madison, and Bollinger— voted to form a regional library. By 1966 the regional library was judged to be giving the citizens of the Ozark Region far better service than they could have obtained from half a dozen inadequate community libraries.

NEBRASKA

220 Lenfest, Grace E. "The Development and Present Status of the Library Movement in Nebraska." Master's thesis, University of Illinois, 1931. 147p.

Development of the following libraries and agencies is considered: 1) the Nebraska State Library; 2) the libraries of the State Historical Society and the Nebraska Legislative Reference Bureau; 3) the libraries of the University of Nebraska and the four state teachers colleges; 4) the public libraries of the State; 5) the Nebraska Library Association; and 6) the Nebraska Public Library Commission.

221 Kalisch, Philip A. "The Early History of the Omaha Public Library." Master's thesis, University of Omaha, 1964. 149p.

The Omaha Public Library, established in 1887, was a direct outgrowth of two earlier subscription associations (1857-1860, 1871-1877). Although the library board governed the library, fiscal control resided with the city council. A new building and a major special collection were made possible from the benefaction of Byron Reed in the 1890s. Charles Evans cataloged the collection in 1887 and a new building was realized in 1894. By

1900, the library had achieved national prominence as a progressive public institution.

NEW JERSEY

222   Curtis, Cordelia M. "The Development of the Public Library in New Jersey." Master's thesis, Columbia University, 1935. 122p.

Outlines the development of public libraries in New Jersey from 1750 to 1930. Separate chapters detail the evolution of association libraries, public libraries, school libraries, library legislation, and the New Jersey Library Association. A chronological list of New Jersey public libraries before 1900 is appended.

223   Doyle, Sister M. Avila. "A History of the Trenton Free Public Library." Master's thesis, Catholic University of America, 1968. 82p.

In this historical treatment of the Trenton Free Public Library, the writer first considers the background and history of the city itself and then examines which factors gave rise to the desire for free library service. Also reviewed are Trenton's early social and proprietary libraries, circulating, mercantile, and mechanics institutions.

224   Gallant, Estelle F. "The History of the Free Library of Teaneck, New Jersey." Master's thesis, Pratt Institute, 1954. 72p.

The public library in Teaneck traces its beginnings to the small private collection of Mrs. Archibald N. Jordan. Jordan, who had made her books available to many children and adults, in 1912 asked for and was granted a deposit collection of books from the New Jersey State Library. In 1923 Jordan and a group of women formed the Teaneck Library Association and opened a library in an old renovated slave cabin. In 1927 the property was sold at a $15,000 profit, and the money was used to establish the Free Public Library of Teaneck, under municipal control. The author traces the development of services, collections, staff and physical plant to 1953.

225 O'Brien, Sister M. Benigna. "The History of the Development of a Library Plan for Clark, New Jersey." Master's thesis, Catholic University of America, 1965. 42p.

Presents a case history of the development and implementation of a plan for a public library in Clark, New Jersey. A major portion deals with the history of Clark, especially its industrial and educational history. The final portion of the thesis outlines the efforts of interested citizens to pass a referendum establishing a public library in 1960. The referendum was voted upon favorably and the author concludes with a reproduction of the library's first annual report.

NEW YORK

226 Breen, Mary H. "The Traveling Library Service of the New York Public Library in Richmond and the Bronx: A Descriptive History." Master's thesis, Pratt Institute, 1951. 58p.

The author divides her paper into three major sections. The first deals with the development of the traveling library in the United States from 1907, when pioneer librarian Mary Titcomb drove the first book wagon, to the current use of book trucks. The second deals with the Richmond Traveling Library from its inception in 1922 to 1950. The third traces the history of the Bronx Traveling Library from its beginnings in 1928. Both areas used wagons until bookmobiles became available. The author also discusses the physical development of the bookmobile.

227 Bullock, Judy Y. "A Résumé of the History, Growth, and Development of Library Service to Hospital Patients by the Queens Borough (New York) Public Library." Master's thesis, Atlanta University, 1962. 37p.

Library service to hospitals gained impetus during World War I when the Department of War induced the ALA to set up libraries in base hospitals to aid in the treatment of disabled veterans. The Queens Borough Public Library began its first service to the Flushing Hospital in 1933; it lasted until 1947 when the hospital was closed. In 1934 service was extended to several other hospitals, and by 1960 the library was serving many shut-ins plus six hospitals in the area.

228 Campbell, Virginia M. "A History of the Lackawanna Public Library." Master's thesis, Canisius College, 1953. 106p.

Traces the history of the Lackawanna (New York) Public Library from 1909 to 1952. More than a decade of civic activity preceded dedication of the Carnegie building in 1922. Library services are emphasized throughout the narrative. A particularly strong children's collection was developed.

229 Dain, Phyllis. "The New York Public Library: A History of Its Founding and Early Years." Doctoral dissertation, Columbia University, 1966. UMI# 67-00789. Published: New York Public Library, 1972.

This study traces the origins, founding, and early growth of the New York Public Library, with emphasis on the years when Dr. John Shaw Billings directed the library (1896-1913). Billings was extremely influential in setting the pattern of growth for the New York Public Library and was a pivotal figure in American librarianship. His contributions are examined, and the basic character of the library during his tenure is carefully analyzed.

230 Davis, Joan M. "Chemung County Library: Past, Present, and Future." Master's thesis, Pratt Institute, 1954. 76p.

The author devotes the first portion of this paper to the history of the Chemung County Library. In 1923 the county of Chemung agreed to give financial support to the Steele Memorial Library, located in Elmira, in order to provide free library service throughout the county. The first appropriation was $2,000 and the money was used to establish a special department called the Chemung County Library. In 1949 the Steele Memorial Library was absorbed by the county and renamed the Steele Memorial Library of Chemung County. The author describes the development of services, physical plant, and staff.

231 Fannin, Gwendolyn M. "A Résumé of the History, Growth, and Development of the Story Hour in the New York Public Library." Master's thesis, Atlanta University, 1958. 47p.

This paper traces the history of the Story Hour at the New York Public Library from its inception in 1908 to 1958. Since 1908 the Story Hour has been one of the specialities of the New York Public Library and one of the largest such undertakings in America.

232 Folcarelli, Ralph J. "A History and Description of Audiovisual Services and Programs of the Public Library Systems of New York State, 1950-1970." Volumes I-III. Doctoral dissertation, New York University, 1973. 919p. UMI# 7319424.

Traces the origin and development of 18 public library systems and their audiovisual programs and services from 1950 to 1970. Unevenness in the nature and scope of services and disparities in the quantity of media are noted. Inconsistencies are related to size of system population, type of area served (rural or urban), and attitude of the director toward audiovisual services. Other findings include the lack of intersystem cooperation, low priority for audiovisual services, and value of federal funds as a stimulus.

233 Goldstein, Dorothy. "The Library for the Blind of the New York Public Library." Master's thesis, Drexel Institute of Technology, 1953. 49p.

The first part of this paper traces the history of the Library for the Blind, its origin as the privately-funded New York Circulating

Library for the Blind (1896-1903), its union with the New York Public Library, and its development from 1903 to 1951.

234 Harvey, David I. "The Process of Metropolitan Political Integration: A Case Study of the Formation of the Onondaga County Public Library." Doctoral dissertation, Syracuse University, 1978. 428p. UMI# 7908536.

This study focuses on the process by which governments engage in collective action to create service structures more capable of delivering public services on a metropolitan-wide basis. Willis D. Hawley's "Sequential Model" is used as a framework for analysis of the political integration of the Onondaga County (New York) Public Library. During the years 1971-1976, Onondaga County created a federated library system requiring new county library service, transferred a city library to the county, and dissolved a cooperative private library system corporation.

235 Milliken, Sister Mary C. "A History of the Rochester Public Library From 1912 to 1936." Master's thesis, Catholic University of America, 1959. 57p.

Rochester's first library, the Rochester Athenaeum, was established in 1820 and survived until 1871. From 1863-1904, a library known as the Central Library was administered by the school superintendent and open to the public. City financial support materialized in 1912 and the Rochester Public Library engaged William F. Yust as its first director in 1912. He moved rapidly to build the collections and to enlarge the staff. John A. Lowe, his successor, secured a permanent library building in 1936. Benefactors Mortimer F. Reynolds and Morton W. Rundel are given prominence in this study.

236 Nichols, Barbara B. "Westchester Library System: The History and Evaluation of a Program of Service." Master's thesis, Southern Connecticut State College, 1969. 58p.

Thirty-eight public libraries in Westchester County, New York make up the Westchester Library System. This study presents a history of the System from its founding in 1958 to 1968; describes the services offered by the System; and presents brief case studies of nine of the member libraries.

237 Rollins, Ottilie H. "The Hepburn Libraries of the St. Lawrence Valley." Master's thesis, Western Reserve University, 1960. 113p. Published: University of Kentucky Press, Microcard Publications, Series B, Number 44.

A. Barton Hepburn was a wealthy New York philanthropist and banker who between 1912 and 1920 established a number of libraries in northern New York State. This thesis covers the history of the seven main Hepburn libraries, located in Colton, Edwards, Lisbon, Madrid, Norfolk and Wandington, as well as four branches administered by the Canton Free Library. Traces the history of these libraries from 1912 to 1958 and discusses the effects of declining population and decreased revenue on their development. All of the collections remained very small, none of them numbering over 10,000 volumes.

238 Wong, Rita. "A History of the Chatham Square Branch of the New York Public Library." Master's thesis, Pratt Institute, 1955. 68p.

The Chatham Square Branch was opened in 1899, and in 1900 it merged with the New York Public Library. In 1903 it moved to the second Carnegie branch building built in New York. The author surveys the development of the library's services and collections from 1899 to 1953.

239 Young, Barbara A. "A Historical Study of the Countee Cullen Regional Branch Library of the New York Public Library System: Its Inception, Trends, Developments." Master's thesis, Southern Connecticut State College, 1969. 58p.

The author traces the history of the library from 1905 to 1967. The Countee Cullen Regional Branch Library was originally called the 135th Street Branch Library and served a population comprised primarily of Jews, Irish, and Germans. By 1917 the clientele had become primarily Negro. In 1925 the famous Schomburg Collection of Negro History and Literature was acquired. In 1967, the federal government funded the North Manhattan Library Project, a project designed to test the library's effectiveness in serving a disadvantaged community.

NORTH CAROLINA

240 Aldrich, Willie L. "The History of Public Library Service to Negroes in Salisbury, North Carolina, 1937-1963." Master's thesis, Atlanta University, 1964. 72p.

The first library service for Negroes in Salisbury was organized in 1937 when two rooms in a frame house in a predominatly white neighborhood were designated the Negro Branch Library. The author found that the library service offered to Salisbury's Negroes, some 28 percent of the city's population, was always inferior to that offered to whites. In 1952, a new segregated Negro Branch was built on the site of the old Main Library. In 1961 the library facilities in Salisbury were desegregated.

241 Batten, Sara S. "The History of the Johnston County Public Library System, 1941-1951." Master's thesis, University of North Carolina, 1960. 88p.

The author first discusses the precursors of the Johnston County Library, North Carolina, 1915-1940, and then devotes the major portion of her study to the growth of the system from 1941 to 1959. The General Assembly passed a bill providing state aid for public libraries in 1941, and under this impetus the citizens of Johnston County moved to unite the county's libraries into a general system. That same year a county librarian was hired and the library began operations with a budget of $3,000. The author describes the difficulties encountered by the new system through the war years, and then traces its consistent development until 1959.

242 Cooke, Adele M. "A History of the Public Library in Murphy, North Carolina." Master's thesis, Florida State University, 1962. 72p.

The public library of Murphy, North Carolina, opened in 1922 through the efforts of the local Women's Club. Josephine Heighway, the second librarian, served as director from 1923 to 1962, a period of steady if undramatic growth. Effects of the great depression were alleviated by a contract between the library and the Tennessee Valley Authority (TVA) which provided funds for the library to serve the special needs of TVA employees. Beginning in 1940 the Murphy Library cooperated in a variety of projects with the Nanthala Regional Library.

243 Eury, William. "The Citizen's Library Movement in North Carolina." Master's thesis, George Peabody College for Teachers, 1951. 75p.

This paper commences with a brief history of libraries in North Carolina to 1926. The citizen's library movement had its origin in the North Carolina Library Association, but under the leadership of interested citizens it functioned as a citizens' library movement in the real sense of the word. The state was divided into districts, and these districts formed the working units for bringing the need for more and better libraries to the people. The movement advanced slowly. By 1950, 95 percent of the state's population had access to libraries, and long-needed Negro library service had been instituted.

244 Garrison, Barbara S. "A History of the Concord Public Library of Concord, North Carolina." Master's thesis, University of North Carolina, 1965. 126p.

The author begins this study with a brief history of Concord and Cabarrus counties in North Carolina. In 1911 several local women's book clubs banded together to found the Concord Library Association. The women held numerous sales to raise money for the library, but found that their efforts were barely sufficient to run the library at even a minimum level. The first "librarian's" salary was $15 a month. By 1922 the struggling library had only 4,000 books, many of them dilapidated. The library somehow struggled through the depression and war years, but made little significant headway. In 1960 the book collection was less than half of the size suggested by the ALA standards.

245 Hunter, Carolyn P. "A History of the Olivia Raney Library, 1899-1959." Master's thesis, University of North Carolina, 1964. 84p.

The Olivia Raney Library was founded as a public library by Richard Beverly Raney in memory of his first wife. The North Carolina General Assembly granted it a charter in 1899, specifying that it was to serve the white population of the city of Raleigh. In 1927 this charter was amended to extend the library's services to the Negro population. The county appropriated funds to help the library establish county library service in 1926. The author emphasizes the development of the services of the library under three head librarians: Miss Jennie Coffin, J. S. Atkinson, and Miss Clyde Smith.

246 Memory, Marjorie W. "A History of the Randolph Public Library, 1935-1967." Master's thesis, University of North Carolina, 1968. 97p.

This historical study of the Randolph Public Library examines factors contributing to the development and progress of the library, including persons and organizations involved. Also discussed are the services offered by the institution as a social and cultural agency as well as support given to the library by the citizens. The building programs of the fifties and sixties are also considered.

247 Moore, Bennie L. "A History of Public Library Service to Negroes in Winston-Salem, North Carolina, 1927-1951." Master's thesis, Atlanta University, 1961. 57p.

The Public Library of Winston-Salem was built with Carnegie funds in 1903. It was not until 1927 that the Moses Horton Branch was opened on a trial basis to serve Negro citizens. In 1931 an old one-room store was rented for the Negro branch. By 1951 the Negro branch contained 10,344 books and circulated 45,415.

248 Murphy, Sunshine B. "The History of the Rockingham County Library, 1930-1955." Master's thesis, University of North Carolina, 1956. 123p.

The author begins with a survey of library development in Rockingham County, North Carolina from 1892, when the first circulating library was established, until 1930. The library owed its origin to Mrs. B. F. McBane, who in 1930 donated 300 books, a furnished cottage to house the books, and funds for a staff. In 1934 the library became known as the Public Library of Rockingham County and began to receive county funds. In 1937 a new headquarters building was constructed and by 1955 eight branch libraries had been built.

249 Scoggin, Rebecca B. "The Development of Public Library Services in Chowan, Tyrrell and Washington Counties." Master's thesis, University of North Carolina, 1967. 69p.

The author outlines the development of libraries in Chowan, Tyrell, and Washington Counties, North Carolina from the colonial era to 1967, with emphasis on the social, economic, and cultural forces which influenced library growth and encouraged the development of public libraries in the area. Special attention is devoted to the Pettigrew Regional Library which has served the tri-county area since 1955.

250 Stewart, William L., Jr. "A History of the High Point, North Carolina Public Library." Master's thesis, University of North Carolina, 1963. 76p.

This paper traces the history of the High Point Public Library from its establishment in 1926 through 1959. It took fourteen years of sustained effort to get the library started, and from then on matters became more difficult rather than simpler. From the very beginning the library lacked the support of the municipal leaders of High Point. From 1926 until 1950 they placed numerous obstacles in the path of the library's development. The author describes the often frustrating efforts of library-conscious individuals to overcome this resistance.

251 Taylor, Joann. "Public Library Legislation in the State of North Carolina, 1897-June 30, 1956." Master's thesis, University of North Carolina, 1958. 89p. Published: University of Kentucky, Microcard Publications, Series B, Number 29.

Traces the history of the public, public-local, and private laws relating to public libraries in North Carolina and analyzes the effects of these laws on library development in the state. The study covers 57 years—from 1897, when the first public library was established by law, to June 30, 1956, when the North Carolina Library Commission was abolished. An appendix contains a chronological list of legislation relating to North Carolina libraries.

252 von Oesen, Elaine. "Public Library Service in North Carolina and the W.P.A." Master's thesis, University of North Carolina, 1951. 119p.

The first section of this thesis reviews public library development in North Carolina from 1897 to the 1930s. Next, the many contributions of the Works Progress Administration (WPA) between 1935 and 1942 are summarized. During this period the areas served by public libraries advanced from 38 percent to 85 percent. WPA workers, numbering 1,200 in 1942, were engaged in such activities as cataloging, mending, staff assistance, and bookmobile service. The WPA experience accelerated the growth of public libraries, promoted regional cooperation, brought improved service to the Negro population, and stimulated a program of state aid following dissolution of the federal programs.

253 Whedbee, Mabel M. "A History of the Development and Expan-

sion of Bookmobile Service in North Carolina, 1923-1960." Master's thesis, University of North Carolina, 1962. 60p.

Traces the origins and evolution of bookmobile service in North Carolina from its start in Durham County in 1923 to 1960. The author attempts to determine the factors that stimulated or retarded this development. Special emphasis is placed on the demonstrations by the Library Commission's book truck, the WPA book trucks, and on state and federal aid.

NORTH DAKOTA

254 Brudvig, Glenn L. "Public Libraries in North Dakota: The Formative Years, 1880-1920." Master's thesis, University of Minnesota, 1962. 129p. Summary published: *North Dakota Quarterly* 39 (1963): 61-66.

Libraries came to North Dakota in the 1870s, but the public libraries had little success until the turn of the twentieth century. The author finds that women's clubs were instrumental in establishing libraries in North Dakota and that they were responsible for obtaining a library tax levy from the legislature in 1900. Further aid was provided by the Carnegie grants in the late nineteenth century. By 1920 public library development had reached a plateau in North Dakota with libraries in all of the major cities and in many of the small towns.

OHIO
(Other than Cleveland)

255 Arthur, Adah W. "A History of the Warder Public Library, Springfield, Ohio." Master's thesis, Kent State University, 1955. 51p.

This paper traces the history of Springfield and its Warder Public Library. Brief attention is given to library development from 1841, when the first subscription library was established, to

1890, when Benjamin Warder paid for the construction of a free public library building. The major portion of the paper is devoted to Mr. Warder's library, 1890-1954.

256   Barnett, Louise F. "A History of the Akron Public Library, 1874-1942." Master's thesis, Kent State University, 1974. 130p.

The Akron Public Library, successor of two earlier social libraries, received municipal approval in 1874. The early development of the library was guided by Mary Pauline Edgerton, director from 1889 to 1920. New quarters were obtained in 1904 with funds secured from the Carnegie Corporation. Despite modest improvements in the collection and staff, the library was chronically short of funds most of the time and the subject of numerous stories in the local press. The contributions of the Works Progress Administration and the introduction of children's services and branches are described.

257   Battles, Frances M. "An Account of the Development of the Public Library Movement in Ohio with Special Reference to Some Outstanding Libraries." Master's thesis, University of Illinois, 1928. 212p.

The author sketches the development of the predecessors of public libraries in Ohio, and then discusses in detail the rise of a number of prominent public libraries including those in Cincinnati, Dayton, Cleveland, Toledo, and Youngstown. Two other chapters deal with library legislation in the state and the development of the Ohio State Library.

258   Baughman, Ruth O. "Fifty-three Years of Progress: Public Libraries in Lima, Ohio 1855-1908." Master's thesis, Western Reserve University, 1954. 92p.

This study traces the evolution of library service in Lima, Ohio, from the establishment of the first school district libraries in the middle of the nineteenth century to the institution of a free public library in 1901, and from there to 1906, when the

Carnegie library building was built. It includes a list of book titles in one of the library's early published catalogs.

259 Boone, Helen H. "A History of the Salem (Ohio) Public Library." Master's thesis, Kent State University, 1962. Published: University of Kentucky Press, Microcard Publications, Series B, Number 53.

This paper is divided into three major parts: 1) history of early subscription libraries in Salem from 1814 to 1898; 2) history of the tax-supported Salem Public Library from 1898 to 1961, with emphasis on the growth of the physical plant and services; and 3) the growth of financial support for the library and the development of the book stock.

260 Bowden, Clyde N. "The History of Lane Public Library, Hamilton, Ohio." Master's thesis, Western Reserve University, 1955. 36p.

The Lane Library is one of the oldest public libraries in Ohio. Special state legislation in 1868 permitted the city of Hamilton to accept the gift of a library from one of its citizens, Clark Lane. A brief biography of Mr. Lane and a survey of precursors of the Lane Library are presented in the early chapters. The author then goes on to trace the library's history, 1868-1954.

261 Burton, Arlynn S. "The Cuyahoga County (Ohio) Library System: A History." Master's thesis, Western Reserve University, 1952. 122p.

This study traces the history of the Cuyahoga County Library from its conception in 1921 with the passage of the County District Library Bill to its development as one of the largest county libraries in the United States. The administrations of librarians Amy Winslow (1941-1946) and Raymond C. Lindquist (1946-) are treated in depth.

262 Buzzard, Ruth A. "History of Bookmobile Service, Dayton Public Library, Dayton, Ohio." Master's thesis, Western Reserve University, 1953. 47p.

This paper treats the history of bookmobile service in Dayton, Ohio, and in Montgomery County, Ohio, from 1923 to the end of 1952. Special emphasis is placed on the ideas and influence of Electra C. Doren, librarian in Dayton 1896-1905 and 1913-1927. A leading library pioneer, she instituted the library's bookwagon—the first in the state and one of the earliest in the nation.

263 Collins, Lucile T. "A History of the East Cleveland Public Library." Master's thesis, Western Reserve University, 1951. 41p.

This study covers the period 1904 to 1950, with emphasis on the years 1904-1916. The author offers a brief history of Cleveland and traces the history of the library movement in the United States and Ohio.

264 Crammer, Jack C. "History and Development of Library Services in the Township of Hudson, Summit County, Ohio." Master's thesis, Kent State University, 1950. 80p.

Chronicles the development of library service in Hudson Township from the first subscription libraries of George Kilbourne and David Hudson (established 1802) through the founding and development of the Hudson Library and Historical Society. In 1910 Mrs. Caroline Babcock presented a $100,000 endowment for the establishment of the Hudson Library and Historical Society, having in mind the initiation of a historical museum and the establishment of a free circulating library to serve the residents of Hudson Township. In addition to a history of the library the author analyzes its relationship with the Western Reserve Academy Library.

265 Donze, Sara L. "A History of the Dr. Sloan Library." Master's thesis, Western Reserve University, 1958. 54p.

Traces the development of a public library established and endowed by "Dr." Earl Sloan, the inventor of "Dr. Sloan's liniment" which was billed as "good for man and beast" and eventually made its inventor a millionaire. In 1914, Sloan built and endowed the little library in Zanesfield, Ohio and named four "lifetime trustees." The library has always been small, never able to afford a professional librarian, but has been fairly well patronized by Zanesfield's residents.

266 Eckert, Charlotte J. "A History of the New Philadelphia-Tuscarawas County (Ohio) District Library." Master's thesis, Western Reserve University, 1955. 53p.

This paper emphasizes the origins and early development of the library from 1900 to 1937. It traces the development and influence of the Philadelphia Union Club Library Association, a women's organization that lent great support to library development.

267 Elias, William D. "History of the Reed Memorial Library, Ravenna, Ohio." Master's thesis, Kent State University, 1961. 60p.

After presenting a brief history of Ravenna from 1799 to 1960, the author traces the history of the Ravenna Public Library from 1913 to 1960. Crowded conditions, financial shortages, and a lack of professional help were the library's problems. In 1960 the library contained 30,000 volumes.

268 Fleischer, Miriam L. "A History of the Rocky River Public Library." Master's thesis, Western Reserve University, 1954. 45p.

The author describes the formation of the North Ridge Literary Society in 1877 and traces its evolution into the Rocky River Public Library in 1925. In 1926 the library was built with a $25,000 gift and a $60,000 bond issue and since that time has developed steadily. In 1952 the library board turned down an offer to become the fourth regional branch of the Cuyahoga County Library.

269 Forney, Dorothy J. "The History of the East Palestine Public Library." Master's thesis, Western Reserve University, 1954. 42p.

This study covers the span of 34 years from 1920 to 1954. The library was started sometime in 1920 with books from the state traveling library. After several defeats of bond issues, the library was able to erect a new building in 1954 as a result of gifts by the citizens.

270 Gooch, Richard E. "History of the Birchard Public Library and Sandusky County Extension Service." Master's thesis, Western Reserve University, 1957. 67p.

This paper surveys the history of the Birchard Public Library in Freemont, Ohio and the Sandusky County Extension Service from 1873, when the library was endowed by Sardis Birchard, through 1956. The author concentrates on the period after 1930.

271 Goodale, Grace. "History of the Portage County Library, Ohio." Master's thesis, Western Reserve University, 1951. 45p.

In 1935 the school board passed a bill creating the Hiram Village School District Public Library. The collection was made up of 150 second-hand books purchased for $35, but soon was augmented by 2,500 books from the state traveling library. In 1942 a large house was purchased for the library's new home. The author carries the story through 1950.

272 Harshe, Cleo E. "Lima Public Library Extension Services: History and Development." Master's thesis, Western Reserve University, 1955. 78p.

Traces the extension activities of the Lima Public Library (Ohio) from 1924 through 1954. By 1954, the library had 22 outlets in the form of bookmobiles, branches, and stations. Information is drawn from library reports, correspondence, and interviews.

273 Harshfield, Lula. "The Wagnall's Memorial." Master's thesis, Western Reserve University, 1957. 100p.

This study describes the events surrounding a gift of nearly a million dollars by Mabel Wagnalls-Jones in honor of her father, Adam W. Wagnalls (co-founder of the Funk and Wagnalls Publishing Company), and her mother, Anna Willis Wagnalls. The $500,000 building, containing some 12,000 volumes, stands in Lithopolis, Ohio, a town of 360 people, and houses such treasures as a number of original O. Henry letters.

274 Havron, H. Julia. "A History of Library Service in Crawford County, Ohio." Master's thesis, Kent State University, 1969. 144p.

A study of library service in Crawford County, Ohio, from 1834, when the first social library was established, to 1969. While all types of library service are covered, the author emphasizes the development of the three public libraries which serve the county.

275 Hazeltine, Robert E. "The History of Birchard Library, Freemont, Ohio 1874-1950." Master's thesis, Western Reserve University, 1950. 56p.

This study traces the development of the Birchard Library from 1873, when Sardis Birchard first pondered the idea, until 1950. Emphasis is laid on the founding and development of the early library. Sardis Birchard donated $50,000 to get the library started. The influence of President (then Governor of Ohio) Rutherford B. Hayes on the development of the library is discussed.

276 Heim, Helen R. "A History of the Lepper Library of Lisbon, Ohio." Master's thesis, Kent State University, 1965. 96p.

This paper presents a history of the Lepper Library from its inception in 1896, due to the efforts of Virginia Lepper, to 1965. The Lepper Library is one of 26 remaining association libraries in Ohio. In 1965 the book collection numbered 50,000 volumes.

277 Hopkins, Laura. "The Development of the Local History and Genealogy Division of the Toledo Public Library." Master's thesis, Western Reserve University, 1957. 74p.

In 1939 the Toledo Public became one of the first libraries in the country to establish a separate history and genealogy division. The first section of the paper is devoted to a brief history of the Toledo Public Library from its origin in 1838 to 1957. The author then traces the history of the Division from 1941 to 1956 and indicates its program aims: 1) to acquire and maintain an excellent history and genealogy collection; 2) to stimulate interest in local history; and 3) to emphasize departmental participation in historical research.

278 Jones, George. "Materials Relating to the Development of a History of Public Libraries in the Western Reserve." Master's thesis, Kent State University, 1957. 81p.

This study examines records of the founding and early activities of public libraries in the Western Reserve territory. Following a brief history and selective description of area libraries, the source documents are listed. Compiled as a resource for further research.

279 Lewis, Mary E. "A History of the Mount Vernon, Ohio, Public Library, 1888-1949." Master's thesis, Western Reserve University, 1950. 56p.

The first three chapters of this paper deal with 1) a sketch of the city of Mount Vernon; 2) early library organizations to 1888; and 3) the public library from its opening in 1888 to 1900. The remaining three chapters cover the period 1900 to 1949.

280 Low, Joanne F. "A History of Cuyahoga Falls Library Association and the Taylor Memorial Association." Master's thesis, Western Reserve University, 1955. 98p.

The Cuyahoga Falls Library Association, founded in 1883 by the poet Edward Rowland Sill, served the community until 1911. It was replaced by the Taylor Memorial Association in 1912. At first a subscription library, Taylor Memorial became a city library during the depression years and is now a county library. The author treats its development to 1954, when the collection numbered 36,000 volumes.

281   MacCampbell, Barbara B. "History of the Kent, Ohio Free Library." Master's thesis, Western Reserve University, 1950. 98p.

Reported missing.

282   Meshot, Genevieve V. "A History of the Hubbard Public Library." Master's thesis, Western Reserve University, 1949. 23p.

This library, actually a school district library, was first established in 1929, and this paper covers its growth until 1948. As with many other American small-town libraries, a women's group, the Hubbard Colloquial Forum, was very influential in its development.

283   Murray, Katherine. "History of the Development of Bookmobile Service, Hamilton County, Ohio." Master's thesis, Western Reserve University, 1951. 37p.

The author traces the development of the bookmobile service instituted by the Cincinnati Public Library in Hamilton County in 1926. The relation of population trends to the expansion of services is statistically illustrated.

284   Mutschler, Herbert F. "The Ohio Public Library and State Aid." Master's thesis, Western Reserve University, 1952. 50p.

This study commences with a survey of early Ohio library history (1795-1851) and then considers chronologically the development of state aid in Ohio. The first real step toward solvency for public libraries was the institution in 1934 of a new source of income—the county intangible tax. Robert A. Taft, then a state senator, sponsored the bill. In 1935, $100,000 was granted by the State Assembly to public libraries in Ohio. Appropriations were made every year thereafter, enabling the public libraries to expand their services.

285 Nestleroad, Rosemary. "A History of Fifty Years of Library Service: Napoleon Public Library, Napoleon, Ohio." Master's thesis, Western Reserve University, 1956. 39p.

The author begins this study with a consideration of the subscription library established in Napoleon in 1906. This library was sponsored by the Women's Christian Temperance Union and the membership fee was 25 cents for a three-month period. One year later another group of women established the Napoleon Library Association, and by 1911 the collection had grown to 1,200 volumes. In 1911 Andrew Carnegie gave the city $10,000 and the Carnegie Free Public Library was built. The author concludes by surveying the administrations of the five librarians who served through 1953.

286 Nolan, C. "The History of the County Library in Ohio." Master's thesis, Western Reserve University, 1949. 31p.

This paper gives a description of Ohio county libraries from 1898 to 1949 with consideration of library legislation and its effects on Ohio library development. The author describes the Brumbach Library in Van Wert County, established in 1898, which is usually considered the first county library in America. Despite the early start, Ohio county libraries developed slowly until 1940, although trends seem to indicate an accelerated pace since then.

287 Reed, Mary M. "History of the Lakewood Public Library, Lakewood, Ohio: The First Twenty-Five Years 1913-1938." Master's thesis, Western Reserve University, 1959. 79p.

The author, after presenting an outline of the history of Lakewood, traces the history of the library in topical form, dealing with such subjects as the book collection, the physical plant, library government, financial support, and personnel. The collection grew to nearly 80,000 volumes by 1938 and the library was operating ten branches in the city schools. The considerable influence of Roena A. Ingham, librarian 1915-1938, is stressed.

288 Satterfield, Helen C. "History of Highland County District Library." Master's thesis, Kent State University, 1960. 60p.

Treats chronologically the history of the Highland County District (Public) Library from its beginnings in 1877 to 1959. The author emphasizes the development of the physical plant and the book collection. Briefly discusses the two branch libraries in Greenfield and Lynchburg.

289 Shewmaker, Janet D. "History of the Willoughby Public Library, Willoughby, Ohio." Master's thesis, Western Reserve University, 1953. 30p.

The study opens with brief sketches of the libraries in Willoughby before 1905, when the public library was established. The author traces the history of the public library to 1952. In 1906 the Circulating Library Society donated its 1,400 books to the new library, and in 1909 a new library building was built with $14,500 given to the city by Andrew Carnegie. In 1947 the library was officially designated the Willoughby Public Library and entered into a contract with the local school board to provide service to the school system.

290 Skidmore, Warren L. "A History of the Peninsula (Ohio) Library and Historical Society, 1941-1967." Master's thesis, Kent State University, 1967. 90p.

The author traces the history of a unique little library in Peninsula, Ohio. This library, established in 1941, had grown to some 18,000 volumes in 1967. The library now is housed in a $149,000 building and has an annual budget of $26,000. The town of Peninsula has slightly over 600 inhabitants.

291 Sommerville, Sally G. "A Brief History of the Public Libraries of Mentor, Ohio." Master's thesis, Kent State University, 1962. Published: University of Kentucky Press, Microcard Publications, Series B, Number 59.

A history of libraries in Mentor, Ohio from 1819 to 1962. Arranged chronologically, this paper treats the following libraries: 1) Mentor Library Company (1819); 2) Mentor Library Association (1875); 3) Mentor Village Library Association (1890); and 4) Garfield Public Library (1927).

292 Spaulding, Verdabelle A. "A History of the Two Public Libraries in Mentor, Ohio." Master's thesis, Western Reserve University, 1950. 31p.

The libraries considered here are the Garfield Public Library, the older of the two, which is covered from 1819 to 1927, and the Mentor Township Public Library, from its inception in 1925 to 1935. The history of the predecessors of both libraries is also sketched.

293 Stratton, George W. "History of Public Library Service in Solon." Master's thesis, Kent State University, 1972. 90p.

This history of the Solon (Ohio) Public Library emphasizes the contributions of the library within the community and the role of community in creating the library. Library service began in Solon in 1924, two years after formation of the Cuyahoga County Library system. The Solon Public Library was housed in the high school and subsequently in the town hall for more than 40 years. A permanent building was realized in 1967 through the efforts of the friends group and community leaders. Service activities, circulation, and the impact of several library directors are discussed.

294 Szkudlarek, Marie E. "Historical Development of Work with Children in the Toledo Public Library." Master's thesis, Western Reserve University, 1954. 37p.

The Toledo Library's Children's Department, established in 1899, was one of the pioneers in this area of public library service. The author traces its history, also that of the library itself and the children's library movement in general. In 1918 Ethel C. Wright was named head of the children's department, and she was instrumental in its organization and in training children's librarians. By 1952 the Children's Department was circulating 874,000 books annually and had a collection of over 150,000 volumes.

295 Teeter, Lulu W. "A Brief History of the Growth and Development of the Youngstown Library Association, Youngstown, Ohio." Master's thesis, Kent State University, 1956. 53p.

A portion of this paper deals with the history of the Association from 1900 to 1950. The rest of the paper deals with current operations.

296 Thomas, Marjorie E. "History of Public Library Service in Jackson County, Ohio." Master's thesis, Kent State University, 1963. 94p.

After a brief history of Jackson County, this paper reviews the historical development of the three Jackson County Public Libraries: Jackson Public Library, Welliston Public Library, and Oak Hill Public Library. The three libraries suffered serious financial difficulties from their early beginnings and are still quite small.

297 Weis, Leah A. "The History of Children's Work at Akron Public Library in Akron, Ohio." Master's thesis, Western Reserve University, 1951. 72p.

After presenting a survey of library history in Akron, the author traces the history of the Children's Department from 1900 into the middle of the twentieth century. The library was fortunate to have such an industrious, forceful children's librarian as Maude Herndon during the years 1900 to 1920. She was able to garner sufficient monetary support to put the department on a sound footing by the time of her retirement. The department slowed after her departure until 1928, when Harriet W. Leaf was named librarian. She was able to reorganize the department, to make large additions to the collection, and to hire numerous children's librarians.

298 Wetzel, Norman P. "Mary P. Martin and the Canton Public Library, 1884-1928: A Study in Library Leadership." Master's thesis, Kent State University, 1969. 153p.

The author presents a history of the Canton Public Library to 1928, with emphasis on Mary P. Martin's role in shaping the library's structure and purpose. Martin served for 42 years as director of the library.

299 Wine, Eugene. "The Development of the Dayton Public Library, Dayton, Ohio 1900-1957." Master's thesis, Western Reserve University, 1958. 38p.

The author treats library development in light of the economic and political background of the area. Four major subjects are considered: 1) the library's economic and political background; 2) the story of the main building; 3) branch library development; and 4) changes in services.

300 Wolcott, Merlin D. "The History and Development of the Sandusky Library Association, Sandusky, Ohio." Master's thesis, Kent State University, 1953. 78p.

Chapter II deals with the social pressures that led to the establishment of libraries in Sandusky as early as 1825. The author traces the evolution of libraries in Sandusky from the Portland Library Association to the Sandusky Lyceum, to the Philomathesian Society, to the Young Men's Christian Association, and finally to the Sandusky Library Association of 1870.

301 Young, Mary Jo. "The Akron Public Library, 1942-1957." Master's thesis, Western Reserve University, 1958. 66p.

This paper describes one of the most active periods of growth in the Akron Public Library's history. The author surveys Akron library history from 1834 to 1942 before beginning a detailed history of the period 1942-1957. Emphasis is placed on the physical features of development. Little space is given to library personalities; however, the influence of librarian Russell Munn is readily discernible.

302 Young, Sefville S. "History of the Norwalk Public Library from 1853-1927." Master's thesis, Western Reserve University, 1954. 106p.

This paper actually is a history of the antecedents of the Norwalk Public Library. In 1853 the library came to life as an integral part of the Whittlessey Academy of Arts and Sciences. The collection grew slowly and in 1866 it was merged with the collection of the Young Men's Library and Reading Room Association. In 1870 the collection of the Firelands Historical Society was added. In 1903 Andrew Carnegie granted the city $15,000 for a building, and in 1927 the Association turned the building and its collections over to a new School District Public Library.

OHIO (Cleveland)

303 Bradley, Nellie B. "The Development of Service to Children in the Cleveland Public Library, with Special Reference to Perkins Library." Master's thesis, Western Reserve University, 1951. 57p.

Chapter I of this study surveys the evolution of children's library service in America. Chapter II evaluates the influence of William H. Brett, Caroline Burnite, the Library League, and Effie L. Power on children's work in Cleveland. Chapters III and IV deal with the history of the Perkins Library, which at its opening in 1908 was the first in Cleveland devoted exclusively to children.

304 Butrick, May W. "History of the Foreign Literature Department of the Cleveland Public Library, 1925-1972." Master's thesis, Kent State University, 1974. 89p.

Describes the growth of Cleveland's foreign literature department and its service to the ethnic community. Major foreign language collections were acquired in German, French, Hungarian, Spanish, Russian, Czech, Yiddish, Polish, and many others. By 1972, the department held 174,000 volumes in 39 languages and operated with a staff of five. When collection size and circulation patterns are compared to population distributions, the author concludes that external pressures, perhaps from academic institutions, account for the variances in some language holdings.

305 Copeland, Elizabeth F. "A History of the Carnegie West Branch of the Cleveland Public Library." Master's thesis, Western Reserve University, 1954. 51p.

This branch of the Cleveland Public Library was opened in 1892 in a rented room on the second floor of a building on Pearl Street. The author describes the changing conditions the library faced over a 60-year period. At first the library served only a wealthy and established class of readers. However, at the turn of the century, large groups of transient workers, attracted by burgeoning industry, settled in the area. The author describes the changes made in library service to meet the demands of the new population.

306 Greene, James T. "A History and Description of the Literature Division of the Cleveland Public Library." Master's thesis, Western Reserve University, 1954. 110p.

The Literature Division got its start when William Howard Brett initiated a plan for the departmentalization of the Cleveland Public Library. Circulation began to soar in 1928 as spreading unemployment provided more time for reading. With the passing of the depression in 1935, circulation and reference figures decreased. Over the years the staff of the Division has become increasingly involved in community life through sponsorship of poetry readings, book talks to clubs, and membership in civic organizations.

307   Ingalls, Mary E. "The History and Description of the Philosophy and Religion Division of the Cleveland Public Library." Master's thesis, Western Reserve University, 1954. 50p.

Established in 1913, the Philosophy and Religion Division has expanded from its original alcove to a large room on the third floor of the main library, crowded with a collection numbering some 70,000 volumes. The first section of this paper is historical in nature; the remainder is a description of present services.

308   Murray, Mary E. "The Branch Library: A Mirror of Its Community, with Case Histories of Several Branches of the Cleveland Public Library." Master's thesis, Western Reserve University, 1951. 50p.

This study devotes the first three sections to the history of branch libraries in Cleveland. After presenting a general introduction, the author traces the history of the following branches: Broadway, Carnegie West, Collinwood, Eastman, Euclid-100th Street, Glenville, Hough, Norwood, Nottingham, Quincy, South Brooklyn, Sterling, Superior, and West Park.

309   Nagy, Mary C. "History and Relationship of the Rice Branch Library to Its Hungarian Patrons." Master's thesis, Western Reserve University, 1952. 28p.

The author begins by outlining the history of the Hungarian population of Cleveland and then traces the history of the Rice Branch's service to Hungarian patrons since 1916. The author discovered three major groups using the library: 1) the aged who never had or would learn English; 2) newcomers who might later master English; and 3) people who knew English but read Hungarian literature to stay familiar with their original language. The period after 1945 saw a tremendous influx of displaced Hungarians into Cleveland, and this greatly increased demands for Hungarian materials.

310   Phillips, Virginia. "Fifty-six Years of Service to the Foreign-born by the Cleveland Public Library." Master's thesis, Western Reserve University, 1957. 55p.

The author describes the efforts of the Cleveland Public Library from 1900 to 1956 to aid the foreign-born in their attempts to become Americanized. Two librarians in the Cleveland area were prominent in this work: May Sweet, librarian at the Alta Branch (1906-1938) in the Italian district, and Eleanor Ledbetter, librarian at the Broadway Branch in the Bohemian and Polish area from 1910-1938. The development of services such as home visits and special library programs is covered. After 1940 a shortage of personnel and shifts in the urban population forced the library to change its approach.

311   Rodstein, Frances M. "The East 79th Street Branch of the Cleveland Public Library: An Historical Overview 1909-1970." Master's thesis, Kent State University, 1971. 99p.

The author portrays the ways in which this medium-sized branch of the Cleveland Public Library met the demands of a constantly changing clientele, while at the same time trying to properly place this story in the context of larger social and economic conditions. After presenting a demographic analysis of the community 1909-1970, the author sketches the early history of the 79th Street Branch, and then looks in detail at adult services, young adult services, and children's services.

312   Schryver, Norma E. "A History of the Business Information Bureau of the Cleveland Public Library." Master's thesis, Western Reserve University, 1950. 51p.

The Business Information Bureau was initiated in response to the demand for a special library service to businessmen. In 1928, Rose Vormelker was brought in to organize and administer the department. The author outlines her contributions and traces the development of the department through 1950. The department became one of the best known services of the Cleveland Public Library. It was directly responsible for bringing a number of industries to Cleveland because of the fine business information service available.

313 Shamp, B. Kathleen. "The Music Section of the Cleveland Public Library." Master's thesis, Western Reserve University, 1954. 53p.

The music section began in 1920 with slightly over a thousand volumes and a budget of $200-$400. In the late 1920s came the domination of the music field by radio, and the author describes how the library met this awkward situation. A similar situation arose with phonograph records in the 1940s. In the fifties the library's holdings numbered over 20,000 items. The author concludes with a discussion of gifts to the library.

314 Sheffield, Helen G. "A Report on the History and Development of the Library for the Blind of the Cleveland Public Library." Master's thesis, Western Reserve University, 1951. 29p.

The first effort at providing reading material for the blind in the Cleveland Public Library was made in 1903, when a small collection of Braille books was made available for loan. Librarian Linda A. Eastman pressed for increased services and by 1913 the collection contained 665 volumes. The appropriations were relatively small until 1932, when the Cleveland Public Library was chosen as a regional center for the reception of Braille books from the government. Under this program the collection grew to 30,647 volumes in 1950.

315 Silver, Robert A. "A Description and History of the Foreign Literature Division of the Cleveland Public Library." Master's thesis, Western Reserve University, 1953. 63p.

In the final portion of this paper the author traces the history of the Division from the early 1900s to 1950. The Foreign Literature

Division gained full status in 1925. The author describes the influence on the Division of the wars and the concomitant influx of the foreign born.

316 Yockey, Robert. "The Winged Bequest: An Account of the Cleveland Public Library's Service to the Incapacitated." Master's thesis, Western Reserve University, 1949.

This paper describes the efforts of the Cleveland Public Library to distribute books to the handicapped. The service began in 1936 with aid from the Works Progress Administration. Shut-ins and invalids were visited and given books. In 1941 the Frederick W. and Henrietta Slocum Judd Fund was established with $519,000 to support the program so that "those who cannot run may read." Services were greatly expanded, and in the last year covered by this study nearly 4,000 shut-ins were helped.

OKLAHOMA

317 Henke, Esther M. "The History of the Public Libraries in Oklahoma." Master's thesis, University of Oklahoma, 1954. 160p.

Beginning with a general history of the public library in America, the author then outlines the factors influencing library development in Oklahoma. Women's clubs, local school districts, and Carnegie grants were the major stimuli. The major portion of the study is devoted to mini-histories of 73 public libraries. Oklahoma lagged behind national standards because of excessive volunteerism and self-perpetuating boards.

OREGON

318 Barrett, Myran. "History of Oregon Public Libraries." Master's thesis, University of Oregon, 1940. 121p.

The development of public libraries in Oregon is traced from the establishment of the Library Association of Portland in 1864 to 1940. Development was relatively slow. At the turn of the century, when the women's clubs of the state pushed a law for the tax support of libraries through the legislature, only nine libraries were able to take advantage of it. However, this law stimulated library growth in the state, and by 1913, when the State Library was organized, there were 45 libraries in Oregon. The author discusses financial and personnel developments in the public libraries of Oregon to 1940, and devotes one chapter to library housing.

319 Kembel, Dorothy. "The Development and Activities of the Library Association of Portland." Master's thesis, University of Portland, 1954. 87p.

The Library Association of Portland (Oregon) was founded in 1864 as a subscription library. Conversion to a tax-supported public library was accomplished in 1901. Branch service to three districts began in 1907. A new building was erected in 1913. Mary Frances Isom served as director from 1902 until her death in 1920. It was a period of progress and innovation. From 1920 to 1945 the library assisted the local school system with its library program. Current activities and services are described in some detail.

320 Kirchem, Charleen E. "Library Development in Clackamas County, Oregon." Master's thesis, University of Washington, 1952. 68p.

The author devotes the first twenty pages of this study to a survey of library developments in Oregon from the early 1840s to 1950. The final portion is devoted to short historical accounts of the ten public libraries in Clackamas County.

PENNSYLVANIA

321 Ambler, Barbara H. "History of the Children's Department of the

Free Library of Philadelphia, 1898-1953." Master's thesis, Drexel Institute of Technology, 1956. 60p.

Reported missing.

322 Barker, Jeanne W. "The History and Development of the Monessen Public Library, Monessen, Pennsylvania." Master's thesis, Western Reserve University, 1953. 61p.

The study begins with a survey of the town and its environment. Part two traces the history of the Public Library from 1934, when the Monessen Women's Club pushed to establish a library program for the city, to 1953. The Club merged its meager collection with the school district library and thus provided library service to the whole community.

323 Diana, Joan P. "History of the Osterhout Free Library, 1889-1961." Master's thesis, Marywood College (Scranton, Pennsylvania), 1961. 41p.

This paper traces the development of the Osterhout Free Library of Wilkes-Barre, Pennsylvania, from its beginnings in 1889 to 1961. The library was given to the city in 1882 by Isaac Smith Osterhout, a wealthy businessman. When opened it contained some 10,500 books and was staffed by six people. In 1961 the collection had grown to over 120,000 volumes and the staff numbered 28. The author finds that the Osterhout Library was the beginning of the free public library movement in northeastern Pennsylvania.

324 DiPietro, Lawrence N. "The Free Library of Philadelphia: Its Formation and Early Physical Growth from 1891 to 1917." Master's thesis, Drexel Institute of Technology, 1952. 46p.

The library conference of 1876, held in Philadelphia, planted the idea of a public library in the minds of the people of that city. However, the city administration seemed satisfied with the numerous semi-public libraries already available to Philadelphia residents. Thus it was not until 1889, when George Pepper presented $250,000 to the city for a public library, that any action was taken. The library system began official operation in 1891, and in 1894 the 14,356-volume book stock registered a phenomenal circulation of over 60,000. The author discusses the development of the branch system, the services offered by the library, and its efforts to build up the collection.

325   Egolf, Jean L. "A History of the Bethlehem Public Library, Bethlehem, Pennsylvania, 1901 to 1954." Master's thesis, Drexel Institute of Technology, 1955. 63p.

The author surveys the history of Bethlehem, Pennsylvania, and discusses the predecessors of the Bethlehem Public Library. In 1900 a group of local women organized the Bethlehem Library Association and started a public subscription library. For the next 20 years subscriptions and gifts were the library's sole means of support, and it encountered numerous financial difficulties. In 1920 the library began to receive public tax funds, and by 1950 was circulating over 120,000 books yearly. The author describes the development of children's work, a branch library system, the physical plant, and the staff.

326   Girvin, Catherine M. "The Allentown Free Library, A History of Its Growth and Services." Master's thesis, Drexel Institute of Technology, 1954. 58p.

The first part of this paper is devoted to a survey of early library development in Allentown, Pennsylvania. The author reports that as early as 1810 libraries were being established in the city. Treats the history of the Allentown Free Library in three chronological sections: early development, 1912-1929; later development, 1930-1942; and recent growth, 1943-1953. Within each section emphasis is placed on the physical plant, financial support, book collection, staff, and library services.

327   Keim, Aldine. "The History of Cambria Free Library, Johnstown,

Pennsylvania, 1925-1951." Master's thesis, Drexel Institute of Technology, 1952. 46p.

This paper presents a brief summary of the early history of the Cambria Free Library (1870-1925), a description of the community it served, and a history of the institution from 1925 to 1951. Emphasized are administrative organization, financing, and special services such as children's services, bookmobile services, and special collections.

328 Klugiewicz, Esther. "Short History of the Erie (Penn) Public Library." Master's thesis, Western Reserve University, 1953. 33p.

Reported missing.

329 Meyer, William P. "A History of the Reading, Pennsylvania, Public Library, and Its Services to the Community, 1898-1952." Master's thesis, Drexel Institute of Technology, 1953. 55p.

The author traces library history in Reading from 1808, when a subscription library was founded, to 1952. The subscription library later evolved into the Reading Library (1868), and in 1898 was opened to the public and renamed the Reading Public Library. Each of five chronological chapters emphasizes the development of staff, facilities, collections, and services.

330 Potera, Edward J. "History of the Back Mountain Memorial Library, Dallas, Pennsylvania." Master's thesis, Marywood College (Scranton, Pennsylvania), 1969. 50p.

This study traces the history of the Back Mountain Memorial Library from 1945, when it was founded, to 1967. The main emphasis is on the continued harmony between the community and its library.

331 Ryberg, Herman T., Jr. "Warren Public Library: A History." Master's thesis, Western Reserve University, 1957. 53p.

Discusses the development of the Warren Public Library, which originated in a library association founded in 1831. The library suffered serious financial difficulties, but many benefactors helped ease the burden. In 1902 a Children's Room was opened, and in 1956 the collection numbered 80,000 volumes.

332 Smith, Mabel H. "Three Rural Libraries of Chester County, Pennsylvania: A Historical Survey of Their Development and Services of the Community." Master's thesis, Drexel Institute of Technology, 1950. 42p.

This study traces the history of three rural libraries within fifteen miles of each other in Chester County, Pennsylvania. The libraries treated are the Oxford Public Library, the West Grove Library, and the Bayard Taylor Library of Kennett Square. All three libraries were established around 1900, and they have remained quite small.

333 Tuck, Rhoda S. "Evolution of the Chester County Library: A History." Master's thesis, Drexel Institute of Technology, 1954. 65p.

This paper is divided into three major portions: 1) a history of Chester County, Pennsylvania; 2) a history of the immediate predecessor of the Chester County Library—the Public School Circulating Library (1897-1930); and 3) the history of the Chester County Library, 1928-1954. The author finds the County Library was a young institution in an old and conservative community and that progress and change were effected very slowly.

334 Whitney, Ellen M. "History of the Norristown (Penn.) Public Library." Master's thesis, Drexel Institute of Technology, 1955. 51p.

This paper traces the history of the Norristown Public Library from its beginnings as a subscription library in 1794 to its status as a public library in 1955. After a brief historical sketch of Norristown, the author treats the library in three chronological periods, with emphasis on the following points: housing, collections, circulation, financial support, and staff.

335 Winger, Anna K. "History of the Huntingdon County Library, Huntingdon, Pennsylvania, 1935-1953." Master's thesis, Drexel Institute of Technology, 1954. 52p.

This paper includes a brief analysis of the Huntingdon County Library, a description of the county it serves, and a history of the library for its 18 years of existence, 1935-1953. The library in 1953 was unable to gain much support from the public and thus failed to win a referendum calling for increased library appropriations.

RHODE ISLAND

336 Harding, Sister Mary F. "A History of the Providence Public Library, Providence, Rhode Island, from 1878 to 1960." Master's thesis, Catholic University of America, 1964. 75p.

The author begins by sketching the early history of libraries in Providence from 1838 to 1859. In 1838, Francis Wayland, who promoted one of the earliest tax-supported libraries in America, spoke before the members of the Providence Athenaeum and urged them to extend their facilities to all the citizens of Providence. Despite his efforts, the city had to wait until 1878 before a public library was established. It began service with some 10,000 volumes and a full-time librarian. The author discusses the development of the collections, the construction of a new building in 1896-1900, and the services.

SOUTH CAROLINA

337 Jarrell, Penelope H. "The Development of the County Library System in South Carolina from 1929 to 1943." Master's thesis, University of North Carolina, 1955. 70p.

This paper traces the history of county library development in South Carolina from 1929, when the State Public Library Association was established by law, to 1943, when the first appropriations were made. The author finds that in the early stages of development, the people were indifferent toward the service until the WPA gave extensive support to the program in 1930. The author is concerned mainly with broad trends and mentions individual libraries only when they influenced state wide patterns.

SOUTH DAKOTA

338 Crouch, Mary L. "The Library Movement in South Dakota with Special Reference to Some Outstanding Libraries." Master's thesis, University of Illinois, 1930. 152p.

Traces the development of the library movement in South Dakota from Territorial days to 1930, with attention to advancement through library legislation. A general survey of library development in South Dakota is presented, with a more detailed account of several representative libraries. Emphasis is placed on library service and administrative methods. The libraries receiving detailed treatment are the university libraries at the University of South Dakota and at South Dakota State, and the public libraries in Aberdeen, Ipswich, Lead, Rapid City, Sioux Falls, and Tyndall.

TENNESSEE

339 Buck, James P. "A History of the Library Resources of Putnam County." Master's thesis, Tennessee Polytechnic Institute, 1961. 87p.

The first part of this study deals with the early school resources of Putnam County that might have influenced the development of libraries. Andrew College, Washington Academy, and Dixie College are among the schools discussed. The second part deals with the early public library resources that have influenced the present system. The early schools had few libraries and the students had to depend on faculty libraries. Lack of financial support, which led to the demise of many private schools, also hampered library development.

340   Gordon, Douglas K. "The Thomas Hughes Free Public Library, Rugby, Tennessee: A History and Practical Bibliography." Doctoral dissertation, University of Tennessee, 1974. 226p. UMI# 75- 3597. Published: Rugby Restoration Press, 1979.

Reconstructs the history and significance of the Hughes Public Library (1800-1899) in the formation and design of the Rugby Colony of Thomas Hughes. The initial benefactor was Dana Estes, Boston publisher of children's literature. The library's catalog, holdings, rules, and use are described. A systematic bibliography of the phrase and poetry collection is included.

341   Govan, James F. "The History of the Chattanooga Public Library, 1905-1950." Master's thesis, Emory University, 1955. 141p.

The author traces the antecedents of the Chattanooga Public Library and describes socio-economic conditions in the city. In 1902 Andrew Carnegie pledged $50,000 for a public library in Chattanooga, and in 1905 the library opened with a collection of 3,700 volumes. In 1906 a children's room was opened, and in 25 years it circulated nearly 700,000 volumes. It was not until 1913 that a Negro branch was established. The author describes the library's unique cooperative arrangements with the University of Chattanooga, the efforts of Julius Rosenwald on behalf of the library during the depression, and the development of a school library branch.

342   Hansbrough, Irene C. "Public Library Service to Negroes in Knoxville, Tennessee." Master's thesis, Atlanta University, 1959. 66p.

The author begins by briefly sketching the history of library service to Negroes in the United States. She then outlines the history of the Knoxville Public Library System from 1885 to 1957, and traces the history of public library service to Negroes in Knoxville, 1917-1957. Library service to Negroes was centered in the two Negro branch libraries (Murphy and Carnegie) until 1950, when Knoxville's libraries were integrated.

343   Hoffman, Rheba P. "A History of Public Library Services to Negroes in Memphis, Tennessee." Master's thesis, Atlanta University, 1955. 54p.

This study traces the history of library service to Negroes in Memphis from its beginnings in the early 1900s to 1955. The author finds that services to Negro readers have been haphazard and insignificant, and that Memphis has lagged far behind other southern cities in the provision of library service to its Negro residents.

344   McCrary, Mary E. "A History of Public Library Service to Negroes in Nashville, Tennessee, 1916-1958." Master's thesis, Atlanta University, 1959. 42p.

The first library in Nashville was established in 1844 as a mercantile library; it became a free public library in 1901 through a donation from Andrew Carnegie. Negroes were not allowed the use of this library, and it was not until 1916 that a Negro branch was finally opened in Nashville. This library proved unsatisfactory for a number of reasons and it was sold in 1949. In 1950 the Nashville Public Library and all of its branches were opened to Negroes.

TEXAS

345   Agnew, Eloise. "The Texas Collection in the Houston Public Library, 1791-1871." Master's thesis, University of Texas, 1941. 122p.

Following a brief history of Houston, the several predecessors of the Houston Public Library are discussed. The Philosophical

Society of Texas was founded in 1837 and its successor, the Houston Lyceum, was established in 1848. The Houston Public Library first received municipal support in 1899. The Texas Collection began with a 15,000 volume gift from Major John Ephraim Thomas Milsap after the Civil War. Appended is a complete bibliographical listing of the 330 rare books, pamphlets, maps, newspapers, and musical scores represented in the collection which have imprint dates ranging from 1791 to 1871.

346 Allen, Dorothy L. "The Kemp Public Library: A History, 1896-1963." Master's thesis, University of Texas, 1965. 138p.

Traces the origin and development of the Kemp Public Library, Wichita Falls, Texas. First attempts to found a library in the latter part of the nineteenth century culminated in the early part of the twentieth century with the building of the present library. The growth of this library to 1963, with emphasis on collections and services, is discussed.

347 Barnes, Glynell S. "A History of Public Library Service to Negroes in Galveston, Texas 1904-1955." Master's thesis, Atlanta University, 1957. 40p.

The intent of this study is to: 1) examine the establishment and historical development of the main library in Galveston; 2) review the development of library service to Negroes in the city; and 3) to evaluate the current state of public library service to Negroes. This study considers the founding and growth of the Rosenberg Library Colored Branch from 1904-1955. The author also compares services to Negroes to the standards set by the American Library Association.

348 Cody, Ninna B. "Historical Development of Public Libraries in Gregg County, Texas." Master's thesis, East Texas State College, 1959. 83p.

This study traces the history of the public libraries in Gregg County from the beginnings in the early 1930s until 1959. The

Woman's Chamber of Commerce worked for establishment of the county's first public library in 1930. The collection opened with around 1,000 volumes and circulated over 7,000 the first year. Later Mr. and Mrs. W. R. Nicholson gave the city a building and $1,000 for a Nicholson Memorial Library. The three main libraries of the county—Nicholson Memorial Library (1932), the Kilgore Public Library (1939), and the Gladewater Public Library (1937)—were merged into the Gregg County Library System in 1944.

349 Downing, Marvin L. "The P.W.A. and the Efforts to Secure the Fort Worth Public Library Building, 1933-1939." Master's thesis, Texas Christian University, 1963. 78p. Summary published: *Texas Libraries* 27 (1965):126-32+.

This study chronicles the six-year struggle to obtain a new library building in Fort Worth. The City's Carnegie Library, erected in 1901, needed replacement by the 1920s, and the funds made available through the Public Works Administration encouraged library supporters to secure a new facility. Mrs. Charles Scheuber, the library's dynamic director, and the library board labored for many years before construction began in 1939. Delays were innumerable, including clashes with the city council, wrangles with PWA officials, and litigation over site selection.

350 Gillespie, Richard C. "La Retama Public Library: Its Origin and Development, 1909-1952." Master's thesis, University of Texas, 1953. 96p.

This study traces the development of the La Retama Public Library in Corpus Christi, Texas from 1909 to 1952. Chapter I analyzes the historical, cultural, and economic conditions out of which the library grew. Chapter II covers the library's embryo stage and its many difficulties. The third chapter deals with the library's becoming, in 1927, a unit of the city government. Chapter IV treats the library's building program, which aroused considerable public controversy. Concludes that after 43 years of existence, the library had not reached a very successful position, and then presents the reasons for the library's slow and erratic development.

351 Jeffress, Iris P. "The Friends of the Sequin Guadalupe County Public Library: History and Analysis, 1954-66." Master's thesis, University of Texas, 1967. 140p.

This history of the Friends begins in 1955 and continues through the dedication of the new library building in 1965, and concludes with the resignation of the first librarian—the author's husband—in 1966. The history of the Friends is followed by an analysis of the organization—its membership, leaders, financial affairs, and promotional programs. Publicity efforts are singled out for special attention.

352 Lee, Robert E. "Texas Library Development: Its Relation to the Carnegie Movement, 1898-1915." Master's thesis, University of Texas, 1959. 78p.

This thesis is a study of Carnegie's interest in philanthropy, especially as regards libraries, the public's reaction, and the results of the Carnegie gifts in Texas from 1898 to 1915. Also considered are the actions of local governments after the erection of their libraries.

353 Mason, Lena G. "The Founding of the Beaumont, Texas Public Library, 1850-1926." Master's thesis, Texas State College, 1951. 65p.

The author examines the events that led to the establishment of the Tyrrell Public Library, Beaumont, Texas in 1926. The first chapter is devoted to a socio-economic survey of the community 1850-1926, and the next several chapters deal with the events immediately preceding the establishment of the library in 1926. The author was particularly interested in finding out if individual philanthropy, or a strong desire on the part of many people, was the main influence on library development in Beaumont. Both factors were present.

354 Mays, Fayrene N. "A History of Public Library Service to Negroes in Houston, Texas, 1907-1962." Master's thesis, Atlanta University, 1964. 55p.

Public library service to the Negro population became available in 1907 with the establishment of a branch in a high school. In 1915 a separate building was erected from Carnegie funds. Circulation figures and expenditures for materials are enumerated. Negro access to the Houston Central Library has been available since 1953.

355 McCracken, Pearl C. "History and Present Status of the County Library in Texas." Master's thesis, Southern Methodist University, 1927. 106p.

The county library concept is first defined in terms of functions and advantages and then traced historically throughout the nation. County libraries arrived in Texas rather late; enabling legislation was passed in 1919. Despite progressive legislation, there were only seven county libraries in Texas by 1927. Slow progress is attributed to the lack of fiscal support, the absence of community improvement, and the shortage of trained librarians.

356 Smith, Mary H.K. "A History of the Libraries of Bonham, Texas." Master's thesis, East Texas State College, 1963. 109p.

Bonham, Texas had a population of only 7,357 people in 1960, and yet had five distinct types of library services available to its citizens. The author covers the history of the following libraries: 1) the Bonham public school libraries; 2) the Bonham Public Library (1901-1963); 3) the library of the Veteran's Administration Center; 4) the Sam Rayburn Library (1957-1963); and 5) four church libraries.

357 Stoneham, Frances M. "History of the County Library Movement of Texas." Master's thesis, Sam Houston State Teachers College, 1939. 118p.

This thesis records the history of the county library movement in Texas, relates the growth of county libraries to the national movement, and notes present trends. Twenty-five county libraries were formed since passage of the enabling legislation in 1919. The Federated Clubwomen are credited as the driving force behind the establishment of county libraries. County libraries developed rather slowly because of the agricultural economy and lack of state encouragement. Brief sketches of the county libraries are included.

358 Suhler, Samuel A. "The Austin Public Library 1926-1956." Master's thesis, University of Texas, 1959. 72p.

The author briefly traces a 25-year effort to establish a public library in Austin, Texas, an effort frustrated by legislative opposition, a lack of city funds, and a lack of widespread popular support. A small subscription library finally was opened in 1926; in 1928 it became the Austin Public Library. For the next five years library development was rapid, but tended to slow down after 1933. The author analyzes this gradual growth period (1933-1956), and discusses the development of staff, book collections, physical plant, and services.

359 Swogetinsky, Betty A. "A Study of Censorial Demands on Texas Libraries, 1952-1957." Master's thesis, University of Texas, 1967. 202p.

After briefly sketching the history of censorship in the U.S. and Texas in the twentieth century, the author devotes the majority of her paper to an analysis of reported censorial demands on Texas libraries, 1952-1957. The objective was to identify patterns 1) in demands; 2) in communities and people; 3) in results as revealed by citizen reaction; and 4) in the final resolution of the case. Seventeen reported cases were identified in nine Texas cities. A careful interpretation of these cases, with over 20 tables, is presented.

360 Teague, Anne H. "Carnegie Library Building Grants to Texas

Communities: A Brief Account and a Comparison." Master's thesis, University of Texas, 1967. 132p.

This study traces the history of the Carnegie building program as it was applied in Texas, reviews the increase in resources in Carnegie libraries in Texas from founding to 1935; and compares present day library resources in selected Texas communities which received Carnegie gifts with those Texas communities of similar size which did not receive Carnegie libraries. The author found that Carnegie had granted some $645,000 over a seventeen-year period for the construction of 31 public libraries in Texas. Smaller communities which were given libraries were often unable to support them and were often forced to default on their promise to Carnegie.

VIRGINIA

361 Brandt, Beverly S. "The Alexandria, Virginia, Library: Its History, Present Facilities, and Future Program." Master's thesis, Catholic University of America, 1950. 94p.

The author has divided the subject into three major periods. The first covers the history of the library from its hesitant beginnings as a subscription library in 1794 to the dispersal of the library's collection during the Civil War. The second period covers the attempts to revive the library after the Civil War and the establishment of the public library in the 1930s. The final section treats the public library's development until 1950. Since 1937 the library has shown a steady growth to nearly 27,000 volumes.

362 Elliott, Mary E. "The Development of Library Service in Fairfax County, Virginia, since 1939." Master's thesis, Drexel Institute of Technology, 1951. 57p.

This study traces the development of the Fairfax County Public Library System from 1939 to 1951. The Fairfax County Public Library System, as it was established in 1939, offered the first organized library program in the county. Progress of the library was rapid and extensive. Circulation grew from 24,000 in 1940-1941 to 170,000 in 1949-1950. The author pinpoints problems and successes in the library's history and concludes with suggestions for improving the system.

363   Moyers, Joyce C. "History of the Rockingham Public Library, Harrisonburg, Virginia." Master's thesis, University of North Carolina, 1959. 116p.

The Rockingham Public Library is a regional library serving the city of Harrisonburg and the counties of Rockingham and Page in Virginia. The Harrisonburg Kiwanis Club was instrumental in promoting the organization of the Rockingham Library Association in 1928, and in 1952 a new library building was constructed entirely from funds derived from public subscriptions. Originally the library was supported by donations, but later received public funds. The author traces the development of the planning of the new building and the efforts to expand services through state aid.

WASHINGTON

364   Hake, Shirley D. "A History of Library Development in Kittitas County, Washington." Master's thesis, University of Washington, 1953. 55p.

Kittitas County was settled in 1867 and the author briefly chronicles its development from that time until 1953. The author then traces library development in the county from 1890, when W. W. Bonney opened a newspaper reading room in Ellensburg, until 1950. Three libraries are covered in some detail: the Carnegie Library of Ellensburg, begun in 1908; the Cleelum Public Library, begun in 1914; and the Roslyn Public Library, which got its start in 1898. All three libraries developed slowly and suffered from serious financial shortages.

365   Newsom, Harry E. "Fort Vancouver Regional Library; A Study of

the Development of Public Library Service in Clark and Skamania Counties, Washington." Master's thesis, University of Washington, 1954. 144p.

A brief overview of Clark and Skamania Counties is presented and the author traces the history of early library development in the two counties. Emphasis is on the development of the Fort Vancouver Regional Library, 1940-1954. This study describes the operations of the headquarters library and the steps that led to the unification and development of services in the two counties.

366 Orr, Maryde F. "Development of the Walla Walla Public Library." Master's thesis, University of Washington, 1953. 62p.

This paper traces the development of library interest in Walla Walla, Washington from 1865, when the Walla Walla Library Association was founded, to 1950. The first library, established in 1867, fell into neglect in 1890. It was not until 1896, when the Women's Reading Club of Walla Walla raised $2,000 to establish a library, that the city again had library service. In 1904 the Walla Walla Public Library was established and Andrew Carnegie gave $25,000 to the city for the construction of a building. Describes the financial and space problems the library encountered from 1945 to 1950.

367 Pitcher, Patricia M. "A Historical Study of Library Development in Chelan County, Washington." Master's thesis, University of Washington, 1952. 67p.

The author analyzes the relation between economic development in Chelan County and the growth of libraries. One third of this paper is devoted to the economic development of the county. The remainder contains individual treatments of five town libraries and the twenty branches of the Chelan County Library, which was established in 1944.

368 Strother, Jane V. "The Development and the Adequacy of the

Library as an Institution in the State of Washington." Master's thesis, University of Washington, 1938. 156p.

The first 25 pages of this paper are devoted to a survey of the development of the State Library of Washington and the other public libraries of the state. The State Library was established in 1853, while the first public libraries appeared in the 1890s.

369 Suzuki, Adele N. "The Foundations and Development of the Yakima Valley Regional Library." Master's thesis, Southern Connecticut State College, 1973. 243p.

The earliest library service in the Yakima Valley (Washington) was a reading room sponsored by the Woman's Christian Temperance Union in 1889. Two years later the North Yakima Library Association was formed. By 1904, the private library association became the Yakima Public Library. A grant from the Carnegie Corporation enabled the community to erect a new building in 1907. A county library system was established in 1944, resulting in some overlap of services and friction. The two libraries merged in 1951 to form the Yakima Regional Library. Official documents related to the library's history are appended.

370 Ward, Barbara A. "A History of Public Library Development in Whitman County, Washington." Master's thesis, University of Washington, 1960. 155p.

Traces the development of public libraries in Whitman County, Washington, from the establishment of the first libraries in the 1860s, to 1960. The study is broken into three major segments: 1) the cultural, economic, and social influences that affected the development of public libraries in the county from 1880 to 1905; 2) the introduction of the public library, its early organization and development, 1906-1940; and 3) the trend toward larger units of service and the rise of extension work, 1940-1960.

WEST VIRGINIA

371 Wade, Barbara A. "History of the Waitman Barbe Public Library of Morgantown, West Virginia; 1926-1956." Master's thesis, Western Reserve University, 1957. 46p.

The purposes of this study are to bring together materials dealing with the Waitman Barbe Public Library; to preserve the information for future use; and to bring the library to the attention of the Morgantown citizens. The history covers the beginnings of the library through 1956. Appendices include coverage of librarians of the library, statistics of the library, and the West Virginia Public Library Law.

372 White, Alice W. "The Public Library Movement in West Virginia." Master's thesis, Columbia University, 1935. 76p.

At the time of this study, 88 percent of the West Virginia population lacked library facilities and more than half of the counties operated without a public library. Early private libraries, literary societies, and lyceums are briefly reviewed. Slow to develop public libraries due to a scattered population and a coal-dependent industry, West Virginia had only one public library, the Wheeling Public Library, before 1900. The West Virginia Library Association successfully lobbied for a state law in 1915 which permitted tax-supported public libraries. Elimination of local school districts and the formation of county districts diverted financial resources from public libraries.

WISCONSIN

373 Colson, John. "The Public Library Movement in Wisconsin, 1836-1900." Doctoral dissertation, University of Chicago, 1973.

The creation of the public library is seen as a process which involved the transplanting of the New England social library to Wisconsin, and its gradual atrophication and replacement by a public institution modeled after the social library. The social library in Wisconsin began and remained an institution dominated by New England migrants; its replacement by the public library was effected by New Englanders. The social library was promoted by laymen, as was the public library; the creation of the latter institution, however, resulted in the establishment of a professional cadre who at the end of the century began to assume direction of public library development, largely through the means of a state agency—the Free Library Commission— and with the assistance of the Wisconsin Library Association.

374 Dengler, Thomas P. "The Public Library in School Library Service, Madison, Wisconsin, 1902-1953." Master's thesis, University of Chicago, 1967. 114p.

Examines the role of the Madison Public Library in providing school library service and chronicles the eventual separation of the two services.

375 Evans, David W. "The Early History of the Appleton, Wisconsin Public Library, 1887-1900." Master's thesis, University of Wisconsin-Oshkosh, 1981. 118p.

The formative years of the Appleton, Wisconsin library movement from the first reading room in 1887 to the completion of the library's permanent home in 1900 are detailed in this study. Although most citizens of the community supported a public library, the building and funding became mired in a struggle over site selection and political advantage. The city eventually prevailed in the courts, but the twenty-seven-year-old pro-library mayor committed suicide in 1900.

376 Loeh, Bonita B. "History of the Joseph Mann Library, Two Rivers, Wisconsin, 1890-1979." Master's thesis, University of Wisconsin-Oshkosh, 1980. 106 p.

Members of the Two Rivers Branch of the Chautauqua Reading Circle were instrumental in establishing the Joseph Mann

Library Association in 1891. Two years later the Association deeded the library to the city on condition of financial support and the right to nominate members of the library board. Funds were secured for a Carnegie building in 1913. A controversy arose in 1954 between the city council and the Association over the original deed and nominations to the library board. The case went to the supreme court of Wisconsin which rendered a decision calling for a shared nomination procedure.

377 Macleod, David I. "Carnegie Libraries in Wisconsin." Master's thesis, University of Wisconsin, 1967. Published: The State Historical Society of Wisconsin for the Department of History of the University of Wisconsin, 1968.

A detailed analysis of Carnegie's objectives in giving libraries to the people of Wisconsin, how effective his gifts turned out to be, and what influence his philanthropy had on the progress of libraries in Wisconsin.

378 Saucerman, Kathryn. "A Study of the Wisconsin Library Movement, 1850-1900." Master's thesis, University of Wisconsin, 1944.

Reported missing.

III. COLLEGE AND UNIVERSITY LIBRARIES

A. General Studies

379   Boll, John J. "Library Architecture 1800-1875: A Comparison of Theory and Buildings with Emphasis on New England College Libraries." Doctoral dissertation, University of Illinois, 1961. 447p. UMI# 61-4263.

Boll devotes the first part of this study to background material, the second to influential contemporary foreign literature, and the third to the buildings themselves, plus important library planners. The author chose seven colleges for his study: Amherst, Brown, Harvard, Yale, Mount Holyoke, Wesleyan, and Williams. He found that writers and planners were very concerned with the protection of the library's collection, and that this influenced them greatly during the period 1800-1875.

380   Brough, Kenneth J. "Evolving Conceptions of Library Service in Four American Universities: Chicago, Columbia, Harvard, and Yale, 1876-1946." Doctoral dissertation, Stanford University, 1949. Published: University of Illinois Press, 1953. Reprinted: Gregg Press, 1972.

After briefly sketching the history of American college library development to 1876, Brough analyzes the evolution of concepts of library administration in four American universities from 1876 to 1946. The significance of the four libraries, their book collections, their librarians, their clientele, and the services offered are discussed.

381 Church, Frances E. "A Historical Survey of the Libraries in a Group of State Normal Schools Prior to 1900." Master's thesis, Columbia University, 1931. 118p.

This study examines library development in a varied group of state normal schools. The East is represented by two states, Massachusetts and New York, where some of the earliest normal schools were established. Alabama and Texas were chosen to represent the South. Indiana, Michigan, Kansas, Colorado and Nebraska represent the Middle West, where the greatest development has come about. California and Washington represent the Pacific Slope. The author describes fourteen libraries in terms of the book collection and its administration, the librarian, and the library room.

382 Erickson, Ernest W. "College and University Library Surveys, 1938-1952." Doctoral dissertation, University of Illinois, 1958. UMI# 58-05412. Published: American Library Association, 1961.

This study traces the effectiveness of library surveys by experts in bringing about beneficial results to the surveyed library. Twelve surveys were studied, beginning with the first major survey in America at the University of Georgia in 1938. The author found that the surveys were successful in a majority of instances in influencing change, and in prompting an increased library consciousness on the part of librarians, faculty, and administration.

383 Flanagan, Cathleen C. "Sound Recordings, Private Collectors, and Academic Research Libraries." Doctoral dissertation, University of Illinois, 1976. 175p. UMI# 76-24,082.

Factors which influenced the establishment of historical sound recordings collections are examined in this study of eight research libraries. The influence of private collectors rather than faculty is highlighted. Six forms of collector influence are identified: 1) promoting establishment of an institutional collection; 2) donating a personal collection; 3) encouraging institution to share collector's concern for preservation; 4) continuing source of support; 5) setting an example for other collectors; and 6) acting as a determinant of institution collection profiles. The most common form of influence was making a personal collection available to the institution.

384 Gelfand, Morris A. "A Historical Study of the Evaluation of Libraries in Higher Institutions by the Middle States Association of Colleges and Secondary Schools." Doctoral dissertation, New York University, 1960. 449p. UMI# 61-324.

This study is an historical analysis of the evolution and influence of the policies and procedures used to evaluate libraries in colleges and universities seeking accreditation from the Middle States Association. The author examines practices of the Association to 1960, and then presents recommendations based on his findings, part of which were derived from a questionnaire sent to the librarians of all institutional members of the Association.

385 Hardin, Willie. "An Analysis of the Growth Patterns in Select Black Land-Grant Colleges and Universities: Five Case Studies." Doctoral dissertation, Simmons College, 1979. 155p.

This study investigates the developmental patterns of five black land-grant college and university libraries to determine the major factors which affected the growth of library resources during the period 1946-1976. Institutions selected for review are University of Arkansas at Pine Bluff, Alcorn State University (Mississippi), Southern University (Louisiana), Tennessee State University and Prairie View University (Texas). Each institution's growth pattern is examined in terms of external factors such as federal library support and civil rights and internal dynamics such as curriculum and enrollment. The expansion of graduate programs is cited as perhaps the most important stimulus of library growth.

386 Harding, Thomas S. "College Literary Societies: Their Contribution to Higher Education in the United States, 1815-1876."

Doctoral dissertation, University of Chicago, 1957. Published: Pageant Press International, 1971.

Several chapters of this work deal with the influence of college literary societies on academic library development.

387 Johnson, Edward R. "The Development of the Subject-Divisional Plan in American University Libraries." Doctoral dissertation, University of Wisconsin, 1974. 240p. UMI# 75-5936. Summary published: *Library Quarterly* 47 (January 1977): 23-42.

The subject divisional plan in American university libraries substituted broad subjects for functions as the basis for specialization. William F. Poole was an early advocate and influential libraries included the Boston Public Library, the University of Chicago Library, and the Johns Hopkins University Library. By 1967 at least twenty-six university libraries were organized along subject-divisional lines. Subject divisional plans prospered because of influential library leaders, trends in higher education, and widespread publicity. Factors contributing to the decline of this configuration included physical constraints, faculty pressure for decentralized collections, and the rapid growth of knowledge.

388 Kansfield, Norman J. "The Origins of Protestant Theological Seminary Libraries in the United States." Master's thesis, University of Chicago, 1970.

Not examined.

389 Kansfield, Norman J. "'Study the Most Approved Authors': The Role of the Seminary Library in Nineteenth-Century American Protestant Ministerial Education." Doctoral dissertation, University of Chicago, 1981. 340p.

Chapter I delineates the image of the Protestant pastor in nineteenth-century America as it relates to theological scholarship, ministerial training, and reliance on books. Seminary library ideals are discussed in Chapter II. Chapter III concentrates on seminary library development, including collections, facilities, staff, and access. The final chapter is devoted to student use of seminary libraries.

390 Knoer, Sister Mary M.A. "A Historical Survey of the Libraries of Certain Catholic Institutions of Learning in the United States." Master's thesis, University of Illinois, 1930. 114p.

Studies briefly the development of libraries in sixteen Catholic colleges and universities to 1930. The author found that collections were usually small, dated, and used mainly by the faculty. Major improvements were made after the organization of the Library Section of the Catholic Educational Association in 1923.

391 Kraus, Joe W. "Book Collections of Five Colonial College Libraries: A Subject Analysis." Doctoral dissertation, University of Illinois, 1960. 312p. UMI# 60-1661. Portion published: *Library Quarterly* 43 (1973): 142-59.

This study focuses on the availability of books and the nature of book ownership in five colonial colleges: Yale, William and Mary, Harvard, Princeton and Brown. The author sets out to answer three questions: 1) what books were available; 2) what subjects predominated in these collections; and 3) what use was made of the books. This study challenges earlier work, and concludes that the libraries studied were better equipped and more widely used than was once thought.

392 Kulp, Arthur C. "The Historical Development of Storage Libraries in America." Master's thesis, University of Illinois, 1953. Published: Association of College and Research Libraries Microcard, Number 12.

After a brief survey of book storage problems from ancient to modern times, the author describes present-day compact book storage techniques. Six working systems are described in some detail: 1) Iowa State College Library; 2) Cornell University

Library Storage Collections; 3) University of Kentucky; 4) New England Deposit Library; 5) Mid-West Inter-Library Center; and 6) Hampshire Inter-Library Center.

393 Lowell, Mildred H. "College and University Library Consolidations." Master's thesis, University of Chicago, 1939. 179p.

The author brings together a number of examples of college and university consolidations, traces the history of each, analyzes the unique features of each, and contrasts them. Approximately a dozen such consolidations are considered, all of them made after 1924.

394 McGowan, Frank M. "The Association of Research Libraries, 1932-1962." Doctoral dissertation, University of Pittsburgh, 1972. 262p. UMI# 73-12,360.

The author traces the history of the Association of Research Libraries (ARL) from 1932, when 42 large research libraries organized the group, to 1962. By that time the ARL had achieved some major successes in stimulating library cooperation; in encouraging a number of major bibliographic projects; and in fostering a growing interest in the nation's major research libraries. At the same time the ARL was frequently accused of being an elitist club, and indeed, the author concludes that one reason for the achievements of ARL was that those who contributed the most to the organization represented the most influential and productive element among American library administrators.

395 Martens, Alice. "A Study of the History and Development of the Protestant Theological Seminary Library Movement in the United States." Master's thesis, Southern Connecticut State College, 1958. 73p.

The author has three objectives in mind: 1) to outline the history of Protestant theological seminary libraries in the United States; 2) to analyze the development of some of the major Protestant theological libraries in the country; and 3) to trace the slow recognition of the library's central role in theological education, a movement which culminated in the establishment of the American Theological Library Association in 1947.

396 Massman, Virgil F. "Responsibilities and Benefits of Faculty Status for Librarians: A Review of Related Literature and a Survey of Librarians and Faculty Members in Nineteen State Colleges and Universities in Michigan, Minnesota, and Wisconsin." Doctoral dissertation, University of Michigan, 1970. 319p. UMI# 71-4674. Published: Scarecrow Press, 1972.

The purpose of this study is to review the literature of faculty status for librarians and to determine by a survey whether librarians meet the requirements and receive the benefits of faculty status. The literature review encompasses definitions, conditions, reasons for seeking faculty status, responsibilities, and benefits. Survey results are discussed in the remainder of the study. Concludes that librarians with faculty status receive equitable treatment when education and scholarly activity are considered.

397 Meckler, Alan M. "Scholarly Micropublishing in America, 1938-1979." Doctoral dissertation, Columbia University, 1980. 237p. UMI# 8222447. Portion published: *Scholarly Publishing* 12 (1981): 339-54.

Scholarly micropublishing in America commenced in 1938 with the founding of University Microfilms in Ann Arbor, Michigan. Early photographic developments from 1600 to 1900 and the individuals and organizations which transformed scholarly micropublishing from an idea to a business are discussed. Detailed treatment is given the early organizations: Eugene Power of University Microfilms; Albert Boni of Readex Microprint; Fremont Rider of Microcard Editions; and Samuel Freedman of Micro Photo. Additional chapters summarize the contemporary micropublishing industry.

398 Miller, Lawrence A. "Changing Patterns of Circulation Services

in University Libraries." Doctoral dissertation, Florida State University, 1971. 188p. UMI# 72-10,058.

The author analyzes the evolution of the concept and reality of circulation services in academic libraries in the United States. Prior to 1920 there was little specialization in "public services" in most academic libraries; reference and circulation were usually carried out at the same desk and by the same staff. The author traces the slow but steady separation of these two functions and concludes with an examination of a number of factors which appear to have been causal elements in the evolution of the academic library circulation department.

399 Orr, Robert S. "Financing and Philanthropy in the Building of Academic Libraries Constructed Between 1919 and 1958." Master's thesis, Western Reserve University, 1959. 87p.

The author discusses the means of financing 61 college and university library buildings built between 1919-1958. Large benefactions characterized the period prior to 1930, while during the 1930s many state colleges and universities gained libraries through the use of Works Progress Administration funds. After 1940, WPA was curtailed and little building was done until after the war. From then to 1958 most state institutions built libraries with state funds, while private institutions usually depended on a large gift from one individual.

400 Osburn, Charles B., Jr. "National Patterns of Academic Research and the Provision of Library Resources." Doctoral dissertation, University of Michigan, 1978. 330p. UMI# 7822980. Published: Greenwood Press, 1979.

This study examines the unprecedented expansion of academic research following World War II and its impact on academic librarianship. Special attention is devoted to the massive infusion of federal funds and the influence of the scientific sector on the social sciences and humanities. During this period "ivory tower" research diminished as studies focused on societal problems. Concludes that a more scholarly approach to collection development is needed to accommodate these changes.

401 Overmier, Judith A. "Scientific Rare Book Collections in Academic and Research Libraries in Twentieth Century America." Doctoral dissertation, University of Minnesota, 1985. 257p. UMI# 8528830.

This study deals with the development of scientific rare book collections in academic and research libraries in twentieth century America. Three questions are addressed. Is scientific book collection a twentieth century phenomenon? Does it reflect general trends in rare book collecting? Does it follow traditional rare book acquisitions practice? Thirty-six collections were surveyed and the collections of three institutions—University of Minnesota, University of Oklahoma, and the Smithsonian Institution—were studied in depth. The three guiding questions were answered in the affirmative.

402 Perrins, Barbara C. "Business and Industrial Reference Service by Academic Libraries, 1900-1965." Master's thesis, Southern Connecticut State College, 1967. 71p.

This study is a description and analysis of the history of business and industrial reference service in four academic libraries whose business schools are members of the American Association of Collegiate Schools of Business—Cornell, Harvard, Massachusetts Institute of Technology, and Stanford. Discusses recent developments in policies, scope, and clientele as well as the problems and early history of each of the institution's libraries.

403 Powell, Benjamin E. "The Development of Libraries in Southern State Universities to 1920." Doctoral dissertation, University of Chicago, 1946. 233p. Portion published: *Wilson Library Bulletin* 31 (1956): 250-54.

Surveys the history of libraries in the state universities of Alabama, Georgia, Louisiana, Mississippi, North Carolina, South

Carolina, Tennessee and Virginia from 1795 to 1920. The author finds that although libraries were considered vital by most of the universities, they were beset by financial difficulties through the nineteenth century. The Civil War, Reconstruction, low per capita incomes, segregation, and the establishment of specialized institutions also contributed to the retardation of library development in southern state universities until 1900. A final chapter compares data from the eight libraries studied with state university libraries in California, Illinois, Michigan, Minnesota, and Wisconsin.

404 Radford, Neil A. "The Carnegie Corporation and the Development of American College Libraries, 1928-1941." Doctoral dissertation, University of Chicago, 1972. 312p. Published: American Library Association, 1984.

This study examines the involvement of the Carnegie Corporation of New York with American college libraries from 1928 to 1941. During this period, 248 institutions received grants totalling $1,636,800 to develop book collections for undergraduate students. Book lists, collection standards, and central purchasing were among the projects stimulated by the grants. Three individuals dominate the narrative: William Warner Bishop, University of Michigan; Frederick Paul Keppel, president of the Carnegie Corporation of New York; and Robert M. Lester, assistant to the president and later secretary of the Carnegie Corporation of New York.

405 Reynolds, Helen M. "University Library Buildings in the United States, 1890-1939." Master's thesis, University of Illinois, 1946. 88p. Summary published: *College & Research Libraries* 14 (1953): 149-57.

Presents a historical interpretation of the development of university library buildings in the United States from 1890 to 1939. Twenty-seven universities and their 38 library buildings are discussed. The author outlines the extensive development library buildings underwent, from very simple structures in which the library usually occupied one floor, to complex buildings of several stories with up to 28 stack levels. Includes numerous plates illustrating the buildings described.

406 Shafer, Henry. "College Libraries in the United States from 1790-1830." Master's thesis, Columbia University, 1927. 45p.

General study of college libraries during the early national period. Covers collections, organization, and regulations. Colleges were heavily dependent upon donations and their library holdings reflected denominational influence.

407 Shiflett, Orvin L. "The Origins of American Academic Librarianship." Doctoral dissertation, Florida State University, 1979. 372p. UMI# 7926818. Published: Ablex, 1981.

Explores the formative period of academic librarianship from the classical college to the 1920s. University expansion, graduate education, and scholarly specialization did not correspond to the practical orientation of Melvil Dewey and the public library movement. Librarians embraced alternatives such as the honorary doctorate and a teaching role in generalized undergraduate education. Doctoral education for librarians did not begin until 1926 at the University of Chicago. By that time the undergraduate preparation provided by library schools was accepted as appropriate for academic librarians.

408 Shores, Louis. "Origins of the American College Library, 1638-1800." Doctoral dissertation, George Peabody College for Teachers, 1934. Published: Barnes and Noble, 1934; Reprinted: Shoestring Press, 1966. Reprinted: Gregg Press, 1972.

This work is the pioneering study of colonial college library history. Shores describes the origins, growth, and administration of the nine college libraries founded in the Colonies prior to 1800. The colleges considered are: Harvard, William and Mary, Yale, Princeton, Columbia, Pennsylvania, Brown, Rutgers, and Dartmouth.

409 Smith, Jessie C. "Patterns of Growth in Library Resources in Certain Land-Grant Universities." Doctoral dissertation, University of Illinois, 1964. 227p. UMI# 65-917.

Compares the development of library resources in selected land-grant and major state universities during the period 1870-1960. Institutions represented in the study are Purdue and Indiana, Michigan State and the University of Michigan, Iowa State and Iowa, the University of Illinois, and Ohio State University. Factors affecting the growth of library resources subject to analysis include curricula, financial support, department collections. Major state university libraries acquired significantly more volumes than land-grant libraries between 1870 and 1960. Curricular expansion in the areas of science and technology did not correlate with growth in library resources.

410 Storie, Catharine. "What Contributions Did the American College Society Library Make to the History of the American College Library?" Master's thesis, Columbia University, 1938. 116p. Summary published: *College & Research Libraries* 4 (1943): 240-48.

The author had a fourfold purpose in mind: 1) general study of the value of college society libraries; 2) specific analysis of the collections of the Peithologian and Philolexian Societies at Columbia University; 3) a preliminary investigation to determine which colleges had societies, and hence probably society libraries; and 4) which of these society libraries had catalogs, especially printed catalogs, and where they were located. Finds that the society library developed to fill needs resulting from a rigid and limited curriculum, and that it appeared to be a substitute for, rather than a supplement to, the main library. It was determined that 80 percent of all the colleges flourishing in 1830 had society libraries, and nearly half of these had collections larger than their college libraries.

411 Strauss, Lovell H. "The Liberal Arts College Library, 1929-1940: A Comparative Interpretation of Financial Statistics of Sixty-Eight Representative and Twenty Selected Liberal Arts College Libraries." Master's thesis, University of Chicago, 1942. 125p.

This study interprets the financial statistics of 88 liberal arts college libraries from 1929 to 1940. It traces changes in college library support through an analysis of standard recorded statistics. Such factors as enrollments, library expenditures, size of library staff, book budgets, size of collections, growth per year, are considered. Data were gathered from questionnaires and published reports.

412   Terwilliger, Gloria H.P. "The Library-College; A Movement for Experimental and Innovative Learning Concepts; Applications and Implications for Higher Education. (Volumes One and Two)." Doctoral dissertation, University of Maryland, 1975. 251p. UMI# 76-8446.

The term "library-college" refers to the merging of instruction with library resources. This study examines the development of the library-college idea in postsecondary education. Leadership and diffusion of the movement are emphasized. The organizational arm of the movement, the Library-College Associates, is fully explored. Key leaders of the concept—Louis Shores, Helen Sheehan, Howard Clayton, Robert Jordan, and Dan Sillers— receive extended treatment. The library-college idea was an experimental model which was not empirically tested. Fragments such as the "generic book" survive.

413   Thurber, Evangeline. "The Library of the Land-Grant College, 1862-1900: A Preliminary Study." Master's thesis, Columbia University, 1928. 84p.

The founding of agricultural colleges, early experiment station activity, and federal aid through the Morrill Act (1862) are reviewed in the first section. Land-grant college libraries often benefitted from the collections of agricultural society libraries and literary society libraries which were on or adjacent to the new institutions. Early land-grant college libraries were administrated by the teaching faculty and hours of operation were modest. By the 1870s librarians influenced the selection and organization of materials, and reoriented libraries from heterogeneous collections of books to vital laboratories in support of the curricula and research.

414 Waldo, Michael J. "A Comparative Analysis of Nineteenth-Century Academic and Literary Society Library Collections in the Midwest." Doctoral dissertation, Indiana University, 1985. 235p. UMI# 8527040.

Ten college and thirteen literary society libraries located at twelve Midwestern college campuses were selected to determine if the collections were substantially different. Characteristics evaluated included subject composition of the collections, the number of popular titles, the number of commonly held titles, and publication dates. Certain components of the subject profiles of the two types of collections differed, but many categories were similar. College collections generally contained as many subjects which were well represented in the society collections. College libraries also contained well-rounded collections, including popular and recent titles.

415 West, Emilie K. "A History of the Bibliographic Center for Research; Rocky Mountain Region, 1942-1966." Master's thesis, Long Island University, 1970. 73p.

This study surveys the history of the Bibliographic Center for Research (BCR), an institution designed to encourage cooperation among member libraries in bibliographic aspects. The author assesses the achievements and failures of the BCR.

416 Yueh, Norma N. "The Development of Library Collections at Former State Teacher Education Institutions: 1920-1970, with Special Consideration of Six New Jersey State Colleges." Doctoral dissertation, Columbia University, 1974. 316p. UMI# 76-30,171.

Study of the library collections of six former New Jersey state teacher training institutions during the period of their transformation into multipurpose institutions. Data from 193 other teaching training schools was also obtained and analyzed. In the majority of cases, collection development was not governed by acquisition policies and faculty consultation—a positive correlation was noted between prior consultation with the library and the age of a multipurpose institution on the one hand and collection development. Quality collections depend upon active involvement of the library in academic planning.

B. Studies Arranged by State

ARIZONA

417 Heisser, Wilma A. "A Historical Survey of the Phoenix College Library; Phoenix, Arizona 1925-1957." Master's thesis, Arizona State College, 1958. 80p.

This study presents a history of the Phoenix College Library from its inception in 1925 to 1956. For five years after its establishment in 1920, the college had no library; students had to use the high school library. In 1925, 250 books were transferred from the Phoenix High School Library, and the college library got its start. By 1930 the book stock was up to 4,000 volumes and in 1937 a $3,000 grant from the Carnegie Foundation greatly added to the library's holdings. The author discusses the problems faced by the college library, mainly financial, and concludes with a survey of current services.

CALIFORNIA

418 Brundin, Robert E. "Changing Patterns of Library Service in Five California Junior Colleges, 1907-1967." Doctoral dissertation, Stanford University, 1970. 303p. UMI# 71-12,866.

Examines the history of library service in five California junior colleges over a sixty year period. The year 1907 marks the beginning of junior college history in the state, but the emphasis in this study is on the period after 1930. The schools studied are: Fullerton Junior College, Long Beach City College, Los Angeles City College, Modesto Junior College, and Pasadena City College.

419 Laudine, Sister Mary. "The Honnold Library of Claremont College: Its History and Services 1952-1961." Master's thesis, Immaculate Heart College, 1961. 66p.

The Honnold Library of Claremont College in Claremont, California was built with money given to the school by William L. Honnold, a California mining engineer, and was opened in 1952. The author deals with the origins and development of the library in several early chapters with later chapters devoted to the description of services and problems.

420 Peterson, Kenneth G. "The History of the University of California Library at Berkeley 1900-1945." Doctoral dissertation, University of California at Berkeley, 1968. UMI# 69-03673. Published: University of California Press, 1970.

The author traces the history of one of America's largest research libraries during its most crucial years of development. During these years the library's collection grew from under 100,000 volumes to well over 1,000,000. Chapters deal with finances, collection development, personnel, building and equipment, classification and cataloging, and services offered by the library.

421 Smith, Dora. "History of the University of California Library to 1900." Master's thesis, University of California, 1930. Published: Association of College and Research Libraries Microcard, Number 21.

After briefly sketching the history of the library from its beginnings in 1862, as part of the College of California, to 1900. The author treats her subject under three major heads: the general administration of the library, the collections, and the staff.

CONNECTICUT

422 Brooks, Robert E. "The Yale University Law School Library: Its History, Organization, and Development 1824 to 1962." Master's thesis, Southern Connecticut State College, 1964. 115p.

Established in 1824 with a collection of 2,000 volumes, the growth of the Law Library paralleled developments of the school it served. Most nineteenth century librarians were either students or members of the faculty. Librarians credited with major contributions are Philip P. Wells (1896-1906), creator of the first card catalog; Edwin M. Borchard (1917-1928), developer of the international law collection; Frederick C. Hicks (1928-1945), deviser of a functional classification scheme; and Harry Bitner (1957-), exponent of legal research. Evolution of the collections, services, and classification scheme are addressed.

423 Colla, Sister Maria B. "A History of the Pope Pius XII Library, St. Joseph College, West Hartford, Connecticut 1932-1962." Master's thesis, Catholic University of America, 1964. 108p.

This study is a historical and statistical study of the library of a small women's college. Chapters dealing with the following topics are included: 1) housing; 2) administration and finances; 3) book and periodical collection; 4) technical services; and 5) public services.

424 Kelly, Sister Thomas A. "The History, Growth, and Development of the Albertus Magnus College Library, New Haven, Connecticut 1925-1970." Master's thesis, Southern Connecticut State College, 1972. 195p.

Albertus Magnus College, a liberal arts institution for women, was founded in 1925. This account covers the growth of the library from that time until 1970. Collections, staff, and services are described in detail. The library is evaluated against ALA's "Guidelines for College Libraries." Along with supporting the educational program of the college, the library assumed the role of a modern information center.

425 Kennett, Sister Marguerite E. "Annhurst College Library, South Woodstock, Connecticut 1941-1967." Master's thesis, Southern Connecticut State College, 1968. 145p.

The purpose of this study is to examine the development of the Annhurst College Library in relation to the instructional program of the college and to compare and contrast the trends noted with those of similar Catholic four-year colleges in the U.S. The author covers major developments of Catholic colleges in the U.S. and points out the factors responsible for growth of Catholic college libraries. Included here are consideration of philosophy of education, historical development of curriculum as related to the library administration, and finances.

426 Lahey, Judith. "The University of Connecticut Law School Library: History, Organization, and Development, 1921-1972." Master's thesis, Southern Connecticut State College, 1972. 72p.

The University of Connecticut School of Law traces its origins to the evening school founded in 1921 known as the Hartford College of Law. In 1943 Hartford College became a part of the University of Connecticut. By 1970 the law library held 85,000 volumes and ranked 68th of 148 accredited law schools. The contributions of various librarians, collections, services, and arrangement of materials are enumerated.

427 Lewis, Leonore L. "The History and Use of the Bookplate in College Libraries in Connecticut." Master's thesis, Southern Connecticut State College, 1972. 184p.

Presents a general history of the bookplate in Europe and America, together with a discussion of the major literature on the subject. Sample bookplates, 160 in all, are drawn from nine Connecticut college libraries: Albertus Magnus College, Connecticut College, Fairfield University, Southern Connecticut

State College, Trinity College, University of Hartford, Wesleyan University, and Yale University.

428   O'Connor, Thomas F. "The Yale University Library, 1865-1931." Doctoral dissertation, Columbia University, 1984. 612p. UMI# 8427442. Portion published: *Journal of Library History* 22 (1987): 164-89.

Three librarians guided the Yale University Library from 1865 to 1931: Addison Van Name, who emphasized collection development; John C. Schwab, who improved the organizational structure; and Andrew Keogh, who assisted in planning the Sterling Memorial Library. Endowment funds and gifts played a significant role. Librarians had more control over collection development at Yale than most academic libraries. Yale accepted only limited standardization in cataloging. Staff specialization accelerated at the turn of the century, as did physical decentralization.

DELAWARE

429   Bauersfeld, Stephanie H. "The Growth and Development of the University of Delaware Library, Newark, Delaware 1833-1965." Master's thesis, Catholic University of America, 1967. 141p.

This study is a historical examination of the University of Delaware Library beginning with the Newark Academy to the present. It includes consideration of literary societies, housing of the library in its various locations and buildings, finances, book and periodical collections, department libraries, public services, objectives of the library, and future plans. Included in the appendix is a "Catalogue of the Books Belonging to the Library of Delaware College and Academy, 1843."

DISTRICT OF COLUMBIA

430   Beach, Sister Francis M. "A History of the Library of Trinity

College, Washington, D.C." Master's thesis, Catholic University of America, 1951. 76p. Published: Association of College & Research Libraries Microcard, Number 41.

Presents a historical and statistical picture of the development of the library of a Catholic liberal arts college for women from 1900 to 1950. The author analyzes the growth of its book collection in comparison to the growth and curriculum development of Trinity College. Also discusses how the library faced administrative, housing, and financial problems.

431 Chamberlain, Lawrence C. "Georgetown University Library, 1789-1937." Master's thesis, Catholic University of America, 1962. 104p.

The author divides his paper into three major sections. The first deals with the library from its beginnings in 1789 to the Civil War. The second covers the period from the close of the Civil War to 1889, and the third traces the library's history from 1889 to 1937. In the beginning the library's growth was stimulated by gifts and donations, especially those of the founder of the Georgetown College, John Carroll. By 1831, the 12,000 volumes in the collection ranked Georgetown University's library in the top ten in America. The author also analyzes the contributions of librarians Henry Shandelle (1895-1922) and Arthur O'Leary (1924-1935).

432 Duncan, Anne M. "History of Howard University Library 1867-1919." Master's thesis, Catholic University of America, 1951. 97p. Published: Association of College & Research Libraries Microcard, Number 42.

Traces the history of the Howard University Library from its inception in 1867 to 1929. The library began with a few books located in one room, but by 1929 contained nearly 50,000 volumes. A new building was provided by a Carnegie grant in 1910. The author analyzes the influence of librarian Edward C. Williams on the library's development and outlines the influence of Congressional support after 1879.

FLORIDA

433 Adams, Katharine B. "The Growth and Development of the University of Florida Libraries 1940-1958." Master's thesis, Catholic University of America, 1959. 80p.

The University of Florida was established at Gainesville in 1905, and engaged a full-time librarian in 1918. An extensive survey of the library was conducted in 1940 by Louis R. Wilson, A.F. Kuhlman, and Guy R. Lyle. Major problems were an inadequate building, insufficient staff, lack of a union catalog, serious gaps in the collection, and deficiencies in the administrative organization. In a span of sixteen years (1940-1956), the library advanced from thirteenth place in the region with sixteen staff and 144,277 volumes to fifth place in the region with 131 staff and 736,855 volumes. Separate chapters are devoted to governance, finances, technical operations, public services, staff, and collections.

434 Husselbee, Margaret V. "The History of the University of Miami Libraries from 1925 to 1960." Master's thesis, University of North Carolina, 1962. 52p.

The University of Miami was established in 1925 and the first professionally qualified librarian was appointed in 1933. Despite financial problems, the library was nurtured by civic-minded citizens and concerned faculty. With the appointment of Archie McNeal as director of libraries in 1952, the library grew dramatically. A new building was completed in 1962 and the collections reflected careful development in such areas as Latin American and Slavic studies.

GEORGIA

435 LaBoone, Elizabeth. "History of the University of Georgia Library." Master's thesis, University of Georgia, 1954. 178p.

Although chartered in 1785, the University of Georgia did not prosper for several decades. A catastrophic fire destroyed most of the collection in 1830 and by the eve of the Civil War, the library held only 10,718 volumes. The first professional librarian was appointed in 1904 and the collection reached 30,000 volumes. Beginning in the 1930s the library developed rapidly through increased financial support and major donations. Collection development, staffing, services, technical processes, and finances are discussed throughout the narrative.

436 Satterfield, Virginia. "The History of College Libraries in Georgia as Interpreted from the Study of Seven Selected Libraries." Master's thesis, Columbia University, 1936. 49p.

This study relates the significant steps in the development of libraries in Georgia, with emphasis on college and university libraries. The seven libraries selected were those at the University of Georgia, Emory University, Mercer University, Wesleyan College, Agnes Scott College, Georgia State College for Women, and Georgia School of Technology. All of the libraries suffered from inadequate financial support and were forced to depend largely on donations in the beginning. It was not until the turn of the twentieth century that separate buildings were erected, professional librarians appointed, and increased budgets secured.

ILLINOIS

437 Archer, Horace R. "Some Aspects of the Acquisition Program at the University of Chicago: 1892-1928." Doctoral dissertation, University of Chicago, 1954. 394p.

After chronologically tracing the history of the University of Chicago Library 1892-1928, the author gives an account of the development of the acquisition department at the University. Emphasis is placed on the various ways in which the library acquired books, such as foreign purchases, gifts, large block acquisitions, and exchanges.

438 Ducker, Dorothy C. "The Ebenezer S. Lane Library: A Study in Nineteenth-Century Reading Tastes." Master's thesis, University of Chicago, 1983. 415p.

The 9,000 volume Ebenezer S. Lane collection, presented to the University of Chicago in 1911, is reconstructed to ascertain Midwest American literary culture of the bourgeois class. Circumstances surrounding acquisition of the collection by the University, formation and growth of the collection, and a content analysis of the library are described in detail. A catalog of the collection is appended.

439 Heckman, Marlin L. "A History of the Library of Bethany Biblical Seminary, Chicago, Illinois." Master's thesis, University of Chicago, 1963. 112p.

The author traces the history of the library at Bethany from its inception in 1905, at which time the students used the books in the private collection of one of the founders, E.B. Hoff, to the 1960s, when the collection numbered some 44,000 volumes. He analyzes the influence of a number of factors, including the board of directors, the administration and faculty, and the standards set by the American Association of Theological Schools.

440 Johnson, Elinor C. "A History of the Theological Book Collection in the Library of Augustana College and Theological Seminary." Master's thesis, University of Chicago, 1957. 122p.

This study traces the development of the library from its beginnings in 1860 to 1948. The author analyzes the growth of the library in relation to its role as a laboratory for students in theological training. Collection building, physical problems, and faculty influences on library development are some of the factors discussed.

441 Lundean, Joel W. "History of the Library of the Chicago Lutheran

Theological Seminary of Maywood, Illinois." Master's thesis, University of Chicago, 1967. 210p.

Traces the history of the Maywood Seminary and its library from 1891, when the Seminary was founded, to 1967.

442 McMullen, Charles H. "The Administration of the University of Chicago Libraries, 1892-1928." Doctoral dissertation, University of Chicago, 1949. 204p. Summary published: *Library Quarterly* 12 (1952): 325-34; (1953): 23-32.

Traces the history of the University of Chicago libraries in terms of administration, with emphasis on collections, staff, financial support, and technical services. Due to faculty insistence, the library system was originally made up of a number of autonomous departmental libraries and a general library. Until 1910 there was no head librarian at the University of Chicago, and after that time the library was headed by faculty members with professional librarians serving as associate librarians. One of the most serious problems was the lack of uniform cataloging programs, which later forced the library to recatalog its collections.

443 Miller, Arthur H., Jr. "The Harriet Monroe Modern Poetry Library: Origins and Growth to 1960." Master's thesis, University of Chicago, 1968. 88p.

This study is the history of a collection of books, manuscripts and letters given to the University of Chicago by Harriet Monroe, the founder of *Poetry: A Magazine of Verse*, and a prominent figure in the history of modern poetry. In 1958 the Harriet Monroe Library was dedicated and contained some 2,500 volumes.

444 Ratcliffe, Thomas E., Jr. "Development of the Buildings, Policy, Collections of the University of Illinois Library in Urbana 1895-1940." Master's thesis, University of Illinois, 1949. 111p.

The phases treated are limited to a description of the development of the physical plant, the body of regulations and policy, growth of the collection and financial support, and the special collections. The paper covers the period from 1897, when Katharine L. Sharp became director, to 1940, when Phineas L. Windsor retired as librarian.

445 Wilcox, Lucile E. "History of the University of Illinois Library, 1868-1897." Master's thesis, University of Illinois, 1931. 77p.

Surveys the development of the library of the University of Illinois from its beginning to 1897, when the library building was erected. The library began with 644 volumes shelved in a recitation room, but was soon large enough to move to rooms in University Hall. By 1897 the collection, which grew quite slowly, contained some 30,000 items. All of the early librarians were from the teaching faculty, and it was not until 1897 that a professional librarian, Katharine L. Sharp, was engaged.

446 Yenawine, Wayne S. "The Influence of Scholars on Research Library Development at the University of Illinois." Doctoral dissertation, University of Illinois, 1955. 294p. UMI# 55-1114.

The University of Illinois Library, one of the finest in the world, took tremendous strides toward its present stature during the period 1900-1930. Yenawine first investigates the state of scholarship at the University during the same period. He found that the increased status of scholarship at Illinois and the pressures by scholars for the development of a large research library were instrumental in the library's swift development. At the same time the library was fortunate to have two dynamic and highly respected librarians at the helm during this period: Katharine L. Sharp and Phineas L. Windsor.

INDIANA

447 Lowell, Mildred H. "Indiana University Libraries, 1829-1942." Doctoral dissertation, University of Chicago, 1957. 453p. Sum-

mary published: *College & Research Libraries* 22 (1961): 423-29; 262-64.

The author considers the development of the Indiana University libraries in terms of the social and economic forces that influenced them. Part one traces the development of the main library from its beginnings to 1943; part two covers the histories of the individual branch libraries. The author finds that from the beginning the library was seen as a vital part of the University environment. However, its development for many years was haphazard and few regular appropriations were made for its upkeep and growth. It was not until 1937 that the University administration took deliberate steps to reorganize and stabilize the library system.

448 Stanley, Ellen L. "The Earlham College Library: A History of Its Relation to the College 1847-1947." Master's thesis, University of Illinois, 1947. 79p.

Earlham College Library is analyzed in relation to its parent institution from its founding in 1847 to 1947. Factors which affected both the college and its library were examined: 1) the government and administration of college; 2) changes in educational theory, curriculum, and emphasis; and 3) the changing size of the student body.

IOWA

449 Slavens, Thomas P. "A History of the Drake University Libraries." Master's thesis, University of Minnesota, 1962. 128p.

The author traces the evolution of the Drake University Library in Des Moines, Iowa from its beginnings as the library of Askaloosa College in the early 1860s. In 1881 the institution moved to Des Moines and became Drake University, but still owned only 13,000 volumes by 1907. This paper is arranged chronologically according to the tenure of each of the librarians. The last librarian covered is J. Elias Jones, who took office in

1957, by which time the collection had grown to nearly 170,000 volumes.

450 Throne, Mildred. "The History of The State University of Iowa: The University Libraries." Master's thesis, University of Iowa, 1943. 121p.

Established in 1855, the University of Iowa Library developed in a pattern similar to other state university libraries. A tragic fire destroyed two-thirds of the collection in 1897. Long-term space problems and insufficient acquisitions plagued the library well into the twentieth century. Major progress is attributed to Malcom G. Wyer, director from 1904 to 1913. Collections, services, and catalogs are described. Expenditures and circulation figures are provided for the central library and departmental libraries.

KANSAS

451 Stephens, Harold H. "A Study of the Growth and Development of the Library of Kansas State Teachers College, Emporia, 1875-1930." Master's thesis, Kansas State Teachers College, 1935. 99p.

The purpose of this thesis is to trace the growth, resources, and functions of the Kellogg Library with the intention of creating an understanding and appreciation of the significant role it has played in the development of the school. The writer looks at early library quarters, resources and funds, librarians, the development of the library school, the mail loan service, and current needs of the library.

452 Williams, Marjorie G. "The William Allen White Memorial Library of Kansas State Teacher's College, Emporia 1930-1959." Master's thesis, Kansas State Teachers College, 1959. 64p.

The William Allen White Library grew rapidly during this period, culminating in a new building dedicated in 1952. Collections and services are described in some detail. Biographical vignettes of the library staff and a descriptive brochure supplement the text.

KENTUCKY

453 Bruner, Joyce E. "The History of the University of Louisville Libraries." Master's thesis, University of North Carolina, 1953. Published: Association of College & Research Libraries Microcard, Number 60.

After briefly sketching the history of the University of Louisville, the author presents individual histories of the following University of Louisville libraries: the School of Medicine Library, the School of Law Library, the General Library, the School of Dentistry Library, the Speed Scientific School Library, the School of Music Library, and the Louisville Municipal College Library. The first library in what is now the University of Louisville was a small medical library established in 1837.

454 Coyte, Donna E. "A History of the University of Louisville School of Law Library 1846-1966." Master's thesis, University of North Carolina, 1968. 103p.

This paper contains four chapters. The first deals with the beginnings of the Law School and its library in 1846, and traces their development to 1940. The second chapter covers the library's history to 1967. Chapter three deals with technical processes in the Law School Library, and chapter four discusses the relative merits of centralization versus autonomy in law school libraries.

455 Scott, Ellen. "The History and Influence of the Old Library of Transylvania University." Master's thesis, University of Kentucky, 1929. 60p.

Transylvania College of Lexington, Kentucky was the first school of higher education established west of the Mountains, and its library, long one of the best in the Ohio Valley, was formed in the East in 1783 and later transported to Lexington. The author of this study treats the history of the "old" library from 1783 to 1860, when the University was temporarily closed because of the Civil War.

LOUISIANA

456 Knighten, Loma. "A History of the Library of Southwestern Louisiana Institute 1900-1948." Master's thesis, Columbia University, 1949. 97p.

This study traces the development of the Library of Southwestern Louisiana Institute in Lafayette, from the beginning of the college in 1901 to the end of 1948. The paper includes a brief history of the college, information about the founding of the library, an analysis of the book collection, a treatment of the growth of staff and housing, and a history of the administration of the library.

MAINE

457 Michener, Roger. "The Bowdoin College Library: From Its Beginning to the Present Day." Master's thesis, University of Chicago, 1972. 236p. Published: *Library Quarterly* 43 (July 1973): 215-26; *Journal of Library History* 10 (July 1975): 214-30.

Eleven chapters are devoted to a detailed reconstruction of the Bowdoin College Library from 1811 to 1968. Early Bowdoin literary societies, the incumbency of librarian Henry Wadsworth Longfellow (1829-1835), the catalog of 1863, and the period 1883-1968 are afforded prominent treatment.

458 Rush, Nixon O. "The History of College Libraries in Maine." Master's thesis, Columbia University, 1945. Published: Clark University Library, Worcester, Massachusetts, 1946.

This paper is concerned with histories of the libraries of the five institutions of higher education in Maine. It covers a span of 137 years, from 1802 to 1939. Each library is treated individually. The author provides information on origins and development, collection building, use and function of the libraries, physical facilities, and financial support. The five schools covered are Bowdoin, Bangor Theological Seminary, Colby, Bates, and the University of Maine. The author finds that church-related groups were influential in establishing most of the schools, and that the library at Bowdoin got the earliest start (1802).

MARYLAND

459   Greer, James J. "A History of the Library of Woodstock College of Baltimore County, Maryland from 1869 to 1957." Master's thesis, Drexel Institute of Technology, 1957. 84p.

The library of Woodstock College (Jesuit) was founded in 1869. The author devotes his first chapter to a history of the Jesuit scholasticates in Maryland to 1957. He then discusses the library in a Jesuit house. Chapter III deals with the library of the Georgetown Scholasticate. The final three chapters trace the history of the Woodstock College Library from 1869 to 1957. The author discusses collection development, physical plant, organization of the collection, and services.

460   Griswold, Ardyce M. "A History of the Columbia Union College Library, Takoma Park, Maryland 1904-1954." Master's thesis, Catholic University of America, 1964.

This study presents a descriptive and statistical survey of the Columbia Union College Library, Takoma Park, Maryland from its very meager beginnings in 1904 to 1954, when it formed a significant part of the Seventh-Day Adventist liberal arts college. The author traces the history of both the college and its library. By 1954 the library's collections numbered nearly 60,000 volumes.

461 Hoff, Alethea. "A History of the Library of Western Maryland College." Master's thesis, Drexel Institute of Technology, 1954. 49p.

This study commences with the founding of Western Maryland College in 1867 and traces the development of the library to 1954. When the college opened in 1867 the only book collection available to students was that owned by Dr. James T. Hall, first president of the school. The library grew slowly and not until 1910 was the first professional librarian appointed. By 1954 the collection had grown to 50,000 volumes, and the library was housed in its own building.

462 Kirby, Madge B. "A History of the Goucher College Library, Baltimore, Maryland 1885-1949." Master's thesis, Catholic University of America, 1952. Published: Association of College & Research Libraries Microcard, Number 26.

The Goucher College Library remained quite small for many years. From 1885 to 1914 the few books were housed in a classroom in Goucher Hall, and faculty members served as librarians. Library growth was hindered by a number of factors after 1915, such as the depression of the 1930s, World War II, a split campus, and a general lack of funds. Despite these difficulties the library grew consistently and was preparing to occupy a new building in 1952. The contributions of librarian Eleanor N. Falley are considered.

463 Klein, Sarah J. "The History and Present Status of the Library of St. John's College, Annapolis." Master's thesis, Catholic University of America, 1952. 53p.

The library originated in a collection of books sent to Maryland in 1697 by the Rev. Thomas Bray. Many of these books, which were not enthusiastically received by the colony, found their way to the St. John's College Library. No organized book purchasing was done by the college library until 1792, when 275 pounds were expended for books and other equipment. The collection grew at a snail's pace; when St. John's College became the Department of Arts and Sciences of the University of Maryland in 1909 the library contained only 9,000 volumes. The author briefly traces the library's development from that time to 1950.

464 Koudelka, Janet B. "A History of the Johns Hopkins Medical Libraries 1889-1935." Master's thesis, Catholic University of America, 1963. 96p.

The author divides her study into three major portions. The first deals with the early medical libraries at Johns Hopkins: the hospital library, 1889-1929; the library of the School of Medicine, 1893-1929; and the library of the School of Hygiene and Public Health, 1919-1929. The second portion traces the developments that led to the establishment of a centralized medical library, the William W. Welch Medical Library in 1929. The third portion treats the Welch Medical Library under the directorship of Fielding H. Garrison, 1930-1934.

465 Luckett, George R. "A History of the United States Naval Academy Library 1845-1907." Master's thesis, Catholic University of America, 1951. 39p.

This paper traces the history of the United States Naval Academy Library from its beginnings in 1845, when it was a small collection of about 300 volumes to 1904, when the collection had grown to nearly 50,000 volumes. Although the library's development parallels somewhat the histories of other American libraries of the nineteenth century, the author believes that its history is more closely connected with the history of the United States. The United States Naval Academy and its library prospered when the Navy was popular and declined when the people lost interest in the Navy.

466 Nichols, Mary E. "Historical Survey of the Library of the College of Notre Dame of Maryland." Master's thesis, Catholic University of America, 1957.

Reported missing.

467 Ownings, Vivian B. "A History of the Library of Morgan State College from 1867 to 1939." Master's thesis, Catholic University of America, 1952. 32p.

Morgan State College in Baltimore, Maryland began in 1867 as the Centenary Biblical Institute. It was one of the many educational endeavors aimed at the newly emancipated American Negro. The first library collection available to students was the private holdings of Dr. J. Emory Round, first president of the Centenary Institute. It was not until 1920 that any extensive library development took place, stimulated by a grant from the Carnegie Foundation and the appointment of the first professional librarian at the college. The author surveys book budgets, staff development, physical plant, and services.

468 Rohdy, Sister Ruth. "A History of Saint Joseph College Library 1902-1955." Master's thesis, Catholic University of America, 1956. 103p.

The author has written this history of the Saint Joseph College Library from 1902-1953 under the following major headings: 1) a brief history of the college; 2) housing; 3) finances; 4) growth and development of the book and periodical collections; 5) administration; 6) staffing; and 7) organization of the collection. Saint Joseph's gained authorization to function as a college in 1902 and from that time on the college had a library, although it remained quite small. In 1955 the budget was only $5,000 and the collection numbered 20,000 volumes.

MASSACHUSETTS

469 Engley, Donald B. "The Emergence of the Amherst College Library 1821-1911." Master's thesis, University of Chicago, 1947. 155p.

The Amherst College Library progressed slowly at first. Faced by a shortage of funds and a seemingly disinterested attitude on the part of the faculty, little progress was made before 1845. Under the energetic guidance of President Edward Hitchcock the first library building was provided in 1853. In the 1870s Melvil Dewey spent a short time at Amherst and developed the beginnings of his classification scheme. However, the great growth of the library took place under the leadership of one of America's leading nineteenth-century librarians, William I. Fletcher, who served the Amherst Library from 1883 to 1911.

470 Terrell, Darrell. "History of the Dumbarton Oaks Research Library of Harvard University 1940-1950." Master's thesis, Catholic University of America, 1954. 51p.

Traces the history of the Dumbarton Oaks Research Library at Harvard, which is devoted to the study of Byzantine history and culture. The first chapter discusses the early development of the library by its founders, Mr. and Mrs. Robert Woods Elise. In 1940 the library building, the collection of some 14,000 books, and 16 acres of land (the whole gift valued at over $1,000,000) were given to Harvard University. Chapter two deals with the library's development after 1940, with special emphasis on administration, services, and the collection. Chapter three deals with special collections and reference tools developed at the library.

471 Wang, Shu-ching Y. "Harvard-Yenching Library: Harvard University, History and Development." Master's thesis, Southern Connecticut State College, 1967. 104p.

The first dozen or so pages of this study trace the history of the Yenching Library at Harvard, 1927-1966.

MICHIGAN

472 Bidlack, Russell E. "The University of Michigan General Library: A History of Its Beginnings 1837-1852." Doctoral dissertation, University of Michigan, 1954. Published: University of Michigan, Department of Library Science, 1962.

This study covers the history of the library, which had its inception together with the University in 1837. The Rev. Henry Colelazer, a local clergyman, was the first librarian. He served in that capacity until 1845, at which time he was replaced by Professor George P. Williams. Williams worked up a classification for the collection adapted from Thomas Jefferson's plan, and he printed a catalog in 1846.

473 Maxwell, Margaret N.F. "Anatomy of a Book Collector: William L. Clements and the Clements Library." Doctoral dissertation, University of Michigan, 1971. 429p. UMI# 72-4931. Published: N. Israel (Amsterdam), 1973.

This study focuses on the book collecting and library founding aspects of the life of William Lawrence Clements (1861-1934), the wealthy industrialist who collected a magnificent library of Americana and then gave it and a building to house it to the University of Michigan in 1923. The author traces Clements' growing interest in book collecting, analyzes his relationship with two prominent book dealers, Lathrop Harper and Henry Stevens, and discusses his warm friendship with librarians George Parker Winship, Worthington C. Ford, and Clarence E. Brigham. Finally, Clements' collection interests after 1923 are treated.

MINNESOTA

474 Fortin, Charles C. "A History of the St. Thomas College Library." Master's thesis, University of Minnesota, 1951. 187p.

The author first traces the history of St. Thomas College in St. Paul, Minnesota. A library was available when the college opened as St. Thomas Aquinas Seminary in 1885, but little is known about it until 1918, when Mary Griffin was named the first full-time librarian. The author divides his history of the library into chronological segments corresponding to the tenure of the librarians: Mary Griffin (1918-1926), Bonita McElmeel (1926-1931), Blaise Hospodor (1931-1932), Leonard Pogge (1923-

1937), Bernadette Becker (1937-1944) and David Watkins (1944-). The author finds that the library was plagued from the beginning by difficulties in preparing a catalog and problems relating to physical facilities.

475 Genaway, David C. "Quasi-Departmental Libraries: Their Origin, Function and Relationship to the University Library System—A Case Study of the University of Minnesota Twin Cities Campus." Doctoral dissertation, University of Minnesota, 1975. 234p. UMI# 76-14,890. Portion published: *College & Research Libraries* 38 (1977): 187-94.

Unofficial libraries sponsored by academic departments are a common phenomena in many universities. Two hypotheses are tested: 1) the emergence and/or maintenance of quasi-departmental libraries are related to use of and attitude toward the university library; and 2) unofficial departmental libraries emerge out of a need for resources not furnished by the central library. Support for the second hypothesis was stronger than for the first. These libraries originated from either gifts or deliberate planning.

476 Miller, Virginia P. "A History of the Library of Gustavus Adolphus College, St. Peter, Minnesota." Master's thesis, University of Minnesota, 1961. 192p.

This paper first presents a chronological history of the development of the library at Gustavus Adolphus College from its beginnings in 1862 until the summer of 1960. The library was managed for some 60 years by faculty librarians, and the author gives extensive coverage to their contributions to library development. The first professionally trained librarian was appointed in the 1920s. The rest of the paper is developed around the three librarians who served from 1919 to 1960: Victoria Johnston (1919-1943), Grant D. Hanson (1945-1950), and Odrun Peterson (1950-). The library was moved to a new building in 1948 and in 1960 contained more than 65,000 volumes.

477 Roloff, Ronald W. "St. John's University Library: A Historical Evaluation." Master's thesis, University of Minnesota, 1953. Published: Association of College & Research Libraries Microcard, Number 34.

Traces the evolution of the St. John's University Library in Collegeville, Minnesota from its beginnings in 1867 to 1953. The library grew out of a small and secluded collection of books, overwhelmingly theological in content. By 1950 the library had grown to 80,000 volumes, but was still plagued by a lack of funds and space.

MISSISSIPPI

478 Nichols, Mary E. "Early Development of the University of Mississippi Library." Master's thesis, University of Mississippi, 1957. Published: Association of College & Research Libraries Microcard, Number 111.

This study traces the history of the University of Mississippi Library from 1849 to 1910. The first years of the University's history were characterized by extreme financial difficulties and the library suffered accordingly. The first librarian, a faculty member, was named in 1853, but it was not until 1886 that a full-time librarian was appointed. The library was damaged during the Civil War and lay dormant during the turbulent Reconstruction period. The library reached a period of relatively smooth growth by 1910.

MISSOURI

479 Hoyer, Mina. "The History of Automation in the University of Missouri Library, 1947-1963." Master's thesis, Indiana University, 1965. Published: Association of College & Research Libraries Microcard, Number 166.

This paper traces the history of automation at the University of

Missouri from 1947, when Ralph Parker became librarian, to 1963. Parker has been a pioneer in library automation, and the author analyzes his efforts in this area. Steps in planning, changes made, and current planning for future development are discussed. The author has not attempted to theorize about all possible types of library machines, but treats only those that are being used or that seem best fitted to future application at the University of Missouri Library.

NEW JERSEY

480 Berberian, Kevorek R. "Princeton University Library, 1746-1860." Master's thesis, Jersey City State College, 1976. 84p. Published: Creative Graphic Art Service, 1980.

Princeton's library began with a gift of 474 volumes from Governor Jonathan Belcher in 1757 and occupied permanent quarters, Nassau Hall, in 1762. In 1760, the first book catalog was issued. The librarian's position was a part-time assignment filled by a faculty member until the Civil War. Collections developed slowly and the library was open only one day a week until 1868. The library was destroyed twice, once during the Revolution and a second time by fire in 1805. By 1865, the library had accumulated 15,000 volumes, far short of Harvard's 74,000. Two literary societies, the Whig and Clisophic, boasted large collections which supplemented the university library's holdings.

NEW MEXICO

481 Bandy, Cheryl N.L. "The First Fifty Years of the New Mexico State University Library, 1889-1939." Master's thesis, University of Oklahoma, 1971. 70p.

For three decades beginning in 1889, the New Mexico State University Library experienced steady growth, new facilities, departmentalization, and rapid turnover in the director's position. In 1929 a new library was constructed and a reclassification to the Library of Congress classification was completed. The library was named for Judge R. L. Young of Las Cruces in 1933 and received two murals by Tom Lea, Jr. of Santa Fe. By 1939 the library contained 37,776 volumes and operated on a 63-hour per week schedule. The lack of adequate staff and funds for the collection were recurring problems.

NEW YORK

482   Allan, John M. "The Library of Hamilton College, Clinton, New York from January, 1793 to January, 1963: The Development of an American Liberal Arts College-Library." Thesis, The Library Association, 1968. 595p.

The history of the Hamilton College Library begins with an account of the foundation of the Hamilton-Oneida Academy in 1793. When Hamilton College was founded in 1812, the library held 186 volumes. By 1963, the library had acquired 255,000 volumes. Library development at Hamilton College is related to national trends in higher education and librarianship. Society libraries at Hamilton are allotted extensive coverage. The directorship of J. D. Ibbetson (1911-1936) is given prominence.

483   Bogart, Ruth E. "College Library Development in New York State During the 19th Century." Master's thesis, Columbia University, 1948. 155p.

The author presents a history of the development of college libraries in New York during the nineteenth century. She treats her subject topically and covers the following major areas: 1) early provisions for college libraries; 2) methods of expanding libraries; 3) growth of the collections; 4) restrictions on acquisitions; 5) housing; 6) library organization; and 7) library instruction. The author finds that religion had some influence on college libraries in New York, though less extensive than in the 1700s. The Civil War did not cause serious problems for college libraries in New York.

484 Boudreau, Allan. "The Growth and Development of the Urban University Research Library Resources at the Washington Center of New York University." Doctoral dissertation, New York University, 1973. 286p. UMI# 73-19,409.

Opens with a description of the place of the library in the University and notes the changing commitments of American education. Various influences on the development of the New York University Library are identified: Jeffersonian ideals; the public library movement; and the changing urban population. Evolving patterns of study and research, together with the emergence of professional schools, are correlated to the growth of the New York University Library.

485 Imberman, Angela. "The History of the Vassar College Library, 1861-1968." Master's thesis, University of Chicago, 1969. 103p.

Recounts the rise of women's education, the growth of the Vassar College Library, and the contributions of director Fanny Borden (1927-1945).

486 Jones, Ruth. "A History of the Library of Teachers College, Columbia University, 1887-1952." Master's thesis, Drexel Institute of Technology, 1953. Published: Association of College & Research Libraries Microcard, Number 39.

After briefly tracing the history of Columbia Teachers College, the author covers the history of the library in three time periods. The library got a tremendous boost when Columbia College transferred over 20,000 volumes on education to the Bryson Library at the Teachers College in 1903. By 1952 the collection, which numbered 500 volumes in 1888, had grown to over 250,000.

487 Kato, Mother Ayako. "A History of Brady Memorial Library, Manhattanville College of the Sacred Heart, Purchase, New York 1841-1957." Master's thesis, Catholic University of America, 1959. 143p.

The author has concentrated on the history of the library of Manhattanville College, a small Catholic liberal arts college for women, but has also made a serious effort to contrast this library's development with others in America. Special emphasis is placed on tracing the active influence the library has exerted on the educational role of Manhattanville College. The author follows a topical arrangement concerned with five major subjects: physical plant, administration, book collection, technical services, and public services.

488 Linderman, Winifred B. "History of the Columbia University Library, 1876-1926." Doctoral dissertation, Columbia University, 1959. 619p. UMI# 59-2859.

The author has chosen to cover the period 1876-1926 because these years witnessed the transition from college to major university. The many difficulties involved in this transition—such matters as collection building, personnel problems, administrative practices and physical plant planning—are considered. The librarians of Columbia were among the most significant of their day. Melvil Dewey established the country's first library school to train assistants for the Columbia University Library. George H. Baker, Dewey's successor, was noted for his collection building efforts. In 1926 the noted library educator and administration, Charles C. Williamson, was named Director of Libraries and Dean of the School of Library Service.

489 Slavens, Thomas P. "The Library of Union Theological Seminary in the City of New York, 1836 to the Present." Doctoral dissertation, University of Michigan, 1965. 358p. UMI# 66-06705. Portions published: *Library History Seminar*, Number 3, edited by Martha Jane K. Zachert, School of Library Science, Florida State University, 1968, p. 26-34; *Journal of Library History* 4 (1969): 321-29.

The author has two purposes in mind: 1) to determine the ways in which the collection was developed, and 2) to demonstrate how other libraries might benefit from Union's experience.

490 Stewart, Nathaniel J. "A History of the Library of the College of the City of New York." Master's thesis, College of the City of New York, 1935. 146p.

The College of the City of New York was first known as the Free Academy (1847-1866). During this period members of the faculty served as librarian, one of whom later committed suicide with sulphuric acid. An important early donor was Seth Grosvenor. Charles G. Herbermann, a prominent classicist, directed the library from 1873 to 1915. He introduced systematic record keeping, published a catalog, and oriented the library toward service. The period 1907-1930 was characterized by the growth of departmental libraries, the increase in the number of staff, the attraction of many gifts, and the struggle for a new building. The author laments that Henry E. Bliss, a gifted cataloger, was bypassed for the directorship in 1918.

491 Tutt, Celestine. "Library Service to the Columbia University School of Social Work, 1898-1979." Doctoral dissertation, Columbia University, 1983. 401p. UMI# 8406559.

The history and philosophy of social welfare in the United States, the evolution of social work as a profession, and education for social work are treated in the first part of this study. Next is a brief review of the nature and role of social work libraries. The school's early years and supporting library services are reviewed in detail, including the merger of the library with others to form the Russell Sage Foundation Library. By 1979 the New York School of Social Work became an integral part of Columbia University.

NORTH CAROLINA

492 Battle, Margaret E. "A History of the Carnegie Library at Johnson C. Smith University." Master's thesis, University of North Carolina, 1960. 55p.

This study traces the development of the Carnegie Library at

Johnson C. Smith University, a Negro college in Charlotte, North Carolina, from the latter part of the nineteenth century to 1958. By 1890 it had reached nearly 5,000 volumes, most of them theological in nature. In 1903 Andrew Carnegie offered to donate $12,500 for a library building if the University could match this amount for upkeep. The University managed by 1911 to raise the money. In 1958 the collection numbered some 30,000 volumes.

493   Clymer, Benjamin F., Jr. "The History of the Division of Health Affairs Library of the University of North Carolina." Master's thesis, University of North Carolina, 1959. 118p.

The origins of the Division of Health Affairs Library are traced back to 1800, to the book collections of the University and the libraries of its two literary societies. The collections contained few medical books, and those few were obsolete gifts. In 1912 the collection, some 3,000 outdated volumes, was housed in a "library room" in the medical building. The collection grew slowly and spasmodically due to a lack of funds. In 1936, the collection was made a departmental library of the University Library and from that time on took on some semblance of organized growth. By 1959 the library had grown to nearly 50,000 volumes and had a staff of four.

494   Cranford, Janet P. "The Documents Collection of the University of North Carolina Library from its Beginning through 1963." Master's thesis, University of North Carolina, 1965. 47p.

Traces the history of the documents collection from its establishment in 1795 to 1963, when the library was named a regional Federal Depository for North Carolina.

495   Diaz, Albert J. "A History of the Latin American Collection of the University of North Carolina Library." Master's thesis, University of North Carolina, 1956. 83p.

The first section deals with the historical development of the collection. Until 1940 the growth of the collection was irregular, hampered by a lack of funds. From 1940 to 1945 the collection was greatly increased with $25,000 provided by the Rockefeller Foundation. In 1947 the Carnegie Corporation provided $14,000 over a five-year period for acquisitions. In 1952 the library had grown to 20,000 volumes and from that time on was financed by the University. Part two deals with the problems faced in acquiring and processing the collection. Part three is a critical evaluation of the development of the collection.

496 Eaton, Joan D. "A History and Evaluation of the Hanes Collection in the Louis R. Wilson Library, University of North Carolina." Master's thesis, University of North Carolina, 1957. 115p.

This paper traces the history of the Hanes Collection from the time of Louis Round Wilson's first conception of it until 1957. Wilson had long hoped to establish a special collection of materials relating to the history of books and bookmaking, but it was not until 1929 that his plans bore fruit. At that time the Hanes Foundation for the study of the origin and development of the book was established by the children of John Wesley and Anna Hodgin Hanes. Thirty thousand dollars was given to the University, $20,000 of which was to be spent for the purchase of 369 incunabula owned by Dr. Aaron Burtis Hunter of Raleigh. Since that time, the collection has grown steadily and now stands as one of the best of its kind in the South.

497 Farrow, Mildred. "The History of Guilford College Library, 1837-1955." Master's thesis, University of North Carolina, 1959. Published: Association of College and Research Libraries Microcard, Number 120.

The history of Guilford College Library, Greensboro, North Carolina, is closely linked with the efforts of the North Carolina Society of Friends to provide books for meeting libraries in the 1830s. The Friends presented the Library with many gifts and by 1866 the collection numbered over 20,000 volumes. The library was destroyed by fire in 1908, but was quickly rebuilt and with the help of a Carnegie grant was able to acquire over 20,000 volumes by 1850.

498 Heindel, Sally W. "A History of the Institute of Government Library of the University of North Carolina." Master's thesis, University of North Carolina, 1965. 107p.

Founded in the 1920s as a research and service agency at the University of North Carolina, the Institute progressed rapidly and became affiliated with the University in 1942. The first full-time librarian was engaged in 1955. By 1965 the collection of state and local materials consisted of 36,000 pamphlets and 11,000 volumes. Access to the library and certain technical processes suffered from its uncertain relationship to the University library.

499 Holder, Elizabeth J. "A History of the Library of the Woman's College of the University of North Carolina, 1892-1945." Master's thesis, University of North Carolina, 1955. Published: Association of College & Research Libraries Microcard, Number 86.

After briefly tracing the history of the school funded in 1891 in Greensboro, North Carolina, the author presents the history of the library from its inception in 1892 to 1945. Chapters are devoted to: 1) the general history of the library; 2) the influence of Carnegie funds on library development; 3) the Department of Library Science, 1927-1931; 4) special collections and gifts; 5) periodical collections; and 6) the library fire of 1932.

500 List, Barbara T. "The Friends of the University of North Carolina Library, 1932-1962." Master's thesis, University of North Carolina, 1965. 65p.

The first section of this paper contains a history of the rise of "Friends of the Library" throughout the United States. The first of these groups was founded in 1923. The author then turns her attention to the Friends of the University of North Carolina, which developed under the guidance of the noted librarian Louis R. Wilson. The author finds that the group has had a significant influence on the library's development. Such issues as the purchase of special collections, lobbying for new buildings or larger budgets, and general support of the library's programs are cited.

501 Moore, Gay G. "The Southern Historical Collection in the Louis Round Wilson Library of the University of North Carolina from the Beginning of the Collection Through 1948." Master's thesis, University of North Carolina, 1958. 83p.

The Southern Historical Collection includes all of the relevant manuscript holdings of the University Library at Chapel Hill. The collection was developed through the efforts of Dr. Joseph G. de Roulhac Hamilton, who was one of the first to realize the services needed for a large, well organized collection of manuscript material on Southern history. The collection was formally recognized in 1930 and Hamilton was named director. By 1943, when he retired, the collection was considered one of the best in the United States.

502 Nicholson, James M., Jr. "A History of the Wake Forest College Library, 1878-1946." Master's thesis, University of North Carolina, 1954. Published: Association of College & Research Libraries Microcard, Number 78.

The chapters of this paper deal with the following subjects: 1) the introduction of "New Education" methods into American education and their affect on Wake Forest College before 1900; 2) the library during the period of transition from the controlling influence of the classical curriculum to the equivalent status of "New Education" courses, 1879-1905; 3) the library during the administration of William L. Poteat, 1905-1927; and 4) the library and two benefactors—Andrew Carnegie and E. Smith Reynolds, 1928-1946.

503 Pearsall, Thelma F. "History of the North Carolina Agricultural and Technical College Library." Master's thesis, Western Reserve University, 1955. 48p.

After surveying the development of Greensboro, North Carolina, and its college, the author divides the history of the library into four sections: 1) the librarians, from Ferdinand D. Bluford in 1912 to Miss Morrow (1937-); 2) the library buildings, including the old library that was destroyed in 1929, the new quarters provided in 1931, and the new building erected in 1954; 3) the library's collections; and 4) library services.

504 Perkins, Theodore E. "The History of Elon College Library, 1890-1957." Master's thesis, University of North Carolina, 1962. 148p.

This study presents the history, 1890-1957, of the library of Elon College, located in Elon, North Carolina. The author divides his study into seven parts. The first part consists of a brief history of the Christian Church (Congregational Christian) from which the college sprang, and a brief history of the college itself. Part two deals with the early history of the library and its numerous difficulties. The third part deals with the library's staff. The fourth part analyzes the development of the library's services. The fifth part analyzes the development of the library's collection. Part six deals with cataloging and classification, and part seven describes the use made of the Elon College Library during the period covered.

505 Tarlton, Shirley M. "The Development of the Library of Charlotte College, 1946-July 1, 1965." Master's thesis, University of North Carolina, 1966. 72p.

Traces the history of the library of Charlotte College, in Charlotte, North Carolina, from its small beginnings in 1946 with 12 books to 1965 when the J. Murray Atkins Library opened with some 100,000 volumes in the collection.

OHIO

506 Barnett, Mildred F. "A History of the Baldwin-Wallace College Library, 1913-1964." Master's thesis, Kent State University, 1967. 159p.

The author traces the history of the library from the union of Wallace College and Baldwin University in 1913 to 1964. The library, originally managed by student librarians, grew to some

100,000 volumes in the 1960s. A new building was completed in 1959.

507 Bobinski, George S. "A Brief History of the Libraries of Western Reserve University, 1826-1952." Master's thesis, Western Reserve University, 1952. Published: Association of College & Research Libraries Microcard, Number 50.

The author describes the evolution of the Western Reserve University Library from a collection of 100 volumes in 1826 to some 700,000 in 1952. The continuous efforts to meet ever-increasing demands for space and the need for unifying the library system are two major themes in the paper. A significant portion of the paper treats the development of the Adelbert College Library of the University from 1882 to 1924.

508 Brookover, Barbara. "A History of the Leonard Case Library, Cleveland, Ohio, 1846-1941." Master's thesis, Western Reserve University, 1957. 37p.

Few libraries have had so varied a history as the Case Library. It traces its beginning to the establishment of the Young Men's Literary Association in 1846. In 1867 it moved to the new library rooms of the Cleveland Library Association, founded and paid for by Leonard Case in memory of his brother William. The library continued to develop with the aid of Mr. Case for many years. In 1924 the library merged with Western Reserve University and Adelbert College.

509 Clinefeller, Ruth W. "A History of Bierce Library of the University of Akron." Master's thesis, Kent State University, 1956. 200p.

This paper traces the history of the library, which began as part of Buchtel College, from 1852 to 1955. Library development was slow, especially after the financial crisis of 1893. In 1916 a new library was built and the collection began to expand. In 1949 a special library on rubber was established with funds from the Rubber Division of the American Chemical Society. By 1955 the Bierce Library held 100,000 volumes.

510 Fry, James W. "The Ohio State University Library, 1913-1928." Master's thesis, Ohio State University, 1971. 65p. Published: Ohio State University Library, 1972.

Following a brief sketch of the Ohio State University Library during the nineteenth century, the author examines the period 1913-1928 in some detail. Throughout this period Olive Branch Jones served as director (1893-1927). A new facility was erected in 1913 but proved inadequate by 1920. Throughout the 1920s Ohio State rated low among Big Ten institutions in terms of its overall library budget and acquisition rate. Although budgets were periodically increased, the library did not improve its relative standing. Protracted ill health of the director and the failure of legislative support are cited as reasons for lack of dynamic growth.

511 Harper, John R. "A History of Mount Union College Library." Master's thesis, Kent State University, 1968. 134p.

This thesis is a study of the history of the Mount Union College Library from its beginnings in the 1840s to the present. It includes examination of literary societies, the growth of holdings and special collections, library service and management, the new library, and the librarians of the college.

512 Irwin, Maurine. "History of the Ohio Wesleyan University Library, 1844-1940." Master's thesis, University of California, 1941. 263p.

The library developed slowly until William Starges donated $10,000 in 1853 to increase the collection. This gift enabled the University to purchase a nucleus of some 3,000 volumes for the library—a collection that was slowly enlarged, as was the case with most college libraries. The Ohio Wesleyan University Library had an irregular and insufficient budget. Most acquisitions came through gifts. In the twentieth century the library developed along more organized lines, but was still hampered by serious financial difficulties in 1940.

513   Mathews, Stanley G. "The Marian Library of the University of Dayton: Origin and Development." Master's thesis, Western Reserve University, 1952. 58p.

The Marian Library of the University of Dayton was organized in 1943 as a centennial project of the Society of Mary (Marianists) in America. A local variant of the Dewey classification was developed to accommodate the unique collection. The library maintains an international union list, provides reference services, and publishes a newsletter. By 1952, the collection consisted of 3,200 books and 800 pamphlets.

514   Meyers, Judith K. "A History of the Antioch College Library, 1850-1929." Master's thesis, Kent State University, 1963. Published: Association of College & Research Libraries Microcard, Number 150.

Examines the history of the Antioch College Library, Yellow Springs, Ohio in relation to broad social, political, economic, and cultural currents of the times. This study covers the library's history from its founding to 1920. The author finds that significant shortages of money, space, and personnel hampered the growth of the library. By 1920 the library contained about 30,000 volumes.

515   Musser, Adah. "A History of Muskingum College Library." Master's thesis, Kent State University, 1963. 77p.

A Presbyterian College established in 1837, Muskingum developed as a liberal arts institution. The first professional librarian was hired in 1923 and the collection reached 62,000 volumes in 1962. Briefly summarizes staffing, faculty, collection, and circulation patterns. Copious photographs accompany the text. Draws from library reports and archival records.

516 Saviers, Samuel H. "The Literary Societies and Their Libraries at Hiram College." Master's thesis, Kent State University, 1958. 277p.

This paper is developed in three parts: 1) the history of the literary societies of Hiram College, 1850-1950; 2) their purposes, organization, and activities; and 3) their libraries. The libraries are studied in depth and their contributions to Hiram College are analyzed. In the nineteenth century the society libraries arose as a result of the inadequacy of the college library, and the author finds their contributions to the college library exceedingly important.

517 Schink, Ronald J. "A History of the Youngstown University and Its Library." Master's thesis, Western Reserve University, 1956. 65p.

This study is mainly concerned with a history of the University. The latter portion of the paper does trace in some detail the development of the library from 1937 to 1950. In 1943 the school was refused accreditation because the library facilities were inadequate. The library made considerable progress after 1943; the author traces its development with emphasis on the events surrounding the construction of the new library in 1950-1951.

518 Silva, Sister M.F.C. "A History of the Ursuline College Library, Cleveland, Ohio, 1922-1957." Master's thesis, Western Reserve University, 1958. Published: Association of College & Research Libraries Microcard, Number 108.

Briefly covers the history of Ursuline College and then discusses the library's history from its beginnings in 1922 to 1957. The treatment is chronological with special consideration given to budget, collection, buildings, organization, and services. By 1957 the library contained more than 20,000 volumes.

519 Skipper, James E. "The Ohio State University Library, 1873-

1913." Doctoral dissertation, University of Michigan, 1960. 330p. UMI# 60-6937.

Part one of this study considers the problems of the physical plant, faculty-library relations, and development of the library's collections from 1873-1893. Part two deals with the history of the library from 1893 until 1913, when the first permanent library building was completed. During the 40-year period covered, the growth of the University Library was restricted by lack of legislative support.

520 Stein, John H. "The Development of the Hiram College Library from the Literary Societies Which Formed Its Nucleus." Master's thesis, Kent State University, 1950. 105p.

Traces the history of the Hiram College Library, Hiram, Ohio, from the beginnings of the literary society libraries in the 1850s to 1940. The author places special emphasis on the factors influencing acquisition policies in the college library. The literary society libraries were found to be the only good libraries on campus until after 1900, and they proved vital to the academic program of the University.

521 Tucker, Jennie S. "Oberlin College Library, 1833-1885." Master's thesis, Western Reserve University, 1953. Published: Association of College & Research Libraries Microcard, Number 45.

The Oberlin College Library experienced its greatest growth after 1885, but the author has chosen its early period for the subject of this paper. The library got official recognition in 1834, and for the next 40 years it was under the able direction of of Dr. James Dascomb, Professor of Chemistry, Physiology and Botany. The author found ledgers recording the books checked out to students in 1836 and presents a list of the titles. A number of literary society libraries were established and they are discussed.

522 Vermilya, Nancy C. "A History of the Otterbein College Library."

Master's thesis, Western Reserve University, 1955. Published: Association of College & Research Libraries Microcard, Number 58.

Traces the history of the Otterbein College Library, Westerville, Ohio from its inception in 1858 to 1955. The paper is divided into two parts: 1) the history of the literary societies and their four libraries at Otterbein; and 2) history of the development of the college library in its five locations. In 1955 the new library building held nearly 50,000 volumes.

PENNSYLVANIA

523 Earnshaw, Jeannine. "A History of the Henry Lea Library at the University of Pennsylvania." Master's thesis, Drexel Institute of Technology, 1955. 41p.

Henry Lea was a Philadelphia scholar interested in medieval law. He collected a remarkable library while doing his research. A survey of his collection in 1878 indicated that he owned over 15,000 books and an impressive collection of manuscripts. It soon became, and remained, one of the best collections on the Inquisition, medieval jurisprudence, and the ecclesiastical courts. Upon his death he left his library to the University of Pennsylvania; in 1925 a new wing was added to the University's main library to hold the collection.

524 Girvin, Anne G. "The Albright Alumni Memorial Library." Master's thesis, Drexel Institute of Technology, 1954. 65p.

This paper surveys the history of the Albright Alumni Memorial Library, located in Albright College, Reading, Pennsylvania. The library at Albright College reflects consolidation of the collections of three earlier colleges: the Union Seminary, Schuylkill College, and Albright Collegiate Institution. This study covers the history of these libraries chronologically from 1853 to 1953, dealing with the early history of the institutions, with the libraries of the three background institutions, and finally with the Albright College Library to 1953.

525   Kraft, Sister M. Immaculata. "A History of the Library of Chestnut Hill College: Philadelphia, Pennsylvania, 1890-1965." Master's thesis, Catholic University of America, 1967. 100p.

A descriptive and statistical history of a small Catholic liberal arts college library with emphasis on: 1) educational development projected against the community background; 2) library standards compared with holdings; and 3) the use of the library.

526   McFarland, Martha M. "History of the Development of Bucknell University Library, Lewisburg, Pennsylvania." Master's thesis, Drexel Institute of Technology, 1955.

Reported missing.

527   McTaggart, John B. "The History of the Eastern Baptist Theological Seminary Library, 1925-1953." Master's thesis, Drexel Institute of Technology, 1954. 63p.

This paper traces the historical development of the Eastern Baptist Theological Seminary Library, Philadelphia, Pennsylvania from its beginning in 1925 until 1953. The study does not attempt a critical analysis of the library and its holdings are not covered in detail. Emphasis has been placed on the library's physical facilities and staff rather than on its services.

528   Meyerend, Maude H. "A History and Survey of the Fine Arts Library of the University of Pennsylvania from Its Founding to 1953." Master's thesis, Drexel Institute of Technology, 1955. 92p.

The first part of this study reviews the history of the Fine Arts Department and its library at the University of Pennsylvania from 1906 to 1953. The rest of the paper is devoted to a survey of present conditions.

529 Osborne, John T. "The Ursinus College Library, 1869-1953." Master's thesis, Drexel Institute of Technology, 1954. 44p.

Presents the history of the Ursinus College Library, Collegeville, Pennsylvania from the founding of the College in 1869 until the end of 1953. The first chapter covers the history of the college, the next three chapters cover the development of the library, and a final chapter discusses the construction of the Alumni Memorial Library building.

530 Richardson, Ellen R. "The La Salle College Library, Philadelphia, 1930-1953." Master's thesis, Drexel Institute of Technology, 1953. 43p.

This study traces the growth of the library from 1930 to 1953 with special emphasis on the plans for the new building and its occupancy. From the beginning the collection was small and poorly housed. The first librarian bought his make-shift book shelves at a local hardware store and installed them himself. In 1950 the college administration agreed to spend $400,000 on a new main library building. The author traces the development of the plans for this building.

531 Schuetz, Augustine R. "A History of the St. Vincent Archabbey-College Libraries." Master's thesis, Catholic University of America, 1959. 75p.

St. Vincent, founded in 1846 by the Benedictines, consists of three programs: preparatory school, liberal arts college, and seminary. Collections, technical processes, and circulation patterns are discussed in some detail. The three libraries were placed under central administration in 1939. The seminary library followed a classification scheme adapted from the Benedictine Monastery at Engelberg, Switzerland, while the college and preparatory school employed the Dewey classification. In 1958 the libraries moved to a central building and the college and monastery collections were reclassified into the Library of Congress classification.

532 Smith, Dorothy J. "The Early History of the Library of Allegheny College, Meadville, Pennsylvania." Master's thesis, Western Reserve University, 1953. Published: Association of College & Research Libraries Microcard, Number 61.

In 1815, and for several years thereafter, the library was the only asset of the new college. Timothy Alden, founder and first president of the college, was an ardent book collector and solicited gifts from such noted New Englanders as John Adams, William Bentley, Isaiah Thomas, and James Winthrop. The author discusses these benefactions and others, the development of the physical plant, the production of the catalog of 1823, and concludes with the year 1837.

533 Valentine, Sister M. "Holy Family College Library: The First Decade." Master's thesis, Marywood College (Scranton, Pennsylvania), 1956. 36p.

This work provides a history of the origins and growth of the Holy Family College Library from 1944, the year the College was founded, to 1954.

534 Wagner, Lloyd F. "A Descriptive History of the Library Facilities of Lafayette College, Easton, Pennsylvania, 1826-1941." Master's thesis, Catholic University of America, 1951. Published: Association of College & Research Libraries Microcard, Number 27.

This paper is a descriptive and statistical study covering the following subjects: 1) the impact of Lafayette College and library administrators, and especially of the students, on library development; 2) the development of library facilities, financial support, and services; 3) the influence of student literary societies at Lafayette College from 1832 to 1900; 4) the increasing significance of the library to the educational programs; and 5) a comparison of the Lafayette College Library with others of similar size, character, and origin.

535 Williams, Carrie W. "A History of the Krauth Memorial Library

and Staff of the Lutheran Theological Seminary at Philadelphia, From 1864 to 1951." Master's thesis, Drexel Institute of Technology, 1952. 65p.

The steady growth of a special library serving the needs of a theological seminary is chronicled in this study. Brief summaries of the collections, staff, finances, and technical operations are provided. Various benefactors and the library's unique classification developed by Luther D. Reed are described. Floor plans and photographs are included.

RHODE ISLAND

536   Desjarlais-Leuth, Christine. "Brown University and Its Library: A Study of the Beginnings of an Academic Library." Doctoral dissertation, University of Illinois, 1985. 212p. UMI# 8521753.

Brown University and its library were selected for examination to counterbalance the frequent studies of the more prestigious institutions. Brown, in fact, was found to be a pace-setter in the development of academic librarianship. It was the first library to create a permanent collection fund (1831) and the first to hire a full-time librarian, Charles C. Jewett, in 1842. Extensive treatment is accorded Reuben A. Guild, librarian from 1847 to 1893. The twenty-seven year tenure of President Francis Wayland (1827-1855) is credited with transforming the library from a passive colonial college library into a pre-modern academic library.

537   Everhart, Sister M. "A Historical Survey of the Annmary Brown Memorial, Providence, Rhode Island." Master's thesis, Catholic University of America, 1957. 45p.

Brigadier General Rush Hawkins (1831-1920) endowed the Annmary Brown Memorial in 1907 as a memorial to his wife. A lawyer, bibliophile, and author, Hawkins amassed one of America's premier collections of incunabula. Early specimens were purchased to document the spread of printing and its impact on civilization. From 1917 to 1953 noted bibliographer

Margaret B. Stillwell served as the curator. Since 1954 the Memorial has been administered by Brown University.

SOUTH CAROLINA

538   Hahn, Stephen S. "A History of the Lutheran Theological Southern Seminary and its Library, 1830-1934." Master's thesis, University of Chicago, 1977. 142p. Portion published: *South Carolina Historical Magazine* 80 (1979): 36-49.

This study traces the fortunes of the library of the Lutheran Theological Southern Seminary, Columbia, South Carolina from the founding in 1830 to construction of the first card catalog in 1934. Multiple relocations plagued the seminary during the early years and the library became a vital resource only during the latter period.

TENNESSEE

539   Atkins, Eliza. "A History of Fisk University Library and Its Standing in Relation to the Libraries of Other Comparable Institutions." Master's thesis, University of California, 1936. 83p.

Traces the historical development of the Fisk University Library from its beginnings in the early 1870s to 1935. The author found that the library developed slowly until 1905, when Carnegie gave $20,000 to the University for a new building. Another major watershed occurred in 1926 when a new University administration took office and began to provide increased support for the library. The author concludes with a comparison of the Fisk Library with those of seven other outstanding Negro schools.

540   Duncan, Ruth B. "A History of the George Peabody College Library, 1785-1910." Master's thesis, George Peabody College for Teachers, 1940. 95p.

The author presents a history of the George Peabody College Library from its beginnings in 1785 to 1910. Its major purpose is to describe, analyze, and evaluate the state of the library in the colleges (Davidson Academy, Cumberland College, Nashville University) that evolved into the George Peabody College.

TEXAS

541   Cochran, Mary A. "The University of Texas Package Loan Library, 1914-1954." Master's thesis, University of Texas, 1956. 206p.

Prior to 1914 the loan of packages of debate materials was part of the extension services of the University of Texas. In 1914 this service was taken over by a new package loan library, patterned after one at the University of Wisconsin. Besides supporting the University extension courses, the package loan library assumed the responsibility of providing information on current subjects to all of the citizens of Texas. The author describes the development of the package loan library and then surveys its current condition.

542   Couch, Cecil R., Jr. "The DeGolyer Foundation Library." Master's thesis, University of Texas, 1967. 42p.

Essentially concerned with a description of the DeGolyer Library located on the campus of Southern Methodist University in Dallas. The author outlines the history of the book-collecting activities of E. L. DeGolyer, a prominent businessman, geophysicist, and philanthropist, and the eventual donation of his library on Southwestern history and "geology" to Southern Methodist University in 1958.

543   Dyess, Stewart W. "A History and Analysis of Library Formula Funding in Texas Public Higher Education." Doctoral dissertation, Texas Tech University, 1977. 99p. UMI# 77-25,504.

Chronicles the inception and development of library funding in

Texas public higher education from 1960 to 1974. Expenditure patterns of 18 institutions are examined. Concludes that equitable funding, free of political manipulation, has not been realized. No organic defects in the concept were identified.

544 Lee, Joe B. "A History of the Library of Texas College of Arts and Industries, 1925-1955." Master's thesis, University of Texas, 1958. 148p.

This study examines the library of the Texas College of Arts and Industries, in Kingsville, Texas from 1925 to 1955. It emphasizes the development of the library's resources—financial, staff, collections, and physical plant. Little attention is paid to such aspects as government, reader services, and the use of the library. The author points out that his emphasis is on the latter part of the period 1925-1955 because of a lack of materials relating to earlier years.

545 Moloney, Louis C. "A History of the University Library at the University of Texas, 1883-1934." Doctoral dissertation, Columbia University, 1970. 404p. UMI# 71-17,525.

This study traces the history of the University of Texas Library from its establishment in 1883 until 1934. The author divides the study on the basis of the terms of the librarians who directed the library during the period: Benjamin Wyche (1897-1903); Phineas Lawrence Windsor (1903-1909); and Ernest William Winkler (1923-1934). Within each chapter the author interprets the historical record as it relates to such factors as financial support, personnel, collection development, services, physical plant, and library government.

546 Proctor, Mamie M. "Historical Survey of the Law School Library of Texas Southern University, Houston, Texas." Master's thesis, Catholic University of America, 1966. 105p.

Reviews the history of the Law School and its library at the Texas State University for Negroes, now Texas Southern University, from 1947-1960. Of special interest due to the influence of several court cases and the intrusion of political considerations into the issue.

547 Rogers, Alfred E. "Swante Palm: With Notes on the Library of a Nineteenth Century Texas Book Collector." Master's thesis, University of Texas, 1966. 80p.

Palm gathered the largest private library (10,000 volumes) in nineteenth century Texas. In 1897 he gave his library to the University of Texas and requested only that he be allowed to work with his books and assist in their use. The author describes the development of the collection and analyzes its contents and growth at the University of Texas.

548 Rouse, Roscoe, Jr. "A History of the Baylor University Library, 1845-1919." Doctoral dissertation, University of Michigan, 1962. 390p. UMI# 62-3257.

The author examines the development of the library from its inception to the retirement of librarian Willard P. Lewis in 1919, at which time the library was viewed as an established service institution in the University. The history of libraries within Baylor University literary and debating societies is provided. The librarians of the University, the first appointed in 1888, are considered in the light of their contributions to the university and their profession. The physical plant is covered with special emphasis on the events surrounding the gift of the F.L. Carroll Chapel and Library in 1901.

549 Sitter, Clara L. "The History and Development of the Rare Books Collections of the University of Texas Based on Recollections of Miss Fannie Ratchford." Master's thesis, University of Texas, 1966. 116p.

Traces the history and development of the rare books collections at the University of Texas based on the recollections of

Fannie Elizabeth Ratchford, who directed the rare books library for the first 40 years of its existence, 1917-1957.

VIRGINIA

550   Edsall, Margaret H. "History of the Library of the Protestant Episcopal Theological Seminary in Virginia, 1823-1955." Master's thesis, Catholic University of America, 1955. 66p.

The author begins this history with a brief survey of the seminary and then traces the evolution of the seminary's library from 1823 to 1955. This study emphasizes the positive role enlightened giving can play in building the book collection of a library with a very small book budget. By 1955 the collection had grown to 40,000 volumes—many of them gifts.

551   Hudson, Jeanne P. "A History of the Roanoke College Library, 1842-1959." Master's thesis, University of North Carolina, 1963. 80p.

The author presents the 117-year history of the library of Roanoke College and analyzes certain trends and influences. The paper is arranged chronologically under four major headings: 1) founding of the library; 2) the new building; 3) the library comes of age; and 4) continued growth. The author found that the college library suffered considerably from a lack of sound financial backing, but made extensive progress due to the continuous support of the college's presidents.

552   Jennings, John M. "The First Hundred Years of the Library of the College of William and Mary in Virginia, 1693-1793." Master's thesis, American University, 1948. Published: University Press of Virginia, 1968.

Presents a chronological history of the library of the College of William and Mary from the establishment of the school in 1693. The College itself is the second oldest in the United States, and its library had grown to sizeable proportions by 1793 when this study ends. Within the century covered the library nourished the minds of such famous Virginians as Thomas Jefferson and James Monroe.

553 Orr, Helen A. "The History of the Emory and Henry College Library, 1839-1954." Master's thesis, East Tennessee State College, 1954. 51p.

Established in 1836 by the Methodist Church, Emory and Henry College has remained a small liberal arts institution throughout its history. By the Civil War the library and literary societies boasted 12,000 volumes. Early librarians were members of the teaching faculty. A fire consumed the library in 1928. By 1954 the library held 32,000 volumes and occupied a modern facility.

WASHINGTON

554 Golicz, Lawrence J. "A History of Washington State University Libraries From 1946 to 1949." Master's thesis, Washington State University, 1968. 97p.

Describes the transformation of the library at Washington State University from the perspective of academic leaders and the librarian. Significant changes were made during the period 1946-1949 by president Wilson N. Compton and librarian G. Donald Smith. Departmental collections and budget authority were transferred to the central library. After much controversy, a new facility was obtained in 1947.

555 Gorchels, Clarence C. "A Land-Grant University Library: The History of the Library of the Washington State University, 1892-1946." Doctoral dissertation, Columbia University, 1971. 427p. UMI# 74- 8179.

Between 1892 and 1946 the Washington State University Library grew from modest beginnings to a collection of more than

500,000 volumes. This dramatic growth coincided with the directorship of William W. Foote, Jr., who served from 1915 to 1946. The library's successful acquisitions program resulted in space problems and make-shift cataloging methods. Also covered are services, cataloging, financial support, staffing, and administrative issues.

556 Potter, Jessica C. "The History of the University of Washington Library." Master's thesis, University of Washington, 1954. Published: Association of College & Research Libraries Microcard, Number 56.

Presents a history of the University of Washington Library from its small beginning in 1862, as part of the Territorial University, to 1950. The arrangement is chronological, except for two chapters dealing with coordination of the library system and cooperation with other libraries.

WEST VIRGINIA

557 Amos, Autumn. "A History of Robert F. Kidd Library." Master's thesis, Western Reserve University, 1953. 45p.

The author describes the development of the library at Glenville State College, Glenville, West Virginia from 1879 to 1952. Topics covered are: 1) the librarians, with emphasis on librarian Alma Janet Arbuckle; 2) the library buildings, with emphasis on the Kidd Library built in 1930; and 3) the book collection.

558 Harris, Virgie. "Library Development in Five Denominational Colleges in West Virginia." Master's thesis, Western Reserve University, 1952. 106p.

The five college libraries studied are those of Bethany College, Salem College, West Virginia Wesleyan College, Anderson-Broaddus College, and Davis and Elkins College. This study covers the period 1842-1952; emphasis, due to a lack of early records, is on the twentieth century. The author studies the relationship of the initial or early book collections to the role of the college, then compares the development of the libraries in terms of holdings, staff, budgets, and circulation. Several of the early collections were owned by literary societies and the author traces their transition from society library to college library.

559 Munn, Robert F. "West Virginia University Library, 1867-1917." Doctoral dissertation, University of Michigan, 1962. 260p. UMI# 62-2770.

Munn considers the development of this library in the context of the University's evolution. Like most university libraries it encountered considerable difficulties from the start. Housed in small and poorly suited quarters, run by a professor-librarian who devoted only a minimum of time to his library duties, and plagued by a shortage of funds, the library developed slowly until 1897. At that time Jerome H. Raymond, an ardent believer in good libraries, was named president of the University. He hired the University's first professional librarian, Eliza J. Skinner, and he was successful in increasing library appropriations and in obtaining a new building.

560 Powell, Ruth A. "A History of the Fairmont State College Library, 1867-1967." Master's thesis, Kent State University, 1967. 149p.

The author presents a history of the Fairmont State College Library in the context of the social, political, economic, and cultural conditions which influenced the college's development. She first presents a summary of the early development of the college and its library to 1928. The bulk of the paper is devoted to the library's history from 1928, the year when Vivian Boughter became the first professional librarian to serve at the college.

WISCONSIN

561 Hubbard, Corinne. "History of Wisconsin State College, Osh-

kosh, Library, September, 1871-August, 1943." Master's thesis, Drexel Institute of Technology, 1954. 69p.

The author begins with a brief survey of the Wisconsin State College in Oshkosh and then traces the history of the college's library from its inception in 1871 to 1943. The library grew quite rapidly, due mainly to a number of large gifts, but most of it was lost in a fire in 1916. By 1953 the collection had been rebuilt to nearly 50,000 volumes and was housed in a new building. The author divides her paper into four major sections: 1) housing of the library; 2) collection; 3) library science classes; and 4) the librarians.

562 Krueger, Hanna E. "History of the Carroll College Library." Master's thesis, University of Chicago, 1943. 164p.

This study begins with a history of Carroll College of Waukesha, Wisconsin from 1846 to 1942. The author then traces the history of the library, 1851-1942. The founders of Carroll College recognized the need for library facilities from the beginning; however, few funds were appropriated for collection building until after 1900. Not until 1911 was a full-time librarian appointed, and it was not until 1926 that the first professionally trained librarian was named. Appendix A includes a chronological table of important dates in the history of the college and of the library.

IV. SPECIAL LIBRARIES

A. Business and Industrial Libraries

563 Axelrod, Helene B. "The History, Development, and Organization of the New York Times Library and Contributions of the Times to Scholarship." Master's thesis, Southern Connecticut State College, 1965. 161p.

The author of this study has three basic objectives: 1) to present a history of the New York Times Library in the light of the company's information needs (1851-1965); 2) to identify those library services which assist the company in meeting its objectives; and 3) to assess the contributions the Times and its library have made to learning and scholarship through the production of bibliographic tools, the preservation of information, and exploration of new communication media.

564 Brown, James V. "History of the Industrial Relations Research Libraries." Master's thesis, Western Reserve University, 1958. 87p.

This paper presents short histories of the industrial relations libraries at the United States Department of Labor, Princeton, University of Michigan, Stanford, Massachusetts Institute of Technology, California Institute of Technology, Loyola, Harvard, St. Joseph's College, Yale, University of Denver, Cornell, University of Chicago, University of California, LeMoyne College, University of Minnesota, University of Illinois, University of Washington, San Jose State, Michigan State, University of Wisconsin, Rutgers, University of Hawaii, and State University of Iowa. A final chapter is a chronological outline of the activities of the Committee of University Industrial Relations Librarians.

565 Harris, Jeanette F. "The Newspaper Library: Its History, Function, and Value with Special Reference to the New York Herald Tribune." Master's thesis, Southern Connecticut State College, 1959. 46p.

The author devotes the first 20 pages of this paper to the history of the newspaper library of the *New York Herald*, which later merged with the *New York Tribune* to become the *New York Herald Tribune*. Emphasis is placed on the special problems encountered by the librarians of a large metropolitan newspaper.

566 Kruzas, Anthony T. "The Development of Special Libraries for American Business and Industry." Doctoral dissertation, University of Michigan, 1960. Published: Special Libraries Association, 1965.

Kruzas based his research on the analysis of data contained in ten special libraries directories published between 1910 and 1957. He lists five major organizational groups maintaining special libraries: 1) business and industrial companies; 2) nonprofit associations and institutions; 3) government agencies; 4) institutions of higher learning; and 5) large public library systems. By 1957 the largest number (47.6 percent) of special libraries were company libraries. The origins of the company libraries, their collections, significant librarians, and patterns of development, are surveyed.

567 Laubach, Harriet. "Library Service to Business, Labor and Industry: Its Development in Libraries at Princeton, Akron, and Pittsburgh." Master's thesis, Carnegie Institute of Technology, 1952. 117p.

This paper is primarily a consideration of current library procedures and services. The author presents a historical discussion of each library before analyzing its present status. The libraries covered are: 1) Industrial Relations Section, Princeton University; 2) Business and Labor Service, Akron Public Library; 3) University of Pittsburgh; and 4) Business Branch of the Carnegie Library of Pittsburgh.

B. Correctional Institution Libraries

568   Johnson, Ruth E. "Libraries in Correctional Institutions." Master's thesis, Western Reserve University, 1959. 123p.

Section II of this paper deals with the history of prison libraries in the United States. This history extends from 1802, when the Kentucky State Reformatory began library service, to the middle of the twentieth century. After a general introduction the author presents brief histories of the libraries at the following penal institutions: 1) U.S. Penitentiary at Atlanta; 2) Menard Division of the Illinois State Penitentiary; 3) Sing Sing Prison; and 4) San Quentin.

569   Petty, Wanda E. "The History of the Ohio Penitentiary Library." Master's thesis, Western Reserve University, 1949. 67p.

In 1839, the Reverend Charles Fitch saw the need for books for inmates of the Ohio Penitentiary and pushed for the establishment of a prison library. His work was carried on by the Rev. J.B. Finley, who canvassed prison contractors and others and ran ads in newspapers until he had increased the collection from 300 to several thousand volumes. By 1885 a school library and a Catholic library had been added to the main library, which with no official appropriations had grown to 10,000 volumes.

570   Reynolds, Ruth C. "The Role of Librarianship in Penal Institutions: A Historical Review and a Survey of Contemporary Training Programs." Master's thesis, California State University, San Jose, 1973. 100p.

This study recounts the history of library education, traces the development of standards for prison libraries, and surveys the field programs of library schools which focus on unserved populations. Examines the work of ALA's Committee on Institutions and notable early leaders Miriam E. Carey and E. Kathleen Jones. The American Prison Association prodded ALA to assume a more active role in prison library service beginning in the 1920s. In the final chapter, training offered by six library schools in the area of penal librarianship is described.

C. Medical, Dental, Hospital Libraries

571 Bernier, Beverly R. "A History of the Art Collection of the National Library of Medicine." Master's thesis, University of North Carolina, 1962. 43p.

This study examines the development, organization, and services of the art collection maintained by the National Library of Medicine. Beginning in the late nineteenth century, the art collection acquired prints, negatives, woodcuts, engravings, etchings, and lithographs. Stamps, maps, charts, anatomical illustrations and other media are also obtained and processed. All items are cataloged, and access to the collection is facilitated by reference and photoduplication services. By 1961 there were over 63,000 items in this important collection.

572 Bracken, Marilyn C. "An Analysis of the Evolution of the National Library of Medicine: Implications for the Development of Scientific and Technical Information Networks." Doctoral dissertation, American University, 1971. 312p. UMI# 71-25,285.

This study examines the evolutionary development of the National Library of Medicine from a traditional library to a comprehensive biomedical communications network. An information systems development model is used to analyze the evolution and impact of the medical network.

573 Cunning, Ellen T. "A History of Jefferson Medical College

Library, 1898-1973." Master's thesis, Drexel Institute of Technology, 1954. 36p.

This study begins with a brief history of the Medical College which was first established in 1825. In 1898 the Women's Auxiliary of the Jefferson Medical College of Philadelphia was formed and began work that led to the establishment of a reading room for the students of that college. In 1906 a new library building was built with part of a $1,250,000 gift by Samuel Parsons Scott. The author traces the development of the collection, services, and physical plant to 1953.

574 Donley, Virginia. "A Chronology of Medical Libraries in the United States with Some Bibliographic Notes Pertaining to Their Early History." Master's thesis, Western Reserve University, 1957. 83p.

This study is a chronological history of important medical libraries. Information given for each includes: 1) date of establishment; 2) any disputed dates; 3) latest available size of collection; 4) name of person or organization responsible for original establishment; and 5) bibliographic notes on sources of information.

575 Freund, Clare E. "The Library of the College of Physicians of Philadelphia." Master's thesis, Drexel Institute of Technology, 1951. 58p.

In 1863 the College of Physicians moved to its first real home and in 1864 acquired the 2,500-volume Lewis collection. By 1950 the collection had grown to some 170,000 volumes and the college and its library were now housed in a new building financed by a $100,000 grant from Andrew Carnegie. The library serves all the major branches of medicine except veterinary science and dentistry, which are covered by the University of Pennsylvania. The library of the College of Physicians has long considered it an obligation to provide a historical record of medicine and thus its collection is rich in the older classics.

576 McColl, Margaret C. "The Evans Dental Library, University of Pennsylvania: History and Service." Master's thesis, Drexel Institute of Technology, 1955. 38p.

Chapter I traces the development of dental history, literature, and libraries. Although the department of dentistry, University of Pennsylvania, was established in 1878, an alcove collection of dental literature in the main library did not materialize until 1900. A major bequest from Thomas V. Evans led to a separate facility for the dental school in 1915 and a major departmental library became a reality. Dean Edward C. Kirk donated his significant personal collection of 4,000 volumes. Between 1900 and 1954, the library grew from 5,000 volumes to 17,000 volumes.

577 Nonacs, Merija. "The Kornhauser Memorial Medical Library: Its History and Development." Master's thesis, University of Texas, 1966. 64p.

Traces the history of the Kornhauser Memorial Medical Library of the University of Louisville from its inception in 1837 to 1966. In part one, the author analyzes the library's holdings of 1847 based on the catalog issued that year and compares the Kornhauser Library's holdings and regulations with other medical libraries of the same period.

578 Opler, Pauline S. "The Origin and Trend of Bibliotherapy as a Device in American Mental Hospital Libraries." Master's thesis, San Jose State College, 1969. 78p.

Bibliotherapy, the use of books as therapy, is traced historically from the early 1900s to the 1960s. The literature is exhaustively reviewed and the trends identified. To ascertain the current status of bibliotherapy in the health community, a questionnaire was dispatched to 217 state mental hospitals. Although most hospitals confirmed the value of bibliotherapy, few had organized programs or librarians to administer such treatment.

579 Sevy, Barbara. "Temple University School of Medicine Library,

1910-1954." Master's thesis, Drexel Institute of Technology, 1955. 61p.

This study is divided into five sections: 1) a history of the Temple College Library from 1892-1900; 2) a history of the Medical School and the Medical Library, 1921-1929; 3) the library of the professional schools (Dentistry, Medicine, and Pharmacy), 1921-1929; 4) the Samaritan Hospital Library, 1929-1930; and 5) the School of Medicine Library, 1930-1954.

580 Thomas, Elizabeth H. "A History of the National Institute of Health Library, 1901-1954." Master's thesis, Catholic University of America, 1956. 72p.

The National Institute of Health (NIH) Library serves a rapidly expanding organization devoted to scientific research in the public health arena. Five chapters, chronologically delimited by the terms of library directors, describe the steady growth of this special library. The decentralized nature of laboratory work plagued the library for years. More than 40 years elapsed before a professional librarian was engaged. Scott Adams, appointed director in 1950, initiated substantial improvement in the areas of collection development and bibliographic control. By 1950 the library held 67,000 volumes and operated with a staff of 15 to serve the NIH staff of 2,373.

581 Weakley, Margaret E. "The Origin and History of the Medical Library of the University of Virginia School of Medicine, 1825-1962." Master's thesis, University of North Carolina, 1966. 117p.

The author traces the origins of the University of Virginia School of Medicine Library to 1825, when Thomas Jefferson included a number of medical titles in a list of books he recommended for the University library. The first medical library was organized in 1911, and in 1929 the library was moved into a new building. The author traces the library's 140-year history and points out the problems arising from a lack of state financial support.

D. Museum and Historical Society Libraries

582 Beattie, Sister P.M. "Growth and Development of the Library Collection at the Marine Historical Association, Incorporated, Mystic, Connecticut." Master's thesis, Southern Connecticut State College, 1968. 101p.

The Marine Historical Association was founded in 1929 to preserve America's maritime past for future generations. A model library was formed in the first year to house books, charts, logbooks, commerce records, diaries, and letters. Growth was slow until the 1940s when collection development was accelerated. By 1965 the Library held 20,000 books and 135,000 manuscripts. Formal dedication ceremonies for a separate facility, renamed the G.W. Blunt White Library, took place in 1965.

583 Brennan, Paula M. "A History of the Library of the Rhode Island Historical Society of Providence, R.I." Master's thesis, Catholic University of America, 1959. 128p.

The Rhode Island Historical Society was established in 1822 to procure and preserve materials relating to the state's history. The Society's progress is treated in the first chapter and the library's role is chronicled in the second. Despite periods of inattention, the library has become the premier repository of imprints and manuscripts for the study of Rhode Island history. The collections of early imprints and newspapers are especially noteworthy. Librarians who contributed significantly to the Society's programs and scholarship included Amos Perry (1880-1899), Clarence S. Brigham (1899-1908), and Howard M. Chapin (1918-1940).

584 Duniway, David C. "The Administration of Six Selected State Historical Society Libraries: A Historical Study." Master's thesis, University of California, 1939. 80p.

The author traces the development of the libraries of the following historical societies: Massachusetts Historical Society, New

York Historical Society, Pennsylvania Historical Society, Wisconsin Historical Society, Minnesota Historical Society, and the Society of California Pioneers. Major emphasis is on administration, with some consideration of the development of collections.

585   Heskin, Mary K. "The Philadelphia Commercial Museum Library, 1896-1952." Master's thesis, Drexel Institute of Technology, 1952. 40p.

The author traces the evolution of the library from a small reference department for the Bureau of Foreign Trade to its position in 1952 as an internationally known free library. The library was handicapped from the beginning by a lack of funds, but still managed to acquire one of the world's best collections relating to trade and commerce. By 1952 the collection numbered some 65,000 volumes.

586   Libby, David C. "The Library of the Chicago Historical Society: A Study." Master's thesis, University of Chicago, 1948. 136p.

The urge to preserve and perpetuate the American tradition in the early nineteenth century has been one of the major causal factors in the development of the American public library. Libby traces the development of the Chicago Historical Society's library from its establishment in 1856 to the 1940s. He points out that the library was a public one, open to all qualified users, and that the Society's collections formed a major part of the Chicago library scene.

587   Pressing, Kirk L. "The Library of the Historical Society of Delaware." Master's thesis, Drexel Institute of Technology, 1954. 51p.

Presents the history of the development of the Historical Society of Delaware and its library from 1864 to 1953. It is divided into three sections: 1) history of the Society; 2) history of the library; and 3) development of publication activities of the Society, now under the library's jurisdiction.

588 Putnam, Lee A. "The Library of the Field Museum of Natural History." Master's thesis, University of Chicago, 1971. 150p.

The first chapter of this work traces the history of the Field Museum in Chicago and the second examines the development of its excellent library.

589 Reed, Lawrence L. "The Development of the Manuscript Collections at the State Historical Society of Wisconsin Through 1969." Doctoral dissertation, University of Wisconsin, 1983. 312p. UMI# 8315022.

This study focuses on the strategy of collection development—the decision to collect, the subject area, and the factors which influenced the collecting. Uses a chronological approach to review the growth of the State Historical Society of Wisconsin, and to examine the origins and results of six major collecting projects. Concludes that the Society had a major role in past projects and that major influences were exerted by the availability of grant monies, the interrelatedness of manuscript materials, and the initiation of graduate students.

590 Schnitzler, Nelle L. "The Mennonite Historical Society and the Reconstruction of Mennonite History Library and Publishing Program at Goshen, Indiana." Master's thesis, University of Chicago, 1969. 126p.

This study traces the Mennonite Historical Society's efforts to reconstruct Mennonite history through the collection of a library and the promotion of a publishing program. Goshen College and the contributions of Harold S. Bender, Dean of Goshen College, figure prominently in the development of the historical library and publishing program. By 1968, the library held 21,000 books and periodicals. Many unique items are held by the library.

591 Sims, Elizabeth E. "The Allen Memorial Art Museum Library, Oberlin, Ohio: A Study." Master's thesis, Western Reserve University, 1952. 73p.

This study traces the development of the collection from 1917. At that time the collection, which was quite small, was transferred to the Allen Art Museum. By 1952 the collection had grown to over 15,000 volumes and had been recognized as outstanding by leading authorities. The author devoted part of this paper to the library's history, while another part is devoted to a survey of current conditions in the library.

592 Smit, Pamela R. "The New-York Historical Society Library: A History, 1804-1978." Doctoral dissertation, Columbia University, 1979. 236p. UMI# 7916448. Published: Shoe String Press, 1984.

At the time of its founding in 1804 the New-York Historical Society was only one of two organizations in the nation primarily concerned with collecting the records of American history. After the Civil War the library entered a period of decline due to financial difficulty, inadequate quarters, and excessive concentration on genealogy. Beginning in 1921 under the librarianship of Alexander Wall, the library modernized its procedures and achieved financial stability. R.W.G. Vail, director from 1944 to 1959, solidified the gains of his predecessor. Despite its rich collection, the library has not found a comfortable balance between the roles of special resource and popular library.

593 Waldron, Rodney K. "A History of the Library of the State Historical Society of Colorado, 1879-1940." Master's thesis, University of Denver, 1950. 167p.

Chronologically traces the main steps in the evolution of the library of the State Historical Society of Colorado, and analyzes the contributions of a few highly influential people—especially Will C. Ferrill, long-time curator of the collection. The author concerns himself mainly with the library's collections and personnel. He finds that the library's growth was slow and very uneven, and that so little interest was evinced by the public and the library's early administration that the library almost ceased to exist. A consistent shortage of funds and numerous factional disputes further hampered the library's growth.

594 Walker, Muriel H. "The Library of the Western Reserve Historical Society." Master's thesis, Kent State University, 1952. 121p.

The first half of this paper deals with the history of the library of the Western Reserve Historical Society from its inception in 1867 to 1950. The author analyzes the reasons for the library's rapid growth, its efforts to secure adequate quarters, the historical evolution of its special collections, and presents short biographical sketches of significant contributors.

595 Wells, Inez S. "A History of the D.A.R. Genealogical Library: Its Objectives, Policies, and Services as a Library of Americana." Master's thesis, Catholic University of America, 1958. 107p.

The Genealogical Library of the National Society of the Daughters of the American Revolution serves as the reference library of this patriotic association which was chartered in 1896. Collections encompass genealogy, biography, heraldry, and local history. Special microfilming projects have been undertaken. By 1957 the library held 45,000 volumes. A roster of librarians, collection statistics, floor plans, and photographs are incorporated.

596 Wolf, Naomi E. "The Library of the Genealogical Society of Pennsylvania, 1892-1952." Master's thesis, Drexel Institute of Technology, 1953.

Traces the history of the Genealogical Society of Pennsylvania, and then describes the history of the library, 1892-1952. One chapter is devoted to the influence of three members of the Leech family on the development of the library.

E. Governmental Libraries and Programs

597 Bartis, Peter T. "A History of the Archive of Folk Song at the Library of Congress: The First Fifty Years." Doctoral dissertation, University of Pennsylvania, 1982. 342p. UMI# 8217081.

Traces the impact of the Library of Congress' Archive of Folk Song (1928-1978) on the fields of folklore, folklife, and ethnomusicological studies. Utilizes correspondence, reports and requisitions to examine collection development and special projects, notably the coordinate role which the Archive served for the Works Progress Administration. Later developments such as preservation are also addressed.

598 Breisacher, Renata. "A History and Survey of the Library of the National Bureau of Standards." Master's thesis, Catholic University of America, 1953. 51p.

The first 20 pages trace the history of the National Bureau of Standards Library from its beginning in 1900 to 1953. The library was organized in answer to the Bureau's needs for a collection to support its research. By 1903 it contained some 1,000 volumes and by 1910 it reached nearly 6,000 volumes. The author describes the development of the library's organization, function, financial support, and physical plant.

599 Brinkley, Clara. "Army Post Library Service: An Inquiry Into Its Origin and Development, Present Organization, and Future." Master's thesis, University of Washington, 1952. 67p.

The first half of this paper deals with the development of the Army Post Library Service from the Civil War, when the first organized efforts were made, to the end of the Second World War. At times the Army Post Library System has stood as the largest public library system in the world. During World War I over 6,000,000 books were brought together for distribution to American soldiers. At the same time some 36 post libraries were constructed with funds from a Carnegie grant. The Army Library Service has traditionally been curtailed during peace time and plunged into feverish activity at time of war.

600 Dutch, Theresa C. "The History and Present Status of the Library of the United States Department of Justice." Master's thesis, Catholic University of America, 1960. 76p.

Established as the Office of the Attorney General in 1789, the Department of Justice did not receive cabinet status until 1870. Regular appropriations for the library began in 1831 and a printed catalog was published in 1863. The first librarian, Henry A. Klopper (1865-1882), labored to produce the second printed catalog and James A. Finch (1891-1894, 1895-1907) prepared a catalog of foreign titles in the Department. Under Mathew A. McKavitt (1937- 1954) the collection of 80,000 volumes was reclassified and technical operations consolidated. Under the progressive administration of Harry Bitner (1954-1957), reader services and management procedures improved significantly.

601 El-Erian, Tahany S. "The Public Law 480 Program in American Libraries." Doctoral dissertation, Columbia University, 1972. 289p. UMI# 372-31,205.

This study provides an overview of the PL 480 program, the only national cooperative acquisition program, which acquires mostly non-western language materials. By 1964, 46 libraries participated in the program. Participating libraries funded a centralized cataloging project until it was merged into the National Program for Cataloging and Acquisitions (NPAC) in 1968. By the end of 1969, the Library of Congress had cataloged 77 percent of the PL 480 monographs. Most participants, however, cataloged less than 25 percent of materials received.

602 Elson, Beverly L. "The Library of Congress: A Merger of American Functionalism and Cosmopolitan Eclecticism." Doctoral dissertation, University of Maryland, 1981. 448p. UMI# 8213807.

The architecture of the Library of Congress is evaluated from the perspectives of functionalism and eclecticism. The nineteenth-century Beaux-Arts structure housing the Library of Congress combines utility within its Renaissance-Baroque style. It is viewed as a monument to America's pre-eminence, particularly in the arts and sciences. A union of aesthetic sense and utility was achieved by the architect.

603 Gecas, Judith G. "The Depository Act of 1962: A Legislative History and Survey of Implementation." Master's thesis, University of Chicago, 1975. 58p.

Early depository legislation and the Depository Act of 1962 are reviewed in terms of legislative history, implementation, and strengths and weaknesses.

604 Goldman, Sylvia. "History of the United States Weather Bureau Library." Master's thesis, Catholic University of America, 1959. 95p.

In 85 years the Weather Bureau Library grew from a small reference collection in the study room of the Chief Signal Offices of the War Department in Washington to a large collection of over 100,000 volumes, maps, photographs, motion pictures and slides. This thesis describes that development from 1870 to 1960. It is divided into three major sections: 1) the history of the Weather Bureau; 2) history of the Weather Bureau Library; and 3) present-day functions of the library at its new location in Suitland, Maryland.

605 Hench, Marcia. "The Library of the Supreme Court of the United States." Master's thesis, Drexel Institute of Technology, 1951. 43p.

This study begins with a brief history of the Court, stressing only the important points from its establishment in 1789. The period from 1789 to 1801 is not covered since during this time the Court used the library facilities of Philadelphia and New York, and no individual court library was established. Until 1807 the Clerk of the Court acted as librarian, but in that year the first librarian, Henry D. Clarke, was appointed. The author emphasizes the history of the library from 1887 to 1932.

606 Horgan, Mary. "Survey of Library Facilities in the Department of the Interior." Master's thesis, Catholic University of America, 1953. 69p.

This study traces the growth of libraries within the Department of the Interior from its establishment in 1849 to the consolidation of its collections in 1949. Among the specialized libraries maintained by the Department are those for the Geological Survey, Law, Fish and Wildlife, Bureau of Mines, National Park Service, and Bureau of Indian Affairs. When the dispersed collections were finally centralized, the library contained 415,000 volumes.

607 Hu, Shu C. "The Development of the Chinese Collection in the Library of Congress." Doctoral dissertation, Florida State University, 1977. 350p. UMI# 77-24,768. Published: Westview, 1979.

From its beginning in 1869 to 1912, the Chinese Collection in the Library of Congress was primarily developed through gifts and exchanges. Between 1913 and 1949 a planned program of acquisitions secured three-fifths of the present 411,963 volumes, particularly in the areas of gazetteers, reprints, and rare books. Two persons guided acquisitions during these productive years: Walter T. Swingle (1913-1927) and Arthur W. Hummel (1928-1949). After World War II, collection development shifted from classical literature to current materials and publications were unavailable from the Peoples' Republic of China.

608 Hudon, Edward G. "The Library Facilities of the Supreme Court of the United States: A Historical Study." Master's thesis, Catholic University of America, 1956. Published: Association of College & Research Libraries Microcard, Number 84. Summary published: *Law Library Journal* 59 (1966): 166-76.

This study traces the evolution of the library of the Supreme Court from 1790 to 1955. For several years after 1790 there was no library for the Supreme Court, and it was not until Marshall became Chief Justice that the library made its feeble start. Since then its growth has been slow but steady, culminating in some 180,000 volumes in two libraries.

609 Jackson, Cynthia. "The Library of Congress' National Program

for Acquisitions and Cataloging: Its Historical Perspective." Master's thesis, University of Chicago, 1972. 128p.

Following a review of early cooperative ventures, the conceptualization and establishment of the National Program for Acquisitions and Cataloging (NPAC, 1965) are addressed. Funding, programs, and effectiveness of NPAC are emphasized.

610 Miller, Sarah J. "The Depository Library System: A History of the Distribution of Federal Government Publications to Libraries of the United States from the Early Years of the Nation to 1895." Doctoral dissertation, Columbia University, 1980. 728p. UMI# 8023529.

Laws governing the distribution of government publications date from an 1813 enactment which authorized sending selected Congressional publications to specified types of institutions. Between 1857 and 1859 a series of laws provided for the designation of depositories based upon Congressional districts and broadened the distribution to libraries. Library leaders supported reforms which culminated in the 1895 Printing Act. Prominent among these reformers were Melvil Dewey, Samuel Swett Green, and Richard R. Bowker.

611 North, Norma. "O.A.E.S.L.; A History of the Library of the Ohio Agricultural Experiment Station at Wooster, Ohio." Master's thesis, Western Reserve University, 1953. 60p.

First established in 1882, this library developed very slowly and did not merit a librarian until 1911. William K. Greenbank was the first official librarian, and the author describes his administration (1911-1922) in detail. The period from 1923 to 1947 saw a succession of four librarians, who were unable to stop a deterioration of the library over the 20-year period. The author explains that this condition was probably due to the fact that the station was not associated with a college or university as were many of the better station libraries.

612 Pandiri, Ananda M. "A Study of the History, Growth, and Development of the Public Law 480 Program and Its Impact on American Academic Libraries with Special Reference to Yale University Library." Master's thesis, Southern Connecticut State College, 1976. 179p.

The Public Law 480 program which became operational in 1962 was a cooperative acquisition program which brought thousands of volumes from Africa, Asia, and the Middle East to more than 40 U.S. research libraries. This study traces the origins, development, and impact of the PL480 program with special emphasis on acquisitions from India. Cataloging, accession lists, and an evaluation of materials are discussed. The final section is devoted to an analysis of Yale University and the impact of PL480 on its teaching and research programs.

613 Scott, Catherine D. "The History and Present Status of the Library of the United States Tariff Commission." Master's thesis, Catholic University of America, 1955. Published: Association of College & Research Libraries Microcard, Number 53.

Traces the history of the Tariff Commission Library from its inception in 1917 to 1955. Originally for the use of the Commission's experts, the Tariff Library has tended to serve an ever-widening clientele. Since 1921 it has done extensive interlibrary loan work and now serves the public as well as government employees. The author finds that the Tariff Library was amply supported from its inception and that its growth has been steady.

614 Smith, Patricia C. "The Tennessee Valley Authority and Its Influence in the Development of Regional Libraries in the South." Master's thesis, University of North Carolina, 1954. 103p.

The Tennessee Valley Authority (TVA) was created by the federal government in 1933 to control floods, to produce electrical power, to develop natural resources, and to promote the economic welfare of the region. Various experimental social programs, including library service, were initiated through local institutions. Regional libraries were established in Alabama,

North Carolina, and Tennessee. Under the guidance of Mary U. Rothrock, director of TVA's library program, these regional libraries emphasized extension services and cooperative arrangements.

615 Stewart, Richard A. "The Development of National Library Functions in the British Museum and the Library of Congress." Master's thesis, University of Chicago, 1978. 144p.

Not examined.

616 Stillman, Mary E. "The United States Air Force Library Service: Its History, Organization, and Administration." Doctoral dissertation, University of Illinois, 1966. 292p. UMI# 67-6743.

The author analyzes the origins, development, purpose, administration, and history of the United States Air Force Library Service, one of the largest and most complex library systems in the world. The libraries contained some six million volumes and employed some 1,700 people in 1966. The author found that the earliest Air Force libraries began in 1918, but major developments came after World War II when the Army Air Force took control of all libraries on air bases.

617 Willis, Dawn E. "The History and Present Status of the Library of the United States Geological Survey." Master's thesis, Catholic University of America, 1953. 62p.

Traces the history of the Geological Survey Library from 1882 when it was established to 1953. By 1953 the library had grown from a small collection of 1,000 volumes to one of the world's best geological libraries, containing over 250,000 volumes and 100,000 maps. Special emphasis is placed on the development of staff, collections, and quarters. A short history of the U.S. Geological Survey is included.

F. Other Special Libraries

618 Bromiley, Francis. "The History and Organization of the Franklin D. Roosevelt Library, Hyde Park, New York." Master's thesis, Western Reserve University, 1959. Published: Association of College & Research Libraries Microcard, Number 117.

Chronicles development of the Roosevelt Library from 1939, when the bill to accept the library for maintenance by the U.S. Government was defeated in the House of Representatives by a vote of 139 to 229, to 1959. Emphasizes services, collections, and physical plant.

619 Brown, Ruth E. "History of Special Libraries in Denver, Colorado, 1861-1953." Master's thesis, University of Chicago, 1955. 225p.

Traces the development of special libraries in Denver from their rather slow beginning with only nine established by 1900, to 1953 when the city had 62 full-fledged special libraries. The author covers almost every phase of library service in Denver, including public library service under the leadership of such librarians as John Cotton Dana and Chalmers Hadley. Treats college and university libraries (i.e., departmental). Appendix I is a chronological list of special libraries established in Denver, 1861-1953.

620 Buckley, Amelia K. "The Keeneland Association Library." Master's thesis, University of Kentucky, 1957. 183p.

The Keeneland Association (Kentucky) was formed as a non-profit corporation in 1935 to promote the sport of horse racing through programs of research and education. The nucleus for a turf library was made possible through a gift of 2,000 volumes from William A. Hanger in 1939. A major collection of 15,000 photographic negatives was acquired in 1954. The fixed location subject arrangement and the various catalogs are described. Over 900 volumes in the collection are listed in extensive bibliographic detail.

Special Libraries

621 Cowles, Lois H. "The First Century of the Library of the New Britain Institute." Master's thesis, Western Reserve University, 1951. 92p.

After first surveying the history of libraries in New Britain, Connecticut, to 1850, the author reviews the history of the New Britain Institute Library from 1853 to 1953. The author treats the development of the Institute's library in detail, outlining its difficulties and achievements. In 1901 a new building was erected, at which time the city agreed to finance the library with $4,000 annually. The period 1901-1921 saw the collection grow rapidly; however, the rate of growth decreased with the advent of the depression and another war. Nevertheless, in 1950 the collection numbered over 90,000 volumes.

622 Dale, Doris C. "The Origin and Development of the United Nations Library." Doctoral dissertation, Columbia University, 1968. UMI# 72-01293. Published: American Library Association, 1970.

Emphasis is placed on the history of the United Nations Library from its establishment in 1945 to the dedication of the Hammarskjold Library building in 1961. A first chapter deals with the library's historical development, while others deal with administrative organization, physical plant, and policy making and implementation.

623 Gladeck, Alberta A. "The Library of the Franklin Institute." Master's thesis, Drexel Institute of Technology, 1953. Published: Association of College & Research Libraries Microcard, Number 37.

Traces the history of the library of the Franklin Institute (founded 1820) from a small collection kept in the homes of the library committee to a scientific library of over 200,000 volumes housed in a wing of the Franklin Institute in Philadelphia. The *Journal of the Franklin Institute* and the library's cataloging and classification system are given special attention.

624 Holloway, Donald P. "A History of the Akron Law Library Association, with Special Attention to Pertinent Legislation." Master's thesis, Kent State University, 1962. 62p.

The Akron Law Library Association, which is the county law library, was established in 1888. Its history is chronicled from trustee minutes. A professional librarian was appointed in 1948 and the collection reached 40,000 volumes in 1960.

625 Kahn, Rose A. "A History of the Peabody Institute Library, Baltimore, Maryland 1857-1916." Master's thesis, Catholic University of America, 1953. Published: Association of College & Research Libraries Microcard, Number 16.

After a brief survey of library development in Baltimore prior to the Civil War and a short account of the life of George Peabody, the author traces the history of the Peabody Institute Library from its inception in 1857 to 1916. The author finds that throughout the library's history the public had been critical of its services. She points out that Peabody planned the library as a reference collection and never intended that it be a popular library, and that the administration of the Peabody Institute Library complied with his wishes.

626 Leasure, Marilyn F. "A History of the Libraries of the Baltimore and Ohio Railroad Company." Master's thesis, Drexel Institute of Technology, 1954. 31p.

This paper is divided into five parts: 1) a brief history of the Baltimore and Ohio Railroad; 2) the history of the railroad's early circulating library (1885-1931); 3) the early development of the research library now called the Employee's Library (1944-1951); 4) the library 1951-1954; and 5) conclusion. The author found that the library established in 1885 was dependent upon the well-being of the B&O Railroad. In the depression of 1931 the library was closed. In 1944 a central library was opened to provide services to anyone desiring information on the B&O.

627　Mallison, David W. "Henry Lewis Bullen and the Typographic Library and Museum of the American Type Founders Company." Doctoral dissertation, Columbia University, 1976. 329p. UMI# 76-18,474.

Founded in 1892 and located in New Jersey, the American Type Founders Company (ATFC) became the world's largest producer of foundry type. The ATFC Library and Museum was developed and nurtured by librarian Henry Lewis Bullen from 1908 to 1936. Special strengths include type specimen books, history of printing, Frankliniana, and incunabula. Columbia University acquired the 17,000 volume collection in 1936 and subsequently disbursed the holdings to several divisions.

628　Mount, Ellis. "History of the Engineering Societies Library, 1913-1973." Doctoral dissertation, Columbia University, 1979. 393p. UMI# 7924947. Published: Shoe String Press, 1982.

This dissertation covers the origin and growth of the Engineering Societies Library, located in New York City. Collections, services, and cataloging are fully described. The terms of three library directors—Harrison W. Craver, Ralph H. Phelps, and S.K. Cabeen—are examined in detail. The relationship between the Library and the *Engineering Index* is explored.

629　Mullins, James L. "A Study of Selected Factors Affecting Growth Rates in American Law School Libraries, 1932-1976." Doctoral dissertation, Indiana University, 1984. 100p. UMI# 8425079.

Data from 75 law libraries were compiled to determine if a correlation existed between the growth rates of law libraries administered within university library systems (integrated) and law libraries which are aligned with law schools (autonomous). Other factors analyzed were source of funding, influence of the library director, facilities, and status as a depository for government publications. The main hypothesis was not confirmed. The influence of the law dean, law librarian, and university librarian produced a positive correlation with the rate of growth.

630 Paul, Gary N. "The Development of the Hoover Institution on War, Revolution and Peace Library, 1919-1944." Doctoral dissertation, University of California, Berkeley, 1974. 274p. UMI# 74-19,597.

The Hoover Library was founded by Professor E.D. Adams of Stanford University and Herbert Hoover, former president of the United States. Funding for the building, completed in 1941, and much of the collection came from the various relief agencies directed by Hoover. Collection activities emphasized the acquisition of archival-based holdings. For many years the rate of acquisitions exceeded the staff's capacity to process it. The separate nature of the library caused some tensions with Stanford's academic community.

631 Smail, H. Arlene. "A History of the Eleanor Squire Memorial Library of the Garden Center of Greater Cleveland." Master's thesis, Western Reserve University, 1955. 63p.

This history of a unique special library spans a period of 25 years, 1930-1955. It originally served only as a reference and research collection, but in 1957 a small lending collection was established. Librarian Marjorie B. Clelland guided the collection from 1938 to 1940 and prepared a *Classification Scheme for a Garden Center Library of Books*, which was published in 1940. The collection today numbers 7,000 volumes, many of them rare, and serves a valuable research function in Cleveland.

632 Strable, Edward G. "The Origin, Development, and Present Status of Advertising Agency Libraries in the United States." Master's thesis, University of Chicago, 1954. 156p.

Advertising agency libraries constitute a type of special library which have received little scholarly attention. The introductory chapter traces the history of advertising agency libraries. The remainder of the text is a survey of the collections, procedures, and staffing of 31 large advertising libraries.

633 Thomas, Evelyn F. "The Origin and Development of the Society of the Four Arts Library, Palm Beach, Florida." Master's thesis, Florida State University, 1958. 55p.

This study traces the evolution of the library of the Society of the Four Arts from its beginnings in 1940 to 1957. The paper is divided into three parts: 1) a description of the character of Palm Beach; 2) a history of the library's development; and 3) an analysis of the library's status in 1957. In 1940 the library was little more than a collection of books, but by 1957 it had grown to a good size, with a children's room, listening rooms, and other physical improvements. The collection has always stressed the fine and decorative arts, but has developed other areas as well.

634 Varner, Sister C. "The Development of Special Libraries in St. Paul and Minneapolis, Minnesota, 1849-1949." Master's thesis, University of Chicago, 1950. 152p.

This study is a history of all types of library service in St. Paul-Minneapolis for the period covered. University, college, and public library development are treated, as well as special libraries. However, the emphasis is on special library development in St. Paul-Minneapolis in the twentieth century. A chronological list of special libraries, 1849-1949, is included.

V. SCHOOL LIBRARIES

A. General Studies

635 Alvey, Richard G. "The Historical Development of Organized Story-Telling to Children in the United States." Doctoral dissertation, University of Pennsylvania, 1974. 908p. UMI# 75-2695.

The author defines storytelling as the application of "folklore art to modern situations." Storytelling is analyzed from the historical perspective as it has been employed by librarians, educators, religious leaders, and recreation specialists. Various models for implementing storytelling activities are examined. The art of storytelling has often been infused with the organizational goals of sponsoring groups. To be successful, storytelling must be performed in an artistic manner free from manipulation.

636 Barr, Janet C. "The Immigrant in Children's Fictional Books Recommended for American Libraries, 1883-1939." Doctoral dissertation, Indiana University, 1976. 185p. UMI# 76-21,525.

Between 1883 and 1939 the great wave of immigration accelerated the development of library services for children and the production of fiction reading lists. A content analysis of recommended fiction titles was performed to determine the nature and extent of immigrant portrayal. Only 30 books were found which met the criteria. There was an inverse relationship between the level of immigration and the number of books. Characters of Anglo-Saxon and Nordic descent exceeded the immigrant flow from these areas. Overall, immigrant characters were depicted in a positive manner.

637 Branyan, Brenda M. "Outstanding Women Who Promoted the Concept of the Unified School Library and Audiovisual Programs, 1950 Through 1975." Doctoral dissertation, Southern Illinois University, 1978. 380p. UMI# 7813533.

This study identified women in the school library or audiovisual fields who advocated the merger of print and audiovisual materials and their associated services into what became known as the school media center. Thirty-five women were surveyed. Key conclusions based upon responses from the leaders were: 1) major contributions have been in the areas of organization of media centers; 2) promoting individualized instruction was a priority; 3) lack of funds was the major administrative obstacle; and 4) future planning will require improvements in higher education programs.

638 Campbell, Rosemae W. "The Development of Public School Librarianship in the United States." Master's thesis, Colorado College, 1953. 67p.

The first school libraries grew out of small classroom libraries, many of them on loan from public libraries. It was not until 1896, when Melvil Dewey pushed for a library department within the N.E.A., that much progress was made. The first professional school librarian was appointed in 1900, and after 1923 school libraries gained a firm footing in America. The author traces the development of quarters, standards, and training of such men as Melvil Dewey, C.C. Certain, and C.C. Williamson.

639 Hammitt, Frances E. "School Library Legislation in Indiana, Illinois, and Wisconsin: A Historical Study." Doctoral dissertation, University of Chicago, 1948. 266p.

Begins by tracing the development of school libraries, especially in the Mid-West, and then devotes three chapters to a discussion of school library legislation in each state to 1940. The final chapter is a synthesis of the data. The author finds many similarities in the approach to school library legislation taken by the three states; however, Wisconsin got a somewhat slower start than did the other two. An appendix includes a chronological list of library laws for the three states to 1940.

640 Herrin, Barbara R. "A History and Analysis of the William Allen White Children's Book Award." Doctoral dissertation, Kansas State University, 1979. 417p. UMI# 8003691.

Established in 1952, the William Allen White Book Award honors a small-town Kansas newspaper editor who attained national prominence. Kansas students in grades four through eight select their favorite book from a master list of several dozen titles. The winning author receives a medallion and meets with children's parents, educators, and librarians. Success of the award is attributed to its simplicity and the involvement of educators across the state. Emporia State University is the award's sponsor.

641 Hill, Myles E. "The Philosophical Aspects of the Newbery Medal Award Books, 1922-1971." Doctoral dissertation, Arizona State University, 1974. 560p. UMI# 74-9886.

The philosophical aspects of the Newbery Medal Award books are uncovered through a content analysis of the books. Among the philosophical dimensions applied by the author were depictions of reality as metaphysical, nature and source of truth, value patterns, and gratification versus deferred satisfaction. The books reflected traditional American values and the WASP ethos.

642 Lanier, Gene D. "The Transformation of School Libraries Into Instructional Materials Centers." Doctoral dissertation, University of North Carolina, 1968. 271p. UMI# 69-10,179.

The author traces the transformation of the school library in the United States over the last several decades into an instructional materials center. He analyzes the battle to modernize school libraries; that is, to make them units which work with all instructional media rather than just the print media.

643 Lemley, Dawson E. "The Development and Evaluation of Administrative Policies and Practices in Public School Library Service as Evidenced in City School Surveys, 1907-1947." Doctoral dissertation, University of Pittsburgh, 1949.

The author studies some 134 city school surveys and the published literature in order to find trends in the administration of school library service in the United States from 1907-1941.

644 Lord, Julia W. "The Cosmic World of Childhood: The Ideology of the Children's Librarians, 1900-1965." Doctoral dissertation, Emory University, 1968. 270p. UMI# 69-5237.

Examines the belief system of children's librarians and the instrumental use of ideas by the profession to assert control and authority over the reading of children. The author contends that librarians embrace the cosmic world of childhood—the egocentric sphere—to impose an ideal order on the world by appealing to the child's nature. This commitment to moral society resulted in standards and selection practices which encouraged the literature fantasy and rebuffed literary themes which might stimulate feelings of guilt, hate, passion, and intimate love. Children's librarians have directed the reading interests of children by manipulating the types of materials available in libraries and influencing publishing decisions.

645 McClenahan, Stella. "Growth of School Libraries in America." Master's thesis, Colorado State Teachers College, 1932. 235p.

Opening with a history of libraries from prehistoric times to the twentieth century, the author then devotes two major chapters to the origin, purpose, and progress of school libraries in America. Special attention is devoted to organization, standardization, architecture, collections, instruction, and student use. Concludes that school libraries, once considered an extravagance, are now viewed as a valuable educational investment.

646 Rufsvold, Margaret I. "Library Service to Schools in the South

Since 1900." Master's thesis, George Peabody College for Teachers, 1933. Published: Peabody Contributions to Librarianship Number 1, 1934.

Traces the history of school libraries in the South from 1900 to 1933. The author finds that school library development was slow and haphazard to 1925, but that remarkable growth was effected from 1925 to 1933. Two factors were central to this growth: 1) the adoption of revised high school library standards in 1929; and 2) the interest of the Julius Rosenwald Fund in school and county library development. Despite rapid growth, the school libraries of the South were still only in the beginning stages of development in 1933.

647 Smith, Mabel. "Development of the Elementary School Library." Master's thesis, University of Mississippi, 1967. 34p.

Contains a brief survey of school library service in this country.

648 Thomas, Fannette H. "The Genesis of Children's Services in the American Public Library: 1875-1906." Doctoral dissertation, University of Wisconsin, 1982. 376p. UMI# 8301891.

The evolution of children's work in the American public library is studied within the framework of five components: 1) emergence of the separate juvenile book collection; 2) appearance of the separate children's room; 3) designation of the children's librarian as a specialist; 4) mechanisms for interagency cooperation; and 5) development of the techniques of readers' services to children.

649 Vinson, Rhonda J. "School Library Media Service for Handicapped Students, 1950-1980." Doctoral dissertation, Southern Illinois University, 1983. 165p. UMI# 8321473.

Library media center service for handicapped students involves the areas of special education and librarianship. These areas developed separately until a convergence of factors in the late

1970s brought them together. The equal rights movement, federal legislation for handicapped children, and sensitivity of the library profession to special needs all contributed to the emergence of library media center services for handicapped students. A nationwide survey of services available in 1979-80 is incorporated.

B. Studies Arranged by State

CALIFORNIA

650 Hall, Elizabeth A. "Public Elementary and Secondary School Library Development in California, 1850-1966." Doctoral dissertation, Columbia University, 1974. 381p. UMI# 75-12,314.

To ascertain the conditions which facilitated and retarded the growth of public elementary and secondary school libraries in California, the author highlights the role played by the state legislature, the California Department of Education, the State Library, and the professional organizations. Although district school libraries were introduced in the 1860s, there were no public school libraries in the nineteenth century. County public librarians often filled the void. Beginning in the 1940s, county superintendents of schools took over school library services from the county libraries. As of 1963 only 38 percent of California's elementary schools operated libraries.

CONNECTICUT

651 Adams, Rita T. "A History of School Libraries in Connecticut, 1948-1967." Master's thesis, Southern Connecticut State College, 1968. 109p.

The purpose of this thesis is to survey the history of Connecticut school libraries and to complete studies done by three other persons. The study considers the school library in relation to the public library, state financial assistance, reorganization of Connecticut libraries, and education acts which influenced libraries.

652 Bell, Dorothy. "History of School Libraries in Connecticut, 1839-1860." Master's thesis, Southern Connecticut State College, 1964. 123p.

The author begins with a description of Henry Barnard's efforts to establish school libraries in Connecticut from 1839 to 1842, and then turns to an analysis of the work of two other superintendents, John D. Philbrick, 1855-1857, and David N. Camp, 1857-1860. In 1839, Barnard noted only six school libraries in Connecticut's 1,400 schools. By 1860 there were nearly 600, with collections totaling over 40,000 volumes. Catalogs of several of the collections are included in the appendix.

653 Rukus, Anne T. "History of School Libraries in Connecticut, 1917-1947." Master's thesis, Southern Connecticut State College, 1968. 102p.

The author traces the development of school libraries in Connecticut from 1917 to 1947 when the influential Public Library Committee was abolished. The study focuses on the interrelationships between four statewide bodies concerned with school libraries: 1) the Connecticut Public Library Committee; 2) the Connecticut State Board of Education; 3) the Connecticut Library Association; and 4) the Connecticut School Library Association.

654 Singer, Anita R. "History of School Libraries in Connecticut, 1871-1916." Master's thesis, Southern Connecticut State College, 1966. 127p.

This study analyzes the erratic growth of school libraries in Connecticut from 1856, when a School Library Law was passed to 1916, when the Public Library Committee, recognizing the critical state of school library services, voted to sponsor and stock branches in Connecticut schools.

GEORGIA

655 Songer, Florence H. "Development of Public School Libraries in Georgia, 1890-1950." Master's thesis, University of North Carolina, 1955. 143p.

Reviews the history of public school library development in Georgia from the first efforts of the Georgia Teacher's Association in 1894 to initiate a reading circle in the public schools to 1950. The growth of school library service in Georgia was slow until 1940. From 1940 to 1950 growth was greatly accelerated due to state financial support and supervisory direction.

ILLINOIS

656 Noonan, Mabel Z. "The Development of Libraries in the Chicago Public Elementary Schools." Master's thesis, De Paul University, 1953. 99p.

This paper chronicles the development of libraries of the Chicago elementary schools from 1899 to 1952. The author finds that from 1883 to 1952 the Chicago Public Library was instrumental in providing loan collections for the elementary schools, and it still plays a vital role, although not to such a great extent. The WPA project in Chicago elementary schools gave great impetus to library development from 1935 to 1941.

INDIANA

657 Carroll, Floy C. "School Library Development in Indiana." Master's thesis, University of Illinois, 1929. 69p.

Describes the growth and decline of township school libraries in Indiana and analyzes the causes of their successes and failures. The period covered is from the establishment of township school libraries in 1852 to 1899, when legislation was passed that led to the demise of the earlier township library system. A brief survey of library development in the state from 1806 to 1852 is included. Public indifference and a consistent lack of funds are considered the basic causes for the failure of the township libraries.

IOWA

658 Buckingham, Betty J. "The Role of Professional Associations in the Development of School Librarians in Iowa." Doctoral dissertation, University of Minnesota, 1978. 301p. UMI# 7911980.

The impact of three Iowa professional associations on school librarians and services from 1890 to 1972 is evaluated: Iowa Library Association; Iowa Association of School Librarians; and Audiovisual Education Association of Iowa. Schools librarians were assisted at the local level more by the Iowa Association of School Librarians than by the other groups. Modest cooperation between the organizations was noted. None of the groups had an overwhelming impact on school libraries. Some influence on state agencies was achieved.

KENTUCKY

659 Galloway, M. Louise. "The Historical Development and Present Status of Public High School Libraries in Kentucky; 1908 to 1950." Master's thesis, Columbia University, 1951. Published: *Education Bulletin* 20 (1952): 5-121.

This study is an analysis of white and Negro public high school libraries in Kentucky from the inception of a statewide system of high schools in 1908 to 1950. The author says that information relating to high school libraries in Kentucky was fragmentary and difficult to locate, but it seems that the first full-time high school librarians were employed in Louisville in 1916. Library development received considerable impetus from the adoption, in 1923, of state regulations for school libraries. Development of high school library services in Kentucky remained slow until 1950, with the most serious retardation occurring during World War II.

LOUISIANA

660 Cookston, James S. "Development of Louisiana Public School Libraries, 1929-1965." Doctoral dissertation, Louisiana State University, 1971. 355p. UMI# 71-29,354.

The author examines the rise of school libraries in Louisiana from 1929, when the first State Supervisor of School Libraries was employed, to 1965, with emphasis on the pivotal role played by the Louisiana State Department of Education. Three articulate women served as State Supervisors of School Libraries during this period: Lois F. Shortess (1929-1940); Sue Hefley (1940-1949); and Lena Y. de Grummond (1950-1965).

MARYLAND

661 Williams, Mary L. "History and Description of the Baltimore Archdiocesan Library Council." Master's thesis, Catholic University of America, 1960. 102p.

Appraises the work of the Baltimore Archdiocesan Library Council from 1946 to 1958. The study focuses on three areas: goals, activities, and relations with external organizations. Presentation of the library and the stimulation of reading in all of the Catholic schools were the primary objectives. These objectives were implemented through reading lists, book fairs, book review contests, and advocacy of central libraries. Except for a continuing relation with the Enoch Pratt Free Library, the Library Council operated in relative isolation.

MINNESOTA

662 Briggs, Margaret I. "The Development of Public School Libraries in Minnesota, 1861-1938." Master's thesis, University of Chicago, 1945. 136p. Summary published: *Minnesota Libraries* 15 (1948): 372-75.

Few books or other educational materials were available to Minnesota school children in the nineteenth century. The first state appropriation was made in 1887. At the same time a public school library commission was established, and by 1900 over 300,000 volumes had been purchased. The author traces the history of these collections and points out the importance of the work of two librarians, Clara Baldwin and Martha Wilson, who prepared book lists, inspected libraries, and gave instruction to would-be school librarians until courses for credit were provided at the University of Minnesota in 1923.

MISSOURI

663 Pentlin, Floyd C. "The Evolution of Public School Libraries in Missouri and the 1901 Library Law." Education Specialist Thesis, Central Missouri State University, 1982. 92p.

Public school libraries developed slowly in nineteenth century Missouri, especially in rural areas. The library law of 1901 stimulated the growth of school libraries by requiring the expenditure of at least 5 cents per pupil. School libraries flourished in many communities, but there was no penalty for flouting the law. Other positive ramifications included better professional practices and the emergence of a trained cadre of school librarians.

NEW JERSEY

664 Lane, Margaret. "The Development of Library Service to Public Schools in New Jersey." Master's thesis, Columbia University,

1938. 177p. Summary published: *New Jersey School Librarian* (formerly *School Library Quarterly*) 1948-1950.

This study covers the development of school libraries in New Jersey from the mid-1800s to 1937. Development was very slow until 1913, with few good collections being established. The 25-year period from 1913-1937 saw some 245 high school libraries established in New Jersey, but elementary school library development was less marked. Such matters as the training and certification of school librarians, state aid, and the development of county library service are also examined.

NEW YORK

665 Tinklepaugh, Doris K. "School Libraries in New York State: Their History from 1890 to 1930." Master's thesis, Columbia University, 1937. 113p.

Examines the history of school library development in New York State, showing the general growth of school libraries from the days when no restrictions or qualifications were imposed to the time when standards for school library service were defined and enforced throughout the state. Discusses the aid and encouragement that state government gave to school library development, and analyzes the role of the school library in the state of New York from 1890 to 1930.

NORTH CAROLINA

666 Burge, Nancy T. "Development of High School Libraries in North Carolina, 1900-1947." Master's thesis, George Peabody College for Teachers, 1948. 107p.

This study traces the development of North Carolina high school libraries through an analysis of four key factors: educational setting; legislative and financial support; standards; and state supervision. Between 1900 and 1930 very little progress was achieved due to insufficient funds and lack of understanding by administrators and teachers of the library's value. By 1947, uniform standards, especially those developed by the Southern Association, and leadership at the state level contributed to the growth of high school libraries.

667 Redding, Bobbie N. "The Developmental History of the Elementary School Libraries in Guilford County, North Carolina." Master's thesis, University of North Carolina, 1957. 71p.

The author assesses the development of the elementary school libraries in three Guilford County school systems—Greensboro, Guilford County, and High Point—through the use of statistics from the State School Library Advisor's Office. These statistics were studied at five-year intervals from 1935-1936 to 1955-1956. Special areas covered are enrollment, librarians, expenditures, collections, circulation, and quarters. The author also examines the impact of centralized authority in each of the systems.

OHIO

668 Aldrich, Frederic D. "History of Ohio Public School Library Legislation." Doctoral dissertation, Western Reserve University, 1953. Published: Scarecrow Press, 1959.

This study deals with Ohio legislation for elementary and secondary school libraries from 1785 to 1953. In 1853 Ohio reorganized its school system and set up a state-wide school district system. It met considerable opposition because of the increased tax burden, the small collections, and the difficulties encountered in servicing rural areas. These difficulties led to the complete abandonment of the libraries in 1868. School libraries did not gain real strength again until after 1902.

PENNSYLVANIA

669 Melvin, Sister M.C. "A History of School Libraries in Pennsylvania." Doctoral dissertation, University of Chicago, 1962. Published: *Approaches to Library History*, edited by John David Marshall (Tallahassee: Journal of Library History, 1966): 106-18.

A history of school libraries in the public school system of Pennsylvania, with emphasis on four factors viewed to be highly influential: 1) legislation; 2) administration of the state; 3) professional organizations; and 4) accrediting agencies. School library service in Pittsburgh and Philadelphia is singled out for special attention.

SOUTH CAROLINA

670 Wofford, Azile. "The History and Present Status of School Libraries in South Carolina, 1868-1938." Master's thesis, Columbia University, 1938. 134p.

This paper covers the history of school libraries in South Carolina beginning with the establishment of public schools in 1868 and ending with 1938. Brief attention is given to libraries in South Carolina before the Civil War, and no coverage is given to libraries in Negro schools. The author presents reasons why school libraries developed more slowly in South Carolina than in any of the other Southern states, the most notable reason being the lack of state aid.

TENNESSEE

671 Taylor, Ila M. "Development of School Library Service in Tennessee, 1796 to 1947." Master's thesis, George Peabody College for Teachers, 1947. 90p.

Until 1900, ineffective legislation, indifference of leaders toward education, and economic factors retarded the development of adequate school library service. Legal provision for the support of school libraries was enacted in 1909 and state supervision commenced in 1913. The Southern Association and state standards are credited with increasing the number of libraries and improving library resources. Further stimulation came from grants bestowed by the Julius Rosenwald Fund and the General Education Board.

TEXAS

672 Donaldson, LaNelle L. "A Decade and a Half with the School Libraries of Texas." Master's thesis, Texas State College, 1954. 84p. Summary published: *Texas Library Journal* 30 (1954): 203-6.

School libraries in Texas were slow to develop. The greatest growth has occurred since 1940 despite the interruptions caused by World War II. This study surveys the events that contributed to school library development in the state, such as standards and legislation, with little coverage of individual libraries or librarians.

673 Feeney, Renee B. "The History and Development of the Library in the Public Schools of Houston, Texas." Master's thesis, Texas State College, 1954. 82p.

This paper traces the development of school libraries in Houston from the first establishment of a small classroom collection in 1882 through 1953. In the beginning students were encouraged to bring their own reading matter from home, but this soon proved unworkable. Later the Houston Public Library stepped in to fill the gap and served as a school materials center for many years. The first full-time school librarian was appointed in 1924.

674 Hembree, Myrtle M. "The Growth and Development of Libraries in the Elementary Schools of Texas." Master's thesis, Southern Methodist University, 1937. 126p.

School library development in Texas is traced from the early 1900s to the depression era. Lack of significant progress is attributed to numerous small districts and the absence of vigorous leadership at the state level. As of 1937, Texas had no school library law to foster development. A survey of library services and organization is included.

675 Holden, Opal. "The History of Library Service in Austin Public Schools." Master's thesis, University of Texas, 1962. 72p.

This study chronicles the library services offered in the Austin, Texas public schools from 1886 to 1962. The first school library in Austin was located in the Austin High School. It had its beginnings in a resolution passed by the School Board in 1886 appropriating $25.00 for the purchase of "classical literature of American and English Authors." From 1900, the Austin public schools grew rapidly and library development paralleled that growth. In 1960, every one of the 60 schools in the Austin public school system had a library with a trained librarian.

676 Moore, Mattie R. "Southern Association, State and Local Leadership for Library Service in Texas Schools." Master's thesis, University of Texas, 1955. 101p.

The historical portion of this paper describes the kind of leadership that has appeared for the improvement of library service in Texas schools. The author also examines the history of regional and state leadership for school library service and traces the transfer of major responsibility from the region to the state and local school districts. The time span covered is 1895-1953.

677 Seth, Olga C. "The Development of School Library Standards in Texas." Master's thesis, University of Texas, 1961. 111p.

Chapters in this study treat the establishment of tax-supported schools and libraries, formation of related state agencies and associations, and formulation and adoption of school library standards (1915-1961). School systems developed slowly in

Texas, especially in the rural areas. Urban high schools and their libraries proliferated following establishment of the University of Texas in 1881. National concern for a system of modern school libraries emerged in 1915. The first national standards were adopted by ALA in 1920 and endorsed by the Texas Department of Education in 1925.

VERMONT

678 Adams, Nancy E. "A Study of Regional Library Services for Children in Rural Vermont, 1930-1950." Master's thesis, Drexel Institute of Technology, 1952. 38p.

This study reviews the development of regional library service for children in Vermont during the twenty-year period beginning in 1930. In that year the Carnegie Corporation funded a two-year experiment in the northwest section of Vermont to encourage centralization, cooperation, and state financing. The Free Public Library Commission was established in 1937, a direct result of the experimental project. Five regional centers, staffed by professionals, were opened between 1937 and 1948. Each regional center furnished bookmobile service, provided technical assistance, supported programs of reader guidance, and arranged for story hours.

VIRGINA

679 Dunkley, Grace C. "Development of Public School Libraries in Virginia with Emphasis on the Period 1958-1959 Through 1963-1964." Master's thesis, University of North Carolina, 1965. 82p.

The author reviews the first 50 years of school library history in Virginia, supplying a detailed quantitative analysis of school library development for the years 1958-1959 through 1963-1964. School library progress in Virginia was mainly due to the financial aid provided by the state. School library growth was also stimulated by the appointment of a State School Library Supervisor in 1923. The author finds that there has been a distinct trend toward the establishment of central libraries in elementary schools, but that the majority of school libraries in Virginia are still located in the high schools.

680 Hoyle, Nancy E. "A Study of the Development of Library Service in the Public Schools of Virginia." Master's thesis, Columbia University, 1938. 168p.

This study reviews the development of library service for the public schools of Virginia from 1870 to 1938. The author points out how social, economic, and educational conditions, and the lack of public library provision, influenced the development of school libraries in Virginia. There was little interest in establishing school libraries in Virginia until a law was passed in 1906 setting up public high schools. Development was slow until 1931, but increased rapidly thereafter. The author discusses the development of standards, education for school librarians, state aid to public school libraries, and other influential factors.

WASHINGTON

681 Foster, Patricia M. "An Historical and Descriptive Study of the Bellevue Public School Library System and of its Administrative Pattern with Implications for the Future." Master's thesis, University of Washington, 1959. 63p.

This study contains a brief history of the development of school libraries in Bellevue, Washington, from 1923, when the first was established, to 1958.

WISCONSIN

682 Skaar, Martha O. "Public School Libraries in Wisconsin: A Historical Study of School Libraries Under the Supervision of the

State Department of Public Instruction." Master's thesis, Columbia University, 1938. 93p.

The author reviews the history of school libraries in Wisconsin from 1848, when the first feeble efforts were made, until 1937, when they were relatively well-established. The first 40 years (1848-1887) of the school library movement in Wisconsin formed a period of struggle and uncertainty, while the 50-year period from 1887 to 1937 was one of slow but steady progress.

VI. STATE LIBRARIES

CALIFORNIA

683 Kunkle, Hannah J. "A Historical Study of the Extension Activities of the California State Library with Particular Emphasis on its Role in Rural Library Development, 1850-1966." Doctoral dissertation, Florida State University, 1969. 365p. UMI# 70-03821.

The author traces the evolution of the California State Library from its early years as a legislative reference library to its later growth into a strong force for adult education in the state. In 1899, James L. Gillis became State Librarian in California and insisted that the State Library should serve all of the State's citizens on an equal basis. Gillis was able to get California's famous county library law passed in 1911, and made a number of notable contributions to library development in California. This study follows the State Library's development to 1966, when it was ranked among the finest in America.

COLORADO

684 VanMale, John E. "A History of Library Extension in Colorado, 1890-1930." Master's thesis, University of Denver, 1940. 100p.

The author begins his study with a brief survey of the "library extension idea" in America. He then traces the development of library extension services in Colorado, which began with John Cotton Dana's efforts in 1890 to serve rural patrons of the Denver Public Library. The first serious efforts at statewide extension services took place after 1900, with a Clubwomen's Commission handling the administration of the traveling libraries. In 1930 the Clubwomen's Commission and the Colorado Library Commission were consolidated and given a budget of $9,000. The author describes the pioneering efforts of Chalmers Hadley and Malcolm Wyer, both librarians at the Denver Public Library.

CONNECTICUT

685 Handy, Catherine H. "The Connecticut State Library, 1851-1936." Master's thesis, Southern Connecticut State College, 1965. 115p.

The author begins with a history of American state libraries from their origins in the eighteenth century through the twentieth, and then considers the reasons for the founding of the Connecticut State Library. It evolved from state needs concerning the care of the book collection, the keeping of records, and the management of systems of exchange. A library committee was set up in 1851 and the first Connecticut State Librarian was appointed in 1854. The story of the library's development from that time until 1936 is divided into sections: 1) I. Hammond Trumbull, 1854-1855; 2) Charles J. Hoadly, 1855-1900; and 3) George S. Goddard, 1900-1936.

DELAWARE

686 Thomas, Mary A. "The Delaware State Archives: 1931-1951." Master's thesis, Drexel Institute of Technology, 1952. 53p.

Presents an account of the development and activities of the Delaware State Archives, 1931-1951. A brief introduction describes archival methods in Delaware before 1905 and the founding and early work of the Public Archives Commission.

FLORIDA

687   Chalker, William J. "The Historical Development of the Florida State Library, 1845-1959." Master's thesis, George Peabody College for Teachers, 1951. 70p.

This study briefly examines the state library in the United States and follows with a history of the Florida State Library to 1949. The Florida State Library, like so many before it, began with miscellaneous collections of books accumulated in the offices of various state officials. In 1855 the Secretary of State was made the official state librarian and $100 was appropriated for binding and shelving the books. In 1925 an act was passed establishing the present Florida State Library. In 1927 W.T. Cash was appointed State Librarian and inherited a collection of 2,500 volumes. Growth was rapid under his directorship despite a serious shortage of funds.

ILLINOIS

688   Bird, Margaret F. "History of the Demonstration Program of the Illinois State Library." Master's thesis, University of Chicago, 1952. 90p.

In 1945, the Illinois Legislature passed a bill authorizing some $300,000 to be spent for the establishment of library demonstration projects conducted by the Illinois State Library. The demonstrations were intended primarily to reach the rural population of the state and encourage the permanent establishment of library service in rural areas. This study analyzes the events leading to the passage of the Demonstration Bill, and traces the development of the program in the six areas chosen for demonstration projects during 1945-1951.

INDIANA

689 Barr, Larry J. "The Indiana State Library, 1825-1925." Doctoral dissertation, Indiana University, 1976. 409p. UMI# 76-21,526.

Created in 1825, the Indiana State Library evolved from a legislative library into a statewide resource during its first century. Between 1825 and 1841 the Secretary of State served as the State Librarian and from 1841 to 1895 the position of State Librarian was held by legislative appointees. By 1925 the State Library was assuming the role of a general library for all citizens. Circulation records are examined for patterns of use.

LOUISIANA

690 Stephenson, Harriet S. "History of the Louisiana State Library, Formerly Louisiana Library Commission." Doctoral dissertation, Louisiana State University, 1957. 492p. UMI# 58-4705.

This study traces the impact of the Louisiana State Library, from its inception in 1920 as the Louisiana Library Commission, on public library development in the state. The first section surveys the condition of public libraries in Louisiana in the early twentieth century. Passage of a modern public library law, the use of demonstration libraries to raise public support, working toward the establishment of a library school at Louisiana State University, the establishment of a statewide reference service for Negroes, and an active public relations program were some of the more significant achievements of the State Library. Examines the career of Essae M. Culver, executive secretary of the Library Commission and president of the American Library Association.

MARYLAND

691 Capozzi, Marian R. "A History of Maryland State Library Agen-

cies, 1902-1945." Master's thesis, Catholic University of America, 1966. 93p.

Examines the development of the state library agencies in Maryland beginning with the State Library Commission in 1902 to its successor, the Maryland Public Library Commission, established in 1920. It in turn was followed by the Maryland Public Library Advisory Commission in 1922. Finally in 1934, the Division of Library Extension was established in the State Department of Education. The author devotes a chapter to each of these agencies.

692 Coover, Robert W. "A History of the Maryland State Library, 1827-1939." Master's thesis, Catholic University of America, 1956. Published: Association of College & Research Libraries Microcard, Number 88.

Chronicles the development of the Maryland State Library from 1827, when it was established, through 1939. The collection grew very slowly; its holdings in 1909 numbered only 40,000 volumes. By 1939 the collection had increased to over 110,000 volumes, primarily law books to serve the Maryland state legislature. The paper discusses the staff, collections, physical plant, and services of the library.

MICHIGAN

693 Larsen, John C. "A Study in Service: The Historical Development of the Michigan State Library and Its Territorial Predecessor, The Legislative Council Library, 1828-1941." Doctoral dissertation, University of Michigan, 1967. 381p. UMI# 67-17,804.

This study covers 113 years in the history of the Michigan State Library. Originally intended as a library to serve the State's legislators, the Michigan State Library slowly evolved into an institution dedicated to providing service to all of the state's residents. This study concludes with 1941, the year when the first professional librarian was appointed to the post of State Librarian in Michigan.

MISSISSIPPI

694 Laughlin, Jeannine L. "The Mississippi Library Commission: A Force for Library Development." Doctoral dissertation, Indiana University, 1983. 221p. UMI# 8317178.

The role of the Mississippi Library Commission in the development of library service in the state from its inception in 1926 to the present is chronicled. As cultural and educational needs dictated more extensive library service, the Commission responded with appropriate organization and leadership. The Commission also sensitized citizens to their advocacy role. Since 1970, the Commission has been largely responsible for public library development and expanded services.

NEBRASKA

695 Suess, Gertrude M. "Library Legislation in Nebraska." Master's thesis, University of Illinois, 1927. 102p.

The evolution of Nebraska library legislation from the territorial period to the 1920s is the focus of this detailed study. Individual chapters are devoted to major types of libraries and administrative bodies: state library; municipal libraries; library commission; legislative reference library; and school district libraries. Significant statutory passages accompany the narrative.

NEW HAMPSHIRE

696 Brown, Carol C. "History of the New Hampshire State Library." Master's thesis, Southern Connecticut State College, 1970. 110p.

This study of the New Hampshire State Library, from its founding in 1818 to 1943, when the functions of a comprehensive state library were being carried out, argues that the New Hampshire State Library was one of the first to recognize the needs of all citizens of the state and was a pioneer in the establishment of a statewide library development program.

NEW JERSEY

697 Johnston, Mary E. "New Jersey State Library: A History of the Development in Public Library Service." Master's thesis, Kent State University, 1952. 54p.

The State Library of New Jersey received legislative authorization in 1813. Over the years, the State Library became a centralized department which administered programs for public and school libraries. County library service, traveling libraries, museum activities, resource sharing, and staff development are discussed in detail.

NEW MEXICO

698 Barrett, Mildred A. "Development of Library Extension in New Mexico." Master's thesis, Western Reserve University, 1958. Published: Association of College & Research Libraries Microcard, Number 97.

Briefly sketches library development and attempts at library extension to 1929; then traces the history of the New Mexico Library Extension Service and its contributions to the New Mexico library scene, from its inception in 1929 to 1958. The service, with no quarters of its own, no book fund, and no books, was a "child of charity" during its early years. However, qualified professional leadership and wide support ensured its success. The author traces the efforts of the service to fulfill its major purpose—promotion of library development in New Mexico.

NEW YORK

699 Vloebergh, Helen E. "A History of the New York State Library from 1818 to 1905." Master's thesis, Catholic University of America, 1956. Published: Association of College & Research Libraries Microcard, Number 83.

This paper reconstructs the history of the New York State Library from its inception in 1818 until 1905, when Melvil Dewey resigned as director. The library was originally founded as a reference collection for state officials, but when Dewey became director in 1888 he extended its services to all the people of New York. The author points out, however, that the State Library always remained essentially a reference library and never functioned as a true public library. The State Library's considerable influence on library development in New York is related, with special reference to school and public library development.

NORTH CAROLINA

700 Babylon, Eugenia R. "History of the North Carolina Library Commission." Master's thesis, University of North Carolina, 1954. 176p.

The author begins by discussing the purpose and background of library extension agencies in the United States and then traces the history of the North Carolina Library Commission, which was established in 1909 as the result of a concerted lobbying effort on the part of the newly formed North Carolina Library Association. The Commission's first chairman was Louis R. Wilson, then Director of Libraries at the University of North Carolina. The author outlines the many ways in which the Commission attempted to stimulate the development of libraries in the state, especially through the use of bookmobile service and grants to libraries.

701 York, Maurice C. "A History of the North Carolina State Library,

1812-1888." Master's thesis, University of North Carolina, 1978. 110p.

Established in 1812, the North Carolina State Library progressed steadily despite the problems of political patronage, loss of the collection through fire, and irregular funding. Separate chapters are devoted to administration, acquisitions, bibliographic control, use, and facilities. During the 1840s, the eminent Joseph Green Cogswell purchased many outstanding titles for the collection. By 1888 the State Library boasted 40,000 volumes, fourth largest of the nation's state libraries.

OHIO

702 Smith, Clara E. "The Growth of the Service of the Ohio State Traveling Library." Master's thesis, University of Cincinnati, 1936. 156p.

This study emphasizes the growth of the Ohio State Traveling Library (1896-1935) and its services to public secondary schools, specifically those of the county district type.

703 Vannorsdall, Mildred M. "The Development of Library Services at the State Level in Ohio, 1817-1896. (Vols. I and II)." Doctoral dissertation, University of Michigan, 1974. 568p. UMI# 74-25,348.

State-level library services in nineteenth-century Ohio and the changing functions of the Ohio State Library are emphasized in this study. The influence of governors, librarians, users and other agencies on library development are considered. Until 1857, when a separate law library was formed, legal and general books were acquired by the State Library. Special services to correctional institutions, blind and handicapped citizens, and universities are reviewed. In 1896, a board of library commissioners was created to oversee the State Library.

OREGON

704 Rowe, Wilbur D. "The Development of the Oregon State Library and Its Contributions to the Public Schools." Master's thesis, University of Oregon, 1939. 104, [4]p.

Describes the program and accomplishments of the Oregon Library Commission from 1905 to 1938. Four service areas are emphasized: 1) book lists; 2) travelling libraries; 3) clearinghouse for public libraries; and 4) reference services. Major strides were made toward expanding school library service, formulating standards, and implementing professional education for libraries. The creative force of the Oregon Library Commission was Cornelia C. Marvin, who served as secretary during the period 1905-1928.

TENNESSEE

705 Settlemire, Claude L. "The Tennessee State Library, 1854-1923." Master's thesis, George Peabody College for Teachers, 1951. 38p.

This paper presents a history of the Tennessee State Library from its establishment in 1854 until it became a division of the State Department of Education in 1923. When the library was established, the Secretary of State acted as librarian, and the first State Librarian was not appointed until 1856. The author emphasizes the legislative development of the State Library.

TEXAS

706 Peace, William K., III. "A History of the Texas State Library with Emphasis on the Period from 1930 to 1958." Master's thesis, University of Texas, 1959. 98p.

Studies the history of the Texas State Library from its inception in

State Libraries

1851 through 1958 with emphasis on the last 28 years. Considers the history of the overall administration of the library, the services and administration of the various divisions, and the administration of the program for developing rural library service under the Library Services Act.

707 Young, Catherine. "The History of the Texas State Library." Master's thesis, University of Texas, 1932. 69p.

The Texas State Library was born in 1839 with a generous appropriation of $10,000. In 1854 the Supreme Court Library was established. For the next 30 years these libraries received meager financial support. The State Library faltered under the requirement that it report to the Secretary of State, and in 1881 the library was destroyed in the capitol fire. Passage of the Texas State Library and Historical Commission Law in 1909 enhanced the State Library's prestige, role and finances. By 1932, the library held 88,800 volumes and operated with a staff of 11.

VII. TYPES OF LIBRARY SERVICE

A. Cataloging and Classification

708   Bates, Nancy P. "The History of the Classification and Cataloging of Maps as Shown in Printed Book Catalogues of Sixteen United States Libraries Issued from 1827 through 1907." Master's thesis, University of North Carolina, 1954. Published: University of Kentucky Press, Microcard Publications, Series B, Number 15.

The author analyzes the method of map cataloging and classification based on 16 catalogs published through 1907. Libraries were rather confused early in the period covered. Entries were generally inconsistent and superficial. In time, however, the author discovered indications of a trend towards standardization and more detailed description.

709   Comaromi, John P. "A History of the Dewey Decimal Classification: Editions One Through Fifteen, 1876-1951." Doctoral dissertation, University of Michigan, 1969. 463p. UMI# 70-14,490. Published: Forest Press, 1976.

This study is the biography of the classification scheme which came in time to be the most popular in the world. The author traces the history of the Dewey scheme from its inception in 1876 through the publication of the very unsuccessful fifteenth edition in 1951. The first half of this study is devoted to an analysis of the development and organization of the first two editions (1876 and 1885), while the second half reviews the subsequent developments with the DDC.

710 Corcoran, Sara R. "A Study of Cataloging Practice Through 1830 as Shown in Printed Book Catalogs of Six Libraries in the City of New York." Master's thesis, Columbia University, 1936. 76p.

The author begins this study with a survey of library history in colonial New York, noting especially the work of the Reverend Thomas Bray. Histories of the six libraries covered in this study are then presented: the New York Society Library; the New York Hospital Library; the New York Historical Society Library; the Apprentices' Library; the Mercantile Library; and the Lyceum of Natural History Library. Trends toward modern cataloging practice were not evident during the period covered (1758-1831), and the author found only one attempt at the establishment of rules for the preparation of a catalog.

711 Davis, Elizabeth R. "Author vs. Title; An Historical Treatment of the Conflict over Choice of Entry for Serials Issued by Corporate Bodies." Master's thesis, University of Chicago, 1973. 54p.

Not examined.

712 Evensen, Robert L. "The Bibliographical Control of Art Exhibition Catalogs: An Historical and Comparative Analysis of Cataloging Rules and Library Procedures in France, Great Britain, and the United States." Master's thesis, University of Chicago, 1974. 82p.

Contemporary exhibition catalogs and the cataloging codes and procedures used by libraries illustrate that the problems involved in establishing entry and obtaining bibliographic control are not new. Inconsistencies found in French and Anglo-American cataloging practices originated in the eighteenth and nineteenth centuries. Modification and simplification are needed to overcome failures of the past.

713 Freedman, Maurice J. "The Functions of the Catalog and the Main Entry as Found in the Work of Panizzi, Jewett, Cutter, and

Lubetzky." Doctoral dissertation, Rutgers University, 1983. 364p. UMI# 8320470.

The alphabetic library catalog encompasses two main functions: 1) identification of a particular publication; and 2) identification of all works and representations by an author. The device by which the relatedness of author's works and the representations of a given work is the concept of main entry. Cutter's definition of the main entry as the full entry was a mistake which plagued the main entry until 1951. Lubetzky defined the main entry functionally as the representation of a particular work by a particular author. Evolution of the catalog and the main entry, including the impact of technology, is addressed.

714 Gillespie, Sarah C. "An Analysis of Certain Notes Used by the Library of Congress in Cataloging Serial Publications, 1898-1942." Master's thesis, Emory University, 1965.

Not examined.

715 Gore, Daniel J., Jr. "The Schomburg Collection and Its Catalog: A Historical Sketch." Master's thesis, University of North Carolina, 1963. 63p.

The author examined the ways in which a library catalog will be affected by the changing character and objectives of the collection it records. The Schomburg collection of Negro Literature and History, a branch of the New York Public Library, is reviewed. The first part of his paper is devoted to a history of the collection's development from 1925 to 1960, while the second part deals with the catalog. Concludes that catalogs of special collections should not be built to a standard, but should be constructed with close regard to the collections they describe.

716 Graziano, Eugene E. "The Philosophy of Hegel as Basis for the Dewey Decimal Classification Schedule." Master's thesis, University of Oklahoma, 1955. 70p. Summary published: *Libri* 9 (1959): 45-52.

This paper begins with a survey of classification in the United States from 1850 to 1856. The author then discusses the pioneering classification scheme devised by William Torrey Harris at the St. Louis Public Library in 1850. The author documents his belief that Harris' classification system was based largely on Hegel's philosophy. He also argues that Dewey adapted his subject divisions from the Harris scheme, and thus the Dewey decimal classification traces its lineage back to Hegel's philosophy, not to Bacon's as is sometimes maintained.

717 Heiss, Ruth M. "The Card Catalog in Libraries of the United States Before 1867." Master's thesis, University of Illinois, 1938. 91p. Summary published: *Cataloger's and Classifier's Yearbook* 8 (1939): 125-26.

The tremendous growth of American libraries in the nineteenth century forced librarians to find new methods of preparing catalogs. After 1853, due to Jewett's pressure for a national catalog using cards and the publicity given card catalogs at the Librarian's Conference of 1853, the card catalog spread across the country. The Philadelphia Library Company pioneered in card catalogs for public use in 1857, and Ezra Abbot and C.A. Cutter produced a model catalog at Harvard in 1861. Foreign influences and the leadership of such Americans as Charles Folsom, Ezra Abbot, Charles Coffin Jewett, and Charles Ammi Cutter are treated.

718 Helfer, Robert S. "Beginning, of Course with A: A Study of Library Filing and the 1980 Filing Codes." Master's thesis, University of Chicago, 1982. 163p.

Compares the *ALA Filing Rules* and the *Library of Congress Filing Rules* within the context of the history of alphabetization practices in American libraries and changing library catalog practices.

719 Hensel, Evelyn M. "History of the Catalog Department of the University of Illinois Library." Master's thesis, University of Illinois, 1936. 100p.

Traces the history of the department from 1868 to 1932 in four chapters. Chapter one discusses cataloging at the library before 1897, when the first professional librarian was hired. Chapter two covers the department from 1897 to 1906, when Katherine Sharp was librarian and Margaret Mann was head (1897-1899) of the Catalog Department. Chapter three treats the period from 1906 to 1932, most of which time Phineas Windsor was Director of the Library. The department grew rapidly from three catalogers in 1906 to 18 in 1932. The fourth chapter covers the history of the Union Catalog at the University of Illinois Library.

720 McHugh, William A. "The Publication of the First Edition of the *Union List of Serials*." Master's thesis, University of Chicago, 1984. 254p.

The first edition of the *Union List of Serials* represented a significant contribution to bibliography and a notable example of library cooperation. The list culminated earlier efforts by the H.W. Wilson Company and the American Library Association (ALA). Harry M. Lydenberg chaired the ALA Committee which commenced preparation in 1921. Guarantor libraries were solicited to support the project. Guidelines for the inclusion and exclusion of titles were a persistent problem. Published in late 1927, supplements appeared in 1931 and 1933.

721 Osborn, Velva J. "A History of Cooperative Cataloging in the United States." Master's thesis, University of Chicago, 1944. 144p.

Beginning with first attempts in 1850, the author reviews the history of cooperative cataloging to the middle of the twentieth century. The first such effort was made in 1850 by Charles Coffin Jewett in his suggestion for making the Smithsonian Institution a national center. His idea failed, and it was not until Cutter, Dewey, Poole, Fletcher and others founded the American Library Association in 1876 that any more work was done in that direction. The important contribution of the Library of Congress is considered.

722 Oswald, Janet F. "The Development of the Medical Subject Heading." Master's thesis, Drexel Institute of Technology, 1955. 65p.

Traces the development of medical subject headings from Dewey in 1876 to 1955 with reference to their use in medical libraries in the United States. The leadership of the Armed Forces Medical Library, and the continuance of its work as the National Medical Library, are emphasized.

723 Palmer, Vivian D. "A Brief History of Cataloging Codes in the United States, 1852-1949." Master's thesis, University of Chicago, 1963. 100p.

The author briefly traces the history of the following codes: 1) Panizzi's; 2) Jewett's; 3) Cutter's; 4) Dewey's; 5) Anglo-American Code; and 6) Library of Congress.

724 Ranz, James. "The History of the Printed Book Catalogue in the United States." Doctoral dissertation, University of Illinois, 1960. 332p. UMI# 60-03980. Published: American Library Association, 1964.

This study, emphasizing the period from the early eighteenth century to the late nineteenth century, is concerned with the rise and fall of the book catalog in America. Examines the development of the first book catalogs in colonial America, the sophistication of catalogs in later periods, and the contributions and conflicts of men like Poole, Abbot, and Jewett. Concludes by discussing the demise of the book catalog in the last quarter of the nineteenth century. Three factors are cited: 1) the rapid growth of library collections; 2) the increased role of the catalog in a service-minded library era; and 3) the development of the Library of Congress card distribution system. Primary sources for the study were over 2,000 printed library catalogs.

725 Rohdy, Margaret A. "Cataloging Anonymous Works: An Histori-

cal and Theoretical Study." Master's thesis, University of Chicago, 1973. 127p.

The development of the catalogers' definition of anonymous works, rules for the entry of such works, and theories for rules and definitions are evaluated in the historical context of Western cataloging traditions. Prominent cataloging authorities cited in the study include Antonio Panizzi, Charles C. Jewett, Charles A. Cutter, and the various American Library Association codes.

726   Ruffin, Mary B. "Some Developments Toward Modern Cataloging Practice in University Libraries as Exemplified in the Printed Book Catalogs of Harvard and Yale Before 1876." Master's thesis, Columbia University, 1935. 68p.

The author examined the printed book catalogs of the college library collection of each university, and also of the various societies and professional schools of Harvard and Yale before 1876. The author found many pioneering steps toward better cataloging before 1876, but they lacked uniformity and were highly localized. Individuality in cataloging was quite prevalent before the day of formal cataloging codes.

727   Schley, Ruth. "Cataloging in the Libraries of Princeton, Columbia, and the University of Pennsylvania Before 1876." Master's thesis, Columbia University, 1946. 117p.

Examines the 15 manuscript and 21 printed catalogs in book form constructed by the main library, departmental libraries, and student society libraries of Princeton, Columbia, and the University of Pennsylvania prior to 1876. Periods of greatest cataloging activity were from 1820 to 1829 and from 1870 to 1876. Librarians gradually supplanted the works of professors in the preparation of catalogs. There was a gradual trend toward modern standards except in the consistent disregard of author entries. Tabular charts and samples from catalogs enhance the text.

728   Servies, James A. "Thomas Jefferson and His Bibliographic

Classification." Master's thesis, University of Chicago, 1950. 119p.

This paper is divided into three major portions. Part one considers several of the major schemes developed during the early period in American history. Part two, the largest section, deals with Jefferson's pragmatic scheme for the classification of knowledge. The author considers its use at the Library of Congress and the University of Virginia, and traces the changes the system underwent at Jefferson's and other classifiers' hands to 1826. The final portion deals with a synthesis of Jefferson's thinking on the classification of knowledge.

729 Straka, Mildred. "A Historical Review of the Cataloging Department of the Columbia University Libraries, 1883-1950." Master's thesis, Columbia University, 1951. 104p.

Examines the historical development of the Cataloging Department at Columbia from 1882 to 1950. The subject is treated under the following headings: 1) organization; 2) staff; 3) working conditions; 4) physical conditions; 5) the catalogs; 6) procedures and routines in the cataloging department; and 7) policies and trends. The author finds that the Cataloging Department at Columbia has shown a willingness to pursue change since Melvil Dewey's tenure as director.

730 Thackston, Frances V. "The Development of Cataloging in the Libraries of Duke University and the University of North Carolina from Their Establishment to 1953." Master's thesis, University of North Carolina, 1959. Published: Association of College & Research Libraries Microcard, Number 124.

After presenting a brief history of the two universities and their libraries from 1795 to 1953, the author traces the development of cataloging in the two libraries. This narrative shows the transition in the two libraries from manuscript book catalogs to the card catalog and from fixed-location symbols to expandable call numbers. Over two million volumes were available in the two libraries in 1953.

731 Wilkins, Madeleine J. "History and Evaluation of Subject Heading Approach in Medicine: A Study of Certain Medical Indexes Published in the United States." Master's thesis, Catholic University of America, 1955. 87p.

The author traces the history of the following medical bibliographies: 1) *Armed Forces Medical Library Catalog*; 2) *Current List of Medical Literature*; and 3) *Quarterly Cumulative Index Medicus*.

732 Willet, Mary M. "A History and Survey of the Nassau County Library Association Union Catalog." Master's thesis, Drexel Institute of Technology, 1955. 46p.

This paper presents a history of the Nassau County Library Association Union Catalog from its inception to 1955. The author finds that the union catalog, usually considered a research tool for large libraries, proved an excellent way for small Nassau County libraries to provide better service to their patrons through mutual cooperation. The cooperative association had nearly 30 members in 1954.

B. Reference

733 Adams, E.M., Jr. "A Study of Reference Librarianship in the American College: 1876-1955." Master's thesis, East Texas State College, 1956. 61p.

Three events that occurred in 1876 stimulated the development of reference service in college libraries: 1) the establishment of the American Library Association; 2) the establishment of the *Library Journal*, with its many aids to reference work; and 3) Samuel S. Green's address to the American Library Association, in which he advocated the radical idea that librarians should help patrons select books and locate information. Green's influence, plus the increase in graduate instruction and the discarding of the single textbook method, pressured libraries into offering reference service. The author finds that organized reference service was slow to develop in many colleges.

734 McBride, Margaret. "Reference Service for Congress Before 1915." Master's thesis, Drexel Institute of Technology, 1955. 67p.

This study investigates the nature and extent of reference services offered by the Library of Congress before the Legislative Reference Service was established in 1915. The author finds that the original reference service, begun by George Waterson in 1815, was limited by the lack of trained staff, finances, research collections, and adequate facilities.

735 Miller, Richard E. "Development of Reference Services in the American Liberal Arts College, 1876-1976." Doctoral dissertation, University of Minnesota, 1984. 218p. UMI# 84185158. Summary published: *RQ* 25 (1986): 460-67.

Prior to 1925, selective liberal colleges largely ignored reference service as a regular activity. Reference service was stimulated by the introduction of independent study and honors programs, the development of bibliographic tools, and the influence of accrediting agencies. Negative influences delaying the adoption of reference service included overreliance on reserve rooms, faculty disdain of librarians, and understaffed libraries. Regular reference service did not become fully accepted at selective liberal art colleges until after World War II.

736 Orr, Adriana P. "A History and Analysis of the Freshman Library Instruction Program Presented at the University of North Carolina." Master's thesis, University of North Carolina, 1958. 94p. Published: Association of College & Research Libraries Microcard, Number 125.

The author devotes the first quarter of this paper to a discussion of the reports and correspondence of the reference librarian and other university personnel concerned with the establishment of a library orientation program. The program grew out of the library staff's frustration over the poor orientation being given freshmen by the English Department in the 1930s, but the library's program was not formally established until 1948.

737   Rothstein, Samuel. "The Development of Reference Services in American Research Libraries." Doctoral dissertation, University of Illinois, 1954. 228p. UMI# 09128. Published: American Library Association, 1955. Reprinted: Gregg Press, 1972.

This study records the history of reference service in research libraries from its early beginnings around 1875 to the middle of the twentieth century. Until the second decade of the twentieth century, little actual reference work was being done. Scholars felt the librarians' duty to be one of acquisitions rather than service, and at the same time felt little need for help in their research. Little aid was given to students and other inexperienced users, for the philosophy of that period was one of encouraging user independence. After 1940, the ever-increasing flow of literature in all research fields led to the establishment of the reference function.

738   Thompson, Madeline C. "History of the Reference Department of the University of Illinois Library." Master's thesis, University of Illinois, 1942. 175p.

This paper presents the history of the development and services of the Reference Department starting from 1897, when the first library building was erected on the campus, the first trained librarian was hired, and the Reference Department was organized. Coverage ceases in 1940, the year which marked the end of Phineas L. Windsor's career as director of the University of Illinois Library.

VIII. LIBRARY EDUCATION

A. General Studies

739 Campion, Anna L. "Education for Special Librarians in the United States and Canada in 1946 and 1952." Master's thesis, Drexel Institute of Technology, 1953. 37p.

The author examines the catalogs of 35 accredited library schools to establish developments in the education of special librarians between 1946 and 1952, and finds a definite trend toward the offering of specific courses in special librarianship. The lack of an adequate teaching literature, facilities, and faculties are cited as problems that have confronted library schools in this area of library education.

740 Carroll, Carmal E. "The Professionalization of Education for Librarianship, with Special Reference to the Years 1940-1960." Doctoral dissertation, University of California, Berkley, 1969. 464p. UMI# 69-18,892. Published: Scarecrow Press, 1970.

This study identifies those forces and events which contributed to the professionalization of library education during the years 1940-1960. Prior to 1940, three events upgraded library education: 1) the Williamson Report, 1923; 2) the founding of the ALA Board of Education for Librarianship; and 3) the establishment of the Graduate Library School, University of Chicago, 1926. The 1951 ALA Standards which accredited only graduate programs in library science accelerated professionalization.

741 Churchwell, Charles D. "Education for Librarianship in the United States: Some Factors Which Influenced Its Development Between 1919 and 1939." Doctoral dissertation, University of Illinois, 1966. 220p. UMI# 66-12,304. Published: American Library Association, 1975.

This study analyzes the movements, events, and influences which contributed to the development of education for librarianship between 1919 and 1939. When the American Library Association identified serious weaknesses in its training agencies, the Board of Education for Librarianship was created to exert a constructive influence upon library education. External factors contributing to the improvement of library education included the phenomenon of specialization, growth of research, pedagogical reevaluation, and regional accrediting associations. The role of the Carnegie Corporation, especially its support of the Graduate Library School at the University of Chicago, is emphasized.

742 Emert, Florence A. "Trends in Thought on the Training of Special Librarians from the Beginning of the Special Libraries Association in 1909 Through 1950." Master's thesis, Western Reserve University, 1952. 55p.

After tracing the early history of the Special Libraries Association, this paper considers the development of a philosophy of education for special librarianship. The author finds it hard to chart a distinct trend, for the period under study has been marked by considerable controversy. The value of a regular library school course for special librarians, and the value of subject specialization over knowledge of library techniques and philosophy were two of the major areas of conflict.

743 Evraiff, Lois A.K. "A Survey of the Development and Emerging Patterns in the Preparation of School Librarians." Doctoral dissertation, Wayne State University, 1969. 273p. UMI# 70-19,055.

The author describes the emergence of curricula for school

librarians beginning in 1926. Library standards and accreditation practices have influenced patterns of preparation of school librarians. Public school personnel and library educators often disagree over the best program of education. Changes in the 1960s are considered pivotally important.

744 Fleischer, Mary B. "Credentials Awarded Through August, 1961, by Agencies Presently or Formerly Approved or Accredited by the American Library Association." Master's thesis, University of Texas, 1963. 60p.

The author identifies the credentials (i.e. degrees) in library science that have been employed by agencies for library education in the United States and Canada from 1887 through August of 1961. She also provides information on the type and number of degrees awarded by each of the agencies now or at one time accredited by the American Library Association. Some 50,000 certificates and degrees have been awarded, 28.5 percent of them during the period 1952-1961. Roughly 60 percent of the total were bachelor's degrees (mostly fifth year), nearly 30 percent were master's degrees, and 11.5 percent were certificates.

745 Lohrer, Mary A. "The Teacher-Librarian Training Program, 1900-1944." Master's thesis, University of Chicago, 1944. 148p.

The development of one training program for teacher-librarians, 1900-1944, the controversy over whether teacher-training agencies or library schools should be responsible for their training, and the changing curriculum for the teacher-librarian are all covered in this study.

746 Roper, Fred W. "A Comparative Analysis of Programs in Medical Library Education in the United States, 1957-1971." Doctoral dissertation, Indiana University, 1971. 191p. UMI# 72-002.

The author analyzes the sixteen specialized programs for the education of medical librarians which have been in existence in the United States since the establishment of the first in 1957 in order to determine: 1) their nature and distinguishing characteristics; 2) the nature of their graduates; and 3) how graduates of the special programs compare to a selected group of medical librarians who did not graduate from the special programs.

747 Siggins, Jack A. "American Influence on Modern Japanese Library Development." Master's thesis, University of Chicago, 1969. 117p.

The author analyzes the considerable American influence on Japanese library development from 1868 to the present. Special attention is placed on the American impact on education for librarianship in Japan since World War II.

748 Singleton, Mildred E. "Reference Teaching in the Pioneer Library Schools, 1883-1903." Master's thesis, Columbia University, 1942. 195p.

Studies reference teaching in four pioneer library schools: Columbia, Pratt Institute in Brooklyn, Drexel Institute in Philadelphia, and Armour Institute in Chicago. Discusses the factors stimulating the development of reference services and reference teaching: 1) the changing emphasis in library work from storage to use; 2) the ever-increasing number of reference books; and 3) the increased use of library collections. The influence of great reference teachers was also significant.

749 Vann, Sarah K. "Training for Librarianship Before 1923, or Prior to the Publication of Williamson's Report on 'Training for Library Service'." Doctoral dissertation, University of Chicago, 1959. Published: American Library Association, 1961.

Presents a detailed analysis of the ideas and concepts of library education that evolved during the "Dewey to Williamson" period, 1887-1923. The author finds that too little attention has been paid to that period, which begins with the founding of the library school at Columbia and ends with the publication of Williamson's report on library education. She argues that the ideas expressed by Williamson, and those frequently identified with him, had actually been quite common throughout the years after the establishment of Dewey's school.

750 Wicklzer, Alice F. "Education for Librarianship: A Brief History, 1886-1953." Master's thesis, Western Reserve University, 1953. 88p.

Examines the history of library education in the United States from the establishment of Dewey's School at Columbia to 1953.

B. **Studies Arranged By State**

GEORGIA

751 Callahan, Betty E. "The Carnegie Library School of Atlanta, 1905-1925." Master's thesis, Emory University, 1961. 94p. Summary published: *Library Quarterly* 37 (1967): 149-79.

Chronicles the origins, purposes, content, and instructional approach of the Carnegie Library School of Atlanta. Established in 1905, the Library School became affiliated in 1925 with Emory University and later developed into the Emory University Division of Librarianship. The school was originally a staff training ground for the Carnegie Library of Atlanta, and the public library needs provided the major influence on curriculum development. The author finds that the school faced constant problems and did not reach maturity until its affiliation with Emory University.

ILLINOIS

752 Richardson, John V., Jr. "The Spirit of Inquiry in Library Science: The Graduate Library School at Chicago, 1921-1951." Doctoral

dissertation, Indiana University, 1978. 437p. UMI# 7900419. Published: American Library Association, 1982.

Library education at the Graduate Library School (GLS), University of Chicago, is reviewed in terms of conception, objectives, and attainments. The GLS was particularly successful in introducing graduate instruction and integrated its program of study with the university. Less successful was the goal of preparing large numbers of library educators. The profession's first research journal, *Library Quarterly*, was launched in 1931. Overall, the lasting impact of the GLS on librarianship was its commitment to a critical spirit of inquiry and willingness to experiment.

NORTH CAROLINA

753 Wing, Mary J. "A History of the School of Library Science of the University of North Carolina: The First Twenty-Five Years." Master's thesis, University of North Carolina, 1958. Published: Association of College & Research Libraries Microcard, Number 119.

Traces the history of the University of North Carolina Library School from 1931 to 1956. Curriculum development, the transition from undergraduate work to graduate work, efforts to win accreditation, and the school's influence on southern and national librarianship are all topics discussed by the author. By 1956 the school had awarded 749 degrees.

OHIO

754 Davenport, Frederick B. "A History of the Western Reserve University Library School, 1904-1954." Master's thesis, Western Reserve University, 1956. 43p.

This study is concerned with the growth of the institution and devotes little space to the influence of various personalities on the school's development. Seven major chapters deal with: 1) requirements for admission; 2) tuition and expenses; 3) general curriculum; 4) work with children and young people; 5) building and books; 6) the summer school; and 7) certificates and degrees. Appendix E compares entrance requirements at three library schools in 1920.

PENNSYLVANIA

755 Nehlig, Mary E. "The History and Development of the Drexel Institute Library School, 1892-1914." Master's thesis, Drexel Institute of Technology, 1952. 48p.

This paper analyzes the development from 1892 to 1914 of the third oldest library school in the United States. The origins of the school, its curriculum, the faculty and their achievements are all discussed by the author. Special emphasis is placed on the period 1913-1914, the last year the school was open until 1922. The school, under the direction of Alice Bertha Kroeger (1892-1909), June Richardson Donnelly (1910-1913), and Corinne Bacon (1913-1914), graduated 317 students, two of them men, by 1914.

756 Osburn, Harriet. "A History of the Library Science Department of the Millersville State Teachers College, Millersville, Pennsylvania." Master's thesis, Drexel Institute of Technology, 1955. 56p.

After briefly surveying the school library situation in Pennsylvania prior to 1921, the author traces the development of the teacher-librarian curriculum at Millersville State from its beginnings in the fall of 1922 to June 1955. The original program required 15 hours, but had grown to 20 by 1955. Graduates of the school are certified by the State Department of Public Instruction to serve in the schools of Pennsylvania.

757 Stanbery, George W., II. "History of the Carnegie Library School; Through Its First Fifty Years." Master's thesis, Carnegie Institute of Technology, 1951. 83p.

Covers the history of the Carnegie Library School from its beginnings in 1901 through the 1950-1951 session. In 1901 Frances Jenkins Olcott organized the Training School for Children's Librarians, which in 1916 became a department of the Carnegie Institute and was renamed the Carnegie Library School. In 1948 the school started its one-year post- B.A. program, which led to a Master of Library Science degree. Short biographical sketches of Frances Olcott, Sara Bogle, Lucy Fay, Nina Brotherton, and Elizabeth Nesbitt are included.

TEXAS

758 Adrian, Janet M. "A History of the Library Science Department of East Texas State College." Master's thesis, East Texas State, 1959. 60p.

This paper is a chronological history of the Library Science Department at East Texas State College from 1947 to 1959. In 1947 the Department began offering a major in library science. One teacher taught all of the classes and 14 students enrolled in the program. From that time to 1959 the Library Science Department awarded 38 Bachelor of Science in Library Science degrees, and 58 Master of Library Science degrees. An appendix contains a list of the recipients and their degrees.

759 Webb, David A. "Local Efforts to Prepare Library Assistants and Librarians in Texas from 1900 to 1942." Doctoral dissertation, University of Chicago, 1963. 356p.

In this study of library education, the author sets the stage by reviewing the history of libraries in Texas from 1900 to 1942. Webb finds that Texas was at least 30 years behind in establishing formal academic programs for the preparation of librarians. It was not until 1919 that the University of Texas opened its library school.

WISCONSIN

760 Fenster, Valmai R. "The University of Wisconsin Library School, A History, 1895-1921." Doctoral dissertation, University of Wisconsin-Madison, 1977. 687p. UMI# 7719758.

The University of Wisconsin Library School was founded in 1906 by the Wisconsin Free Library Commission. Four major factors influenced library education at the University of Wisconsin: national trends; relationship to the Wisconsin Free Library Commission; affiliation with the University of Wisconsin; and the educational philosophy of the school's principal, Mary E. Hazeltine. Although college preparation was suggested, the reality of service in rural areas dictated a high school graduation requirement. Field work and a special program in legislative reference gained national recognition.

IX. LIBRARY ASSOCIATIONS

AMERICAN ASSOCIATION OF LAW LIBRARIES

761 McGregor, J. W. "History of the American Association of Law Libraries from 1906 to 1942." Master's thesis, University of Chicago, 1963. 160p.

Reported missing.

AMERICAN DOCUMENTATION INSTITUTE

762 Farkas-Conn, Irene S. "From Documentation to Information Science: The Origins and Early Development of the American Documentation Institute-American Society for Information Science." Doctoral dissertation, University of Chicago, 1984. 500p.

Identifies the influences, events, and activities which created the American Documentation Institute (ADI) in 1937 as an alliance of representatives from the scholarly, scientific, professional, and government communities. Watson Davis, director of science service, is credited as the visionary early leader of the ADI. Microfilm services and bibliographic projects dominated the first decade. By 1950, the journal *American Documentation* was launched and the ADI began the process of transforming itself into a professional association.

AMERICAN LIBRARY ASSOCIATION

763 Agria, John J. "The American Library Association and the Library Services Act." Doctoral dissertation, University of Chicago, 1966. 196p.

The partnership of the American Library Association (ALA) and the federal government in the formulation, passage, and implementation of the Library Services Act (LSA) is explored in this study. To achieve its goal, the ALA forged alliances with other interest groups and proved to be an adept strategist. Impact of the LSA on federal-state relations, standards, and popular control is viewed as positive.

764 Busbin, O. Mell, Jr. "A Survey of the Writings of the First Fifteen Women Presidents of the American Library Association." Specialist in Arts thesis, Western Michigan University, 1978. 124p.

The publications of the first fifteen women presidents of the American Library Association are analyzed by subject content, type of librarianship, and source. Biographical vignettes, lists of publications, and various citation breakdowns are furnished for each president. Concludes that national leadership was attained due to publishing record, occupational mobility, influence as library school educators, non-ALA elective posts, and career positions. The women presidents are Theresa W. Elmendorf, Mary W. Plummer, Alice S. Tyler, Linda A. Eastman, Josephine A. Rathbone, Gratia A. Countryman, Essae M. Culver, Althea H. Warren, Mary U. Rothrock, Loleta D. Fyan, Flora B. Ludington, Lucille M. Morsch, Frances L. Spain, Florrinell F. Morton, and Mary V. Gaver.

765 Butters, Avery J. "Concepts of Library Purpose in the Professional Works of Seven Founders of the American Library Association." Master's thesis, Catholic University of America, 1951. 57p.

Surveys the principal library concepts espoused by seven founders of the American Library Association: Thomas W. Bicknell, Charles A. Cutter, Melvil Dewey, Samuel S. Green, Frederic B. Perkins, James L. Whitney, and Justin Winsor. The purpose of the library as articulated by the founders was to serve man in "aiding him to learn, to relax, and to earn." In a densely argued analysis, the author concludes that the founders failed to acknowledge any goal beyond the vague and mundane. The "vast expectancy" of the library will only be realized through philosophical introspection and rejection of its naturalistic course.

766 Clement, Evelyn G. "Audiovisual Concerns and Activities in the American Library Association, 1924-1975." Doctoral dissertation, Indiana University, 1975. 171p. UMI# 76-11,411.

The audiovisual activities of the American Library Association, from the formation of Committee on Relations between Libraries and Moving Pictures in 1924 to the demise of the Audiovisual Committee in 1975, are chronicled in this interpretive history. During 1940s and 1950s, the Audiovisual Committee secured several foundation grants and promoted concerns within the ALA and in libraries. Efforts were hampered, however, by poor communication, jurisdictional confusion, and organizational complexity. By 1975 audiovisual activities were so dispersed through ALA that the committee was discontinued.

767 Elliott, Ella M. "Federal Relations of the American Library Association, 1930-1940." Master's thesis, University of Chicago, 1946. 75p.

The relationship between libraries and the federal government, which began in 1816 with the exemption of libraries from import duties on books, is studied here. The author emphasizes the period 1930-1940, when the ALA was actively involved with the federal government. Most efforts were aimed at securing advantages for libraries, but the lack of a coordinated ALA program hampered the efficiency of the work. Three appendices are included: 1) ALA boards and committees involved in federal relations, 1930-1940; 2) statements by ALA representatives at hearings on copyright bills; and 3) ALA activities related to the federal government, 1930-1940.

768 Hale, Charles E. "The Origin and Development of the Association of College and Research Libraries, 1889-1960." Doctoral dissertation, Indiana University, 1976. 294p. UMI# 77-10,937.

The College Library Section of the American Library Association (ALA), the predecessor of the Association of College and Research Libraries (ACRL), was organized in 1890. This study is a history of the division's growth and accomplishments. Originally representing librarians from large academic libraries, the membership devoted much attention to the mechanics of academic librarianship and avoided external relationships. From 1922 to 1939, ACRL cooperated more closely with ALA and concerned itself with standards, surveys, and education for librarianship. Between 1940 and 1960, ACRL addressed such issues as reorganization, democratization, autonomy, and federation.

769 Hanson, Eugene R. "Cataloging and the American Library Association, 1876-1956." Doctoral dissertation, University of Pittsburgh, 1974. 485p. UMI# 74-19,520.

This study opens with a brief history of cataloging before the founding of the American Library Association (ALA) and follows with a comprehensive treatment of cataloging interest groups and major issues considered at annual meetings. Librarians formed the Catalog Section in 1900 and this unit became the Division of Cataloging and Classification in 1941. Recurring issues discussed at the annual meetings in terms of frequency: 1) administration (cooperative/centralized cataloging, personnel, economics); 2) development of rules; and 3) general ramifications (history, research, etc.). Both units, concludes the author, have fulfilled their functions as discussion forums and stimulators of interest and activities.

770 Koch, Charles W. "A History of the American Association of

School Librarians, 1950-1971." Doctoral dissertation, Southern Illinois University, 1976. 870p. UMI# 76-28,753.

This "sanctioned" history of the American Association of School Librarians (AASL), a division of the American Library Association (ALA), centers on five themes: 1) responses to educational needs; 2) development of policies and standards; 3) philosophy of school librarianship; 4) furtherance of professionalism; and 5) cooperative endeavors within ALA units and educational organizations. The alienation of school librarianship resulted in an identity crisis which diverted AASL efforts from professional activities to governance concerns. It has attempted, for the most part, to carry out its activities independently of ALA.

771 Kraske, Gary E. "The American Library Association in the Emergence of U.S. Cultural Diplomacy, 1938-1949." Doctoral dissertation, Columbia University, 1983. 498p. UMI# 8311849. Published: Greenwood Press, 1985.

The American Library Association (ALA) played a significant role in the establishment of an official U.S. cultural relations program with other nations, which began with the creation of the State Department's Division of Cultural Relations in 1938. Forming a partnership with the federal government and philanthropic trusts, the ALA became the leading exponent for books and libraries in the U.S. and abroad. Major programs included the establishment of libraries in foreign countries, especially Latin America; the provision of library materials to foreign institutions; and support for professional training.

772 Molz, Redmond K. "National Planning for Library Service, 1935 to 1975: From the National Plan to the National Program." Doctoral dissertation, Columbia University, 1976. 195p. UMI# 77-255. Published: American Library Association, 1984.

National planning for library service emerged in the depth of the great depression with the publication of *A National Plan for Libraries* by the American Library Association (ALA) in 1935. Socioeconomic planning at the federal level stimulated ALA leaders such as Carl H. Milam, Carleton B. Joeckel, and Louis Round Wilson to define American librarianship in terms of a coordinated system serving the educational, recreational, and educational needs of all Americans. Post-WW II planning, including the crusade for federal funds, and establishment of the National Advisory Commission on Libraries in the 1960s are reviewed.

773 O'Loughlin, Sister M.A.J. "The Emergence of American Librarianship: A Study of Influences Evident in 1876." Doctoral dissertation, Columbia University, 1971. 269p. UMI# 74-8201.

Significant events of 1876 in American librarianship included publication of the monumental *Public Libraries in the United States of America*, issuance of Charles A. Cutter's *Rules for a Printed Catalog* and Melvil Dewey's classification, founding of the American Library Association, and the appearance of the *Library Journal*. In addition to Cutter and Dewey, Justin Winsor, William F. Poole, Frederick Leypoldt, and Richard R. Bowker deeply influenced the convergence of events which ushered in the modern era of librarianship.

774 Pond, Patricia K. "The American Association of School Librarians: The Origins and Development of a National Professional Association for School Librarians, 1896-1951." Doctoral dissertation, University of Chicago, 1982. 2 vols. 824p.

This study traces the origins of the American Association of School Librarians (AASL), the only national professional association for school librarians in the United States. Special emphasis is placed on issues which faced the school library field and the role of National Education Association, the National Council of Teachers of English, and the American Library Association in promoting school library service. Concepts from the sociological literature and the historical method are applied to the school library movement and its associational growth.

775 Roper, Dewitt F. "The American Library Association Subscrip-

tion Books Committee and Its Influence on Encyclopedia Publishing, 1930-1958." Master's thesis, Florida State University, 1960. 123p.

The Subscription Books Committee is analyzed in terms of its membership, method of operation, reaction to sales practices, and relations with publishers. More than one-half of the committee members were public librarians from the northeast and midwest. The committee emphasized continuous revision, yearbooks, and copyright in its deliberations. Lists of recommended encyclopedias and those titles not recommended are appended.

776 Thomison, Dennis V. "The History and Development of the American Library Association 1876-1957." Doctoral dissertation, University of Southern California, 1973. 457p. UMI# 73,18,846. Published: American Library Association, 1978.

The American Library Association (ALA) is the country's major national library organization. Slow growth, lack of grass roots involvement, and financial strains occurred during the early decades. Major accomplishments include the development of library standards and the strengthening of library education. The ALA presidency became subordinate to the permanent secretary and tensions periodically surfaced between ALA and its divisions. Programs, organizational structure, and conferences are highlighted throughout the narrative.

777 Whalum, Claire G. "A Content Analysis of American Library Association Presidential Inaugural Addresses, 1940-1964." Master's thesis, Atlanta University, 1969. 48p.

Of the 25 ALA presidents who served during this period, 17 were men and 8 were women. Midwesterners dominated, with 9 of the presidencies. Addresses are analyzed in terms of references to the ALA and to the profession. The cooperative relationships and the structure of the ALA received consistent attention. Professional issues most frequently mentioned were the insufficient number of trained librarians, low salaries, inadequate library funding, and lack of cooperative endeavors.

778 Young, Arthur P. "The American Library Association and World War I." Doctoral dissertation, University of Illinois, 1976. 315p. UMI# 77-9246. Published: *Library Quarterly* 50 (1980): 191-207; Beta Phi Mu, 1981.

Shortly after the American declaration of war in 1917, the American Library Association (ALA) created the Library War Service under the direction of Herbert Putnam, Librarian of Congress. Between 1917 and 1920, ALA raised $5 million from public donations, erected 36 camp library buildings, distributed 10 million books, and sponsored 1,200 library workers. Service locations included domestic camps, Europe, and naval ships. Censorship, Americanization, reading interests, hospital libraries, and relations with other social welfare agencies are highlighted. Prominent librarians in the Library War Service were Herbert Putnam, Carl Milam, Frank Hill, McKendree Raney, Burton Stevenson, and Caroline Webster.

779 Zubatsky, David S. "'No Book Should Be Out of Reach': The Role of the American Library Association in the Sharing of Resources for Research, 1922-1945." Doctoral dissertation, University of Illinois, 1982. 526p. UMI# 8218602.

This study provides an overview of interlibrary cooperation in the U.S. between 1876 and 1945, an assessment of the American Library Association's (ALA) role in resource sharing during 1922-1945, and an analysis of major issues. Topics include cooperative acquisitions, subject specialization, and bibliographical and physical access. ALA's most conspicuous success related to national union lists, interlibrary loan codes, cooperative cataloging, and regional evaluations of library resources. Microphotography is cited as a failure.

AMERICAN LIBRARY INSTITUTE

780 Piper, Sister Tressa. "The American Library Institute, 1905-1951: An Historical Study and an Analysis of Goals." Specialist paper, University of Wisconsin, 1975. 142p.

In 1904, the American Library Association (ALA) approved the establishment of a separate organization to be named the American Library Institute (ALI). Former presidents of the ALA served as charter members of the ALI, a group of senior leaders who met to discuss significant library problems and issues. Melvil Dewey was a catalyst in the group's formation. The ALI often held meetings in conjunction with ALA conferences. Only 221 Fellows were elected during the ALI's existence as an organization. Most members perceived of the ALI as an honor society and did not participate in its activities. The ALI's goals, conferences, publications, membership, and constitution are treated in considerable detail.

AMERICAN MERCHANT MARINE LIBRARY ASSOCIATION

781 Michelson, Aaron I. "The American Merchant Marine Library Association—Its History and Functions." Master's thesis, Western Reserve University, 1950. 53p.

The American Merchant Marine Library Association was established by Mrs. Henry Howard in 1921. Its origin was prompted by the American Library Association, which had supplied free books to seamen aboard American vessels during World War I. The ALA transferred to the Association some 65,000 volumes and about $5,000 in unexpended funds. In 1924 over 18,000 books were circulated by the Association. In the next decade financial difficulties struck the Association and in 1937 only 163 books were circulated. During World War II circulation jumped greatly—768,500 books and 1,500,000 magazines were distributed to 3,874 ships in 1945.

AMERICAN THEOLOGICAL LIBRARY ASSOCIATION

782 Mehl, Warren R. "The Role of the American Theological Library Association in American Protestant Theological Libraries and Librarianship, 1947-1970." Doctoral dissertation, Indiana University, 1973. 226p. UMI# 73-23, 026.

This study of the American Theological Library Association (ATLA) focuses on the various programs of support for librarians and libraries. Guidance for librarians has covered such areas as library functions, buildings, and personnel. In regard to libraries, ATLA has developed standards, produced the *Index to Religious Periodical Literature*, and promoted various collection development strategies.

ASSOCIATION OF AMERICAN LIBRARY SCHOOLS

783 Davis, Donald G., Jr. "The Association of American Library Schools: An Analytical History." Doctoral dissertation, University of Illinois, 1972. 574p. Published: Scarecrow Press, 1974.

The Association of American Library Schools (AALS) was founded in 1915, and since then has frequently been criticized as being inactive and ineffective in shaping the role of library education in this country. This study has four purposes: 1) to reconstruct the history of the Association from 1915 to 1968; 2) to analyze its role in education for librarianship; 3) to compare the relative goal attainment of the AALS with similar professional bodies; and 4) to describe the ways in which other associations have approached problems similar to those faced by the AALS.

CATHOLIC LIBRARY ASSOCIATION

784 Dunleavy, Sister Consolata M. "The History of the Catholic Library Association, 1921-1961." Master's thesis, Catholic University of America, 1964. 130p.

This study is mainly concerned with an analysis of the achievements of the Catholic Library Association (CLA). The author lists five major characteristics that have led to the independent and progressive nature of the CLA: 1) the foresight and zeal of the founding fathers; 2) interest and initiative of later executives; 3) organization and cooperation; 4) well-planned publications and activities; and 5) a constitution and by-laws that were revisable and expandable. The author also lists the presidents and many other officials of the CLA.

785 Ross, Sister M. Collete. "A Study of the Catholic Library Association Based on Presidential Addresses Made During the Years 1931-1956." Master's thesis, University of Texas, 1958. 137p.

After presenting a concise history of the Catholic Library Association (CLA), the author analyzes the presidential addresses made to the Association from 1931-1956. This analysis is used to identify the objectives and needs of the CLA, describe the Catholic librarian as portrayed by the presidents, and compare the CLA with the American Library Association for the first 25 years in the life of each association, and also during the 25 years in question.

CONNECTICUT LIBRARY ASSOCIATION

786 Marchesseault, Rose E. "A History of the Connecticut Library Association 1891-1955." Master's thesis, Catholic University of America, 1959. 134p.

Beginning in 1891 with a membership of 30 librarians and annual dues of 50 cents, the Connecticut Library Association became a strong professional advocate for the membership and the cause of library development. Records the speeches, activities, and influence of the association. Continuing concerns included professional standards, extension of service, legislative relations, and support of the American Library Association. Among those who served as president may be noted Addison Van Name, Caroline Hewins, Fremont Rider, and David Clift.

DISTRICT OF COLUMBIA LIBRARY ASSOCIATION

787 Seabrook, Martha. "A History of the District of Columbia Library Association, 1894-1954." Master's thesis, Catholic University of America, 1957. 128p.

Traces the history of the District of Columbia Library Association (DCLA) from its founding in 1894 as the Washington Librarians' Club, with 23 members, to 1954. One of the original founders of the group was A.R. Spofford, the Librarian of Congress. The author describes the DCLA's development from 1898, with emphasis on its activities, publications, and relations with the ALA. A chronological list of DCLA publications from 1894 through 1954 is included.

ILLINOIS ASSOCIATION OF SCHOOL LIBRARIANS

788 Cox, Dorothy J. "The Illinois Association of School Librarians: A History." Doctoral dissertation, Southern Illinois University, 1975. 334p. UMI# 76-26, 935.

The Illinois Association of School Librarians and its influential role in the development of school libraries and school librarianship from 1922-1972 is reviewed. The constitution, executive board, finances, and publications are examined in depth. Relations with other professional associations, dissemination of school library ideas, and the formulation of standards and certification requirements receive extensive treatment.

MEDICAL LIBRARY ASSOCIATION

789 Donovan, Margaret J. "Presidential Addresses to the Medical Library Association, 1890-1965; A Thematic Analysis." Master's thesis, Catholic University of America, 1968. 155p.

The purpose of this thesis is to view the growth and changing interests of the Medical Library Association by means of the presidential address, and to determine the nature of change in the educational background and professional status of the presidents. The study includes abstracts of all the presidential addresses which were published as well as biographical data for each person. The addresses are examined thematically and include consideration of the organization of the Association, acquisition materials, organization of the collection, cooperation between libraries, and recruitment and education of medical librarians.

790 Maggetti, Mary T. "The Medical Library Association: Its History and Activities, 1898-1953." Master's thesis, Drexel Institute of Technology, 1955. 43p.

Records briefly the history of the Medical Library Association from its founding in 1898 to the year 1953, including a review of its activities. Special emphasis is placed on the Medical Library Exchange and on the Association's efforts to develop standardization and certification for medical librarians.

MISSOURI ASSOCIATION OF SCHOOL LIBRARIANS

791 Burr, Catherine R.M. "Missouri Association of School Librarians: 1950-1975." Doctoral dissertation, Saint Louis University, 1981. 264p. UMI# 8207389.

An introductory chapter traces the development of Missouri school libraries from 1850 to 1950. The Missouri Association of School Librarians is then examined in terms of goals, organization, officer committees, programs, finances, and publications. State standards have been upgraded due to the unified voice of the Association. The author recommends constitutional revision, cooperative relationships, and legislative workshops.

MUSIC LIBRARY ASSOCIATION

792 Bennett, Janice P. "The Music Library Association 1931-1956." Master's thesis, Western Reserve University, 1957. 23p.

This paper brings together all available material on the Music Library Association and its influence on music librarianship in America. Founded in 1931, at the instigation of Carleton Sprague Smith of the New York Public Library, the Music Library Association had grown to nearly 900 members in 1956. The author surveys noted activities and projects of the Association, such as its *Checklist of Thematic Catalogues*. Important publications, such as the *List of Subject Headings*, *Code for Cataloging*, and the official periodical *Notes*, are discussed.

793 Morroni, June R. "The Music Library Association, 1931-1961." Master's thesis, University of Chicago, 1968. 74p.

The author applies qualitative and quantitative tests, utilizing both historical and sociological data. The early origins of the Association are examined, the organization's structure is analyzed, and the Music Library Association's relation with other library associations is considered.

SOUTHWESTERN LIBRARY ASSOCIATION

794 Walker, Mary J.D. "The Southwestern Library Association, 1922-1954." Master's thesis, University of Texas, 1959. 222p.

Describes the development of the Southwestern Library Association from its establishment in 1922 through 1954. Emphasis is placed on description and analysis of the factors that contributed to its formulation, administration, activities, and problems. Little attention is devoted to the contributions of individual leaders in the Association.

SPECIAL LIBRARIES ASSOCIATION

795   Hendrickson, Ruth M. "The Rio Grande Chapter of the Special Libraries Association." Master's thesis, University of Texas, 1962. 72p.

The first several chapters of this paper deal with the events that led to the organization of the Rio Grande Chapter in 1956. The author finds that the major stimulus was the establishment and expansion of government libraries in New Mexico following World War II. The concomitant increase in research placed greater demands on these small libraries, and the other libraries of the state held little promise of being able to help. The librarians banded together in a special library association to discuss their particular problems and to develop means of cooperation. The chapter was officially recognized in 1956, becoming the 31st member of the Special Libraries Association.

TENNESSEE LIBRARY ASSOCIATION

796   Easterly, Ambrose. "The Tennessee Library Association's First Fifty Years, 1902-1951." Master's thesis, George Peabody College for Teachers, 1954. 119p.

The author is concerned with the history of the Tennessee Library Association (TLA) from its beginnings in 1902 through 1951. Consideration is given to an analysis of the Association's beginnings, objectives, and accomplishments. The paper concludes with recommendations for increasing the TLA's effectiveness as a professional association.

797   Findlay, Stephen M. "The Tennessee Library Association, 1950-1975." Master's thesis, University of Tennessee, 1978. 207p.

This analytical study is framed around four propositions: 1) the Tennessee Library Association (TLA) failed to influence library planning in the state from 1950 to 1975; 2) the TLA did not cooperate with the Tennessee State Library and Archives; 3) the TLA was ineffective in efforts to secure funding from the state legislature; and 4) the enumerated failures were attributable to a lack of continuity in the administration of the TLA. The propositions were supported by the evidence. A series of recommendations are tendered to remedy the problems noted.

TEXAS LIBRARY ASSOCIATION

798   Kell, Beatrice F. "An Analysis of Texas Library Association Membership and Officers, 1902-1956." Master's thesis, University of Texas, 1956.

This study is concerned with an analysis and interpretation of factual changes in membership of the Texas Library Association; changes in the status of the divisional members; and the pattern of office-holding and membership representation, 1902-1956. The author finds that as the Texas Library Association grew, the direction and determination of its policy shifted from the membership as a whole to a selective executive board, and that there often tended to be little communication between the board and the members.

799   McClaren, Dorothy N. "The First Ten Years of the Teenage Library Association of Texas, 1949-1959." Master's thesis, University of Texas, 1966. 65p.

School librarians in Texas found it difficult to recruit student library assistants in the face of competition from other school activities. As a result they founded, in 1949, an association for student library assistants which was intended to make the library assistant's job more appealing. The author discusses the establishment, organization, leadership and membership, objectives, programs, and accomplishments of the Teenage Library Association, 1949-1959. The organization was found to have met with enthusiastic response from librarians and students alike, and by 1959 nearly 6,000 students from Texas junior and senior high schools were members.

800 Prassel, Martha A. "Some Notes Toward a History of the Texas Library Association, 1902-1909." Master's thesis, University of Texas, 1967. 55p.

This study is not a formal history, but is instead intended as a critical essay on the sources for such a history. The author discusses the many manuscript and printed sources of information on the history of the Texas Library Association, and concludes with appendices containing a chronology, a roster of important individuals, and facsimile of the Texas Library Association's original constitution.

X. BIOGRAPHICAL STUDIES

AHERN, MARY E.

801 Mulac, Carolyn M. "'Librarian Militant': Mary Eileen Ahern and *Public Libraries.*" Master's Thesis, University of Chicago, 1978. 46p.

The first section of this study recounts the life and career of Mary Eileen Ahern. The remainder of the study is devoted to a content analysis of *Public Libraries*, a journal edited by Ahern.

ASPLUND, JULIA B.

802 Honea, Ann B. "Julia Brown Asplund: New Mexico Librarian, 1875-1958." Master's thesis, University of Texas, 1967. 58p.

This study outlines Asplund's significant contributions to New Mexico library development. She was employed as a librarian for only seven of her 53 years of service to New Mexico libraries. She taught library school at Drexel, and directed the new library at the University of New Mexico (1901-1905). In 1929 she was employed to organize the State Library extension service. She resigned in 1932. During the years between and after her employment as a librarian she worked aggressively for libraries in New Mexico through a number of women's groups. She was the founder of the New Mexico Library *Bulletin*, a major force in the early years of the New Mexico Library Association, and a major power behind the rise of the Santa Fe Public Library.

BAKER, AUGUSTA

803   Merriman, Maxine M. "Augusta Baker: Exponent of the Oral Art of Storytelling; Utilizing Video as a Medium." Doctoral dissertation, Texas Woman's University, 1983. 257p. UMI# 8401210.

Augusta Baker, master storyteller and longtime children's librarian at the New York Public Library, is the subject of this experimental study. The author sought to: 1) determine if there was a correlation between a storyteller's personality and style, and types of stories selected for telling; 2) examine the premise that a live audience has an impact on the quality of telling stories; and 3) preserve Baker's style and philosophy by producing a videotape. The study consists of background material on past storytellers, a biographical sketch of Baker, material on the techniques of storytelling, and a one-hour videotape of Baker telling two stories.

BATCHELDER, MILDRED L.

804   Anderson, Dorothy J. "Mildred L. Batchelder: A Study in Leadership." Doctoral Dissertation, Texas Woman's University, 1981. 404p. UMI# 820173.

Investigates the life and work of Batchelder, with emphasis on philosophy, leadership style, and impact on the profession. Batchelder was the first school library specialist on the staff of the American Library Association, where she served for 30 years (1936-1966). In addition to her work with school libraries, Batchelder devoted much time to audiovisual materials, intellectual freedom, and international relations.

BISHOP, WILLIAM W.

805   Sparks, Claud G. "William Warner Bishop." Doctoral dissertation, University of Michigan, 1967. 677p. UMI# 68-7732.

William Warner Bishop (1871-1955) was a major force in twentieth century American librarianship. He attained his greatest prominence as director of the University of Michigan Library from 1915-41, and as founder and director of the University of Michigan Department of Library Science, 1926-40. Sparks analyzes Bishop's multi-faceted contribution to the development of American librarianship, including his many published writings and his involvement in professional library organizations.

BLACK LIBRARIANS

806 Rhodes, Lelia G. "A Critical Analysis of the Career Backgrounds of Selected Black Female Librarians." Doctoral dissertation, Florida State University, 1975. 251p. UMI# 75-26810.

This collective biography of 15 black female librarians who held or hold top administrative posts in various types of libraries utilizes oral history to identify career patterns. Major findings: born in the south; 64 years old; attended top schools; middle class background; majored in liberal arts; and librarianship not primary. Recommends additional study of minority librarians.

BLUE, THOMAS F.

807 Wright, Lillian T. "Thomas Fountain Blue, Pioneer Librarian, 1866-1935." Master's thesis, Atlanta University, 1955. 59p.

Thomas Fountain Blue was one of the first Negro library leaders. In 1905 he was named head of the colored branch of the Louisville Free Public Library. From then until 1935 he provided leadership for his own library and also contributed to branch library development in this country. He pioneered in the apprentice training of Negro library assistants and was one of the first organizers of Negro librarians.

BOOTH, MARY J.

808 Lawson, Richard W. "Mary Josephine Booth: A Lifetime of Service, 1904-1945." Doctoral dissertation, Indiana University, 1975. 193p. UMI# 76-2850. Summary published: *Illinois Libraries* 60 (1978): 504-10.

Mary Josephine Booth served as director of the Eastern Illinois University Library from 1904-1945. She was a leader among normal school librarians and clearly in advance of her time in such areas as elementary school librarianship, reference service, and the provision of free and inexpensive educational materials. She held offices in the Illinois Library Association, the American Library Association, and the National Education Association.

BOSTWICK, ARTHUR E.

809 Cunningham, Larry L. "Contributions of Arthur Elmore Bostwick to the Library Profession." Master's thesis, Indiana University, 1962. 95p.

Bostwick is recognized as one of the outstanding figures in American library history and this study pinpoints his ideas on library science and their influence on the development of American librarianship. Bostwick was director of the St. Louis Public Library from 1909 to 1938; the author of numerous books, the most important of which was *The American Public Library*; president of several state library associations and the American Library Association; and a member of the editorial staff of such reference works as the Funk and Wagnalls *Standard Dictionary*. A bibliography of Bostwick's published work is included.

BUFFINGTON, WILLIE L.

810 Carr, Louise D. "The Reverend Willie Lee Buffington's Life and

Contributions to the Development of Rural Libraries in the South." Master's thesis, Atlanta University, 1958. 53p.

In 1931 Reverend Buffington decided to ask for donations of books for Negro pupils in the South. Since his total assets were 10 cents, he was able to mail an appeal to only five people. One person, the Rev. Lorenzo H. King of New York, responded, and several months later over 1,000 books arrived in barrels. There were more than were needed for a school library, so the Rev. Buffington decided to build a school library. With help from the residents of Edgefield, South Carolina, on December 31, 1932 the first of his Faith Cabin Libraries was opened. He went on to establish 26 more libraries in South Carolina and 55 in Georgia.

BUTLER, SUSAN D.

811 Bolden, Ethel E. M. "Susan Dart Butler — Pioneer Librarian." Master's thesis, Atlanta University, 1959. 31p.

Susan Dart Butler, aware of the deficiencies in public library service for Negroes in the South, was instrumental in getting financial assistance from the Julius Rosewald Fund to aid in the establishment of a library for Negroes in Charleston, North Carolina. In 1931 the library was opened and from that date until 1957 she served as its librarian. In 1952 the library, called the Dart Hall Branch Library, circulated some 150,000 volumes. This paper describes her efforts to improve library service to Negroes in Charleston.

CASSEL, ABRAHAM H.

812 Heckman, Marlin L. "Abraham Harley Cassel: Nineteenth-Century American Book Collector." Doctoral dissertation, University of Chicago, 1971. 207p.

Abraham Cassel (1820-1908) was an important American book collector who was most active between 1840-1880. Cassel, a wealthy Pennsylvania farmer and book collector, amassed a collection of some 80,000 items prior to 1880. The author assesses Cassel's book collecting activities, his efforts to make his library available to others, and the dispersal of his collection.

CURRY, ARTHUR R.

813 Winship, Sheila G. "Arthur Ray Curry: A Biography." Master's thesis, University of Texas, 1966.

This study traces the life of Arthur Ray Curry, a graduate of the University of Illinois. After several years as an assistant librarian at the University of Oklahoma he became, in 1923, executive secretary of the Public Library Commission. In 1925 he became director of the Texas Christian University Library. From that time until 1955 he held a variety of positions in Texas, including supervisor of the statewide WPA Library Project.

CUTTER, CHARLES A.

814 Little, Agnes E. "Charles Ammi Cutter, Librarian at Forbes Library, Northampton, Massachusetts, 1894-1903." Master's thesis, University of North Carolina, 1962. 55p.

This biography of Charles Ammi Cutter, one of the greatest American librarians, covers his career as director of the Forbes Library in Northampton from 1894-1903. The author believes that these years were the most personally rewarding of Cutter's life. The four chapters of this paper provide: 1) a brief historical sketch of Northampton; 2) a discussion of the activities and writings of Cutter before he joined the Forbes Library in 1894; 3) Cutter's theories of library management as seen through his administration of the Forbes Library; and 4) a summary of his work at Forbes.

815 Miksa, Francis L. "Charles Ammi Cutter, 1837-1903." Master's thesis, University of Chicago, 1970. 107p.

See next entry.

816 Miksa, Francis L. "Charles Ammi Cutter: Nineteenth-Century Systemizer of Libraries." Doctoral dissertation, University of Chicago, 1974. 2 vols. 893p. Published, in part: Libraries Unlimited, 1977.

This study of Charles Ammi Cutter (1837-1903) ranks him as a commanding figure in nineteenth-century American librarianship. Cutter served in the Harvard College Library (1860-1868), directed the Boston Athenaeum (1869-1893), and headed the Forbes (Massachusetts) Library from 1894 to 1903. He was prominent in the affairs of the American Library Association, corresponded with Melvil Dewey and Richard R. Bowker, and wrote extensively for the *Nation* and *Library Journal.* Cutter's crowning achievement was the *Rules for a Dictionary Catalog*, a work which enhanced access to recorded knowledge and provided the concept of the modern dictionary catalog.

817 Morse, Clarence R. "A Biographical, Bibliographical Study of Charles Ammi Cutter, Librarian." Master's thesis, University of Washington, 1961.

The first part of this study briefly traces Cutter's life from his birth in 1837 to his death in 1903. Cutter was librarian of the Boston Athenaeum for 25 years, and later he was director of Forbes Library at Northampton. The second part of this paper is a chronological listing of some 100 articles by Cutter that appeared in *The Nation* and the *North American Review.* All of the articles, 90 in *The Nation* and three in the *North American Review*, are annotated.

DANA, JOHN C.

818 Cohen, Lucille G. "John Cotton Dana's Library Services for Children in Springfield, Massachusetts." Master's thesis, Southern Connecticut State College, 1966. 88p.

This study reviews John Cotton Dana's efforts to establish children's services at the Springfield Public Library, 1898 to 1902. Dana, who had established one of the earliest children's rooms in the country in Denver in 1894, introduced a number of changes at Springfield. He abolished age limitations for borrowers' cards, separated juvenile literature from adult, provided a special "corner" for children, compiled reading lists for children, and allowed teachers to borrow large numbers of books for classroom libraries. These innovations greatly increased circulation, and Dana's descriptions of children's work in the literature of librarianship were influential in spreading the idea of services to children in American public libraries.

819 Hauserman, Dianne D. "John Cotton Dana: The Militant Minority of One." Master's thesis, New York University, 1965. 79p.

This study highlights the contributions made by John Cotton Dana to the American museum and to reveal the role which he played in support of American contemporary art expression. Chapters cover the social and educational aspects of the museum, the museum as opposed to contemporary art from 1905-1929, and industrial and applied art. Some comments are made concerning Dana's work in the library field.

DAVIS, MARY G.

820 Sword, Elizabeth D. "Mary Gould Davis: Her Contribution to Storytelling." Master's thesis, Southern Connecticut State College, 1972. 69p.

Mary Gould Davis served as the supervisor of storytelling in the

New York Public Library from 1922 to 1944. Davis, a gifted storyteller, author, and reviewer, energized the storytelling program at the New York Public Library. Attendance increased from 47,335 in 1922 to 136,000 in 1944. She wrote nine books, edited a review column for the *Saturday Review of Literature*, and lectured at several library schools.

DAVIS, RAYMOND C.

821 Abbott, John C. "Raymond Cazallis Davis and the University of Michigan General Library, 1877-1905." Doctoral dissertation, University of Michigan, 1957. 315p. UMI# 58-1370.

The first part of this study is devoted to Davis' life, from his birth in 1836 until his death in 1919. In 1868 he was named assistant librarian at the University of Michigan and in 1877 he was named head librarian. Part two is a history of the library during Davis' reign as director, 1877-1905. Davis was faced with numerous difficulties, most serious of which were lack of funds and problems with the catalog. His interest in public services prompted him to institute a credit course in bibliography (the first in this country) in 1883.

DEWEY, MELVIL

822 Haynes, Beulah G. "Melvil Dewey." Master's thesis, George Peobody College for Teachers, 1932. 96p.

This study brings together published facts concerning the career of Melvil Dewey, especially his contributions to education, library service, and business efficiency. There are seven chapters: early years; Decimal Classification; library promoter; Columbia Library School; Dewey as administrator (secretary to the University of the State of New York and State Librarian); Lake Placid Club; and time-saving devices (e.g. simplified spelling).

823 Lee, Michael M. "Melvil Dewey (1851-1931): His Educational Contributions and Reforms." Doctoral dissertation, Loyola University of Chicago, 1979. 309p. UMI# 7910342.

This study examines Dewey's educational ideas, and the social milieu in which they flourished. Dewey's commitment to adult education and simplification are highlighted. His various positions in the American Library Association and the Metric Bureau are discussed. His contributions in the areas of library development and education for librarianship are considered incomparable. Among these achievements may be noted library associations, school libraries, university extension, winter sports, professional education, and service for the blind.

DOWNS, ROBERT B.

824 Suen, Ming Tung. "Robert Bingham Downs and Academic Librarianship." Master's thesis, Southern Connecticut State College, 1967. 75p.

The author assesses Robert Bingham Downs' contributions to academic library development from 1926 to 1967. Downs has been director of libraries at Colby College, University of North Carolina, New York University, and the University of Illinois. He served as president of the Illinois Library Association and the American Library Association. A bibliography of Downs' published work is included.

EASTMAN, LINDA A.

825 Phillips, Cecil O. "Linda Anne Eastman; Librarian." Master's thesis, Western Reserve University, 1953. 46p.

Reported noncirculating.

826 Wright, Alice E. "Linda A. Eastman: Pioneer in Librarianship." Master's thesis, Kent State University, 1952. 83p.

This biography of Linda A. Eastman emphasizes her pioneering efforts on behalf of American librarianship. Eastman served the profession for 43 years. From 1918 to 1938 she was librarian of the Cleveland Public Library. The author devotes chapters to areas where Eastman's influence was great, especially work with the blind, divisional plans in libraries, and adult education.

ELLIOTT, LESLIE R.

827 Benson, Stanley H. "Leslie Robinson Elliott: His Contributions to Theological Librarianship." Master's thesis, University of Texas, 1965. 91p.

Leslie R. Elliott served as the librarian of the Fleming Library, Southwestern Baptist Theological Seminary, from 1922 to until his retirement in 1957. Under his directorship the collections expanded from 8,000 volumes to over 130,000 volumes. Elliott was committed to the library as an educational force throughout his career. His principal external accomplishments included consulting on several dozen library buildings and selection as the first president of the American Theological Library Association. He is considered by many as the pioneering dean of Texas theological librarianship.

EVANS, CHARLES

828 Holley, Edward G. "Charles Evans, American Bibliographer." Doctoral dissertation, University of Illinois, 1961. UMI# 61-04311. Published: University of Illinois Press, 1963.

The first part of this study deals with Evans the librarian. After working under W.F. Poole at the Boston Athenaeum, Evans became director of the Indianapolis Public Library when he was only 22. Holley traces Evans' frustrating library career from that time until 1901, when he was dismissed from his library post at the Chicago Historical Society and decided to devote the rest of his life to his *American Bibliography*. Evans was one of the founders of the American Library Association in 1876, and in 1877 he attended the first international Conference of Librarians in London. The second part of this study deals with his career as a bibliographer.

FOGARTY, JOHN E.

829 Healey, James S. "The Emergence of National Political Leadership For Library Development: The Case of Representative John E. Fogarty." Doctoral dissertation, Columbia University, 1973. 195p. UMI# 76-16,357. Published: Scarecrow Press, 1974.

John E. Fogarty, Democratic member of Congress from Rhode Island, exerted a major influence on federal library legislation during the period 1956-1966. Before entering Congress, Fogarty worked as a bricklayer. His early legislative interest was in the area of public health. Librarians in Rhode Island sensitized Fogarty to the needs of libraries and he championed the use of federal funds to support libraries. In recognition of his significant contribution to the welfare of libraries, the American Library Association bestowed the award of honorary member in 1966.

FOIK, PAUL J.

830 Bresie, Mayellen. "Paul J. Foik, C.S.C., Librarian-Historian." Master's thesis, University of Texas, 1964. 168p.

After briefly sketching Father Foik's early life and education, from his birth in 1879 to 1912, the author deals with his library career. From 1912 to 1924 he served as librarian at Notre Dame, and from 1924 to 1941 he served as librarian at St. Edward's University in Austin, Texas. Father Foik's leadership in establishing the Catholic Library Association, the initiation of the *Catholic Periodical Index*, and his many activities as a Catholic historian are also discussed. A bibliography of his extensive writings is included.

FRANKLIN, BENJAMIN

831 Korty, Margaret B. "Benjamin Franklin and Eighteenth-Century American Libraries." Master's thesis, Catholic University of America, 1964. Published: *Transactions of the American Philosophical Society* (New Series), 55 (1965); and *Journal of Library History* 2 (1967): 271-328.

Describes Franklin's extensive influence on American library development, which began with his establishment of America's first social library in 1731. Besides describing Franklin's efforts on behalf of the Library Company of Philadelphia, the author analyzes his many other library activities: 1) trustee of the Loganian Library; 2) contributor to the libraries of Harvard and Yale; 3) founder of the American Philosophical Society and builder of its library collections; 4) a founder of the Pennsylvania Hospital, home of the first Medical Library in America; and 5) contributor of a library to the town of Franklin, Massachusetts, which eventually evolved into the town's public library.

FRANKLIN, LOUISE

832 Pettigrew, Claudie L. "Louise Franklin: The Education of a Texas Librarian." Master's thesis, University of Texas, 1967. 182p.

This thesis is concerned with the education and professional development of Louise Franklin, a staff member at the Houston Public Library for 40 years (1921-1961). During most of this time she served as head of reference and circulation. However, in tracing Franklin's professional career the author also presents detailed discussions of the University of Texas Department of Library Science, the Houston Public Library, and the Texas Library Association. Appendices include "University of Texas,

Department of Library Science: A History," and "Documents and Records pertaining to the Department of Library Science."

GOODWIN, JOHN E.

833   Salinas, Anna. "John Edward Goodwin: University Librarian." Master's thesis, University of Texas, 1966. 68p.

The author presents, in seven chapters, a biography of John Edward Goodwin, who in a span of nearly 40 years directed both the University of Texas and UCLA Libraries. After working at Stanford, Goodwin became the librarian at the University of Texas in 1944. The author details his administration of these two libraries, and also discusses his significant contribution to professional associations. He served as president of the Texas Library Association, and was active in California and in the American Library Association.

GOREE, EDWIN S.

834   Porter, Margaret L.R. "Edwin Sue Goree, A Biography." Master's thesis, University of Texas, 1965. 118p.

Chronicles the 50-year career of Edwin Sue Goree (1884-1961), who served in a variety of library positions, mostly in Texas. She began as a library assistant at the University of Texas Library, joined the ALA Library War Service, directed the Sante Fe Public Library, served as library organizer with the Texas State Library, worked as executive secretary of the Texas Library Association, accepted a position with the San Antonio Public Library, directed the U.S. Naval Air Station Library at Corpus Christi, and retired as librarian of the Burnet County Free Library. She was prominent in the Texas extension library movement and fought for improved local and state funding.

GRAHAM, BESSIE

835 Campbell, Mildred M. "Bessie Graham, Bibliophile." Master's thesis, Texas State College for Women, 1953. 71p.

Bessie Graham is familiar to all librarians as the author of the *Bookman's Manual.* This paper is divided into two major sections, a biographical study and a chronological analysis of her writings. Bessie Graham attended the Drexel Library School in 1910, and in 1914 she began teaching a course "about books" in the William Penn Evening School. She later taught courses in bibliography at the New York Public Library. She published the first edition of the *Bookman's Manual* in 1921, the same year she became librarian of the Apprentice's Library of Philadelphia. She resigned in 1924 to go to Temple University as head of the Library Science Department, remaining there until 1940. A bibliography of her extensive writings is appended.

GREEN, SAMUEL S.

836 Trombley, Sister M. Francis X. "Samuel Swett Green: His Contribution to the Worcester, Massachusetts, Free Public Library." Southern Connecticut State College, 1972. 51p.

Samuel Swett Green, library pioneer and innovator, served as the director of the Worcester Free Public Library from 1871 to 1909. During this period Green transformed the library "from a semi-private collection of books into a great educational institution." He opened the library on Sundays, promoted cooperation with the schools, used pictures to promote interest in art, established children's and young adult rooms, and introduced interlibrary loan. The author credits Green as either contributor to or initiator of virtually every modern library practice.

GROTHAUS, JULIA

837 Drummond, Donald R. "Julia Grothaus, San Antonio Librarian." Master's thesis, University of Texas, 1964. 100p.

The author traces the life of Grothaus from her birth, through high school, to college at Southwest Texas State Normal School, the University of Tennessee, and the University of Illinois Library School. In 1922 she was named assistant librarian at the San Antonio Public Library, and in 1933 she became its director, a position she held for over 20 years. She instituted many new services there, including the first bookmobile service in the city, the first integrated library service, in-service training for librarians, and an audio-visual department. Her many difficulties with local censors and her courageous defense of the freedom to read in San Antonio is discussed. She served as president of the Texas Library Association, 1940-1941.

GUNTER, LILLIAN

838 Nichols, Margaret I. "Lillian Gunter: Pioneer Texas County Librarian, 1870-1926." Master's thesis, University of Texas, 1958. 81p.

Lillian Gunter was a leader of Texas librarians from 1914 to 1926. She began her career by transforming a small subscription library into the Gainsville Public Library, which she directed for 10 years. She became interested in rural library service and in 1915 drafted the County Free Library Bill. The bill proved ineffective, and in 1919 she fought successfully for its amendment. This success remains her greatest achievement. In 1920 she established and directed the Cook County Library. She was active in the Texas Library Association. This study emphasizes her efforts to establish good rural library service in Texas.

HANSON, J.C.M.

839 Scott, Edith. "J.C.M. Hanson and His Contribution to Twentieth Century Cataloging." Doctoral dissertation, University of Chicago, 1970. 695p.

J.C.M. Hanson (1864-1943), "the dean of American catalogers," will best be remembered for his work on the Anglo-American Cataloging Code and the concomitant standardization of cataloging practice which has since then characterized American libraries. Scott traces Hanson's life with heavy emphasis on his many and varied contributions to cataloging theory and practice.

HARRISON, ALICE S.

840 Herring, Billie G. U. "Alice S. Harrison: Pioneer School Librarian, 1882-1967." Master's thesis, University of Texas, 1968. 115p.

Alice Sinclair Harrison was the first school librarian appointed to serve in the Austin, Texas school system. She worked as a leader in school library development in Austin and throughout the state for 35 years.

HEWINS, CAROLINE M.

841 Deksnis, Alma. "Caroline Maria Hewins: Pioneer in the Development of Library Service for Children." Master's thesis, Southern Connecticut State College, 1959. 58p.

Caroline Hewins joined the library profession at a time when library service for children was in its developmental stages. Her first library job brought her under the tutelage of William F. Poole at the Boston Athenaeum. In 1875 she became librarian of the Young Men's Institute of Hartford, Connecticut, and served there for some 50 years. In 1893 the library became the Hartford Public Library, and in 1904 she persuaded city officials to provide a separate children's room. A founder of the Connecticut Library Association in 1891, she was recognized as a national leader in the field of children's librarianship. Hewins was also a prolific and influential writer.

HOOLE, WILLIAM S.

842 Hoole, Martha D. "William Stanley Hoole, Student-Teacher-Librarian-Author." Master's thesis, Florida State University, 1958. 78p.

The author treats her subject in two parts. The first is a biography while the second is an analysis of Hoole's written contributions. Hoole was born in 1903, was graduated from Wofford College, South Carolina, in 1924, and began teaching high school English the same year. In 1934 he earned a doctor's degree from Duke University. In 1935 he became director of the Phillips Library at Birmingham-Southern College in Alabama. From 1937 to 1939 he served as head of the Baylor University Library and in 1939 he became librarian at North Texas State College. In 1944 he was named Director of Libraries at the University of Alabama. Hoole is one of the most published librarians.

IDESON, JULIA B.

843 McSwain, Mary B. "Julia Bedford Ideson, Houston Librarian, 1880-1945." Master's thesis, University of Texas, 1966. 133p.

A detailed study of the professional career of Julia Bedford Ideson, who served as director of the Houston Public Library for 42 years (1903-1945).

JEFFERSON, THOMAS

844 Peden, William H. "Thomas Jefferson: Book Collector." Doc-

toral dissertation, University of Virginia, 1942. Portions published: *William and Mary Quarterly* 1 (1944): 265-72; *Ibid.* 6 (1949): 631-36.

Analyzes Jefferson's voracious book collecting habits and traces the development of his three libraries, the second of which was sold to the Congress of the United States in 1815.

LEYPOLDT, FREDERICK

845   Beswick, Jay W. "The Work of Frederick Leypoldt, Bibliographer and Publisher." Master's thesis, Columbia University, 1941. 102p. Reprinted: R.R. Bowker, 1942.

Frederick Leypoldt (1835-1884) was a versatile nineteenth-century American publisher and bibliographer who also exerted a significant influence on the development of modern librarianship. A publisher in Philadelphia and then New York, Leypoldt moved into the bibliographic arena with the *Literary Bulletin* in 1868, a monthly listing of American and foreign books. Under his direction the *Publishers' Weekly* appeared in 1872 and the monumental *American Catalog, 1876* in 1881. He launched the *American Library Journal* in 1876. Active in library affairs, he was a founding member of the American Library Association and served as a councillor in the 1880s.

LOWE, JOHN A.

846   O'Flynn, Mary E. "John Adams Lowe: Administrator and Library Planner." Master's thesis, Drexel Institute of Technology, 1955. 46p.

The author treats Lowe's library career in four parts: 1) a summary chapter on his life; 2) Lowe's view on the public library in the community; 3) Lowe as a planner of library buildings; 4) his work after retirement. After receiving his college degree, Lowe served as librarian at Williams College, 1910-1915; Assistant City

Librarian in Brooklyn, 1919-1931; and director of the Rochester Public Library, a position he held for some 20 years (1932-1952). Lowe was also active in library association affairs, both state and national, and gained a reputation as a building planner and administrator. A bibliography of his writings is included.

McDIARMID, ERRETT W.

847 McCulley, Kathleen M. "Dr. Errett Weir McDiarmid's Application of His Philosophy of Library Administration in the University of Minnesota Library, 1943-1951." Master's thesis, University of North Carolina, 1963. 84p.

This study of E.W. McDiarmid, librarian at the University of Minnesota and later Dean of the College of Science, Literature and the Arts at the University of Minnesota, is an effort to ascertain how he introduced and carried out his philosophy of library administration. His philosophy is drawn from his many publications and includes the methods he advocated. No attempt is made at critical analysis, but the author attempts to show how an experienced library administrator must have a definable and flexible philosophy to do his job correctly.

MACDONALD, ANGUS S.

848 Baumann, Charles H. "The Influence of Angus Snead MacDonald and the Snead Bookstack on Library Architecture." Doctoral dissertation, University of Illinois, 1969. 374p. UMI# 70-00787. Published: Scarecrow Press, 1972.

For 40 some years, Angus Snead MacDonald (1883-1961) served as president of Snead and Company, specialists in the design and erection of library bookstacks. Baumann outlines Snead's seminal role in introducing the "modular" library and the convertible stack, elements which led to the construction of much more flexible libraries after World War II.

MANN, HORACE

849 O'Connell, John J. "Horace Mann's Influence on School Libraries in Massachusetts." Master's thesis, Massachusetts State College, 1934. 49p.

Horace Mann's vigorous advocacy of the common-school library during his term (1837-1849) as secretary of Massachusetts State Board of Education is delineated in this study. Mann popularized the idea of school libraries through lectures, articles, and annual reports. His arguments included the paucity of available books, the value of reading to a progressive society, and the role of books in keeping children out of mischief. Between 1839 and 1849 the number of volumes in the state's common-school libraries increased from 10,000 to 91,539 volumes.

MILAM, CARL H.

850 Sullivan, Peggy. "Carl H. Milam and the American Library Association." Doctoral dissertation, University of Chicago, 1972. 488p. Published: American Library Association, 1976.

This study deals with the career of Carl H. Milam, who was the secretary and later executive secretary of the American Library Association from 1920 to 1948. The opening chapter recounts the Association's history from 1876 to 1920. Milam's career as student, university librarian and assistant director of ALA's Library War Service in World War I is treated in the second chapter. Milam's 28 years at ALA headquarters are the subject of the majority of the study. A final chapter deals with his life from 1948 until his death in 1963, a period during which he served as librarian of the United Nations Library in New York.

MONTI, MINNIE S.

851 Hershey, Frederick E. "Minnie Sweet Monti: Her Life and

Influence." Master's thesis, Western Reserve University, 1957. 41p.

This study traces Minnie Sweet Monti's life from her birth on March 22, 1888, to her retirement as order librarian at the Cleveland Public Library in 1956. She was graduated from Western Reserve University in 1908 and then joined the order department at the Cleveland Public Library. In 1950 she was named head of the order department. This paper deals mainly with her labors at Cleveland.

MOORE, ANNE C.

852   Akers, Nancy M. "Anne Carroll Moore; A Study of Her Work with Children's Libraries and Literature." Master's thesis, Pratt Institute, 1951. 49p.

Anne Carroll Moore, a pioneer in children's library work, became in 1896 the first children's librarian at the Pratt Institute Free Library in Brooklyn. Ten years later she became the first superintendent of work with children at the New York Public Library. Moore remained there for 45 years and through example and published writings greatly influenced the development of children's work in America. A bibliography of her publications on librarianship is included.

853   Poor, Anne M. "Anne Carroll Moore: The Velvet Glove of Librarianship." Master's thesis, Southern Connecticut State College, 1966. 122p.

The purpose of this study is to reveal the personality of a famous librarian and her influence on growth and creativity in the field of children's literature. The four sections of the thesis cover: 1) the biographical sketch of Anne Moore; 2) the contributions of Moore as a professional librarian; 3) the influence of Moore's personality on authors and illustrators; and 4) the achievements and significance of her work.

MUDGE, ISADORE G.

854 Waddell, John N. "The Career of Isadore G. Mudge: A Chapter in the History of Reference Librarianship." Doctoral dissertation, Columbia University, 1973. 354p. UMI# 73-29,871.

Isadore G. Mudge (1875-1957) is rated the most successful figure in American reference librarianship due to her editing of the *Guide to Reference Books* and her administration of the reference department at the Columbia University Library from 1911 to 1941. After securing the approval of her superiors, Mudge transformed a passive reference operation into a dynamic, sophisticated service. Her contribution to library education and involvement with the *Guide* are fully examined.

OHIO STATE LIBRARIANS

855 Cohen, Sidney. "Biographical Data on the Librarians of the Ohio State Library, 1817-1960." Master's thesis, Kent State University, 1961. 120p.

This paper contains short biographical sketches of the 28 librarians who have served the Ohio State Library.

OWEN, THOMAS M.

856 Ketchersid, Arthur L. "Thomas McAdory Owen: Archivist." Master's thesis, Florida State University, 1961. 77p.

Thomas M. Owen died in 1920, but his pioneering efforts in archive organization and development are still recognized as highly authoritative. The author traces his life, with special emphasis on his efforts on behalf of historical archives in the South. His major achievement was the creation and development of the Alabama Department of Archives and History. This department set a pattern for archival organization that has been copied extensively throughout the nation.

PATTEN, FRANK C.

857 Jordan, Melbourne. "Frank Chauncy Patten: the Galveston Years." Master's thesis, University of Texas, 1966. 101p.

Frank Chauncy Patten (1855-1934) was a member of the first graduating class of Dewey's library school at Columbia. From 1903 to 1934 he served as director of the Rosenburg Library in Galveston, Texas. Patten, a scholar and one-time student at Harvard, emphasized services designed to aid serious study in his library. Patten also pioneered in several areas, including open stacks and public lectures in the library; and he was responsible for the construction of the first Negro branch in the country.

PEARSON, EDMUND L.

858 Hyland, Laura. "An Interpretation of Edmund Lester Pearson—Librarian Extraordinary, to Which Is Added a Bibliography of His Works." Master's thesis, Carnegie Institute of Technology, 1952. 62p.

This study of Edmund Lester Pearson, librarian, bookman, mystery writer, and wit, places emphasis on Pearson the bookman and author. Pearson never made a great dent on the American library profession, but he was one of those wonderful, rare types who loved books, read them, wrote them, reviewed them—in short, lived them. His *Old Librarians' Almanac* stands as one of the wittiest spoofs on librarianship ever written. Pearson liked to laugh at the "old librarians" and garnered considerable enmity in the process. The author includes a bibliography of Pearson's work.

PIERCE, CORNELIA M.

859 Brisley, Melissa A. "Cornelia Marvin Pierce: Pioneer in Library Extension." Master's thesis, University of Chicago, 1967. Summary published: *Library Quarterly* 38 (1968): 125-53.

Cornelia Marvin Pierce (1873-1957) was a leading figure in library affairs in the West during the first quarter of the 20th century. A graduate of the Armour Institute Library School directed by Katharine Sharp, Cornelia Marvin Pierce served briefly in Wisconsin before she moved to Oregon in 1905 to become head of the Oregon State Library, a post she held with distinction for 24 years.

POOLE, WILLIAM F.

860 Williamson, William L. "William Frederick Poole and the Modern Library Movement." Doctoral dissertation, University of Chicago, 1959. Published: Columbia University Press, 1963.

When the idea of the public library began to develop in the latter half of the 19th century, one man stood out as the acknowledged leader—William Frederick Poole, a pioneer and a highly influential American librarian. Poole's library career led him from the Boston Athenaeum, 1856-1868, to the directorship of the new Cincinnati Public Library, 1869-1873, to the first directorship of the new Chicago Public Library, 1874-1886, and finally to the directorship of the Newberry Library in Chicago, 1887-1894. His most significant publication was Poole's *Index to Periodical Literature*, a forerunner of the *Readers' Guide*. Poole also served as president of the American Library Association and the American Historical Association.

POWER, EFFIE L.

861 Becker, Margaret B. "Effie Louis Power: Pioneer in the Devel-

opment of Library Services for Children." Master's thesis, Western Reserve University, 1950. 76p.

In the first three chapters the author surveys library service to children before 1900, traces the early history of public library service to children at the Cleveland Public Library, and analyzes work with children as it was presented at the annual meetings of the American Library Association from 1889 to 1906. The next four chapters deal with Power's contributions in the varied facets of her career: 1) supervisor of children's work, St. Louis Public, 1911-1914; 2) head of the Children's Department, Carnegie Library, Pittsburgh, 1914-1920; 3) director of work with children, Cleveland Public Library, 1920-1937; and 4) author, bibliographer and compiler.

RAINES, CALDWELL W.

862 Christie, Clara C. "Caldwell Walton Raines, 1839-1906: Historian and Librarian." Master's thesis, University of Texas, 1966. 117p.

Judge Caldwell Walton Raines was a long-time State Librarian in Texas, a founder of both the Texas Library Association (1902) and the Texas Historical Association (1897), and the author of the *Bibliography of Texas*.

RICHARDSON, ERNEST C.

863 Branscomb, Lewis C., Jr. "A Bio-bibliographic Study of Ernest Cushing Richardson, 1860-1939." Doctoral dissertation, University of Chicago, 1954. 143p.

Branscomb traces Richardson's life from his birth in 1860 to his education at Amherst, and from there through his professional career. Beginning as librarian at the Hartford Theological Seminary, Princeton, he became finally a bibliography consultant at the Library of Congress. Richardson was able to exert much influence through his personal contacts, made as president of

ALA, 1904-1905, as chairman of numerous committees of the American Historical Society, and as vice president, 1906-1909, of the Bibliographical Society of America. His first paper appeared in 1883 when he was 23 and his last (the 230th) appeared in 1939. His *Classification Theoretical and Practical* (1901) is highly respected. His work in library history—*Beginnings of Libraries* (1914), *Biblical Libraries* (1914), *Some Old Egyptian Libraries* (1911)—is still read.

RODEN, CARL B.

864 Adkins, Marjorie R. "Carl Bismarck Roden and the Chicago Public Library." Master's thesis, University of Chicago, 1979. 96p.

Carl B. Roden served as director of the Chicago Public Library for 32 years (1918-1950), a period described by many as the "golden years." During his tenure, the Chicago Public Library advanced from a collection of 882,566 volumes and 48 branches to a 2.2 million volume collection distributed over 58 branches. The library's dramatic growth and Roden's "style" of leadership are the central themes of this study.

ROGAN, OCTAVIA F.

865 Banks, Kalani. "Octavia F. Rogan, Texas Librarian." Master's thesis, University of Texas, 1963. 151p.

This biography traces the early life and professional career of Octavia Rogan, a leading figure in Texas library history. Rogan, educated at the University of Texas and the University of Illinois Library School, entered library work in 1911. She served the State Library for 16 years, finally being promoted to State Librarian. In 1927 she left the State Library but continued her work in libraries for some 30 years, most notably with the Houston Public Library, the Texas A & M University Library, and the University of Texas

Library. Her leadership in professional associations is also covered.

ROOT, AZARIAH S.

866 Tucker, John M. "Librarianship as a Community Service: Azariah Smith Root at Oberlin College." Doctoral dissertation, University of Illinois, 1983. 231p. UMI# 84100661.

Azariah Smith Root served as librarian of Oberlin College from 1887 to 1927. He built the largest college library collection in America, taught courses in library use, and administered the Oberlin Public Library beginning in 1908. At Oberlin, Root assumed many nonlibrary duties. Other professional activities included lecturing in library schools, service in professional organizations, and library consulting. Root succeeded as a librarian because he articulated the values of his various communities and functioned as a reconciler of opposing views. Finally, Root is judged an exemplary leader of his day rather than a library trailblazer.

SABIN, JOSEPH

867 Jensen, Gary D. "Joseph Sabin and His Dictionary of Books Relating to America." Doctoral dissertation, George Washington University, 1980. 342p. UMI# 8023855.

Joseph Sabin, pioneer nineteenth-century bibliographer, is best known for his comprehensive bibliography of books relating to America. This study discusses the compilation of the *Dictionary*, which occupied the last 25 years of his life, and its posthumous completion. Sabin's activities as a book seller, publisher, auctioneer, and cataloger are recounted. He published the *American Bibliopolist* which evolved into a journal of literary and bibliographical merit. Sabin's contributions to the antiquarian book trade, American bibliography, and historical scholarship rate a significant place in history.

SCHEUBER, JENNIE S.

868 Taylor, Robert N. "Jennie Scott Scheuber: An Approach to Librarianship." Master's thesis, University of Texas, 1968. 143p.

A pioneering Texas librarian, Scheuber worked with libraries in Fort Worth for some 50 years from 1892-1938. The author traces her involvement from support of the establishment of the Fort Worth Public Library Association in 1892 to retirement as librarian of the Fort Worth Carnegie Library in 1938. A lengthy appendix is devoted to a consideration of Scheuber's contributions to the Texas Library Association.

SCHOMBURG, ARTHUR A.

869 Sinnette, Elinor D. "Arthur Alfonso Schomburg, Black Bibliophile and Curator: His Contribution to the Collection and Dissemination of Materials About Africans and People of African Descent." Doctoral dissertation, Columbia University, 1977. 263p. UMI# 80-17471.

Arthur Alfonso Schomburg, a Puerto Rican of African descent (1874-1938), emigrated to New York City in 1891. This study focuses on four major aspects of his career: 1) early life and involvement with the Puerto Rican and Cuban Nationalist Movement; 2) activities as a lay-historian and member of the American Negro Academy and the Negro Society for Historical Research; 3) bibliophilic contributions to the cultural phenomenon known as the Harlem Renaissance; and 4) role as curator of black collections at Fisk University and the New York Public Library.

SHARP, KATHARINE L.

870 Grotzinger, Laurel Ann. "The Power and the Dignity: Librarianship and Katharine Sharp." Doctoral dissertation, University of Illinois, 1964. UMI# 65-00821. Published: Scarecrow Press, 1966.

Katharine Sharp, 1865-1914, studied under Melvil Dewey and was an influential advocate of his philosophy of library service. The author first surveys Sharp's early life and education and then discusses her very significant contributions to library science. Sharp established and guided the Midwest's first library school, in Chicago, 1893-1897. She was then brought to the University of Illinois, where she served as director of the Library School and Librarian of the University from 1897 to 1906. It was under her direction that the University of Illinois Library School gained the first rank in its field, and her personal example brought new stature to the library profession. In 1907, after working herself to near exhaustion, she resigned to become vice-president of Dewey's New York Lake Placid Club.

SHERA, JESSE H.

871 Ruderman, Laurie P. "Jesse Shera: A Bio-Bibliography." Master's thesis, Kent State University, 1968. 84p.

Jesse Shera must rank among the two or three most prolific and influential authors to take an interest in library science. In addition to short chapters describing Dean Shera's remarkable career, the author provides a bibliography of his 200 published papers, 30 chapters in various books, and 10 books. The author provides a definitive bibliography of reviews, bibliographies, reports, speeches, and a list of his major professional activities over a 40-year period.

SHORTESS, LOIS F.

872 Theroit, Bernice C. "A Study of the Contributions of Lois F. Shortess to Louisiana's Public School Library Development." Master's thesis, University of Southwestern Louisiana, 1968. 86p.

When Lois Shortess began working at Southwestern Louisiana Institute in 1923, she was the first professionally trained librarian employed by a Louisiana College. Not long thereafter, Shortess became Louisiana's first supervisor of school libraries. Her first job was to start from scratch, since there were no functioning school libraries in Louisiana. Her efforts met with remarkable success, and it was unfortunate indeed when she was relieved of her duties in 1940 as a result of a shift in the political power structure in the state.

SONNECK, OSCAR G.

873 Moore, Daniel T. "Oscar G. Sonneck and His Contributions to Music Librarianship and Bibliography." Master's thesis, Southern Connecticut State College, 1973. 100p.

Oscar G. Sonneck (1873-1928) served as chief of the Music Division at the Library of Congress from 1902 to 1917. During this period he devised the classification scheme for music and published several critically acclaimed bibliographies. His career at the Library of Congress and subsequent employment with G. Schirmer, Inc. are described. A select list of his writings are appended.

SPOFFORD, AINSWORTH R.

874 Cole, John Y. "Ainsworth Spofford and the 'National Library.'" Doctoral dissertation, George Washington University, 1971. 170p. UMI# 72-8994. Portions published: *Journal of Library History* 6 (1971): 34-40; *Quarterly Journal of the Library of Congress* 28 (1971): 114-36; Libraries Unlimited, 1975.

Ainsworth Rand Spofford (1825-1908) served as Librarian of Congress for nearly half a century, 1864-1897. He was responsible for bringing the Library of Congress from relative obscurity to a position of unrivaled significance during his tenure. Cole analyzes Spofford's contributions with emphasis on his vision of the Library of Congress as the "National Library" of the United States.

875 Grisso, Karl M. "Ainsworth R. Spofford and the American Library Movement: 1861-1908." Master's thesis, Indiana University, 1966. 122p.

Emphasis on Spofford's leadership of the Library of Congress, and the interrelationships between Spofford and other leaders of the American library movement.

876 Miller, Charles H. "Ainsworth Rand Spofford, 1825-1908." Master's thesis, George Washington University, 1938. 58p.

This is a balanced biography of Spofford, following the future Librarian of Congress through his New England boyhood, his unsuccessful career as bookseller, publisher, and editor in Cincinnati, to the Library of Congress. In addition to covering Spofford's 40-year reign at the Library of Congress, the author presents a careful analysis of Spofford "The Litterateur," as a member of numerous literary societies and other organizations. Appended is a bibliography of Spofford's writings.

877 Schubach, Bernice W. "Ainsworth Rand Spofford and The Library of the United States." Master's thesis, Northern Illinois University, 1965. 133p.

Ainsworth Rand Spofford (1825-1908) served the Library of Congress for 47 years (1861-1908), 33 of them as director. From the beginning of his administration there was a pressing space problem, appropriations were small, and a shortage of help to handle the ever-increasing duties of the library. He increased the staff from six to 42 (1861-1896). He tightened the loopholes in the copyright law, instituted exchanges, and achieved increased appropriations. All this led to a tremendous growth in the size of the library's collection, from 63,000 items in 1861 to around 2,000,000 in 1908.

STANTON, MADELINE E.

878 Blankfort, Joelle R. "Madeline Earle Stanton and the Historical Library of the Yale Medical Library." Master's thesis, Southern Connecticut State College, 1976. 102p.

The Historical Library of the Yale Medical Library was created in 1941 through the efforts of pioneer neurosurgeon and bibliophile Dr. Harvey Cushing. His close friends, Dr. Arnold Klebs and Dr. John Fulton, also contributed their private libraries. Madeline Earle Stanton, Cushing's secretary since 1920, became secretary and then librarian of the Historical Library during the period 1941-1968. Biographical sketches of the donors, descriptions of the holdings, and services of the library are furnished. Stanton was an internationally recognized scholar and medical bibliographer. She served as an editor of the *Journal of the History of Medicine and Allied Sciences*.

TEXAS LIBRARIANS

879 Wheeler, Sally B. "Directory of Early Texas Librarians." Master's thesis, University of Texas, 1965. 58p.

Biographical information on 320 librarians who served in Texas libraries from 1850 to 1920 is presented. Information is gleaned from directories and interviews. Of the total number of entries, 50 percent are public librarians, 36 percent are college librarians, and 14 percent are school and other librarians.

TICKNOR, GEORGE

880 Turner, Harold M. "George Ticknor and the American Library Movement." Doctoral dissertation, New York University, 1972. 263p. UMI# 73-11,779.

George Ticknor's scholarly career and many contributions to the early library movement in America are highlighted in this study. Ticknor studied at Göttingen in 1815 where he mastered the techniques of modern scholarship and embraced the idea of a free library. He returned to Harvard University as a professor of Languages and then became director of the Boston Athenaeum. He built the collection and converted the Athenaeum into a circulating library. His collection of Spanish literature and history became the preeminent private library in America. Ticknor influenced the fledging Boston Public Library in 1852 to become a free library accessible by the average citizen.

TYLER, ALICE S.

881 Richardson, Cora E. "Alice Sarah Tyler: A Biographical Study." Master's thesis, Western Reserve University, 1951. 43p.

Tyler was one of the leading library educators of the early 20th century. This study divides her life into five major segments: 1) early life, education, and first position, 1859-1900; 2) Secretary of the Iowa State Library Commission, 1900-1913; 3) director and dean of the School of Library Service at Western Reserve, 1913-1929; 4) library interests and personal life; and 5) active retirement and death, 1929-1944. Tyler served as president of the Ohio Library Association, 1916-1917; president of the Association of American Library Schools, 1918-1919; and president of the American Library Association, 1920-21.

VATTERMARE, ALEXANDRE

882 Richards, Elizabeth M. "Alexandre Vattermare and His System of International Exchanges." Master's thesis, Columbia University, 1934. Summary published: *Medical Library Association Bulletin* 32 (1944): 413-48.

Vattermare, a prominent French ventriloquist turned intellectual missionary, visited the United States twice, in 1837 and 1849, and spoke convincingly on behalf of a scheme to institute a system of international exchanges. He was influential in stimulating interest in a number of public libraries—most notably the Boston Public Library.

VORMELKER, ROSE L.

883 Magner, Mary J. "The Businessman's Librarian—Rose L. Vormelker." Master's thesis, Western Reserve University, 1957. 106p.

Rose Vormelker is best known for her pioneering efforts toward establishing the Business Information Bureau (BIB) of the Cleveland Public Library. Under her guidance it rapidly became a respected source of business information. This study follows her career through the Detroit Public Library (1919-1922), the Science and Technology Division at the Cleveland Public Library (1922-1925), the White Motor Company (1925-1928), the BIB (1928-1955), to Assistant Director of the Cleveland Public Library (1955-1956), and finally to the Forest City Publishing Company. A bibliography of her extensive publications is appended.

WEST, ELIZABETH H.

884 Hester, Goldia A. "Elizabeth Howard West, Texas Librarian." Master's thesis, University of Texas, 1965. 110p.

Elizabeth Howard West was a pioneer Texas librarian (1873-1948). The most extensive part of this paper is devoted to West's career as a librarian; founder and president of the Texas Library Association; State Librarian and initiator of library service for the blind in Texas; librarian of the Texas Technical College; and a leader in the Texas public library field. Succeeding sections describe the associations she influenced, her publications (library science, American history, Spanish colonial history), and her education. The author lists and analyzes her published works.

WHITE, JOHN G.

885 Reece, Motoko B.Y. "John Griswold White, Trustee, and the White Collection in the Cleveland Public Library." Doctoral dissertation, University of Michigan, 1979. 304p. UMI# 8007818.

John White donated folklore and Orientalia books to the Cleveland Public Library in 1899. He subsequently bequeathed a library of chess and checkers volumes which is recognized as the world's premier special collection in that subject. White's relationship with the library and an analysis of his collection are emphasized.

WILLIAMSON, CHARLES C.

886 Winckler, Paul A. "Charles Clarence Williamson (1877-1965): His Professional Life and Work in Librarianship and Library Education in the United States." Doctoral dissertation, New York University, 1968. 594p. UMI# 69-11,766.

The author examines Williamson's place, influence, and impact on the development of library education and librarianship in the United States. Williamson made many important contributions to the field, but his famous report on library education, prepared for the Carnegie Corporation in 1923, is considered his most influential work. This report, entitled *Training for Library Service*, blamed many of the library profession's shortcomings on training, and argued convincingly for the establishment of formal education programs to replace the apprentice system.

WINSOR, JUSTIN

887 Boromé, Joseph A. "The Life and Letters of Justin Winsor." Doctoral dissertation, Columbia University, 1950. 655p. UMI# 1834.

Justin Winsor (1831-1897), was one of the most influential of America's librarians. In 1868 he became director of the Boston Public Library and in 1877 he resigned to become director of the Harvard University Library, a post he held until his death. Winsor was a prominent historian as well as librarian, and was active in the professional affairs of both groups serving as president of the American Library Association, 1876-85, 1897, and of the American Historical Association.

WYER, MALCOLM G.

888 Parham, Paul M. "Malcolm Glenn Wyer, Western Librarian; A Study in Leadership and Innovation." Doctoral dissertation, University of Denver, 1964. 428p.

Malcolm Glenn Wyer (1877-1965) was a prominent figure in librarianship in the Rocky Mountain area for a quarter of a century. After nearly 25 years as the head of several midwestern university libraries, Wyer moved to Denver where he became director of the Public Library (1924-1951). In addition to his leadership role in the public library field, Wyer was a prolific author and a major force in professional organizations—he served as president of the Iowa, Nebraska, Colorado, and American Library Associations. He was also dean of the University of Denver School of Librarianship (1931-1948).

XI. STUDIES OF THE LITERATURE

889 Afolabi, Michael. "The Literature of a Bibliographical Classification: A Citation Study to Determine the Core Literature." Doctoral dissertation, Indiana University, 1983. 204p. UMI# 8401557.

A total of 4,631 citations were identified from the period 1960-1980 to identify the following elements in the literature of bibliographical classification: a) core journals cited; b) core papers cited; c) core authors cited; and d) characteristics of the cited literature by format, language, subject, and age. Findings revealed six core journals and citation of monographs (57%) over journals (31%). Concludes that there is a strong number of core journals, but a weak core literature.

890 Allanson, Virginia L. "A Comparative and Historical Study of the *Wilson Library Bulletin*." Master's thesis, Kent State University, 1967. 159p.

This thesis is an historical examination of the *Wilson Library Bulletin*. Its purpose is to discover how effective the *Bulletin* has been in meeting the growing needs of libraries and librarians, the means by which these needs were fulfilled, and how these means have been adapted and amended over the years. The study is divided by decades, but examines the publication by editors as well. Only the first 50 years of publication are considered.

891 Bates, Phyllis N. H. "Subject Catalog Use Studies, 1953-1966." Master's thesis, University of Chigago, 1968.

Not examined.

892 Bennett, William C. "The Library in Literature of Sociology," Master's thesis, University of Texas, 1952. 164p.

This study was undertaken to test the hypothesis that the library has received little recognition in the literature of sociology. To ascertain the level of recognition, the author examined 287 books and 34 articles published during the period 1920-1950. References to the library are arranged by sociological discipline (urban, rural, general) and subdivided by type of literature (secondary textbook, college textbook, and general text). Overall, there were 694 references related to the library in 184 sociological works, an average of 3.7 references per title. Extensive discussion of the library was found in only four titles.

893 Benson, Elfrida C. "An Analysis of the Periodical Literature Relative to Book Selection in Public Libraries, 1926-1963." Master's thesis, Atlanta University, 1967.

This study analyzes the literature cited in *Library Literature* for the period 1926 through 1963 to identify the problems encountered by librarians in the selection of books for public libraries. The most frequent problems reflected in the 111 articles were limited funds, censorship, need for a book selection policy, overproduction of books, and inadequate book reviews.

894 Binkowski, Mary. "An Evaluative Survey of the Literature on Public Library Service to Business, 1925-1962." Master's thesis, Catholic University of America, 1965. 81p.

The growth of public library service to the business community is traced through an examination of the secondary literature. John Cotton Dana of the Newark Public Library established the first business branch in 1904. By 1929 there were 31 departments and branches throughout the nation and the service was secure. Between 1904 and the depression, the literature emphasized the promotion of services and collections. Following World War II, business librarians highlighted the value of the library to economic readjustment, accelerated public relations, and promoted cooperative arrangements with other libraries. An annotated bibliography of 157 items is appended.

895   Blough, Nancy L. "Histories of Some Major Library Periodicals." Master's thesis, Western Reserve University, 1955. 67p.

This study presents brief histories of 16 library periodicals: 1) *Booklist*; 2) *ALA Bulletin*; 3) *Subscription Books Bulletin*; 4) *College and Research Libraries*; 5) *Journal of Cataloging and Classification*; 6) *Serial Slants*; 7) *Bulletin of the Medical Library Association*; 8) *Special Libraries*; 9) *Catholic Library World*; 10) *American Documentation*; 11) *Publishers' Weekly*; 12) *Library Journal*; 13) *Wilson Library Bulletin*; 14) *Horn Book Magazine*; 15) *Library Quarterly*; and 16) *Library Trends*. An appendix lists the publications that index each journal and gives chronological listings of the editors for each journal.

896   Boyd, Sister Consolata. "A Survey of Literature on Adult Book - Selection Theory in American Public Libraries, 1900-1950." Master's thesis, Catholic University of America, 1956.

Six chronologically overlapping theories of book selection in the American public library are identified and evaluated: 1) universal betterment; 2) civic enlightenment; 3) group apportionment; 4) value and demand; 5) opinion reinforcement; and 6) total commitment. No theory is found acceptable as an integrating norm, and the author proposes a "composite-reader theory" based upon relevant intrinsic and extrinsic factors.

897   Brace, William. "A Citation Analysis of Doctoral Dissertations in Library and Information Science, 1961-1970." Doctoral dissertation, Case Western Reserve University, 1975. 157p. UMI# 75-19,185. Summary published: *Journal of Library and Information Science* 2 (April 1976): 216-34.

This study analyzes 20,298 citations drawn from 202 library science dissertations written during the decade of the 1960s. Citations are categorized by type of library, central focus, and type of activity. Although some authors were cited frequently, a middle core was not identified. The large number of nonlibrary science titles in the journal distribution suggests the absence of a single core of research literature.

898 Cline, Gloria S. "A Bibliometric Study of Two Selected Journals in Library Science, 1940-1974." Doctoral dissertation, University of Southern California, 1979. Portion published: *College & Research Libraries* 43 (1982): 208-32.

This study hypothesizes that articles appearing in *College & Research Libraries* and *Special Libraries* changed during the period from 1940 through 1974 from characteristics associated with the soft science to those representative of the hard science. Data are collected on 3,522 source documents. Characteristics of the source documents include core of significant contributors, sex, institutional affiliation, collaborative authorship, self-citation rates, subject, percentage of unreferenced documents, and average number of references. Lotka's law, the Bradford-Zipf distribution, and Price's Index were applied to the data. Library literature, as represented in these journals, had not completed the transformation from soft to hard science.

899 Cropper, Mary S. "An Analysis of the Literature of Law Library Administration, 1936-1968." Master's thesis, Atlanta University, 1969. 39p.

A sample of 35 articles from 8 journals was employed to identify trends in law library administration. Twenty-seven of the articles appeared in the *Law Library Journal*. Issues and types of libraries addressed in the articles are summarized. The rank order of problems is planning, cataloging, collections, personnel, reference, selection, clientele, and finances.

900 Daughtrey, Joyce A. "A Content Analysis of Periodical Literature Relating to the Certification of Librarians, 1906 to 1952." Master's thesis, Atlanta University, 1954. 117p.

The author finds that the first move toward certification of librarians came in 1906, when the Minnesota Public Library Commission issued state certificates on the basis of state examinations. The American Library Association did not take much interest in the problem until after Williamson's groundbreaking report in 1923, but from that time on the interest in certification grew. In 1952, 22 states had legal certification, 10 had voluntary certification of librarians, and 15 had no specific certification requirements. The author finds that certification has been confined mainly to secondary school librarians.

901 Dunn, Aileen. "The Nature and Functions of Readers Advisory Service As Revealed by a Survey of the Literature of the Field from 1935-1950." Master's thesis, Western Reserve University, 1950. 32p.

In the early 1920s the first readers advisory services were established. A great number of people, feeling that their education was inadequate, were turning to the library for further study. Librarians were quick to see the need for a serious form of guidance for these new readers and from this recognition came the development of the individualized readers advisory service, which sprang up all over America during the 1920s and 1930s. The author finds that this trend has been reversed since the 1940s and that many libraries had abandoned their formal attempts at reader guidance by 1950.

902 Ferguson, Richard D., Jr. "Information Science: A Bibliometric Evaluation of the Information Analysis Concept." Doctoral dissertation, Boston University, 1980. 307p. UMI# 8024186.

Bibliometric techniques were used to explore the growth of an interdisciplinary information science specialty known as information analysis. Information analysis draws upon concepts from the fields of psychology, sociology, and communication. References and citations from the information analysis literature during the period 1958-1978 were gathered and collated to identify the core literature, key indicators, and linkages between them. Comparisons between the information analysis citation network and other scientific literatures were undertaken. Concludes that polydisciplinarity is a variable which can differentiate knowledge circulation patterns.

903 Foreman, Carolyn. "An Analysis of Publications Issued by the American Library Association, 1907-57." Master's thesis, University of Texas, 1959. 199p.

Publications issued by the American Library Association (ALA) between 1907 and 1957 are analyzed according to format, form, and author, sponsor, intended users, and content. Bibliographies and pamphlet series dominate, and 20 percent of the 1,000 publications intended for librarians were directed to public libraries. Few publications addressed the area of international library cooperation. Library education and the library in society received major emphasis while the publication of research investigations was negligible. Authorship trends reveal a continuing participation of ALA subdivisions, a decline in personal authorship, and an increase in contributions by outside agencies.

904 Graham, Carolyn A. "Trends in Library Cooperation, 1921-1955: An Analysis Based on Library Literature." Master's thesis, University of Texas, 1961. 69p.

The author analyzed some 1,167 citations to papers dealing with library cooperation located under 11 subject headings in *Library Literature* from 1921 to 1955, and describes trends in the publication and emphasis of the items involved.

905 Hankins, Frank D. "The Treatment of Basic Problems in the *Library Journal*, 1900-1930." Master's thesis, University of Texas, 1951. 256p.

To ascertain the basic problems of librarianship from 1900-1930, the author analyzed all issues of the *Library Journal* for the years 1900, 1920, 1930. The author presents, with the aid of many tables, the rising and falling interests of librarians in such issues as bibliographic control, administration, book selection, and the philosophy of librarianship.

906 Hertzel, Dorothy H. "Bibliographical Approach to the History of Idea Development in Bibliometrics." Doctoral dissertation, Case Western Reserve University, 1985. 222p. UMI# 8510095.

Traces the history of the term "bibliometrics" from the expression "statistical bibliography." A prevailing theory of bibliometrics was not identified.

907 Hohman, Agnes C. "An Analysis of the Literature on the Outstanding Issues and Opinions on Censorship, 1940-1950." Master's thesis, Catholic University of America, 1951. 182p.

Examines major censorship episodes involving *Esquire* magazine and the *Nation*. Editorial opinion of the period, largely against censorship, is analyzed. The preponderance of opinion rejected censorship except for pornographic literature.

908 Jackson, Barbara. "An Evaluative Guide to the Literature about Bookmobiles, 1905-1965." Master's thesis, Catholic University of America, 1967. 128p.

The author examines the voluminous literature pertaining to bookmobiles which has appeared between 1905 and 1966. Separate chapters cover history, philosophy, operation, schedules, materials and services, staffing, physical aspects, and the role of bookmobile service. Nearly 300 items are listed in the bibliography. Proponents of the bookmobile emphasize convenience and access while opponents cite the paucity of materials and substandard service. Most of the literature is characterized as descriptive rather than analytical.

909 Kanner, Elliot E. "The Impact of Gerontological Concepts on Principles of Librarianship." Doctoral dissertation, University of Wisconsin, 1972. 167p. UMI# 72-4281.

The author sets out to measure the speed with which research-based information and concepts were transferred from gerontology to library science from 1946, when gerontology became an established discipline, to 1969. Using content analysis as the primary research technique, the author collected and analyzed the literature of library science (from 21 selected journals) in order to establish the extent to which gerontological concepts have influenced the library profession.

910 Killian, Kathleen A. "An Analysis of the Depiction of Libraries and Librarians in Novels Published Between 1965 and 1972." Master's thesis, Southern Connecticut State College, 1976. 195p.

Since novels depicting libraries and librarians contain information useful to adults in making career decisions, nine adult novels were selected for extensive analysis. Evaluative categories used to rate the portrayal in the novels were employment, training, personal qualities, advancement, conditions of work, salary, and employment outlook. Overall, the novels presented a neutral portrait of the library profession. There was no correlation between extent of treatment and the degree of favorability toward the profession.

911 Knutson, Gunnar S. "Content Analysis of Obituaries of Prominent Librarians Recorded in the *New York Times*, 1884-1976." Master's thesis, University of Chicago, 1981. 112p.

Not examined.

912 Kuehn, Clara-Louise. "Catholic Library Practice in the United States, 1930-1949: An Annotated and Classified Bibliography." Master's thesis, Catholic University of America, 1958. 155p.

The author has compiled an extensive annotated bibliography covering the literature of Catholic librarianship for the period 1930-1949. Just over 500 entries are arranged under key headings: general, education, technical services, reader services, library associations, libraries in parochial schools, and special libraries.

913 Landram, Christina O. "A Study of the Changing Concept of American Librarians as Reflected in the Novels of the Twentieth Century." Master's thesis, Texas State College, 1951. 93p.

This study evaluates the hypothesis that there was a change in the image of the librarian as expressed by 20th-century novelists. To see if the librarians who were portrayed in the early part of the century were different from those portrayed in later years, the author located 36 novels in which a librarian was the major character. The results of this historical survey showed that novelists had pictured librarians as young, attractive, single women in most cases. The greatest changes came in the areas of education, specialized training, interest in the profession, and satisfaction in work.

914 Lane, Nancy D. "Characteristics Related to Productivity Among Doctoral Graduates in Librarianship." Doctoral dissertation, University of California, Berkeley, 1975. 264p. UMI# 76-718.

Using a population of 289 graduates who received doctorates in librarianship between 1930 and 1969, this study analyzes the rate of publication activity following graduation and correlated antecedent variables with post-doctoral productivity. Findings indicate that 38% of the doctoral graduates did not publish subsequent to the dissertation, and 73% published four or less times. Application of a predictive statistical model disclosed that the total count of publications and productivity were related most strongly to the number of pre-doctoral publications and number of years elapsed between receipt of the B.A. and Ph.D.

915 Lehnus, Donald J. "Milestones in Cataloging, 1835-1969: An Attempt at an Objective Approach to the Growth of a Subjective Literature." Doctoral dissertation, Case Western Reserve University, 1973. 346p. UMI# 74-10,804. Published: Libraries Unlimited, 1974.

A citation analysis of cataloging works was employed to define a network of 7,209 citations of 2,532 works written by 1,412 authors. A further analysis was applied to 184 works which were cited 8 or more times. Publication dates of the works ranged from 1841 to 1964. A biographical study of the 125 most frequently cited authors revealed that a "chain of contacts existed among 115 of the authors, confirming the 'invisible college' concept of key figures in a field." Classics could be identified by combining citation duration with citation frequency.

916   Long, Lucille E. "The Stereotyped Librarian as Portrayed in Modern American Belles-Lettres." Master's thesis, Kent State University, 1957. 93p.

The many facets of the stereotypical librarian depicted in belles-lettres are explained in this study. Characteristics of the librarian stereotype are described as old maidish, high morals, devoted to work, bookish, routine work, territorial, shy, and noncompetitive. These characteristics appear frequently in the genres of fiction, poetry, short story, essay/oration, and drama. Dozens of works are cited which document the reclusive and tepid demeanor of the librarian. An extensive bibliography of the cited literature secondary sources is appended.

917   Maddox, Lucy J. "Trends and Issues in American Librarianship as Reflected in the Papers and Proceedings of the American Library Association, 1876-1885." Doctoral dissertation, University of Michigan, 1958. 590p. UMI# 58-7763.

The decade from 1876 to 1885 is generally considered the beginning of the modern library movement in America. The techniques and philosophy of librarianship projected then are still widely accepted, and few radical departures from that early period can be found. During that decade the most discussed library subject was cataloging and classification, and the author reviews the six major systems developed. Among other significant topics treated are the rise of public library service for adults; library building problems; cooperative ventures; library legislation; and circulation systems. The author also evaluates the contributions of leading librarians during this decade such as Dewey, Poole, Winsor, Cutter, Green, and Sanders.

918 Nation, Margaret A. "The Librarian in the Short Story: An Analysis and Appraisal." Master's thesis, Florida State University, 1954. 55p.

Forty short stories published between 1900 and 1945 which feature a librarian are examined. Plot summaries and details of librarian characters/library settings are furnished for each story. Twenty-five of the stories are attributed to Edmund Lester Pearson. Overall, the stereotypical image of the librarian predominates: bookworm, versatile, fanatic, spinster, "glamour girl," and nondescript. Libraries are often tangential to the story and their appearance frequently adds a scholarly veneer to an otherwise plebeian tale. The author concludes that the fictional portrait of librarianship remains drab and that the stories do not convey an authentic image of the profession.

919 Neal, Peggy. "Library Problems, 1876-1886; An Analysis of 'Notes and Queries' in 'Library Journal' and 'Proceedings of the American Library Association.'" Master's thesis, Carnegie Institute of Technology, 1954.

Reported missing.

920 Nelson, Mary N.B. "Analysis of the *Texas Library Journal* and Its Predecessor, *News Notes*." Master's thesis, University of Texas, 1958. 184p.

The official publication of the Texas Library Association is examined for the years 1924-1957. A separate chapter is devoted to each of three major periods of development: *News Notes* (1924-1931, 1932-1949) and *Texas Library Journal*, 1950-1957. Chapters include an analysis of editorials, contributions, and news sections. For the first two decades, public librarians dominated the editor's position and news of the association/regional libraries took precedence. Beginning in 1950 more scholarly articles appeared. Twenty-five tables complement the text.

921 O'Connor, Mary A. "Dissemination and Use of Library Science Dissertations in the Periodicals Indexed in the *Social Sciences Citation Index.*" Doctoral dissertation, Florida State University, 1978. 223p. UMI# 7909785.

The extent to which library science dissertations were disseminated and used by authors who published articles in library science and other social science journals is analyzed. Library science dissertations dating from 1925 to 1975, 1,206 in all, were searched in the *Social Sciences Citation Index* volumes for 1970-1975. A total of 789 citations were located to 312 of the dissertations. Library science journals provided 88 percent of the citations, and articles constituted 43 percent of the source items. The subject category of history received the greatest number of cited dissertations.

922 Palmer, Roger C. "Contributor Affiliation and Nature of Contribution Content in U.S. Journal Articles from the Fields of Law, Library Science, and Social Work, 1965-1974." Doctoral dissertation, University of Michigan, 1978. 150p. UMI# 7813717.

Journal articles from the established profession of law and the emerging professions of library science and social work were analyzed to determine bibliometric similarities and differences. The data base consisted of 253 law articles, 297 library science articles, and 393 social work articles. Social work was found to be closer to law in its citation patterns than library science. Women authors are underrepresented in the literature of social work and library science. Law and social work professors contributed twice the volume of articles to their journals as do professors of library science.

923 Peirce, Patricia. "A Study of the Philosophy of Librarianship; A Review of the Relevant Literature, 1930-1950." Master's thesis, Drexel Institute of Technology, 1951. 46p.

A historical and critical review of what was written in the professional literature (1930-1950) about the philosophy of librarianship. An extensive bibliography of such writings is included.

924 Peritz, Bluma C. "Research in Library Science as Reflected in the Core Journals of the Profession: A Quantitative Analysis (1950-1975)." Doctoral dissertation, University of California, Berkeley, 1977. 223p. Portion published: *Library Research* 2 (1980): 251-68; and 3 (1981): 47-65.

Research literature appearing in 39 English language core journals is studied to ascertain methodology, type of library investigated, affiliation of the author, citation characteristics, subject content, and relationship to the philosophy and practice of librarianship. Papers seem to be more process-oriented than client-oriented, and they are more directed toward the professional community than with other groups. Empirical studies written by practitioners dominate the literature, and the average number of citations per paper was lower than other social science disciplines.

925 Rehfus, Ruth O. and Eugene I. Stearns. "The *Library Quarterly*, 1931-1966; An Index With Commentary." Master's thesis, Kent State University, 1967. 267p.

The purpose is to study the *Library Quarterly* using the content analysis method. The goal is to present the *Quarterly* as a reflection of major trends in the field of library science during the period covered. An author, title, and subject index to the *Quarterly's* content accounts for the bulk of this thesis.

926 Schmidt, Valentine L. "The Development of Personnel Selection Procedures and Placement Services in the Professional Staffing of the Library, 1935-1959." Master's thesis, University of North Carolina, 1960. Published: Association of College and Research Libraries Microcard, Number 128.

Based on an analysis of the published literature on the subject, this study is broken down into chapters dealing with such matters as qualification requirements, interviews, employer recruiting, and formal placement services.

927 Scott, Richard P. "A Survey of the Literature on the Financial Aspects of Libraries in the Institutions of Higher Education in the United States, 1926-1956." Master's thesis, Catholic University of America, 1958. 90p.

The financial component of academic library literature is identified and analyzed in this annotated, 253-item bibliography. Books, articles, and theses related to the following topics are included: importance of financial resources, administration of funds, sources of funds, expenditures, and minimum standards. Author, subject, and title indexes are appended.

928 Sparks, Claud G. "Presidential Addresses Made to the American Library Association, 1876-1951: A Content Analysis." Master's thesis, University of Texas, 1952. Published: Association of College and Research Libraries Microcard, Number 131.

This analysis of the major ideas to be found in the presidential addresses to the American Library Association from 1876 to 1951 illustrates the most important issues facing the profession during those years. Such topics as "What a Librarian Should Be" got emphasis before 1930, while most addresses after that year were oriented towards "Libraries and Their Organization." The topic of professional associations was also found to be a frequent subject of presidential addresses.

929 Speiden, Virginia M. "The Image of the Librarian as Seen in Eight Library Career Novels." Master's thesis, University of North Carolina, 1961. 43p.

Not examined.

930 Thomas, Ritchie D. "An Evaluation and Analysis of the Literature on the Newspaper Library, 1900-1957." Master's thesis, Catholic University of America, 1959. 94p.

This bibliographical essay identifies, arranges, and summarizes the literature of newspaper libraries. Articles, books, and theses are included. Separate chapters are devoted to history, administration, classification and filing, indexes, reference collections, and descriptions of individual libraries. Principal findings are that classification and indexing schemes lack uniformity, that the public service role is controversial, and that new storage and retrieval techniques are emerging.

931 Wagner, Marjorie K. "Music Librarianship in the United States, 1876-1955: An Annotated, Classified Bibliography." Master's thesis, Catholic University of America, 1957. 77p.

The secondary literature of music librarianship is recorded in this classified, partially annotated bibliography. Books and articles from 45 journals are cited. Arrangement is by topic, subdivided by year of publication. A list of 37 theses is also included. An author - subject index to the entries rounds out the volume.

932 Wilson, Eunice C. "A Study of Articles on Librarianship in Non-Library Periodicals from 1947 through 1951." Master's thesis, Atlanta University, 1953. 108p.

This study identifies 516 articles derived from four nonlibrary indexes. Articles are analyzed in terms of source journals, area of librarianship, and chronological appearance. Approximately 35% of all articles pertain to school libraries.

XII. CENSORSHIP AND FREEDOM OF INFORMATION

933   Bartlett, Lynne E. "Censorship in the McCarthy Era." Master's thesis, University of Chicago, 1977.

Not examined.

934   Boyer, Paul S. "The Vice Society Movement and Book Censorship in America, 1873-1933." Doctoral dissertation, Harvard University, 1966. Published: Scribner, 1968.

Not examined.

935   Curry, William L. "Comstockery: A Study in the Rise of Censorship with Attention Particularly to the Reports of the New York Society for the Suppression of Vice, to Magazine Articles and to News Items and Editorials in the *New York Times*, Supplementing other Standard Studies on Comstock and Censorship." Doctoral dissertation, Columbia University, 1957. 279p. UMI# 57-2805.

Censorship as espoused by Anthony Comstock and the New York Society for the Suppression of Vice, especially in the late nineteenth century, cannot be explained by a single cause. All of the following variables contributed to censorship: Puritanism, Victorian prudery, fear of changing times, growth of cities, influx of immigrants and alien ideas, and admiration of the entrepreneurs who supported censorship. Future episodes will probably not be directed at communism or obscenity, but rather the violence of juvenile delinquency.

936 Fulchino, Stephen A. "'The Right to Know' and the Library: A Case History in the Popularization of a Slogan." Master's thesis, University of Chicago, 1974. 107p.

The "right to know" slogan was introduced during the 1973 protest over zero-funding of library programs by the federal government. This study explores the origins of the phrase in 1945 and documents its popularization by the media and politicians. Content analysis is used to identify qualitative changes in meaning and context over the years.

937 Line, Bryant W. "A Study of Incidents and Trends in the Censorship of Books Affecting Public and School Libraries in the United States 1954-1964". Master's thesis, Catholic University of America, 1965. 249p.

This study is a comprehensive account of censorship activities during the period 1954-1964. Government censorship, through the Post Office and Customs Bureau, is documented. Key court cases, titles under attack, and various pro-censorship groups are discussed. Over the years, the judicial branch has issued progressively more permissive rulings. The author found a shift from political to moral censorship and noted that librarians are now responsible for the ideological content of collections as well as physical custody.

938 McCoy, Ralph E. "Banned in Boston: The Development of Literary Censorship in Massachusetts." Doctoral dissertation, University of Illinois, 1956. 349p. UMI# 56-3020.

Frustrated by the ascending power of the Irish Catholic immigrant in Boston politics, old-line Protestant families launched a Puritan crusade against the excesses of the "dreadful decade." It is in this setting that the New England Watch and Ward Society was founded in 1878. The group became a powerful force for suppressing literature and sponsored strict obscenity laws. In 1882 the Boston edition of Walt Whitman's *Leaves of Grass* was suppressed. Relief was provided by H.L. Mencken's successful fight to distribute the *American Mercury*. Massachusetts eventually learned to balance the excesses of puritanism and democracy.

939 Smith, V. James. "The Freedom of Information Act of 1966: A Legislative History." Master's thesis, University of Chicago, 1979. 106p.

This study traces the legislative history of the Freedom of Information Act from its origins in the Administrative Procedures Act of 1946 to 1966. The 1966 Act specifies the responsibilities of the federal government with respect to the right of U.S. citizens to government information.

940 Woods, Lemuel B. "Censorship Involving Educational Institutions in the United States, 1966-75." Doctoral dissertation, University of Texas, 1977. Published: Scarecrow Press, 1979.

Censorship incidents in the 1960s and 1970s are analyzed from data located in the *Newsletter on Intellectual Freedom*, published by the American Library Association. A set of questions constitutes the framework of the study, e.g. when, where, how many, and reasons for the censorship attempts. A major increase in the number of incidents was noted from 1966 to 1975. High schools reported the most episodes and more than half of the attempts in all settings were successful.

XIII. AMERICAN INFLUENCE ABROAD

941   Brewster, Beverly J. "An Analysis of American Overseas Library Technical Assistance, 1940-1970." Doctoral dissertation, University of Pittsburgh 1974. UMI# 75-4090. Published: Scarecrow Press, 1976.

Library technical assistance has been closely associated with U.S. foreign assistance since the Point Four program. During the Point Four years, library technical assistance concentrated on the establishment of libraries in new institutes of technical/professional training, the formation of university libraries, and the introduction of workshops on library education. Foundation sponsorship of technical assistance exceeded government aid in the 1960s. The American Library Association had little impact on the location, level, type, or sponsor of international library technical assistance.

942   Horrocks, Norman. "The Carnegie Corporation of New York and Its Impact on Library Development in Australia: A Case study of Foundation Influence." Doctoral dissertation, University of Pittsburgh, 1971. 935p. UMI# 73-27,143.

This study examines the impact of the Carnegie Corporation of New York on the development of library services in Australia. The first grants were for adult education libraries. Following publication of the Munn and Pitt survey in 1935, activity shifted to public libraries. Direct grants to university and state libraries, to the National Library, and to the Library Association of Australia are described.

943 Poste, Leslie I. "The Development of U.S. Protection of Libraries and Archives in Europe During World War II." Doctoral dissertation, University of Chicago, 1958. 427p.

Surveys the efforts of the United States to save Italian and German libraries under the provisions of the War Department's monuments, fine arts, and archives program. The author concludes his study with the closing of the Offenbach Archival Depot in 1949 when the U.S. State Department assumed responsibility for all non-military operations abroad.

944 Rochester, Maxine K. "American Influence in New Zealand Librarianship as Facilitated by the Carnegie Corporation of New York." Doctoral dissertation, University of Wisconsin-Madison, 1981. 388p. UMI# 8117530.

Traces the influence of American librarianship on New Zealand library practice during the 1930s. Four areas are identified: 1) concept of the library as a collection of materials organized intellectually and physically for access by user; 2) library as an educational institution; 3) organized information as a public resource and responsibility; and 4) librarianship as a profession and education for librarianship. Changes in New Zealand librarianship were the product of help from the Carnegie Corporation, government support of library development, and new concepts introduced by those librarians who studied abroad.

945 Suzuki, Yukihisa. "American Influence on the Development of Library Services in Japan, 1860-1941." Doctoral dissertation, University of Michigan, 1974. 223p. UMI# 75-10,312.

Beginning with the Meiji Period (1868-1912), Japanese librarians and educators displayed interest in the American model of librarianship. Japanese students visited the United States and returned to implement what they learned. The experiment was not entirely successful due to indigenous factors. The government considered libraries as ancillary to the educational system. Relations deteriorated in the 1920s and contact lessened. Overall, Japan benefitted from the exposure to U.S. library methods and the U.S. has reciprocated through encouragement and philanthropic activity.

946 Thorp, E. Nina. "The Fulbright Program, 1948-1968: University Lectureships and Advanced Research Awards in Library Science." Master's thesis, University of Chicago, 1973. 189p.

During the period 1948-1968, 91 American librarians held university lectureships or advanced research awards in 38 foreign countries. Despite the relatively low number of awards, the program is judged a success, especially in the more advanced countries in Europe and Middle Eastern countries such as Iran. Twenty-two tables categorize the recipients and their contributions.

XIV. MISCELLANEOUS STUDIES

947 Birdsall, William F. "The American Archivists' Search for Professional Identity, 1909-1936." Doctoral dissertation, University of Wisconsin, 1973. 263p. UMI# 74-7456. Portions published: *American Archivist* 38 (1975): 159-73; *Journal of Library History* 14 (1979): 457-79.

This study traces the movement to establish an archival profession in America. The emergence of professional historians and the proliferation of institutions collecting historical source materials were essential prerequisites to the formation of the archival profession. In 1936, the Society of American Archivists was established. Gradually, archivists delineated the difference between archival administration and library science. Obstacles to the attainment of a cohesive identity included the small number and geographic dispersion of practitioners, the slow growth of archival institutions, and the lack of leadership.

948 Bradley, Carol J. "The Genesis of American Music Librarianship, 1902-1942." (Volumes I, II). Doctoral dissertation, Florida State University, 1978. 839p. UMI# 7822150. Portion published: *Music Library Association Notes* 37 (1981): 763-822.

This study emphasizes the idea that music in American libraries requires extraordinary library techniques which are variant from those associated with the traditional book. Activities in the areas of collection development, classification, and cataloging are comprehensively reviewed. Biographical sketches of eight prominent music librarians enhance the narrative: Otto Kinkeldey, Carl Engel, Carleton Sprague Smith, Harold Spivacke, Oscar

George Theodore Sonneck, George Sherman Dickinson, Eva Judd O'Meara, and Richard S. Angell. A chronology of the establishment of music collections is furnished.

949   Brand, Barbara E. "The Influence of Higher Education on Sex-Typing in Three Professions, 1870-1920: Librarianship, Social Work, and Public Health." Doctoral dissertation, University of Washington, 1978. 467p. UMI# 7820705. Portion published: *Journal of Library History* 18 (1983): 391-406.

Five explanations are offered for the predominance of women in librarianship, social work, and public health: 1) similarity of professional tasks to home and family roles; 2) presence of women as mentors; 3) equation of professional attributes and feminine qualities; 4) lack of barriers to enter the profession; and 5) income levels not suitable for men. The author concludes that higher education fostered a narrow sex-stereotyped view of women's professional roles.

950   Brennan, Sister Mary A. "History and Influence of the Catholic Reading Circle Movement." Master's thesis, University of Delaware, 1930. 72p.

The Catholic reading circle movement began in 1886 under the direction of the Paulist Fathers of New York City. Self-improvement and the diffusion of Catholic literature were the primary goals of the reading groups. Book lists and reader guidance were provided through the *Catholic World* and the *Catholic Reading Circle Review*. By 1900, over 200 reading circles were meeting regularly throughout the United States. Beneficial results of the reading circles included the greater use of public libraries, the establishment of personal collections, the opportunity for the continuing education of women, and the formation of the Catholic Summer School in New York.

951   Cooper, Marianne A. "United States Secondary Information Services in Physical Science and Engineering: Evolution and Trends From Sputnik to Nixon." Doctoral dissertation, Catholic

University of America, 1981. 496p. UMI# 8016912. Portion Published: *Journal of the American Society for Information Science* 33 (1982): 152-56.

Major factors which influenced the evolution of U.S. secondary information services and their producers in physical science and engineering from 1957 to 1971 are studied. Four organizations are examined in detail: H.W. Wilson Company, Engineering Index, Inc., U.S. Atomic Energy Commission, and the Institute for Scientific Information. External factors affecting services and products such as the federal government, new technology, financial support, and the marketplace are extensively reviewed.

952 Corwin, Margaret A. "An Investigation of Female Leadership in State Library Organizations and Local Library Associations, 1876-1923." Master's thesis, University of Chicago, 1973. 89p. Published: *Library Quarterly* 44 (April 1974): 133-44.

This study tested the hypothesis that female librarians did provide leadership in state organizations, local associations, and state programs during the years 1876-1923. Data indicated that women librarians contributed more to the profession on state and local than national levels, although never in proportion to their numbers in the profession.

953 Dick, Archie L. "A Study of a Model of Society's Knowledge System and Its Implications for Librarianship." Master's thesis, University of Washington, 1981. 115p.

Examines the knowledge model and its constituent elements: production; organization and storage; distribution; and application or use. The knowledge model is related to issues of public policy, social change, and libraries. The library is linked to the model and all of its components, not merely its traditional organizational function. Concludes that libraries are imbedded in the knowledge model and social reality. Therefore, libraries cannot be defined as neutral agencies.

954 Ducsay, William J. "A Translation of the 'History of Libraries in the United States of America' From the *Milkau Collection.*" Master's thesis, Western Reserve University, 1959. 160p.

This is a translation of chapter 12, pages 776 to 855, of the second part of the third volume in the *Handbuch der Bibliothewissenschaft*, published 1952-1957.

955 Esterquest, Ralph T. "War Literature and Libraries: The Role of the American Library in Promoting Interest in and Support of the European War, 1914-1918." Master's thesis, University of Illinois, 1940. 214p. Summary published: *Wilson Library Bulletin* 15 (1941): 621-36.

This study analyzes the impact of war and propaganda on the attitudes of librarians and their collections during World War I. Before America's entry into the war, librarians exhibited a pro-Ally sympathy. Collections emphasized the Allied point of view and several hundred thousand books distributed by Wellington House in England found their way into American libraries. After 1917, an examination of a representative group of public libraries revealed a 5 to 1 ratio of pro-Allied to pro-German titles in the collections. The pro-Allied stance of most libraries is attributed to war-time patriotism, government propaganda, and import restrictions on pro-German literature.

956 Harris, Helen J. "A History of Joseph Ruzicka, Inc., Library Bookbinders, 1758-1966". Master's thesis, University of North Carolina, 1966. 72p.

This study traces the growth of Joseph Ruzicka, Inc., a certified library bindery, from its humble origins in Bohemia in 1758 to the operation of two modern plants in America. Joseph Ruzicka emigrated to the United States in 1879 and continued the family tradition of binding by establishing a shop in Baltimore. By 1928 the business expanded to a second plant in Greensboro, North Carolina. Although library binding is the major activity of the firm, hand binding and foredge painting continue to flourish.

The North Carolina Library Association awarded an honorary membership to Ruzicka in 1954.

957 Irvine, Sharon L. "U.S. Library Unionism: An Historical Outline and an Analysis Employing Industrial Relations Models and Techniques." Master's thesis, University of Chicago, 1976. 212p.

This study places library union development in the context of U.S. labor history, examines attitudinal characteristics of libraries, reviews legal constraints, analyzes specific bargaining agents, and comments on the role of the American Library Association. Concludes that the library union movement has only recently entered the mainstream of national union development.

958 Jackson, Ruth L.M. "Origin and Development of Selected Personnel Management Functions in the Field of American Librarianship, 1876-1969." Doctoral dissertation, Indiana University, 1976. 565p. UMI# 76-21,585. Summary published: Sidney L. Jackson, ed., *Century of Service*, American Library Association, 1976.

This study traces the origin of three personnel management functions—job analysis, job evaluation, and personnel testing—in the field of American librarianship. Three hypotheses were formulated: 1) personnel problems have not been discussed within the framework of the behavioral sciences; 2) the impact of management theory upon personnel concepts in librarianship has been limited; and 3) librarians have not developed a body of personnel management literature for their field. All three hypothesis were confirmed.

959 Karetsky, Stephen. "Reading Research and Librarianship to 1940; An Analysis." Doctoral dissertation, Columbia University, 1978. 486p. UMI# 8204500. Published: Greenwood Press, 1982.

The movement within American librarianship to conduct scientific research on the sociological aspects of adult reading flourished in the 1930s, particularly at the Graduate Library School,

University of Chicago. Douglas Waples energized the program of research and study. Behavioral research was fostered by the growing interest in social science research, the de-emphasis of technical routines, and the expanding interest in adult education. Opponents within the profession claimed that librarianship was an art and that the methods of social science were inhumane.

960   Maruskin, Albert F. "An Historical Analysis of OCLC, Inc.: Its Governance, Function, Financing and Technology." Doctoral dissertation, University of Pittsburgh, 1979. 261p. UMI# 7924730. Published: Marcel Dekker, 1980.

Using historical descriptive approaches, this study analyzes the growth of OCLC, Inc., an on-line computerized network headquartered in Columbus, Ohio. Principal findings indicate that the presidents of several Ohio academic institutions formulated initial plans for the network. Originally an Ohio-based group of academic libraries, OCLC is now a national consortium of libraries which participate in the organization's governance. Funding from various granting agencies was critically important to OCLC's early growth. Although six subsystems were promised, only the shared cataloging module was operational.

961   Ogden, Sherelyn. "A Study of the Impact of the Florence Flood on the Development of Library Conservation in the United States: 1966-1976." Master's thesis, University of Chicago, 1978. 113p. Published: *Restaurator* 3 (1979): 1-36.

Not examined.

962   Schrader, Alvin M. "Toward a Theory of Library and Information Science." Doctoral dissertation, Indiana University, 1983. 1,016p. UMI# 8401534. Summary published: *Library and Information Research* 6 (1984): 227-71.

Applies logical and conceptual analysis to the task of defining the domain of library and information science. Over 1,500 definitions from the past 100 years are identified and collated. Confusion, disagreement, and contradiction characterize the definitions. The author applies metatheory, an extension of general systems theory, to the domain of library science. This approach defines library and information science to be a "system of human social practice in which one person facilitates access to selected cultural objects on behalf of another person who is seeking access to them."

963 Walch, David B. "Toward Professionalization in the Media Field." Doctoral dissertation, University of Utah, 1973. 203p. UMI# 73-21,367.

This study examines the dynamic process of professionalization in the media field, an emerging field composed of audiovisual and library science. Five focuses which influenced the movement toward professionalization were identified: 1) increase in quantity and quality of research; 2) emergence of scholarly leaders; 3) development of professional association; 4) federal aid; and 5) growth and development of instructional technology.

964 Wells, Sharon B. "The Feminization of the American Library Profession, 1876 to 1923." Master's thesis, University of Chicago, 1967. 105p.

American librarianship became a feminized profession during the period 1876-1923, largely due to library education, low salaries, and other factors. The author concludes that women never dominated top library positions, never administered the largest libraries, and never received the highest salaries.

PART THREE

PAPERS AND REPORTS

XV. PUBLIC LIBRARIES

A. General Studies

965 Bertrand, Cynthia. "The Americanization of the Immigrant: The Role of the Public Library, 1900-1920." Research paper, Queens College, 1975.

966 Cole, Eva D.H. "A History of Public Library Services to Blacks in the South, 1900-1975." Research paper, Texas Woman's University, 1976.

967 Hollowell, Luther S., II. "Benjamin Franklin and the Subscription Library: The Foundations." Research paper, Texas Woman's University, 1978.

968 Johns, Elizabeth A. "The Development of Automation in the Catalogue Department of Public Libraries in the United States." Research paper, Texas Woman's University, 1975.

969 Keller, Lela E. "The History of Contributions of Blacks to Public Librarianship from 1903-1976." Research paper, Texas Woman's University, 1978.

970 LaFleur, Lisa B. "Librarian's Response to Adverse Economic

Conditions: A Study of Public Libraries in the Great Depression (1929-1938) and the Current Recession (1970-1975)." Research paper, University of Missouri-Columbia, 1975. 36p.

B. Studies Arranged by State

GEORGIA

971 Johnston, Robin P. "The Development of the Decatur-deKalb Regional Library." Master's paper, Emory University, 1964.

972 Moore, Marianna G. "A Study of the History and Development of the Troup-Harris-Coweta Regional Library." Master's paper, Emory University, 1964.

LOUISIANA

973 Howell, David B. "The Historical Development and Foreclosure of a Public Library in Alexandria, Louisiana." Master's paper, University of Mississippi, 1960.

MAINE

974 O'Connor, William. "A History of the Portland (Maine) Public Library, 1763-1969." Research paper, Long Island University, 1971.

MASSACHUSETTS

975 Colodny, Shirley. "A Centennial History of an Association Library, Lenox, Massachusetts, 1856-1956." Research paper, Long Island University, 1970. 64p.

MISSOURI

976 Boeckman, Laurel. "History of the Scotland County Library in Memphis, Missouri." Research paper, University of Missouri, 1974. 73p.

977 Browning, Leona A. "History of the Public Library Movement in Columbia, Missouri." Research paper, University of Missouri, 1969. 92p.

978 Jennings, Kathryn L. "Kansas City Public Library, 1873 to 1898: Its Historical Growth as Related to the Development of the Public School System of Kansas City." Research Paper, University of Missouri, 1971. 50p.

979 Jones, Alfred H. "State Aid to Public Libraries in Missouri 1945-1955." Research paper, University of Missouri, 1973. 20p.

980 O'Driscoll, Patrick D. "History of the Mid-city Branch of the St. Louis (City) Public Library." Research paper, University of Missouri, 1973. 108p.

981 Pittman, Charlene K. "History of the Two Attempts to Establish a Tax-Supported Public Library in Adair County, 1948 and 1967." Research paper, University of Missouri, 1971. 50p.

982 Showalter, George W. "History of Public Libraries in Washington County, Missouri." Research paper, University of Missouri, 1973. 122p.

983 Sommer, June M. "History of the Genealogical Collection of the St. Louis Public Library." Research paper, University of Missouri, 1974. 168p.

984 Strunk, Amy L. "History of the Lucy Wortham James Memorial Library, 1930-1953." Research paper, University of Missouri, 1974. 41p.

NEW YORK

985 Anhalt, Lenore. "The History, Development, and Organization of the Record Collection of the Great Neck (New York) Library." Research paper, Long Island University, 1969. 92p.

986 Appleget, Norma M. "The Grand Old Lady of Grand Street: A History of the White Plains (New York) Public Library, 1812 to 1969." Research paper, Long Island University, 1969. 95p.

987 Bailey, Martha. "An Early History of the Stenson Memorial Library, Sea Cliff, New York." Research paper, Long Island University, 1968.

988 Barnes, Herbert C. "The Valley Stream Public Library, Valley Stream, Long Island, New York: A History." Research paper, Long Island University, 1968.

989 Bell, Carol M. "Grinnell Library Association of Wappingers Falls, New York, 1867-1940." Research paper, Long Island University, 1975.

990 Berde, Maria. "History of the Williston Park (New York) Public Library From the Founding in 1937 to the Present Day." Research paper, Long Island University, 1971.

991 Berkowitz, Silvia. "Historical Study of the Elmont (New York) Public Library, 1939-1965." Research paper, Long Island University, 1967.

992 Bleier, Meta. "A History of the Hewlett-Woodmere (New York) Public Library." Research paper, Long Island University, 1967.

993 Bloomgarden, Clara B. "History of the Port Washington (New York) Public Library, 1892-1967." Research paper, Long Island University, 1968.

994 Brown, Emily T. "An Historical Study of the East Rockaway (New York) Free Library." Research paper, Long Island University, 1968.

995 Brown, Gertrude. "History of the Long Beach (New York) Public Library." Research paper, Long Island University, 1969.

996 Buxton, Karen. "The Emma S. Clark Memorial Library in Setauket, Long Island, New York: A History." Research paper, Long Island University, 1965.

997 Carbino, Nancy. "History of the Plainedge Public Library, Massapequa, New York." Research paper, Long Island University, 1970. 90p.

998 Chapin, Vivian J. "A Historical Study of the Origins of the Library in Huntington, Long Island, New York, 1759-1929." Research paper, Long Island University, 1966.

999 Chichester, Marion. "Library Service for a Growing Population: A History of the Massapequa Public Library, 1953-1965." Research paper, Long Island University, 1966.

1000 Clark, Carol. "An Historical Study of the Various Controversies in which the Farmingdale Public Library has been Engaged since 1963." Research paper, Long Island University, 1970.

1001 Connally, Evelyn. "A History of the Mount Vernon (New York) Public Library from 1948 Through 1968." Research paper, Long Island University, 1969.

1002 Coogan, Inge M. "The Lynbrook (New York) Public Library, 1913-1964: An Historical Study." Research paper, Long Island University, 1967.

1003 Corsaro, James. "History of the Albany Library With an Examination of Reading Vogues in Albany, 1824-1829." Research paper, State University of New York, Albany, 1969. 56p.

1004 Davidoff, Deborah. "History and Development of the Bellmore (New York) Memorial Library from its Establishment in 1948 to 1970." Research paper, Long Island University, 1971.

1005 Dziewiatkowski, Naomi. "History of the Jesse Merritt Memorial

Library at Salisbury Park, L.I." Research paper, Long Island University, 1966.

1006 Ellison, Virginia N. "The History of the Nassau County Law Library." Research paper, Long Island University, 1967.

1007 Erichsen, Ruth H. "History of the Smithtown Library, Smithtown, Long Island, New York, from 1907 to 1967." Research paper, Long Island University, 1968.

1008 Freund, Esta. "A History of the Malverne (New York) Public Library, 1929-1968." Research paper, Long Island University, 1969.

1009 Gavurin, Esther A. "Guide to the Archival Collections in the Public Libraries of Nassau County, New York." Research Paper, Long Island University, 1972. 271p.

1010 Gerard, Helene L. "A History of the Westhampton Free Library, Westhampton Beach, N.Y." Research paper, Long Island University, 1971. 192p. UMI# M-3142.

1011 Gillie, Mildred H. "The History of the Port Jefferson, Long Island, New York, Library, 1908-1966." Research paper, Long Island University, 1967.

1012 Gold, Ethel. "A History of the West Islip (New York) Public Library." Research paper, Long Island University, 1966.

1013 Goldberg, Jeanne. "The History of the Northport - East Northport Public Libraries." Research paper, Long Island University, 1966.

1014 Gordon, Harriet S. "A History of the Crestwood Branch of the Yonkers (New York) Public Library." Research paper, Long Island University, 1969.

1015 Gould, Lillian P. "Historical Study of the East Meadow (New York) Public Library, 1954-1965." Research paper, Long Island University, 1967.

1016 Groves, Marion N. "The History of the Freeport Memorial

Library, 1884-1938." Research paper, Long Island University, 1968.

1017 Haase, Leila. "History of the Manhasset (New York) Public Library, 1945-1965." Research paper, Long Island University, 1966.

1018 Halpin, James R. "A History of the Farmingdale Public Library, Including Background on the Town of Farmingdale." Research paper, Long Island University, 1965.

1019 Hedges, Harold A. "A History of the Mattituck Free Library in Mattituck, New York." Research paper, Long Island University, 1975.

1020 Hisz, Evelyn. "History of the Theatre Collection New York Public Library at Lincoln Center." Research paper, Long Island University, 1969.

1021 Holzer, Stanley. "A History of the Sarah Hull Hallock Free Library, Milton, New York." Research paper, Long Island University, 1970.

1022 Hyman, Toby A. "A History of the Walter Hampden Memorial Library." Research paper, Long Island University, 1968. 79p.

1023 Iber, Elizabeth. "History of the Founding of the Deer Park (New York) Public Library." Research paper, Long Island University, 1971.

1024 Jacobson, Barbara. "History of the New York Public Library for the Blind and Physically Handicapped, 1895-1969." Research paper, Long Island University, 1971.

1025 Jacobson, Sabina. "A Study of the Growth and Development of the Hicksville Public Library, Hicksville, New York." Research paper, Long Island University, 1968.

1026 Jawitz, Marilyn. "History of the Babylon (New York) Public Library, 1895-1970." Research paper, Long Island University, 1971.

1027 Jespersen, Helene. "A History of the Garden City (New York) Public Library." Research paper, Long Island University, 1967.

1028 Karro, Thelma. "Harborfields, New York: A Community without a Public Library." Research paper, Long Island University, 1970.

1029 Katz, Lorraine F. "A History of the Great Neck (New York) Library, 1800-1960." Research paper, Long Island University, 1967.

1030 Kavasch, Dorothy. "History of the Cold Spring Harbor (New York) Library." Research paper, Long Island University, 1966.

1031 Keenan, Beulah M. "A History of the Newspaper Division of the New York Public Library, 1911-1968." Research paper, Long Island University, 1969.

1032 King, Dorothy. "History of the East Hampton Free Library, 1897-1970." Research paper, Long Island University, 1971. 96p.

1033 Kirsch, Silvia. "A History of the Rockville Centre Public Library, Long Island, New York." Research paper, Long Island University, 1967.

1034 Lapidus, Brynar. "A Historical Study of the North Bellmore (New York) Public Library." Research paper, Long Island University, 1968.

1035 Licandro, Margaret L. "History of the Bryant Library, Roslyn, N.Y. (1878-1953)." Research paper, Long Island University, 1968.

1036 Lo, Henry. "History of the Flushing Branch of The Queens Borough Public Library." Research paper, Long Island University, 1970.

1037 Lukoski, Lila L. "History of the Sayville (New York) Library from 1914-1967." Research paper, Long Island University, 1968.

1038 Lusak, Richard. "A History of the Islip Public Library from 1923 to 1965." Research paper, Long Island University, 1968.

1039 Lutrin, Debe B. "History of the Establishment of the North Merrick (New York) Public Library, 1951-1969." Research paper, Long Island University, 1970.

1040 Malino, Edna. "A History of the Bethpage (New York) Public Library from 1927-1966." Research paper, Long Island University, 1968.

1041 Maxian, M. Bruce. "A History of the Morton Penny-packer Library, Long Island, Collection." Research paper, Long Island University, 1966.

1042 Morris, Ruth. "Finkelstein Memorial Library, Spring Valley, New York: An Oral History of the Early Years, 1917-1940." Research paper, Long Island University, 1971. 12p.

1043 Normandeau, Constance. "History of the Brentwood (New York) Public Library." Research paper, Long Island University, 1969. 48p.

1044 O'Brian, Audrey. "A History of the Mineola (New York) Memorial Library." Research paper, Long Island University, 1965.

1045 O'Connor, Sonya. "A History of the John Jermain Memorial Library, Sag Harbor, New York." Research paper, Long Island University, 1971.

1046 Page, John S., Jr. "A History of the Oceanside (New York) Free Library." Research paper, Long Island University, 1967.

1047 Provenzano, Laura. "Study of the Growth and Development of the Library in Huntington, Long Island (New York) 1929-1967." Research paper, Long Island University, 1968.

1048 Quain, Mildred. "A History and Descriptive Study of the Music Division of the Library and Museum of the Performing Arts, The New York Public Library at Lincoln Center, New York, N.Y." Research paper, Long Island University, 1969. 52p.

1049 Resnick, Shirley. "A History and Descriptive Study of the Greenpoint Branch of the Brooklyn (New York) Public Library." Research paper, Long Island University, 1971.

1050 Rigali, Donna L. "History of the Seaford Public Library, Seaford, New York." Research paper, Long Island University, 1968.

1051 Robertson, Marian P. "History of the Westbury Memorial Public Library, Westbury, New York." Research paper, Long Island University, 1967.

1052 Rubin, Phyllis. "History of the Jewish Division of the New York Public Library, 1897-1970." Research paper, Long Island University, 1971.

1053 Sayle, Selma. "A History of the Mamaroneck (New York) Free Library, Inc. from 1951 Through 1969." Research paper, Long Island University, 1970. 103p.

1054 Scanlon, Regina. "A History of the Delancey Floyd-Jones Free Library, Massapequa, New York, From Its Origin, 1896, to the Establishment of the Massapequa Public Library, 1953." Research paper, Long Island University, 1969.

1055 Schneberg, Ben. "The History of the Lindenhurst (New York) Memorial Library, 1945-1970." Research paper, Long Island University, 1971.

1056 Seabury, Jane B. "A History of the Hampton Library in Bridge Hampton, N.Y." Research paper, Long Island University, 1967. 95p.

1057 Seaton, Elaine. "Origins of the Shelter Rock (New York) Public Library." Research paper, Long Island University, 1966.

1058 Seryneck, William P. "The First Fifty Years: A History of the Amityville Free Library, 1907-1957." Research paper, Long Island University, 1965.

1059 Siegel, Helen. "A History of the Plainview-Old Bethpage Public Library from its Beginning to 1965." Research paper, Long Island University, 1967.

1060 Silver, Carol K. "An Historical Study of the Peninsula Public Library in Lawrence, New York, 1950-1967." Research paper, Long Island University, 1968.

1061 Sisson, Laurel K. "A History of the Riverhead (New York) Free Library, Including a Brief History of the Town of Riverhead." Research paper, Long Island University, 1967.

1062 Sokol, Evelyn. "Conflicting Community Interests: The Establishment of the South Huntington, (New York) Public Library." Research paper, Long Island University, 1967.

1063 Timlin, Dorothy S. "A History of the Bay Shore Public Library." Research paper, Long Island University, 1967.

1064 True, Patricia. "A History of the New City Free Library, New York City, New York, from 1936 to 1968." Research paper, Long Island University, 1970.

1066 Vinicombe, Marie. "A History of the Baldwin (New York) Public Library from its Founding in 1919 to the Present Day." Research paper, Long Island University, 1971.

1067 Weber, Harry. "A History of the Merrick (New York) Library, 1891-1965." Research paper, Long Island University, 1968.

1068 Wensley, Dorothy D. "The Children's Library, Robert Bacon Memorial, Westbury, Long Island, 1924-1965; Five Owls and the Winds of Change." Research paper, Long Island University, 1966.

1069 Williamson, Lorraine. "History of the Syosset (New York) Public Library." Research paper, Long Island University, 1970.

NORTH CAROLINA

1070 Sawyer, Mary H. "Most Worthy Child: the Williamsburg Free Public Library, 1909 to 1933." Research paper, University of North Carolina-Chapel Hill, 1981. 96p.

OHIO

1071 Agnoni, Leah V. "Public Library Service in Alliance, Ohio: 1885 to 1956." Research paper, Kent State University, 1976. 87p.

1072 Carter, Betsy. "Taylor Memorial Library, Cuyahoga Falls, Ohio, 1955-1970." Research paper, Long Island University, 1970. 84p.

1073 Cool, Dorothy. "History of the Warren Public Library, 1950-1970." Research paper, Kent State University, 1971. 116p.

1074 Gankoski, Irene F. "History of the Massillon, Ohio, Public Library From 1899 to 1920." Research paper, Kent State University, 1970. 51p.

1075 Lane, Margaret S. "Development of the Public Library in Troy, Ohio." Research paper, Kent State University, 1969. 53p.

1076 Lawson, Louise G. "History of the Books/Jobs Project: Akron Public Library, July 1, 1968-June 30, 1972." Research paper, Kent State University, 1973. 206p.

1077 Lewis, Ronald A. "History of Colburn Library, 1904-1968." Research paper, Kent State University, 1970. 72p.

1078 McKnight, Joyce A. "History of the Wayne County Public Library." Research paper, Kent State University, 1970. 81p.

1079 McQuade, Jayne W. "History of the Mansfield, Ohio, Public Library." Research paper, Kent State University, 1969. 67p.

1080 Pikovnik, Rudolph. "History of the Lorain Public Library to the Year 1926." Research paper, Kent State University, 1971. 42p.

1081 Seabrook, John H. "History of the Worthington, Ohio, Public Library, 1803-1967." Research paper, Kent State University, 1969. 77p.

1082 Tucker, Christine. "Development of Guernsey County District Public Library (Ohio) from 1898 to 1972, with Particular Consideration of the Professional Staff, Physical Facility, and the Library Services to the Community." Research paper, Kent State University, 1973. 67p.

1083 Waters, John K. "History of the Canal Fulton (Ohio) Public Library." Research paper, Kent State University, 1972. 46p.

1084 Woodward, Phyllis K. "History of the Stow Public Library, 1924-1974." Research paper, Kent State University, 1975. 164p.

OREGON

1085 McGuire, Marian P. "The Albina Branch Library Portland, (Oregon); its First Half Century." Research paper, Portland State University, 1962.

TEXAS

1086 Ferguson, Elizabeth O. "The History and Development of Lee Public Library and John Ben Sheppard, Jr. Texana Collection Memorial-Gladewater, Texas." Research paper, Texas Woman's University, 1978.

1087 Field, Judith E.F. "History of Dunlap Memorial Library, Italy, Texas." Research paper, Texas Woman's University, 1977.

1088 Foto, Suzanne T. "The History of the Houston Public Library." Research paper, Texas Woman's University, 1977.

1089 Howe, Marilyn J. "The Public Library of Beaumont, Texas: A History." Research paper, Texas Woman's University, 1977.

1090 Sanders, Lucy M. "Nicholson Memorial Library, Garland, Texas, 1927 to Present." Research paper, Texas Woman's University, 1977.

1091 Waller, Hope C. "A History of the Sherman Public Library, Sherman, Texas, to 1974." Research paper, Texas Woman's University, 1975.

1092 Wells, Mattie L. "Denton Public Library Then and Now." Research paper, Texas Woman's University, 1976.

UTAH

1093 Hepworth, Bobbee M. "Carnegie Libraries in Utah." Research paper, Brigham Young University, 1976.

XVI. COLLEGE AND UNIVERSITY LIBRARIES

A. General Studies

1094 Jones, Vance H. "The Influence of the American College Fraternity on Chapter House Library Development." Master's paper, Emory University, 1964.

1095 Miletic, Ivan. "Major Cooperative Programs of Research Libraries: The Farmington Plan; The Public Law 480 Program and the National Program for Acquisitions and Cataloging." Research paper, Queens College, 1975.

1096 Savary, M. J. "The Latin American Cooperative Acquisitions Project (LACAP)." Research paper, Long Island University, 1966.

B. Studies Arranged By State

FLORIDA

1097 Quinn, Charles. "A History of the St. Vincent DePaul Seminary Library, Boynton Beach, Florida." Research paper, Long Island University, 1971.

MASSACHUSETTS

1098 Greever, Mary F.C. "The Harvard Library in Colonial America." Research paper, Texas Woman's University, 1975.

MISSOURI

1099 Deweese, Barbara J. "History of the Library, University of Missouri-Columbia, 1928-1946." Research paper, University of Missouri, 1973. 75p.

NEW YORK

1100 Morris, Rita. "Case History of the Library of the Nassau Community College." Research paper, Long Island University, 1967.

1101 Oh, Song Ja. "A Study of the Edwin Markham Collection of the Horrman Library of Wagner College, Staten Island, New York, 1940-1969." Research paper, Long Island University, 1969.

1102 O'Shea, John M. "History of the Library of the Suffolk County (New York) Community College." Research paper, Long Island University, 1968.

1103 Paciorek, Loretta A. "The History of the United States Military Academy Library at West Point, New York." Research paper, Long Island University, 1968.

1104 Ross, Norma. "History of the Hofstra University Library, 1935-1970." Research paper, Long Island University, 1971. 158p.

1105 Schwartz, Maxine. "History of the Library of the Jewish Theological Seminary of America." Research paper, Long Island University, 1967.

1106 Sun, Delphine. "History of the Chinese Section of the East Asian Library, Columbia University, New York, New York." Research paper, Long Island University, 1969.

1107 Sussman, Diane. "History of the Brooklyn (New York) College Library From 1930-1966." Research paper, Long Island University, 1967.

XVII. SPECIAL LIBRARIES

A. General Studies

1108 Hedrick, Lila F. "The History and Development of Presidential Libraries." Research paper, Texas Woman's University, 1979.

1109 Johnson, Alice H. "Prison Libraries in the United States 1965-1975." Research paper, Texas Woman's University, 1975.

1110 Moscowitz, Rita. "The History of the U.S.I.A. Overseas Library Program." Research paper, Long Island University, 1970.

1111 Olson, Carol A. "Librarianship in the History of Medicine." Research paper, Brigham Young University, 1976.

1112 Patri, Daniel. "An Annotated, Classified, and Selected Bibliography of American Theatre Libraries and American Theatre Librarians: 1902-1976." Research paper, Queens College, 1978.

B. Studies Arranged by State

CONNECTICUT

1113 Higgins, Marian H. "A History of the Submarine Force Library and Museum in New London, Connecticut." Research paper, Long Island University, 1971.

MASSACHUSETTS

1114   Liu, Nathaniel. "A History of the New England Deposit Library (1942-1962)." Research paper, Long Island University, 1966.

MISSOURI

1115   Sanders, Beverly. "History of the Henry L. Wolfner Memorial Library for the Blind and Physically Handicapped." Research paper, University of Missouri-Columbia, 1974. 22p.

NEW YORK

1116   Albright, Helena. "History of the Research Library of Brookhaven National Laboratory." Research paper, Long Island University, 1968.

1117   Fabian, Sophie. "History of the New York Institute Library." Research paper, Long Island University, 1970.

1118   Marris, Alice. "Franklin D. Roosevelt and the Franklin D. Roosevelt Library." Research paper, State University of New York, Albany, 1971. 38p.

1119   McLoughlin, Eileen C. "History of the Joseph Conrad Memorial Library of the Seaman's Church Institute of New York." Research paper, Long Island University, 1970. 81p.

1120   Skidmore, Suzanne. "History of the Library of The Huntington Historical Society." Research paper, Long Island University, 1967.

1121   Synodis, Edith J. "History of the Library of the Institute of Life Insurance, New York City, N.Y." Research paper, Long Island University, 1969.

1122 Tu, Shih-Soo. "History of the Library of the Grolier Club." Research paper, Long Island University, 1970.

1123 Turnow, William H. "The Engineering Societies Library: A History of its Origins and Early Development, 1852-1928." Research paper, Long Island University, 1967.

1124 Wortman, Leonore J. "A Study of the Library of The New York Academy of Medicine, 1847-1968." Research paper, Long Island University, 1969. 65p.

1125 Young, Robert L. "A History of the Young Men's Christian Association Historical Library, New York, N.Y." Research paper, Long Island University, 1967.

1126 Zaremba, Maurice. "An Historical-Descriptive Study of the Library Archives of the Leo Baeck Institute." Research paper, Long Island University, 1972. 99p. UMI# M-3384.

TEXAS

1127 Griffin, Brenda C. "The History and Development of The Criswell Center for Biblical Studies Library." Research paper, Texas Woman's University, 1978.

XVIII. LIBRARY ASSOCIATIONS, COMMISSIONS, AND CONSORTIA

AMERICAN ASSOCIATION OF LAW LIBRARIES

1128 Bieber, Doris. "History of the American Association of Law Libraries, 1937-1967." Research paper, Long Island University, 1970.

AMERICAN LIBRARY ASSOCIATION

1129 Chin, Jaylene. "A History of School Library Standards Published by the American Library Association." Research paper, Long Island University, 1969.

1130 Clairmont, Shirley A. "Coming of Age of Intellectual Freedom in the American Library Association." Research paper, State University of New York, Albany, 1972. 70p.

1131 Crawford, Debra R. "Black Librarians' Caucus of the American Library Association as Seen by Itself; Materials for a History." Research paper, Kent State University, 1974. 72p.

1132 King, Sandra K. "History and Work of the Social Responsibilities Round Table of the American Library Association." Research paper, Texas Woman's University, 1977.

1133 Theis, Karen A. "The Association of College and Research Libraries: A History." Research paper, Texas Woman's University, 1979.

AMIGOS BIBLIOGRAPHIC COUNCIL

1134 Walters, Pamela L. "A History of the Amigos Bibliographic Council: 1972-1979." Research paper, Texas Woman's University, 1979.

CENTER FOR RESEARCH LIBRARIES

1135 Malik, Abdul. "A History of the Center for Research Libraries (1949-1965)." Research paper, Long Island University, 1969. 72p.

GEORGIA LIBRARY ASSOCIATION

1136 Archer, Nell W. "The Georgia Library Association: The First Forty Years." Master's paper, Emory University, 1962.

LONG ISLAND RESOURCES COUNCIL

1137 Leinoff, Thelma. "A Study of the Long Island Library Resources Council, Inc., 1963-1969." Research paper, Long Island University, 1970. UMI# M-2875.

MEDICAL LIBRARY ASSOCIATION

1138 Guzzo, Linda S. "The Medical Library Association: Its History and Activities." Research paper, Texas Woman's University, 1977.

MISSOURI LIBRARY COMMISSION

1139 Doering, Nancy. "History of the Missouri Library Commission, 1907-1946." Research paper, University of Missouri-Columbia, 1975. 74p.

NASSAU-SUFFOLK LIBRARY ASSOCIATION

1140 Bilinkoff, Helen. "A History of the Nassau-Suffolk School Library Association." Research paper, Long Island University, 1969. 127p.

OHIO COLLEGE LIBRARY CENTER

1141 Post, Kathleen L. "History of the Ohio College Library Center from 1967-1972." Research paper, Kent State University, 1974. 164p.

WEST VIRGINIA LIBRARY COMMISSION

1142 Davis, William P. "The West Virginia Library Commission and Public Library Development Since 1972." Research paper, Texas Woman's University, 1979.

XIX. BIOGRAPHICAL STUDIES

COOLIDGE, ARCHIBALD C.

1143   Olsen, Richard A. "Archibald Cary Coolidge and the Harvard University Library, 1910-1928." Research paper, Long Island University, 1967.

DOWNS, ROBERT B.

1144   Duyka, Anne A. "Robert Bingham Downs: His Life and Works." Research paper, Texas Woman's University, 1976.

FISKE, DANIEL W.

1145   Bierds, Betty K. "Daniel Willard Fiske: His Professional Career and its Influence on the Growth of the Cornell University Libraries." Research paper, Long Island University, 1966.

GILLIS, JAMES L.

1146   Halligan, John T. "James Louis Gillis, California State Librarian, 1899-1917: His Role and Influence in the Growth of California Libraries." Research paper, Long Island University, 1962.

GOODRICH, FRANCIS L.D.

1147 Podolnick, Shirley. "The Administration of the Library of the College of the City of New York by Francis L.D. Goodrich from 1930-1945." Research paper, Long Island University, 1966.

JEWETT, CHARLES C.

1148 Purcell, Bonnie L. "Charles Coffin Jewitt: A Man Ahead of His Times." Research paper, Texas Woman's University, 1979.

KNIGHT, HATTIE M.

1149 Rabner, Lanell B. "Hattie Madson Knight: Leader, Educator, Librarian-Professional Years, 1941-1973." Research paper, Brigham Young University, 1976.

MACLEISH, ARCHIBALD

1150 Schwartz, Betty. "Role of the American Library Association in the Selection of Archibald MacLeish as Librarian of Congress." Research paper, Kent State University, 1970. 77p.

PUTNAM, HERBERT

1151 Krieg, Cynthia J. " Herbert Putnam's Philosophy of Librarianship." Research paper, Long Island University, 1970. 178p. UMI# M-2874

ROOT, AZARIAH

1152 Rubin, Richard. "Azariah Root's Concept of Education for Librarianship." Research paper, Kent State University, 1976. 52p.

SCOGGIN, MARGARET C.

1153 Lowy, Beverly. "Margaret C. Scoggin (1905-1968): Her Professional Life and Work in Young Adult Librarianship." Research paper, Long Island University, 1970. 101p.

STUCKERT, BEATRICE S.

1154 Potts, Ann J. "The Life and Librarianship of Beatrice Stackhouse Stuckert, Director of the Haddonfield Public Library, Haddonfield, New Jersey." Master's paper, Glassboro State College, 1972.

VORMELKER, ROSE L.

1155 Gabriel, Patricia. "Rose L. Vormelker, 1895-1970." Research paper, Kent State University, 1971. 53p.

WINCHELL, CONSTANCE M.

1156 Whyte, Edith. "Constance M. Winchell: Reference Librarian." Research paper, Long Island University, 1971. 70p. UMI# M-3107.

XX. MISCELLANEOUS STUDIES

1157 Detter, Howard. "The Selection and Performance of the Librarian of Congress." Research paper, Queens College, 1975.

1158 Downs, Myrna W. "The Emergence of a Philosophy of Librarianship in the United States." Research paper, Long Island University, 1969. 129p.

1159 Helgerson, Marguerite. "The Development of American Book Fairs, 1899-1949." Research paper, Long Island University, 1964.

1160 Jackson, Carole S. "A History of Censorship Attempts in American Libraries During 1955-1960, Based on Cases Reported in the *New York Times* During this Period." Master's paper, Emory University, 1963.

1161 Lewis, Diane T. "The History of the Publishing of the *National Union Catalog*." Research paper, Texas Woman's University, 1976.

1162 Lippman, Murray. "Background and Organization of the *American Library Directory*." Research paper, Long Island University, 1969. 90p.

1163 Malamud, Sylvia. "Reviews of the Newbery Award Winners 1955-1965: A Statistical Analysis." Research paper, Long Island University, 1969. 69p.

1164 May, Robert H. "Chronicle of Notable Library Facts and Events as Seen by *Library Journal*, 1895-1933." Research paper, Kent State University, 1971. 45p.

1165 Medley, Nora M.D. "Securing the Library: A History." Research paper, Texas Woman's University, 1976.

1166 Pazar, Clara H. "Judicial Decisions in Censorship Cases of the New York Court of Appeals, 1933-1967." Research paper, Long Island University, 1969.

1167 Piscitello, Caroline M. "High School Library Standards, 1918-1949: A Critical Summary of Changes and Developments in the United States." Master's paper, University of Illinois, 1950.

1168 Ruffe, Barbara L. "Dissemination of Information in the American Library, 1900-1925." Research paper, Brigham Young University, 1976.

1169 Scott, Sharon S. "Cataloging in Publication: History and Development." Research paper, Texas Woman's University, 1978.

1170 Smith, Harold B. "The Development of Automation in the Library: 1936-1966." Research paper, Long Island University, 1968.

1171 Starke, Ray. "History of the School of Library and Information Science at the University of Missouri-Columbia." Research paper, University of Missouri-Columbia. 1979. 60p.

1172 Starr, Kerry D. "Educational Philosophies of Early American Librarianship—The Causes for the Lack of Intellectualism." Research paper, Brigham Young University, 1977.

1173 Steele, Ulysses M. "A Study of Characteristics of Graduates of the Division of Librarianship of Emory University, 1931-1953." Master's paper, Emory University, 1960.

1174 Tierney, Catherine M. "Women in American Librarianship: An Annotated Bibliography of Articles in Library Periodicals, 1920-1973." Research paper, Kent State University, 1974. 38p.

AUTHOR INDEX

[Numbers refer to entry numbers]

Abbott, J.C., 821
Adams, E.M., Jr., 733
Adams, K.B., 433
Adams, N.E., 678
Adams, R.T., 651
Adkins, B.M., 160
Adkins, M.R., 864
Adrian, J.M., 758
Afolabi, M., 889
Agard, R.M., 137
Agnew, E., 345
Agnoni, L.V., 1071
Agria, J.J., 763
Akers, N.M., 852
Albright, H., 1116
Aldrich, F.D., 668
Aldrich, W.L.B., 240
Allan, J.M., 482
Allanson, V.L., 890
Allen, D.L., 346
Alvey, R.G., 635
Ambler, B. H., 321
Amos, A., 557
Anders, M.E., 71-72
Anderson, D.J., 804
Anderson, M.T., 1
Anhalt, L., 985
Appleget, N.M., 986
Archer, H.R., 437
Archer, N.W., 1136
Arthur, A.W., 255
Atkins, E., 73, 539

Axelrod, H.B., 563

Babylon, E.R., 700
Backus, J., 34
Baer, E.A., 2
Bailey, M., 987
Bandy, C.N.L., 481
Banks, K., 865
Barfield, I.R., 155
Barker, J.W., 322
Barnes, G.S., 347
Barnes, H.C., 988
Barnett, L.F., 256
Barnett, M.F., 506
Baron, M.S., 203
Barr, J.C., 636
Barr, L.J., 689
Barrett, M., 318
Barrett, M.A., 698
Bartis, P.T., 597
Bartlett, L.E., 933
Bates, N.P., 708
Bates, P.N.H., 891
Batten, S.S., 241
Battle, M.E., 492
Battles, F.M., 257
Bauersfeld, S.H., 429
Baughman, R.O., 258
Baumann, C. H., 848
Beach, Sister F.M., 430
Beamon, M., 175

Beattie, Sister P.M., 582
Becker, M.B., 861
Bell, B.L., 74
Bell, C.M., 989
Bell, D., 652
Benedetti, L.S., 130
Bennett, J.P., 792
Bennett, W.C., 892
Benson, E.C., 893
Benson, S.H., 827
Berberian, K.R., 480
Berde, M., 990
Berg, V.A., 169
Bergen, E., 138
Berkowitz, S., 991
Bernier, B.R., 571
Bertrand, C., 965
Beswick, J.W., 845
Bidlack, R.E., 472
Bieber, D., 1128
Bierds, B.K., 1145
Bilinkoff, H., 1140
Binkowski, M., 894
Bird, M.F., 688
Birdsall, W.F., 947
Black, D.M., 75
Blankfort, J.R., 878
Blanks, E.W., 182
Bleier, M., 992
Blinkhorn, M.E., 195
Bloomgarden, C.B., 993
Blough, N.L., 895
Bobinski, G.S., 76, 507
Boeckman, L., 976
Bogart, R.E., 483
Bolden, E.E.M., 811
Boll, J.J., 379
Boone, H.H., 259
Borome, J.A., 887
Boudreau, A., 484
Bowden, C.N., 260

Boyd, Sister C., 896
Boyd, M.R., 77
Boyd, W.D., Jr., 35
Boyer, P.S., 934
Brace, W., 897
Bracken, M.C., 572
Bradley, C.J., 948
Bradley, N.B., 303
Bradley, R., 3
Brand, B.E., 949
Brandt, B.S., 361
Branscomb, L.C., Jr., 863
Branyan, B.M., 637
Braverman, M.R., 78
Breen, M.H., 226
Breisacher, R., 598
Breish, K.A., 79
Brennan, Sister M.A., 950
Brennan, P.M., 583
Bresie, M., 830
Brewster, B.J., 941
Briggs, M.I., 662
Brinkley, C., 599
Brisley, M.A., 859
Bromiley, F., 618
Brookover, B., 508
Brooks, R.E., 422
Brophy, E.D., 36
Brough, K.J., 380
Brown, C.C., 696
Brown, E.T., 994
Brown, G., 995
Brown, J.V., 564
Brown, R.E., 619
Browning, L.A., 977
Brudvig, G.L., 254
Brundin, R.E., 418
Bruner, J.E., 453
Bryan, B.D., 139
Buchanan, J.B., 204
Buck, J.P., 339

Author Index

Buckingham, B.J., 658
Buckley, A.K., 620
Bullock, E.V., 170
Bullock, J.Y., 227
Burge, N.T., 666
Burich, N.J., 209
Burke, B.L., 37
Burr, C.R.M., 791
Burton, A.S., 261
Busbin, O.M., Jr., 764
Butrick, M.W., 304
Butters, A.J., 765
Buxton, K., 996
Buzzard, R.A., 262
Byrnes, H.W., 38

Caldwell, M.S., 167
Callahan, B.E., 751
Campbell, M.M., 835
Campbell, R.W., 638
Campbell, V.M., 228
Campion, A.L., 739
Cantrell, C.H., 4
Cao, J.F., 131
Capozzi, M.R., 691
Carbino, N., 997
Carr, L.D., 810
Carrier, E.J., 80
Carroll, C.E., 740
Carroll, F.C., 657
Carter, B., 1072
Carter, M., 39
Castegnetti, N.R., 140
Chalker, W.J., 687
Chamberlain, L.C., 431
Chapin, V.J., 998
Chichester, M., 999
Chin, J., 1129
Christie, C.C., 862
Church, F.E., 381

Churchwell, C.D., 741
Clairmont, S.A., 1130
Clark, C., 1000
Clark, R.B., Jr., 205
Clayton, S.A.H., 171
Clement, E.G., 766
Cline, G.S., 898
Clinefeller, R.W., 509
Clopine, J., 81
Clymer, B.F., Jr., 493
Cochran, M.A., 541
Cody, N.B., 348
Coghlan, J.M., 5
Cohen, L.G., 818
Cohen, S., 855
Cole, E.D.H., 966
Cole, J.Y., 874
Colla, Sister M.B., 423
Collier, F.G., 82
Collins, L.T., 263
Colodny, S., 975
Colson, J., 373
Comaromi, J.P., 709
Connally, E., 1001
Coogan, I.M., 1002
Cook, V.R., 152
Cooke, A.M., 242
Cookston, J.S., 660
Cool, D., 1073
Cooper, M.A., 951
Cooper, N.W., 161
Coover, R.W., 692
Copeland, E.F., 305
Corcoran, S.R., 710
Corsaro, J., 1003
Corwin, M.A., 952
Couch, C.R., Jr., 542
Coughlin, B., 183
Cowles, L.H., 621
Cox, D.J., 788
Coyte, D.E., 454

Crammer, J.C., 264
Cranford, J.P., 494
Crawford, D.R., 1131
Crittenden, J.L., 162
Crook, M.R., 6
Cropper, M.S., 899
Cross, W.O., 40
Crouch, M.L., 338
Crumpacker, G.F., 187
Cunning, E.T., 573
Cunningham, L.L., 809
Curry, J.L., 156
Curry, W.L., 935
Curtis, C.M., 222

Dain, P., 229
Dale, D.C., 622
Darby, M.R., 196
Daughtrey, J.A., 900
Davenport, F.B., 754
Davidoff, D., 1004
Davis, D.G., Jr., 783
Davis, E.G., 41
Davis, E.R., 711
Davis, F.C., 83
Davis, J.M., 230
Davis, W.P., 1142
Day, N.J., 42
DeAngelis, P., 141
Deksnis, A., 841
Dengler, T.P., 374
Desjarlais-Leuth, C., 536
Detter, H., 1157
Deweese, B.J., 1099
Di Pietro, L.N., 324
Diana, J.P., 323
Diaz, A.J., 495
Dick, A.L., 953
Dickey, P.W., 216
Ditzion, S.H., 84-85

Dodge, A.C., 43
Doering, N., 1139
Donaldson, L.L., 672
Donley, V., 574
Donovan, M.J., 789
Donze, S.L., 265
Downing, M.L., 349
Downs, M.W., 1158
Doyle, Sister M.A., 223
Drummond, D.R., 837
DuMont, R.R., 86
Ducker, D.C., 438
Ducsay, W.J., 954
Dugger, H.H., 7, 8
Duncan, A.M., 432
Duncan, R.B., 540
Duniway, D.C., 584
Dunkley, G.C., 679
Dunleavy, Sister C.M., 784
Dunn, A., 901
Dutch, T.C., 600
Duyka, A.A., 1144
Dyess, S.W., 543
Dziewiatkowski, N., 1005

Early, S.E., 142
Earnshaw, J., 523
Easterly, A., 796
Eaton, J.D., 496
Eberhart, L., 87
Eckert, C.J., 266
Edgar, W.B., 9
Edsall, M.H., 550
Egolf, J.L., 325
El-Erian, T.S., 601
Elias, W.D., 267
Elliot, E.M., 767
Elliott, M.E., 362
Ellison, V.N., 1006
Elson, B.L., 602

Author Index

Emert, F.A., 742
Engley, D.B., 469
Erichsen, R.H., 1007
Erickson, E.W., 382
Esterquest, R.T., 955
Eury, W., 243
Evans, D.W., 375
Evensen, R.L., 712
Everhart, Sister M., 537
Evraiff, L.A.K., 743
Evtushenko, T.B., 10

Fabian, S., 1117
Fannin, G.M., 231
Farkas-Conn, I.S., 762
Farrow, M.H., 497
Feaster, D.M., 176
Fedder, M.B., 44
Feeney, R.B., 673
Fenster, V.R., 760
Ferguson, E.O., 1086
Ferguson, R.D., Jr., 902
Field, J.E.F., 1087
Findlay, S.M., 797
Flanagan, C.C., 383
Fleischer, M.B., 744
Fleischer, M.L., 268
Flener, J.G., 45
Folcarelli, R.J., 232
Fonville, E.R., 121
Foreman, C., 903
Forney, D.J., 269
Fortin, C.C., 474
Foster, P.M., 681
Foto, S.T., 1088
Freedman, M.J., 713
Freund, C.E., 575
Freund, E., 1008
Fry, J.W., 510
Fulchino, S.A., 936

Fund, C.K., 206

Gabriel, P., 1155
Gaiser, B.F., 188
Gallant, E.F., 224
Galloway, M.L., 659
Gankoski, I.F., 1074
Garrison, B.S., 244
Garrison, L.D., 88
Gaskill, G.A., 46
Gates, E.S., 143
Gates, J.K., 127
Gavurin, E.A., 1009
Gecas, J.G., 603
Gelfand, M.A., 384
Geller, E.G., 89
Genaway, D.C., 475
Gerard, H.L., 1010
Gibson, F.E., 212
Giddings, R.L., 144
Gill, S., 157
Gillespie, R.C., 350
Gillespie, S.C., 714
Gillie, M.H., 1011
Girvin, A.G., 524
Girvin, C.M., 326
Gladeck, A.A., 623
Gold, E., 1012
Goldberg, J., 1013
Goldman, S. 604
Goldstein, D., 233
Golicz, L.J., 554
Gooch, R.E., 270
Goodale, G., 271
Gorchels, C.C., 555
Gordon, D.K., 340
Gordon, H.S., 1014
Gordon, N.S., 27
Gore, D.J., Jr., 715
Goudeau, J.M., 11

Gould, L.P., 1015
Govan, J.F., 341
Graham, C.A., 904
Gray, G., 47
Grayson, B.R., 122
Graziano, E.E., 716
Green, C.S., 90
Green, E.B., 217
Greene, J.T., 306
Greer, J.J., 459
Greever, M.F.C., 1098
Griffin, B.C., 1127
Grimm, D.F., 48
Grisso, K.M., 875
Griswold, A.M., 460
Grotzinger, L.A., 870
Groves, M.N., 1016
Gustafson, R.E., 49
Guyton, T.L., 91
Guzzo, L.S., 1138

Haase, L., 1017
Hahn, S.S., 538
Hake, S.D., 364
Hale, C.E., 768
Hall, E.A., 650
Halligan, J.T., 1146
Halpin, J.R., 1018
Hammitt, F.E., 639
Hamner, P.N., 50
Handy, C.H., 685
Hankins, F.D., 905
Hansbrough, I.C., 342
Hanson, E.R., 769
Hardin, W., 385
Harding, Sister M.F., 336
Harding, T.S., 386
Harper, J.R., 511
Harris, H.J., 956
Harris, J.F., 565

Harris, M.H., 12
Harris, V., 558
Harshe, C.E., 272
Harshfield, L., 273
Harvey, D.I., 234
Hatch, O.W., 51
Hauserman, D.D., 819
Hausmann, A.F., 145
Havron, H.J., 274
Haynes, B.G., 822
Hazeltine, R.E., 275
Healey, J.S., 829
Heckman, M.L., 439, 812
Hedbavny, L., 13
Hedges, H.A., 1019
Hedrick, L.F., 1108
Heim, H.R., 276
Heindel, S.W., 498
Heiss, R.M., 717
Heisser, W.A., 417
Helfer, R.S., 718
Helgerson, M., 1159
Helms, C.E., 210
Hembree, M.M., 674
Hemmer, P.B., 193
Hench, M., 605
Hendrickson, R.M., 795
Henke, E.M., 317
Hensel, E.M., 719
Hepworth, B.M., 1093
Herdman, M.M., 92
Herrin, B.R., 640
Herring, B.G.U., 840
Hershey, F.E., 851
Hertzel, D.H., 906
Heskin, M.K., 585
Hester, G.A., 884
Higgins, M.H., 1113
Hill, M.E., 641
Hisz, E., 1020
Hoesch, M.J., 211

Author Index

Hoff, A., 461
Hoffman, R.P., 343
Hohman, A.C., 907
Holden, O., 675
Holder, E.J., 499
Holley, E.G., 828
Holloway, D.P., 624
Hollowell, L.S., II, 967
Holzer, S., 1021
Honea, A.B., 802
Hoole, M.D., 842
Hopkins, L., 277
Horgan, M., 606
Horrocks, N., 942
Houlette, W.D., 14
Howard, L., 163
Howe, M.J., 1089
Howell, D.B., 973
Hoyer, M., 479
Hoyle, N.E., 680
Hu, S.C., 607
Hubbard, C., 561
Hudon, E.G., 608
Hudson, J.P., 551
Hull, T.V., 177
Hunter, C.P., 245
Hurwitz, J.D., 93
Husselbee, M.V., 434
Hutzler, H.C., 164
Hyland, L., 858
Hyman, T.A., 1022

Iber, E., 1023
Imberman, A., 485
Ingalls, M.E., 307
Irvine, S.L., 957
Irwin, M., 512

Jackson, B., 908

Jackson, C., 609
Jackson, C.S., 1160
Jackson, R.L.M., 958
Jacobson, B., 1024
Jacobson, S., 1025
James, B.L., 132
James, S.E., 94
Jarrell, P.H., 337
Jawitz, M., 1026
Jeffress, I.P., 351
Jennings, J.M., 552
Jennings, K.L., 978
Jensen, G.D., 867
Jespersen, H., 1027
Johns, E.A., 968
Johnson, A.H., 1109
Johnson, E.C., 440
Johnson, E.R., 387
Johnson, R.E., 568
Johnston, M.E., 697
Johnston, R.P., 971
Jones, A.H., 979
Jones, G., 278
Jones, R., 486
Jones, V.H., 1094
Jordan, M., 857

Kahn, R.A., 625
Kalisch, P.A., 197, 221
Kanner, E.E., 909
Kansfield, N.J., 388-389
Karetsky, S., 959
Karro, T., 1028
Kato, Mother A., 487
Katz, L.F., 1029
Kavasch, D., 1030
Keenan, B.M., 1031
Keep, A.B., 52
Keim, A., 327
Kell, B.F., 798

Keller, L.E., 969
Kelly, Sister T.A., 424
Kembel, D., 319
Kennett, Sister M.E., 425
Ketchersid, A.L., 856
Keys, T.E., 15
Killian, K.A., 910
King, D., 1032
King, M.L., 153
King, S.K., 1132
Kirby, M.B., 462
Kirchem, C.E., 320
Kirsch, S., 1033
Kittle, A.T., 95
Klein, S.J., 463
Klopfenstein, M.J., 96
Klugiewicz, E., 328
Knighten, L., 456
Knoer, Sister M.M.A., 390
Knutson, G.S., 911
Koch, C.W., 770
Koch, J.V., 198
Korty, M.B., 831
Koudelka, J.B., 464
Kraft, Sister M.I., 525
Kram, R.I., 172
Kramp, R.S., 97
Kraske, G.E., 771
Kraus, J.W., 391
Krieg, C.J., 1151
Krueger, H.E., 562
Kruzas, A.T., 566
Kuehn, C.L., 912
Kulp, A.C., 392
Kunkle, H.J., 683

LaBoone, E., 435
LaFleur, L.B., 970
Lahey, J., 426
Landram, C.O., 913

Lane, M., 664
Lane, M.S., 1075
Lane, N.D., 914
Lanier, G.D., 642
Lapidus, B., 1034
Larsen, J.C., 693
Laubach, H., 567
Laudine, Sister M., 419
Laugher, C.T., 28
Laughlin, J.L., 694
Lawson, L.G., 1076
Lawson, R.W., 808
Leasure, M.F., 626
Lee, J.B., 544
Lee, M.M., 823
Lee, R.E., 98
Lee, R. Edward, 352
Lehnus, D.J., 915
Leinoff, T., 1137
Lemley, D.E., 643
Lenfest, G.E., 220
Levy, R.G., 123
Lewis, D.F., 178
Lewis, D.T., 1161
Lewis, L.L., 427
Lewis, M.E., 279
Lewis, R.A., 1077
Libby, D.C., 586
Licandro, M.L., 1035
Lincoln, Sister M.E., 213
Linderman, W.B., 488
Line, B.W., 937
Lippman, M., 1162
List, B.T., 500
Little, A.E., 814
Liu, N., 1114
Livingston, H.E., 29
Lo, H., 1036
Loeh, B.B., 376
Lohrer, M.A. 745
Long, L.E., 916

Lord, J.W., 644
Low, J.F., 280
Lowell, M.H., 393, 447
Lowrey, S.G.R., 146
Lowy, B., 1153
Luckett, G.R., 465
Lukowski, L.L., 1037
Lundean, J.W., 441
Lusak, R., 1038
Lutrin, D.B., 1039

MacCampbell, B.B., 281
Macleod, D.I., 377
Maddox, L.J., 917
Maestri, H.L., 53
Maggetti, M.T., 790
Magner, M.J., 883
Mahoney, B.L., 133
Malamud, S., 1163
Malik, A., 1135
Malino, E., 1040
Mallison, D.W., 627
Manint, H.R., 189
Manning, J.W., 16
Maples, H.L., 154
Marchesseault, R.E., 786
Marris, A., 1118
Martens, A., 395
Martin, D.V., 54
Maruskin, A.F., 960
Mason, L.G., 353
Mason, P.R., 158
Massman, V.F., 396
Mathews, S.G., 513
Mauseth, B.J., 124
Maxian, M.B., 1041
Maxwell, M.N.F., 473
May, R.H., 1164
Mayfield, S.N., 17
Mays, F.N., 354

McBride, M., 734
McCauley, E.B., 99
McClaren, D.N., 799
McClenahan, S., 645
McColl, M.C., 576
McCoy, R.E., 938
McCracken, P.C., 355
McCrary, M.E., 344
McCulley, K.M., 847
McFarland, M.M., 526
McGowan, F.M., 394
McGowan, O.T.P., 207
McGregor, J.W., 761
McGuire, L.P., 184
McGuire, M.P., 1085
McHugh, W.A., 720
McKnight, J.A., 1078
McLoughlin, E.C., 1119
McMullen, C. H., 442
McMurty, B.B., 199
McNeil, G., 128
McQuade, J.W., 1079
McSwain, M.B., 843
McTaggart, J.B., 527
Meckler, A.M., 397
Medley, N.M.D., 1165
Mehl, W.R., 782
Melvin, Sister M.C., 669
Memory, M.W., 246
Merriman, M.M., 803
Meshot, G.V., 282
Meyer, W.P., 329
Meyerend, M.H., 528
Meyers, J.K., 514
Michelson, A.I., 781
Michener, R., 457
Miksa, F.L., 815-816
Miletic, I., 1095
Miller, A.H., Jr., 443
Miller, C.H., 876
Miller, L.A., 398

Miller, R.E., 735
Miller, S.J., 610
Miller, V.P., 476
Milliken, Sister M.C., 235
Minnick, N.F., 136
Mitchell, M.W., 147
Molnar, J.E., 18
Moloney, L.C., 545
Molz, J.B., 30
Molz, R.K., 772
Monroe, M.E., 100
Moore, B.L., 247
Moore, D.T., 873
Moore, G.G., 501
Moore, M.G., 972
Moore, M.R., 676
Moore, M.V., 55
Morris, Rita, 1100
Morris, Ruth, 1042
Morroni, J.R., 793
Morse, C.R., 817
Morse, D.B., 190
Moscowitz, R., 1110
Moss, J.R., 101
Mount, E., 628
Moyers, J.C., 363
Mulac, C.M., 801
Mullins, J.L., 629
Munn, R.F., 559
Murphy, S.B., 248
Murray, K., 283
Murray, M.E., 308
Musmann, V.K., 56
Musser, A., 515
Mutschler, H.F., 284

Nagy, M.C., 309
Nation, M.A., 918
Neal, P., 919
Nehlig, M.E., 755

Nelson, M.N.B., 920
Nestleroad, R., 285
Newell, M.M., 102
Newman, W.A., 103
Newsom, H.E., 365
Nichols, B.B., 236
Nichols, M.E., 466, 478
Nichols, M.I., 838
Nicholson, J.M., Jr., 502
Nolan, C., 286
Nonacs, M., 577
Noonan, M.Z., 656
Normandeau, C., 1043
North, N., 611
Nourse, L.M., 104
Nylander, E.P., 214

O'Brian, A., 1044
O'Brien, Sister M.B., 225
O'Connell, J.J., 849
O'Connor, M.A., 921
O'Connor, Sister M.V., 57
O'Connor, S., 1045
O'Connor, T.F., 428
O'Connor, W., 974
O'Driscoll, P.D., 980
O'Flynn, M.E., 846
O'Loughlin, Sister M.A.J., 773
O'Rourke, M.M., 58
O'Shea, J.M., 1102
Oehlerts, D.E., 105
Ogden, S., 961
Oh, S.J., 1101
Olech, J., 106
Olsen, R.A., 1143
Olson, C.A., 1111
Opler, P.S., 578
Orr, A.P., 736
Orr, H.A., 553
Orr, M.F., 366

Author Index

Orr, R.S., 399
Osborn, V.J., 721
Osborne, J.T., 529
Osburn, C.B., Jr., 400
Osburn, H., 756
Ostendorf, P.J., 215
Oswald, J.F., 722
Overmier, J.A., 401
Ownings, V.B., 467

Paciorek, L.A., 1103
Page, J.S., Jr., 1046
Palmer, R.C., 922
Palmer, V.D., 723
Pandiri, A.M., 612
Parham, P.M., 888
Patri, D., 1112
Patrick, W.R., 19
Patterson, J.M., 20
Paul, G.N., 630
Pazar, C.H., 1166
Peace, W.K., III, 706
Pearsall, T.F., 503
Pease, K.R., 185
Peden, W.H. 844
Peirce, P., 923
Pentlin, F.C., 663
Peritz, B.C., 924
Perkins, T.E., 504
Perres, M.J., 159
Perrins, B.C., 402
Peterson, K.G., 420
Pettigrew, C.L., 832
Petty, W.E., 569
Phelps, D.J., 125
Phillips, C.O., 825
Phillips, V., 310
Pikovnik, R., 1080
Piper, Sister T., 780
Piscitello, C.M., 1167

Pitcher, P.M., 367
Pittman, C.K., 981
Podolnick, S., 1147
Poll, B., 107
Pond, P.K., 774
Poor, A.M., 853
Porter, M.L.R., 834
Post, K.L., 1141
Poste, L.I., 943
Potera, E.J., 330
Potter, J.C., 556
Potts, A.J., 1154
Powell, B.E., 403
Powell, N.L., 200
Powell, R.A., 560
Prassel, M.A., 800
Pressing, K.L., 587
Prichard, L.G., 173
Proctor, M.M., 546
Provenzano, L., 1047
Purcell, B.L., 1148
Purdy, B.A., 108
Putnam, L.A., 588

Quain, M., 1048
Quinn, C., 1097

Rabner, L.B., 1149
Radford, N.A., 404
Ranz, J., 724
Ratcliffe, T.E., Jr., 444
Read, K.T., 21
Redd, G.L., 165
Redding, B.N., 667
Reece, M.B.Y., 885
Reed, L.L., 589
Reed, M.M., 287
Rehfus, R.O., 925
Reilly, P.G., 59

Resnick, S., 1049
Reynolds, H.M., 405
Reynolds, R.C., 570
Rhodes, L.G., 806
Ribbens, D.N., 22
Rice, D.M., 201
Richards, E.M., 882
Richards, E.S., 151
Richardson, C.E., 881
Richardson, E.R., 530
Richardson, J.V., Jr., 752
Richie, J.F., 60
Rigali, D.L., 1050
Robertson, M.P., 1051
Robinson, R.W., 61
Rochester, M.K., 944
Roddy, Sister R., 468
Rodstein, F.M., 311
Rogers, A.E., 547
Rohdy, M.A., 725
Rollins, O.H., 237
Roloff, R.W., 477
Roper, D.F., 775
Roper, F.W., 746
Ross, Sister M.C., 785
Ross, N., 1104
Rothstein, S., 737
Rouse, R., Jr., 548
Rouzer, S.M., 109
Rowe, W.D., 704
Rubin, P., 1052
Rubin, R., 1152
Rubinstein, S., 202
Ruderman, L.P., 871
Ruffe, B.L., 1168
Ruffin, M.B., 726
Rufsvold, M.I., 646
Rukus, A.T., 653
Rush, N.O., 458
Rush, S.C., 191
Ryberg, H.T., 331

Sabine, J.E., 62
Sahli, M.S., 31
Salfas, S.G., 208
Salinas, A., 833
Sanders, B., 1115
Sanders, L.M., 1090
Satterfield, H.C., 288
Satterfield, V., 436
Saucerman, K., 378
Savage, A.L., 110
Savary, M.J., 1096
Saviers, S.H., 516
Sawyer, M.H., 1070
Sayle, S., 1053
Scanlon, R., 1054
Schink, R.J., 517
Schley, R., 727
Schmidt, V.L., 926
Schneberg, B., 1055
Schnitzler, N.L., 590
Schrader, A.M., 962
Schryver, N.E., 312
Schubach, B.W., 877
Schuetz, A.R., 531
Schwartz, B., 1150
Schwartz, M., 1105
Scoggin, R.B., 249
Scott, C.D., 613
Scott, Edith, 839
Scott, Ellen, 455
Scott, K.J., 194
Scott, R.P., 927
Scott, S.S., 1169
Seabrook, J.H., 1081
Seabrook, M., 787
Seabury, J.B., 1056
Searcy, H.L., 32
Seaton, E., 1057
Semmler, E.A., 148

Author Index

Servies, J.A., 728
Seryneck, W.P., 1058
Seth, O.C., 677
Settlemire, C.L., 705
Sevy, B., 579
Shafer, H., 406
Shamp, B.K., 313
Shaw, R.R., 23
Sheffield, H.G., 314
Shera, J.H., 63
Shewmaker, J.D., 289
Shiflett, O.L., 407
Shores, L., 408
Showalter, G.W., 982
Siegel, H., 1059
Siggins, J.A., 747
Sigler, R.F., 134
Silva, Sister M.F.C., 518
Silver, C.K., 1060
Silver, R.A., 315
Sims, E.E., 591
Singer, A.R., 654
Singleton, M.E., 748
Sinnette, E.D., 869
Sisson, L.K., 1061
Sitter, C.L., 549
Skaar, M.O., 682
Skidmore, S., 1120
Skidmore, W.L., 290
Skipper, J.E., 519
Slavens, T.P., 449, 489
Sloan, R.M., 111
Smail, H.A., 631
Smit, P.R., 592
Smith, C.E., 702
Smith, D., 421
Smith, D.J., 532
Smith, H.B., 1170
Smith, J.C., 409
Smith, L.E., 24
Smith, M., 647

Smith, M.H., 332
Smith, M.H.K., 356
Smith, P.C., 614
Smith, R.C., 192
Smith, V.J., 939
Snyder, E.B., 186
Sokol, E., 1062
Sommer, J.M., 983
Sommerville, S.G., 291
Songer, F.H., 655
Souza, M.A., 135
Spain, F.L., 64
Sparks, C.G., 805, 928
Sparks, E.C., 218
Spaulding, V.A., 292
Speiden, V.M., 929
Speirs, C.H., 112
Spencer, G.S., 174
Stanbery, G.W., II, 757
Stanley, C.V., 25
Stanley, E.L., 448
Stark, B., 65
Starke, R., 1171
Starr, K.D., 1172
Stearns, E.I., 925
Steele, U.M., 1173
Stein, J.H., 520
Stephens, H.H. 451
Stephenson, H.S., 690
Stevenson, G.M., 113
Stewart, J., 126
Stewart, N.J., 490
Stewart, R.A., 615
Stewart, W.L., Jr., 250
Stibitz, M.T., 114
Stiffler, S.A., 66
Stillman, M.E., 616
Stoneham, F.M., 357
Storie, C., 410
Strable, E.G., 632
Straka, M., 729

Stratton, G.W., 293
Strauss, L.H., 411
Strother, J.V., 368
Strunk, A.L., 984
Suen, M.T., 824
Suess, G.M., 695
Suhler, S.A., 358
Sullivan, P., 850
Sun, D., 1106
Sussman, D., 1107
Suzuki, A.N., 369
Suzuki, Y., 945
Swartz, R.G., 219
Swogetinsky, B.A., 359
Sword, E.D., 820
Synodis, E.J., 1121
Szkudlarek, M.E., 294

Tachihata, C., 168
Tarlton, S.M., 505
Taylor, I.M., 671
Taylor, J., 251
Taylor, M.V., 179
Taylor, R.N., 868
Teague, A.H., 360
Teeter, L.W., 295
Terrell, D., 470
Terwilliger, G.H.P., 412
Thackston, F.V., 730
Theis, K.A., 1133
Theriot, B.C., 872
Thomas, E.F., 633
Thomas, E.H., 580
Thomas, F.H., 648
Thomas, M.A., 686
Thomas, M.E., 296
Thomas, R.D., 930
Thomison, D.V., 776
Thompson, L.B., 115
Thompson, M.C., 738

Thorp, E.N., 946
Throne, M., 450
Thurber, E., 413
Tierney, C.M., 1174
Tietjen, L.M., 67
Tillman, R.H., 129
Timlin, D.S., 1063
Tinklepaugh, D.K., 665
Tracy, W.F., 116
Trombley, Sister M.F.X., 836
True, P., 1064
Tu, S., 1122
Tuck, R.S., 333
Tucker, C., 1082
Tucker, J.M., 866
Tucker, J.S., 521
Turner, H.M., 880
Turnow, W.H., 1123
Tutt, C., 491
Tyne, J., 1065

Unger, C.P., 117

Valentine, Sister M., 533
Van Beynum, W.J., 68
Van Horne, J.C., 33
VanMale, J.E., 684
Vann, S.K., 749
Vannorsdall, M.M., 703
Varner, Sister C., 634
Vattermare, A., 882
Vermilya, N.C., 522
Via, N.S., 149
Vinicombe, M., 1066
Vinson, R.J., 649
Vloebergh, H.E., 699
vonOesen, E., 252

Author Index

Waddell, J.N., 854
Wade, B.A., 371
Wadsworth, R.W., 118
Waggoner, L.B., 150
Wagner, L.F., 534
Wagner, M.K., 931
Walch, D.B., 963
Waldo, M.J., 414
Waldron, R.K., 593
Walker, M.H., 594
Walker, M.J.D., 794
Waller, H.C., 1091
Walters, P.L., 1134
Walther, L.A., 180
Wang, S.Y., 471
Wannarka, M.B., 119
Ward, B.A., 370
Waters, J.K., 1083
Weakley, M.E., 581
Webb, D.A., 759
Weber, H., 1067
Weis, L.A., 297
Welborn, E.C., 69
Wells, I.S., 595
Wells, M.L., 1092
Wells, S.B., 964
Wensley, D.D., 1068
West, E.K., 415
Wetzel, N.P., 298
Whalum, C.G., 777
Whedbee, M.M., 253
Wheeler, J.T., 26
Wheeler, S.B., 879
White, A.W., 372
Whitney, E.M., 334
Whyte, E., 1156
Wicklzer, A.F., 750
Wilcox, H.M., 70
Wilcox, L.E., 445
Wilkins, M.J., 731
Willet, M.M., 732

Williams, B.C., 166
Williams, C.W., 535
Williams, M.L., 661
Williams, M.G., 452
Williams, R.V., 120
Williamson, L., 1069
Williamson, W.L., 860
Willis, D.E., 617
Wilson, E.C., 932
Winckler, P.A., 886
Wine, E., 299
Wing, M.J., 753
Winger, A.K., 335
Winship, S.G., 813
Wofford, A., 670
Wolcott, M.D., 300
Wolf, N.E., 596
Wong, R., 238
Woods, L.B., 940
Woodward, P.K., 1084
Wortmen, L.J., 1124
Wright, A.E., 826
Wright, L.T., 807

Yenawine, W.S., 446
Yockey, R., 316
York, M.C., 701
Young, A.P., 778
Young, B.A., 239
Young, C., 707
Young, M.J., 301
Young, R.L., 1125
Young, S.S., 302
Yueh, N.N., 416

Zaremba, M., 1126
Zimmerman, M., 181
Zubatsky, D.S., 779

SUBJECT INDEX

[Numbers refer to entry numbers]

Abbot, Ezra, 717, 724
Accreditation, 384, 744
Acton Library, CT, 67
Adair County Public Library, MO, 981
Adams, E.D., 630
Adams, John, 532
Adams, Scott, 580
Adult education, 87, 98, 100, 114, 1168
Advertising agency libraries, 632
Agnes Scott College Library, GA, 436
Ahern, Mary E., 801
Akron Law Library Association, OH, 624
Akron Public Library, OH, 256, 297, 301, 567, 1076
Akron, University of, Library, OH, 509
ALA Filing Rules, 718
Alabama, 121-123, 403, 842, 856
Alabama Department of Archives and History, 856
Alabama, University of, Library, 403, 842
Alaska Department of Library Service, 125-126
Alaska, 124-126
Albany Library, NY, 1003
Albertus Magnus College Library, CT, 424, 427
Albright Alumni Memorial Library, PA, 524
Albright College Library, PA, 524
Alcorn State University Library, MS, 385
Alden, Timothy, 532
Alexandria Public Library, LA, 190, 973
Alexandria Public Library, VA, 361
Allegan County, libraries in, MI, 210
Allegheny College Library, PA, 532
Allen Memorial Art Museum Library, OH, 591
Allentown Free Library, PA, 326

Alliance, OH, 1071
American Association of Law Libraries, 761, 1128
American Association of School Librarians, 770, 774
American Bibliopolist, 867
American Catalog, 845
American Documentation Institute, 762
American Historical Association, 887
American influence abroad, 941-946
American Library Association, 720, 740-741, 744, 763-779, 804, 823, 850, 860, 863, 881, 887-888, 903, 917, 928, 957, 1129-1133
American Library Directory, 1162
American Library Institute, 780
American Library Journal, 845
American Merchant Marine Library Association, 781
American Mercury, 938
American Negro Academy, 869
American Prison Association, 570
American Theological Library Association, 395, 782
American Type Founders Company Library, NY, 627
Americanization, 965
Amherst College Library, MA, 379, 469
Amigos Bibliographic Council, TX, 1134
Amityville Free Library, NY, 1058
Anderson-Broaddus College Library, WV, 558
Andrew College, TN, 339
Angell, Richard S., 948
Anglo-American Cataloging Code, 723
Annhurst College Library, CT, 425
Annmary Brown Memorial Library, RI, 537
Antioch College Library, OH, 514
Appleton Public Library, WI, 375
Apprentice's Library, MA, 203
Apprentice's Library, NY, 710
Apprentice's Library, PA, 835
Arbuckle, Alma J., 557
Architecture, 79, 105, 206, 379, 405, 602
Archivists, 947
Arizona, 417
Arkansas, 127-129, 385
Arkansas, University of, Pine Bluff, Library, 385
Armed Forces Medical Library Catalog, 731

Subject Index

Army Post Library System, 599
Art collections, 571
Art exhibition catalogs, 712
Askealoosa College Library, IA, 449
Asplund, Julia B., 802
Association of American Library Schools, 783
Association of College and Research Libraries, 768, 1133
Association of Research Libraries, 394
Astor, John J., 96
Atkinson, J.S., 245
Atlanta Penitentiary Library, GA, 568
Atlanta Public Library, GA, 160
Atlanta University Center Library, GA, 71
Audiovisual Education Association of Iowa, 658
Audiovisual services, 232, 637, 649, 766
Augustana College and Theological Seminary Library, IL, 440
Austin Public Library, TX, 358
Austin, TX, school libraries, 840
Australia, 942
Automation, 479, 1141, 1170

Babcock, Caroline, 264
Babylon Public Library, NY, 1026
Bacon, Francis, 716
Baker, Augusta, 803
Baker, George H., 488
Baldwin, Clara, 215, 662
Baldwin Public Library, NY, 1066
Baldwin-Wallace College Library, OH, 506
Baltimore and Ohio Railroad Company Library, 626
Baltimore Archdiocesan Library Council, MD, 661
Bangor Theological Seminary Library, ME, 458
Barnard, Henry, 96, 652
Bartlesville Public Library, OK, 77
Batchelder, Mildred L., 804
Bates College Library, ME, 458
Bates, Joshua, 96
Bay Shore Public Library, NY, 1063
Bayard Taylor Library of Kennett Square, PA, 332
Baylor University Library, TX, 548, 842

Beaumont Public Library, TX, 353, 1089
Becker, Bernadette, 474
Bedford Social Library, NH, 42
Belcher, Johnathan, 480
Bellevue Public School Library System, WA, 681
Bellmore Memorial Library, NY, 1004
Bender, Harold S., 590
Bentley, William, 532
Bessemer Public Library, AL, 121
Bethany Biblical Seminary Library, IL, 439
Bethany College Library, WV, 558
Bethany Library Association, CT, 149
Bethesda Public Library, MD, 195
Bethlehem Library Association, PA, 325
Bethlehem Public Library, PA, 325
Bethpage Public Library, NY, 1040
Bibliographic Center for Research, 415,
Bibliometrics, 906
Bibliotheca Americana, 49
Bibliotherapy, 578
Bicknell, Thomas W., 765
Bierce Library, OH, 509
Billings, John S., 229
Bindery, 956
Birchard Public Library, OH, 270, 275
Birchard, Sardis, 270, 275
Birmingham-Southern College Library, AL, 842
Bishop, William W., 404, 805
Bitner, Harry, 422
Black Mountain Memorial Library, PA, 330
Blacks, library service to, 73-74, 121-122, 129, 156, 159-162, 165, 191, 216, 240, 247, 342-344, 347, 467, 492, 539, 546, 806-807, 811, 857, 869, 966, 969, 1131
Blind, library service to, 90, 102, 233, 314, 1024
Blue, Thomas F., 807
Bluford, Ferdinand D., 503
Board of Education for Librarianship, 740-741
Bogle, Sarah, 757
Bonham Public Library, TX, 356
Boni, Albert, 397
Bonney, W.W., 364

Subject Index 435

Book catalogs, 710, 724, 726
Book fairs, 1159
Book selection, 115, 893, 896
Book-Company of Durham, CT, 68
Bookman's Manual, 835
Bookmobile service, 253, 262, 283, 908
Bookplates, 427
Booth, Mary J., 808
Borchard, Edwin M., 422
Borden, Fanny, 485
Boston Athenaeum, MA, 40, 815-817, 828, 860, 880
Boston, MA, early libraries, 40, 46
Boston Post, 77
Boston Public Library, MA, 63, 77, 119, 204, 206, 387, 880, 882, 887
Bostwick, Arthur E., 809
Boughter, Vivian, 560
Bowdoin College Library, ME, 457
Bowker, Richard R., 610, 773, 816
Bradford, John, 41
Bray, Thomas, 9, 26-33, 52, 68, 463, 710
Brentwood Public Library, NY, 1043
Brett, William H., 303, 306
Bridgeport Public Library, CT, 138
Brigham, Clarence E., 473, 583
British Museum Library, 615
Brookhaven National Laboratory Library, NY, 1116
Brooklyn College Library, NY, 1107
Brooklyn Public Library, NY, 108, 846, 1049
Brotherton, Nina, 757
Brown University Library, RI, 379, 391, 408, 536-537
Brumbach Library, OH, 286
Bryant Library, NY, 1035
Buchtel College Library, OH, 509
Bucknell University Library, PA, 526
Buffington, Willie L., 810
Bullen, Henry L., 627
Burditt, Margery, 144
Burnet County Free Library, TX, 834
Burnite, Caroline, 303
Business, service to, 106, 312, 402, 883, 894
Butler, Susan D., 811

Byrd, William, II, 14, 25

Cabeen, S.K., 628
Cairo Public Library, GA, 166
California, 3, 34, 56, 104, 130-135, 402, 418-421, 564, 568, 584, 630, 650, 683, 833, 1146
California Institute of Technology Library, 564
California State Library, 683, 1146
California, University of, Berkeley, Library, 420-421, 564
California, University of, Los Angeles, Library, 833
Cambria Free Library, PA, 327
Camp, David N., 652
Camp, Rev. Ichabod, 68
Canal Fulton Public Library, OH, 1083
Canton Public Library, OH, 298
Carey, Miriam, 570
Carnegie, Andrew, 76, 96
Carnegie Corporation, 71-72, 76, 352, 360, 377, 404, 678, 741, 942, 944, 1093
Carnegie Library of Ellensburg, WA, 364
Carnegie Library of Pittsburgh, PA, 567, 861
Carnegie Library School, GA, 751
Carnegie Library School, PA, 757
Carroll College Library, WI, 562
Carroll, John, 431
Carter, Robert, 21
Case, Leonard, 508
Cash, William T., 687
Cassel, Abraham H., 812
Catalog codes, 711
Cataloging and classification, 708-732, 769, 839, 889, 891, 915, 968, 1169
Cathedral Free Circulating Library, NY, 58
Catholic academic libraries, 390
Catholic librarianship, 912, 950
Catholic Library Association, 390, 784-785, 830
Catholic reading circle movement, 950
Censorship, 77, 89, 101, 112, 134, 359, 907, 933-940, 1130, 1160, 1166
Center for Research Libraries, IL, 1135
Central City Public Library, CO, 136
Certain, Casper C., 638
Certification, 900

Subject Index 437

Chapin, Howard M., 583
Charlotte College Library, NC, 505
Chattanooga Public Library, TN, 341
Chelan County Library, WA, 367
Chemung County Library, NY, 230
Cheshire Public Library, CT, 150
Chester County Library, PA, 332-333
Chestnut Hill College, PA, 525
Chicago Historical Society Library, IL, 586
Chicago Lutheran Theological Seminary Library, IL, 441
Chicago Public Library, IL, 172-174, 860, 864
Chicago, University of, Graduate Library School, IL, 740-741, 752, 959
Chicago, University of, Library, IL, 380, 387, 407, 437-438, 442-443, 564
Children's librarians, 644
Children's libraries and services, 108, 294, 297, 303, 321, 374, 635-682, 818, 840-841, 849, 852-853, 861
Chinese collection, 607, 1106
Cincinnati, OH, early libraries, 54
Cincinnati Public Library, OH, 257, 283, 860
Circulating libraries, 6, 26, 52, 55, 63, 67, 84
Circulation services, university libraries, 398
City Library Association, MA, 203
Clackamas County, OR, 320
Claremont College Library, CA, 419
Clark Memorial Library, CT, 149
Clark Public Library, NJ, 225
Clarke, Henry D., 605
Clayton, Howard, 412
Cleelum Public Library, WA, 364
Clelland, Marjorie B., 631
Clements, William L., 473
Cleveland Public Library, OH, 78, 257, 303-316, 825-826, 851, 861, 883, 885
Clift, David, 786
Cliosophic Society Library, NJ, 480
Coffin, Jennie, 245
Cogswell, Joseph G., 701
Colburn Library, OH, 1077
Colby College Library, ME, 458
Cold Spring Harbor Library, NY, 1030
Colelazer, Henry, 472

College & Research Libraries, 895, 898
College of Notre Dame of Maryland Library, 466
College of Physicians Library, PA, 575
College of the City of New York Library, 490, 1147
Collins, Henry, 57
Colonial libraries, 1, 9-10, 14-15, 19-21, 23-33, 36-37, 41-42, 47-48, 52, 55, 57, 61, 63-65, 67-68, 391, 408, 1098
Colorado, 136, 564, 593, 619, 684, 888
Colorado Library Commission, 684
Colorado State Historical Society Library, 593
Columbia Union College Library, MD, 460
Columbia University Library, NY, 53, 380, 408, 410, 486, 488, 491, 627, 727, 729, 854, 1106, 1156
Columbia University, Library School, NY, 822
Columbus Public Library, GA, 162
Committee of University Industrial Relations Librarians, 564
Community college libraries, 418
Compton, Wilson N., 554
Comstockery, 934-935
Concord Public Library, NC, 244
Connecticut, 10, 36-37, 65, 67-68, 137-150, 380, 391, 408, 422-428, 564, 582, 612, 621, 651-654, 685, 786, 841, 878, 1113
Connecticut College Library, 427
Connecticut Library Association, 786
Connecticut State Library, 685
Connecticut, University of, Library, 426
Connell, Wessie, 166
Conservation, 961
Consolidations, 393
Cook County Library, TX, 838
Coolidge, Archibald C., 1143
Cooperation, 393, 779, 904, 960, 1095-1096
Cornell University Library, NY, 392, 402, 564, 1145
Countryman, Gratia A., 215, 764
County libraries, 104, 286, 337, 355, 357
Courts, 116, 1166
Craver, H.W., 628
Crawford County, OH, 274
Crerar, John, 96
Criswell Center for Biblical Studies Library, TX, 1127
Cultural diplomacy, 771

SUBJECT INDEX

Culver, Essae M., 690, 764
Cumberland College Library, TN, 540
Current List of Medical Literature, 731
Curry, Arthur R., 813
Cushing, Harvey, 878
Cutter, Charles A., 713, 717, 721, 723, 725, 765, 773, 814-817, 917
Cuyahoga County Library, OH, 261, 280
Cuyahoga Falls Library Association, OH, 280

Dag Hammarskjold Library, NY, 622
Dana, John C., 119, 203, 619, 684, 818-819
Darby Library Company, PA, 61
Dartmouth College Library, NH, 408
Dascomb, James, 521
Daughters of the American Revolution Genealogical Library, DC, 595
Davenport Public Library, IA, 183-184
Davidson Academy Library, TN, 540
Davis and Elkins College Library, WV, 558
Davis, Mary G., 820
Davis, Raymond C., 821
Davis, Watson, 762
Dayton Public Library, OH, 257, 262, 299
Dayton, University of, Library, OH, 513
Decatur-DeKalb Regional Library, GA, 971
Deer Park Public Library, NY, 1023
DeGolyer, E.L., 542
DeGolyer Foundation Library, TX, 542
Delaware, 151, 429, 587, 686
Delaware Historical Society Library, 587
Delaware State Archives, 686
Delaware, University of, Library, 429
Denton Public Library, TX, 1092
Denver Public Library, CO, 888
Denver, University of, Library, CO, 564, 888
Denver, University of, Library School, CO, 888
Departmental libraries, 475
Depository Act of 1962, 603
Depository library system, 610
Des Moines Public Library, IA, 182, 184, 186
Detroit Public Library, MI, 883

Devereaux, John H., 60
Dewey Decimal Classification, 709, 716, 721, 723, 773, 822
Dewey, Melvil, 407, 469, 488, 610, 638, 699, 709, 716, 721, 723, 729, 765, 773, 780, 816, 822-823, 870, 917
Dickinson, George S., 948
Dictionary of Books Relating to America, 867
District of Columbia, 152-154, 401, 430-432, 564, 595, 597-598, 600, 602, 605-610, 613, 615, 617, 728, 734, 787, 873-877
District of Columbia Library Association, 787
District of Columbia Public Library, 152-153
Ditzion, Sidney, 107
Divisional plan, university libraries, 387
Dixie College, TN, 339
Doctoral dissertations, 897, 914, 921
Doctoral education, 407, 914
Doren, Electra C., 262
Downs, Robert B., 824, 1144
"Dr." Sloan Library, OH, 265
Drake University Library, IA, 449
Drexel Institute Library School, PA, 755
Duke University Library, NC, 730
Duluth Public Library, MN, 214
Dumbarton Oaks Research Library, MA, 470
Dunlap Memorial Library, TX, 1087

Earlham College Library, IN, 448
East Cleveland Public Library, OH, 263
East Hampton Free Library, NY, 1032
East Meadow Public Library, NY, 1015
East Palestine Public Library, OH, 269
East River Library Company, CT, 146
East Rockaway Free Library, NY, 994
East Saint Louis Public Library, IL, 171
East Texas State College, 758
Eastern Baptist Theological Seminary Library, PA, 527
Eastern Illinois University Library, 808
Eastman, Linda A., 314, 764, 825-826
Ebenezer S. Lane Library, IL, 438
E.C. Scranton Library, Madison, CT, 146
Edgerton, Mary P., 256

Edmonds, Emma, 217
Edson, Hanford A., 177
Eleanor Squire Memorial Library, OH, 631
Elise, Robert W., 470
Elliott, Leslie R., 827
Elmendorf, Theresa W., 764
Elmont Public Library, NY, 991
Elon College Library, NC, 504
Emerson, Ralph W., 40
Emma S. Clark Memorial Library, NY, 996
Emory and Henry College Library, VA, 553
Emory University, GA, 751
Emory University Library, GA 436
Emory University, Library School, GA, 1173
Engel, Carl, 948
Engineering books, 23
Engineering Index, 951
Engineering Societies Library, NY, 628, 1123
Enoch Pratt Free Library, MD, 78, 100, 105, 197-198, 202
Erie Public Library, PA, 328
Esquire, 907
Estes, Dana, 340
Evans, Charles, 177, 221
Evans Dental Library, PA, 576
Evans, Thomas V., 576
Everett, Edward, 96, 204

Faculty status, 396, 407
Fairfax County Library, VA, 362
Fairfield Public Library, CT, 139
Fairfield University Library, CT, 427
Fairmont State College Library, WV, 560
Fall River Public Library, MA, 207
Falley, Eleanor N., 462
Farmer's Library, East Guilford, CT, 146
Farmingdale Public Library, NY, 1000, 1018
Farmington Plain Library, Plainville, CT, 148
Farmington plan, 1095
Fay, Lucy, 757
Federal legislation, 103, 767, 829

Ferrill, Will C., 593
Fiction, 80, 636, 910, 913, 916, 918, 929
Field Museum of Natural History Library, IL, 588
Finch, James A., 600
Finkelstein Memorial Library, NY, 1042
Finley, J.B., 569
Fisk University Library, TN, 539, 869
Fiske, Daniel W., 97, 1145
Fitch, Charles, 569
Fitchburg Public Library, MA, 108
Fletcher, William I., 469, 721
Florence, Italy, 961
Florida, 155-159, 433-434, 633, 687, 1097
Florida State Library, 687
Florida, University of, Library, 433
Fogarty, John E., 829
Foik, Paul J., 830
Folger, Henry, 96
Folk song archive, 597
Folsom, Charles, 717
Foote, William W., Jr., 555
Forbes Library, MA, 814-817
Ford, Worthington C., 473
Fort Vancouver Regional Library, WA, 365
Fort Worth Public Library, TX, 349, 868
Franklin, Benjamin, 48, 96, 831, 967
Franklin D. Roosevelt Library, NY, 618, 1118
Franklin Institute Library, PA, 623
Franklin Library Association, CA, 132
Franklin, Louise, 832
Franklin Society and Library Company, VA, 47
Fraternity libraries, 1094
Free Circulating Library of the First Congregational Church, CT, 144
Free Library of Philadelphia, PA, 48, 59, 321, 324
Freedman, Samuel, 397
Freedom of Information Act (1966), 939
Freedom to Read, 89
Freeport Memorial Library, NY, 1016
Fulbright program, 946
Fullerton Junior College Library, CA, 418
Fulton, John, 878

Subject Index

Funding, Texas higher education libraries, 543
Fyan, Loleta D., 764

Gainsville Public Library, TX, 838
Galveston, TX, 347, 857
Garden City Public Library, NY, 1027
Garfield Public Library, OH, 291-292
Garrison, Fielding H., 464
Gaver, Mary V., 764
Genealogical Society of Pennsylvania Library, 596
Genealogy in libraries, 277, 596, 983
General Education Board, 71, 671
Geneva Public Library, IL, 170
George Peabody College Library, TN, 540
Georgetown University Library, DC, 431
Georgia, 160-166, 403, 435-436, 568, 655, 751, 810, 971-972, 1136, 1173
Georgia Library Association, 1136
Georgia School of Technology Library, 436
Georgia State College for Women Library, 436
Georgia, University of, Library, 403, 435-436
Gerontology, 909
Gillis, James L., 683, 1146
Githens, Alfred M., 105
Gladewater Public Library, TX, 348
Glenville State College Library, WV, 557
Goddard, George S., 685
Goodrich, Francis L.D., 1147
Goodwin, John E., 833
Goree, Edwin S., 834
Goucher College Library, MD, 462
Gould, George M., 119
Government publications, 603
Graham, Bessie, 835
Great books movement, 109
Great Neck Library, NY, 985, 1029
Green, Samuel S., 610, 733, 765, 836, 917
Greenbank, William K., 611
Gregg County Library, TX, 348
Griffin, Mary, 474
Grinnel Library Association of Wappingers Falls, NY, 989
Grolier Club Library, NY, 1122

Grosse Pointe Public Library, MI, 211
Grosvenor, Seth, 490
Grothaus, Julia, 837
Grummond, Lena Y. de, 660
Guam, 167
Guam Public Library System, 167
Guernsey County District Public Library, OH, 1082
Guide to Reference Books, 854
Guild, Reuben A., 536
Guilford College Library, NC, 497
Guilford, CT, early libraries, 37, 67
Gunter, Lillian, 838
Gustavus Adolphus College Library, MN, 476
G.W. Blunt White Library, CT, 582

Haddonfield Public Library, NJ, 1154
Hadley, Chalmers, 619, 684
Hall, James T., 461
Hamilton College Library, NY, 482
Hamilton County, OH, 283
Hamilton, Joseph G.R., 501
Hampshire Interlibrary Center, MA, 392
Hampton Library, NY, 1056
Handbuch der Bibliothewissenschaft, 954
Handicapped services, 316, 649
Hanes, Anna H., 496
Hanes Foundation, NC, 496
Hanger, William A., 620
Hanson, Grant D., 476
Hanson, J.C.M., 839
Harborfields, NY, 1028
Harper, Lathrop, 473
Harper, Wilhelmina, 132
Harriet Monroe Modern Poetry Library, IL, 443
Harris, William T., 716
Harrison, Alice S., 840
Hartford Public Library, CT, 841
Hartford, University of, Library, CT, 427
Harvard University Library, MA, 379-380, 391, 402, 408, 470-471, 564,
    726, 816, 887, 1098, 1143

SUBJECT INDEX

Hawaii, 168, 564
Hawaii State Library, 168
Hawaii, University of, Library, 564
Hawkins, Rush, 537
Hawley, Willis D., 234
Hawthorne, Nathaniel, 22
Hayes, Rutherford B., 275
Hazeltine, Mary E., 760
Hefley, Sue, 660
Hegel, Georg W.F., 716
Heighway, Josephine, 242
Henry L. Wolfner Memorial Library, MO, 1115
Henry Lea Library, PA, 523
Hepburn, A. Barton, 237
Hepburn Libraries (St. Lawrence Valley), NY, 237
Herbermann, Charles G., 490
Hewins, Caroline M., 786, 841
Hewlett-Woodmere Public Library, NY, 992
Hicks, Frederick C., 422
Hicksville Public Library, NY, 1025
High Point Public Library, NC, 250
Highland County District Library, OH, 288
Hild, Frederick H., 173
Hill, Frank, 778
Hiram College Library, OH, 516, 520
Hitchcock, Edward, 469
Hoadly, Charles J., 685
Hofstra University Library, NY, 1104
Holy Family College Library, PA, 533
Honnold Library, CA, 419
Honnold, William L., 419
Hoole, William S., 842
Hoover, Herbert, 630
Hoover Institution on War, Revolution and Peace Library, CA, 630
Horse racing, 620
Hospital library service, 227
Hospodor, Blaise, 474
Houston Lyceum, TX, 52, 345
Houston Public Library, TX, 51, 345, 354, 832, 843, 865, 1088
Howard, Mrs. Henry, 781
Howard University Library, DC, 432

Hubbard Public Library, OH, 282
Hudson, David, 264
Hudson Library and Historical Society, OH, 264
Hughes, Thomas, 340
Hummel, Arthur W., 607
Hunter, Aaron B., 496
Huntingdon County Library, PA, 335
Huntington Historical Society Library, NY, 1120
Huntington Library, NY, 1047
Huntington, NY, 998
H.W. Wilson Co., 951

Ibbetson, J.D., 482
Ideson, Julia B., 843
Illinois, 169-174, 380, 392, 409, 437-446, 564, 568, 586, 588, 639, 656, 688, 719, 738, 752, 788, 808, 824, 860, 864, 870-871, 1144
Illinois Association of School Librarians, 788
Illinois State Library, 688
Illinois State Penitentiary Library, 568
Illinois, University of, Library, 409, 444-446, 564, 719, 738, 1144
Illinois, University of, Library School, 870
Immigrant in children's fiction, 636
Index to Periodical Literature, 860
Index to Religious Periodical Literature, 782
Indiana, 12, 175-181, 409, 447-448, 590, 639, 657, 689
Indiana State Library, 179-180, 689
Indiana University Library, 409, 447
Indianapolis Public Library, IN, 175-177, 828
Industrial relations research libraries, 564
Institute for Scientific Information, PA, 951
Institute of Life Insurance Library, NY, 1121
Instructional materials center, 642
International exchanges, 882
International relations, 771
Iowa, 182-186, 392, 409, 449-450, 564, 658
Iowa Association of School Librarians, 658, 881, 888
Iowa Library Association, 658
Iowa State College, 392
Iowa State Library Commission, 881
Iowa State University Library, 409

Iowa, University of, Library, 409, 450, 564, 888
Islip Public Library, NY, 1038
Isom, Mary F., 319

Jackson Public Library, MS, 216
Jackson Public Library, OH, 296
Jacksonville Public Library, FL, 156
Japanese library development, 747, 945
Jefferson Medical College Library, PA, 573
Jefferson, Thomas, 5, 14, 472, 552, 728, 844
Jesse Merritt Memorial Library, NY, 1005
Jewett, Charles C., 536, 713, 717, 721, 723-725, 1148
Jewish Theological Seminary of America Library, NY, 1105
Joeckel, Carleton B., 772
John Jermain Memorial Library, NY, 1045
Johns Hopkins University Library, MD, 387
Johns Hopkins University Medical Library, MD, 464
Johnson C. Smith University Library, NC, 492
Johnston County Public Library System, NC, 241
Johnston, Victoria, 476
Jones, E. Kathleen, 570
Jones, J. Elias, 449
Jones, Olive B., 510
Jordan, Mrs. Archibald N., 224
Jordan, Robert, 412
Joseph Conrad Memorial Library, NY, 1119
Joseph Mann Library, WI, 376
Joseph, Ruzicka, Inc., 956
Journal of the Franklin Institute, 623
Journal of the History of Medicine and Allied Sciences, 878
Julius Rosenwald Fund, 341, 671, 811

Kansas, 187-188, 451-452
Kansas City Public Library, MO, 978
Kansas State Teachers College Library, 451-452
Keayne, Robert, 96
Keeneland Association Library, KY, 620
Kemp Public Library, TX, 346
Kensington, CT, 141

Kent Free Library, OH, 281
Kentucky, 41, 392, 453-455, 577, 620, 659, 807
Kentucky, University of, Library, 392
Keogh, Andrew, 428
Keppel, Frederick P., 404
Ketchikan Public Library, AK, 124
Kilbourne, George, 263
Kilgore Public Library, TX, 348
Killingsworth, CT, 67
Kinkeldey, Otto, 948
Kirk, Edward C., 576
Kittitas County Library, WA, 364
Klebs, Arnold, 878
Klopper, Henry A., 600
Knight, Hattie M., 1149
Knoxville Public Library, TN, 342
Kornhauser Memorial Medical Library, KY, 577
Krauth Memorial Library, PA, 535
Kuhlman, A.F., 433

La Retama Public Library, TX, 350
La Salle College Library, PA, 530
Lackawanna Public Library, NY, 228
Ladies Circulating Library, CT, 67
Ladies' Library Association, MI, 50
Lafayette College Library, PA, 534
Lakewood Public Library, OH, 287
Lancaster Library Company, PA, 61
Land-grant university libraries, 385, 409, 413
Lane, Clark, 260
Lane Public Library, OH, 260
Lanier, Sidney, 22
Lansing Public Library, MI, 209
Latin American Cooperative Acquisitions Project, 1096
Law libraries, 899, 1128
Law profession, 922
Law school libraries, 629
Lawrence, Abbott, 96
Lea, Henry, 523
Leaf, Harriet W., 297

Subject Index 449

Leavenworth Public Library, KS, 188
Leaves of Grass, 938
Lebanon, CT, early libraries, 65
Ledbetter, Eleanor, 310
Lee County Library, MS, 217
Lee Public Library, TX, 1086
Legler, Henry E., 173
LeMoyne College Library, NY, 564
Lenox Association Library, MA, 975
Lenox, James, 96
Leo Beck Institute Library, NY, 1126
Leonard Case Library, OH, 508
Lepper Library, OH, 276
Lepper, Virginia, 276
Lester, Robert M., 76, 404
Lewis, Willard P., 548
Lewiston Public Library, ME, 193
Lexington, KY, libraries in, 41
Leypoldt, Frederick, 773, 845
Liberal arts college libraries, 411, 735
Library and information science, 897, 902, 921-924, 932, 949, 953, 959, 962-964, 1158, 1172
Library assistants, 759
Library Association of Portland, OR, 319
Library Commission of Delaware, 151
Library Company of Philadelphia, PA, 48, 59, 831
Library education, 739-760, 783, 1172-1173
Library finances, 927
Library history, 863
Library instruction, 736
Library Journal, 82, 733, 773, 816, 845, 895, 905, 919, 1164
Library of Congress Cataloging Code, 723
Library of Congress, DC, 24, 597, 602, 607, 609, 615, 714, 718, 723, 728, 778, 863, 873-877, 1150-1151, 1157
Library of Congress Filing Rules, 718
Library of Hawaii, 168
Library of the Sixth District School, CT, 36
Library of the Windsor Congregational Church, CT, 36
Library Quarterly, 752, 895, 925
Library Services Act, 103, 763
Library War Service, 778

Library-college movement, 412
Library-School Council of Wethersfield, CT, 143
Lima Public Library, OH, 258, 272
Lindenhurst Memorial Library, NY, 1055
Lindquist, Raymond C., 261
Literary Bulletin, 845
Literary society libraries, 386, 410, 414, 516, 520
Little Rock Public Library, AR, 129
Logan, James, 25
Long Beach City College Library, CA, 418
Long Beach Public Library, NY, 995
Long Island Library Resources Council, NY, 1137
Longfellow, Henry W., 457
Lorain Public Library, OH, 1080
Los Angeles City College Library, CA, 418
Los Angeles Public Library, CA, 131, 134
Louisiana, 11, 17, 19, 53, 189-192, 385, 403, 456, 660, 690, 872, 973
Louisiana State Library, 192, 690
Louisiana State University Library, 403
Louisville Free Public Library, KY, 807
Louisville, University of, Library, KY, 453-454, 577
Lowe, John A., 235, 846
Loyola University Library, IL, 564
Lubetzky, Seymour, 713
Lucy Wortham James Memorial Library, MO, 984
Ludington, Flora B., 764
Lutheran Theological Seminary Library, PA, 535
Lutheran Theological Southern Seminary Library, SC, 538
Lyceum of Natural History Library, NY, 710
Lydenberg, Harry M., 720
Lyle, Guy R., 433
Lynbrook Public Library, NY, 1002

MacDonald, Angus S., 848
MacLeish, Archibald, 1150
Macon Public Library, GA, 165
Madison, East Guilford, CT, 146
Madison, James, 14, 24
Madison Library Association, CT, 146
Madison Public Library, WI, 374

Subject Index

Maine, 193-194, 457-458, 974
Maine, University of, Library, 458
Malverne Public Library, NY, 1009
Mamaroneck Free Library, NY, 1053
Management theories and libraries, 95
Manhasset Public Library, NY, 1017
Manhattanville College of the Sacred Heart Library, NY, 487
Mann, Horace, 849
Mann, Margaret, 719
Mansfield Public Library, OH, 1079
Manufacturer's and Mechanics' Library Association, ME, 193
Map cataloging, 708
Marian Library, OH, 513
Marin County Free Library, CA, 133
Marine Historical Association Library, CT, 582
Marion County Library, IN, 178
Martin, Lowell, 107
Martin, Mary P., 298
Marvin, Cornelia C., 704
Maryland, 26, 30-31, 78, 195-202, 459-468, 564, 571, 580, 604, 625, 661, 691-692
Maryland State Library, 691-692
Massachusetts, 40, 46, 63, 77, 108, 203-208, 380, 391-392, 402, 408, 469-471, 564, 584, 814, 816-818, 836, 849, 860, 880, 887, 938, 975, 1098, 1114, 1143
Massachusetts Historical Society Library, 584
Massachusetts Institute of Technology Library, 402, 564
Massachusetts State Board of Education, 849
Massapequa Public Library, NY, 999, 1054
Massillon Public Library, OH, 1074
Mather, Cotton, 25
Mattituck Free Library, NY, 1019
McBane, Mrs. B.F., 248
McCarthyism, 933
McDiarmid, Errett W., 847
McElmeel, Bonita, 474
McKavitt, Mathew A., 600
McKim, Charles F., 206
McNeal, Archie, 434
Media, professionalization, 963
Media services, 232, 637, 649

Medical libraries, 464, 493, 571-581, 722, 878, 1111
Medical Library Association, 119, 789-790, 1138
Medical library education, 746
Medical subject headings, 722, 731
Memphis, TN, 343
Mennonite Historical Society Library, IN, 590
Mentor Library Association, OH, 291
Mentor Library Company, OH, 291
Mentor Public Library, OH, 291-292
Mentor Village Library Association, OH, 291
Mercantile libraries, 35, 39, 46, 59, 84
Mercantile Library Association of Boston, MA, 46
Mercer University Library, GA, 436
Merrick Library, NY, 1067
Metric Bureau, 823
Miami Public Library, FL, 155, 157
Miami, University of, Library, FL, 434
Michigan, 50, 209-211, 409, 472-473, 564, 693, 805, 821
Michigan State Library, 409, 693
Michigan State University Library, 564
Michigan, University of, Library, 409, 472-473, 564, 805, 821
Micro Photo, 397
Microcard Editions, 397
Micropublishing, 397
Middle States Association of Colleges and Secondary Schools, 384
Midwest Interlibrary Center, IL, 392
Milam, Carl H., 622, 772, 778, 850
Milford, CT, 142
Mill town libraries, 99
Millersville State Teachers College, PA, 756
Milsap, John E.T., 345
Mineola Memorial Library, NY, 1044
Minneapolis, MN, 634
Minneapolis Public Library, MN, 212-213
Minnesota, 212-215, 401, 474-477, 564, 584, 634, 662, 847
Minnesota Federation of Women's Clubs, 215
Minnesota Historical Society Library, 584
Minnesota, University of, Library, 401, 475, 564, 847
Mississippi, 216-218, 385, 403, 478, 694
Mississippi Library Commission, 694
Mississippi, University of, Library, 403, 478

Subject Index 453

Missouri, 2, 7, 8, 708, 219, 479, 663, 791, 809, 976-984, 1097, 1099, 1115, 1139, 1171
Missouri Association of School Librarians, 791
Missouri Library Commission, 1139
Missouri, University of, Library, 479, 1099
Missouri, University of, Library School, 1171
Mitelin, Thomas, 24
Modesto Junior College Library, CA, 418
Monessen Public Library, PA, 322
Monroe, Harriet, 443
Monroe, James, 552
Monroe Public Library, LA, 191
Montgomery Public Library, AL, 122
Monti, Minnie S., 851
Moore, Anne C., 852-853
Morgan State College, MD, 467
Morsch, Lucile M., 764
Morton, Florrinell F., 764
Morton Penny-Packer Collection, NY, 1041
Mount Holyoke College, MA, 379
Mount Union College Library, OH, 511
Mount Vernon Public Library, NY, 1001
Mount Vernon Public Library, OH, 279
Mudge, Isadore G., 854
Munn, Russell, 301
Murphy Public Library, NC, 242
Museums, 819
Music libraries and librarianship, 111, 118, 873, 931, 948, 1048
Music Library Association, 792-793
Muskingum College Library, OH, 515

Napoleon Public Library, OH, 285
Nashville Public Library, TN, 344
Nashville University Library, TN, 540
Nassau County Law Library, NY, 1006
Nassau County Library Association Union Catalog, NY, 732
Nassau County, NY, 1009
Nassau-Suffolk Library Association, NY, 1140
Nation, 816, 907
National Advisory Commission on Libraries, 772

National Bureau of Standards Library, MD, 598
National Council of Teachers of English, 774
National Education Association, 774
National Institutes of Health Library, MD, 580
National Library of Medicine, MD, 571-572, 722
National Plan for Libraries (1935), 772
National Program for Cataloging and Acquisitions, 601, 609, 1095
National Union Catalog, 1161
Nebraska, 220-221, 695
Nebraska State Library, 220
Nebraska, University of, Library, 888
Negro Society for Historical Research, 869
Negroes. *See* Blacks
Nesbitt, Elizabeth, 757
Networks, 960
New Britain Institute Library, CT, 621
New City Free Library, NY, 1064
New England Deposit Library, MA, 391, 1114
New Hampshire, 42, 408, 696
New Hampshire State Library, 696
New Haven Free Public Library, CT, 145
New Jersey, 62, 104, 222-225, 391, 408, 416, 480, 564, 567, 664, 697, 727, 863, 1154
New Jersey Library Association, 222
New Jersey State Library, 697
New Mexico, 481, 698, 802
New Mexico, library extension, 698, 802
New Mexico State University Library, 481
New Mexico, University of, Library, 802
New Orleans Commercial Library Society, LA, 53
New Orleans, LA, early libraries, 17, 53
New Orleans Public Library, LA, 189
New Philadelphia-Tuscarawas County District Library, OH, 266
New York, 13, 43, 52, 58, 78, 108, 226-239, 380, 392, 402, 408, 482-491, 563-565, 568, 584, 592, 618, 622, 627-628, 665, 699, 710, 715, 727, 729, 732, 803, 820, 822-823, 845-846, 852-854, 869, 911, 985-1069, 1100-1107, 1116-1126, 1137, 1141, 1145, 1147, 1153, 1156, 1160, 1166
New York Academy of Medicine Library, 1124
New York Circulating Library for the Blind, 233
New York Herald Tribune, Library, 565

SUBJECT INDEX 455

New York Hospital Library, 710
New York Institute Library, 1117
New York Mercantile Library, 710
New York Public Library, 58, 78, 100, 226, 229, 231, 233, 238-239, 715, 803, 820, 852-853, 869, 1024, 1031, 1052, 1155
New York Public Library, Lincoln Center, 1020, 1048
New York Society for the Suppression of Vice, 77, 934-935
New York Society Library, 52, 710
New York State Library, 699
New York Times, 563, 911, 1160
New York University Library, 484
New-York Historical Society Library, 584, 592, 710
New Zealand, 944
Newark Public Library, NJ, 62
Newberry Library, IL, 860
Newbery Medal Award, 641, 1163
Newbery, Walter, 96, 641
Newsletter on Intellectual Freedom, 940
Newspaper Libraries, 2, 930, 1031
Newton Library Company, PA, 61
Nicholson Memorial Library, TX, 348, 1090
Normal School Libraries, 381, 416
Norristown Public Library, PA, 334
North American Review, 816-817
North Bellmore Public Library, NY, 1034
North Bristol Library, CT, 146
North Carolina, 240-253, 403, 492-505, 666-667, 700-701, 730, 736, 753, 811, 956, 1070
North Carolina Agriculture and Technical College Library, 503
North Carolina Library Association, 243
North Carolina Library Commission, 251, 700
North Carolina State Library, 701
North Carolina, University of, Library, 403, 493-496, 498, 500-501, 730, 736
North Carolina, University of, School of Library Science, 753
North Carolina, University of, Woman's College Library, Greensboro, NC, 499
North Dakota, 254
North Merrick Public Library, NY, 1039
North Texas State College Library, 842

Northeast Regional Library, MS, 218
Northport-East Northport Public Libraries, NY, 1013
Norwalk Public Library, OH, 302
Notre Dame, University of, Library, IN, 830

Oak Hill Public Library, OH, 296
Oberlin College Library, OH, 521, 866, 1152
Obituaries, prominent librarians, 911
Oceanside Free Library, NY, 1046
Ohio, 39, 54, 60, 66, 78, 255-316, 409, 506-522, 567, 569, 591, 594, 611, 624, 632, 668, 702-703, 754, 825-826, 852, 855, 860-861, 866, 871, 881, 883, 885, 960, 1071-1084, 1141, 1152
Ohio Agricultural Experiment Station Library, 611
Ohio College Library Center, 960, 1141
Ohio State Library, 257, 703, 855
Ohio State Penitentiary Library, 569
Ohio State Traveling Library, 702
Ohio State University Library, 409, 510, 519
Ohio Wesleyan University Library, 512
Oklahoma, 77, 317, 401
Oklahoma, University of, Library, 401
Olcott, Frances J., 757
Old Librarians' Almanac, 858
Old Lyme, CT, 67
Old Saybrook, CT, 67
O'Leary, Arthur, 431
Olivia Raney Library, NC, 245
Omaha Public Library, NB, 221
O'Meara, Eva J., 948
Onondaga County Public Library, NY, 234
Oregon, 6, 16, 318-320, 704, 859, 1085
Oregon State Library, 704, 859
Osterhout Free Library, PA, 323
Osterhout, Isaac S., 323
Otterbein College Library, OH, 522
Owen, Thomas M., 856
Oxford Public Library, PA, 332
Ozark Regional Library, MO, 219

Subject Index 457

Palm, Swante, 547
Panizzi, Anthony, 713, 723, 725
Parish libraries, 14
Parker, Ralph, 479
Parochial libraries. See Bray, Thomas
Pasadena City College Library, CA, 418
Patten, Frank C., 857
Peabody, George, 96, 625
Peabody Institute Library, MD, 625
Peabody Library, DC, 154
Pearson, Edmund L., 858
Peithologian Society, NY, 410
Peninsula Library and Historical Society, OH, 290
Peninsula Public Library, NY, 1060
Pennsylvania, 48, 59, 61, 321-335, 408, 523-535, 567, 573, 575-576, 579, 584-585, 596, 623, 669, 727, 755-757, 812, 831, 835, 845, 967
Pennsylvania Historical Society Library, 584
Pennsylvania, University of, Library, 408, 523, 528, 575-576, 727
Pensacola Public Library, FL, 159
People's Library, CT, 146
People's University, 93
Pepper, George, 324
Perkins, Frederic B., 765
Perkins Library, OH, 303
Perry, Amos, 583
Personnel, 926, 958
Peterson, Odrun, 476
Pettigrew Regional Library, NC, 249
Phelps, Ralph H., 628
Philadelphia Apprentice's Library, PA, 59
Philadelphia Athenaeum, PA, 59
Philadelphia City Institute Library, PA, 59
Philadelphia Commercial Museum Library, PA, 585
Philadelphia, early libraries, PA, 48, 59
Philadelphia German Society Library, PA, 59
Philadelphia Union Club Library Association, OH, 266
Philagrammatican Library, CT, 65
Philanthropy, academic libraries, 399. *See also* Carnegie and Peabody
Philbrick, John D., 652
Philolexian Society, NY, 410
Philomathesian Society, OH, 300

Philosophical Society of Texas, 345
Philosophy of library science, 1158, 1172
Phoenix College Library, AZ, 417
Phonograph records. See Music libraries
Pierce, Cornelia M., 859
Pittsburgh, University of, Library, PA, 567
Plainedge Public Library, NY, 997
Plainview-Old Bethpage Public Library, NY, 1059
Plainville Public Library, CT, 148
Plummer, Mary W., 764
Pogge, Leonard, 474
Poole, William F., 173, 387, 721, 724, 773, 860, 917
Pope Pius XII Library, CT, 423
Poquonock Social Library, CT, 36
Port Jefferson Library, NY, 1011
Port Washington Public Library, NY, 993
Portage County Library, OH, 271
Portland Library Association, OH, 300
Portland Public Library, ME, 194, 974
Portland Public Library, OR, 1085
Power, Effie L., 303, 861
Power, Eugene, 397
Prairie View University, TX, 385
Pratt, Enoch, 96
Pratt Institute Free Library, NY, 852-853
Presidential libraries, 1108, 1118
Prince George's County Public Library, MD, 196, 199
Princeton University Library, NJ, 391, 408, 480, 564, 567, 727, 863
Prison libraries, 1109
Protestant Episcopal Theological Seminary Library, VA, 550
Providence Public Library, RI, 336
Public health, 949
Public Law 480 Program, 601, 612, 1095
Public Libraries, 801
Public libraries: adult education, 87, 98, 100, 114; architecture, 105; benefactors, 96; blacks, 969; business, 106; causal factors, 84-85; censorship, 112; collections, 118; Congress, 104; courts, 116; depression, 92, 970; economic conditions, 92, 94, 97; freedom to read, 89; Great Books movement, 109; housed in schools, 117; immigrants, 965; leaders, 88; management, 95; medical collections, 119; notables, 75; People's University, 93; social institutions, 110;

SUBJECT INDEX 459

unions, 91; working class origin, 108
Public Libraries in the U.S. (1876), 82, 113, 773
Public Library Commission of Indiana, 179
Public Library Inquiry (1950), 113
Public Works Administration, 349
Publishers' Weekly, 845
Purdue University, IN, 409
Putnam County, TN, 339
Putnam, Herbert, 778, 1151

Quarterly Cumulative Index Medicus, 731
Queens Borough Public Library, NY, 227, 1036

Railroad reading rooms, OH, 60
Raines, Caldwell W., 862
Randolph Public Library, NC, 246
Raney, McKendree L., 778
Raney, Richard B., 245
Rare book collections, 401
Ratchford, Fannie E., 549
Rathbone, Josephine A., 764
Ravenna Public Library, OH, 267
Raymond, Jerome H., 559
Reader advisory service, 901
Readers' Guide to Periodical Literature, 860
Readex Microprint, 397
Reading Public Library, PA, 329
Reading research, 959
Reading tastes, 2, 4-9, 11-12, 15-22, 25-26
Redwood, Abraham, 57
Redwood City Library Association, CA, 132
Redwood City Public Library, CA, 132
Redwood Library and Athenaeum, RI, 57
Reed, Byron, 221
Reed Memorial Library, OH, 267
Reference instruction, courses in library schools, 748
Reference services, 733-738, 854, 901, 951, 1156, 1168
Research and library resources, 400
Reynolds, E. Smith, 502

Reynolds, Mortimer F., 235
Rhode Island, 57, 336, 391, 408, 536-537, 583, 829
Rhode Island Historical Association Library, 583
Richardson, Ernest C., 863
Richardson, Henry H., 79
Rider, Fremont, 397, 786
Rio Grande Chapter of the Special Libraries Association, 795
Riverhead Free Library, NY, 1061
Roanoke College Library, VA, 551
Robert Bacon Memorial Library, NY, 108, 1068
Robert F. Kidd Library, WV, 557
Rochester Athenaeum, NY, 235
Rochester Public Library, NY, 235, 846
Rockefeller, John D., 96
Rockingham County Library, NC, 248
Rockingham Public Library, VA, 363
Rockville Centre Public Library, NY, 1033
Rocky River Public Library, OH, 268
Roden, Carl B., 173, 864
Rogan, Octavia F., 865
Rome Public Library, GA, 164
Roorbach, Orville, 49
Roosevelt, Franklin D., 618
Root, Azariah S., 866, 1152
Rosenberg Library, TX, 857
Rosenwald, Julius, 341, 671
Roslyn Public Library, WA, 364
Rothrock, Mary U., 614, 764
Round, J. Emory, 467
Rundel, Morton W., 235
Rural libraries, 810, 838
Russell Library Company, CT, 140
Russell Sage Foundation Library, NY, 491
Rutgers University Library, NJ, 408, 564

Sabin, Joseph, 867
Saint Joseph College Library, MD, 468, 564
Salem College Library, WV, 558
Salem Public Library, OH, 259
Salisbury Public Library, NC, 240

Subject Index 461

Sam Rayburn Library, TX, 356
San Antonio Public Library, TX, 77, 834, 837
San Francisco, CA, early libraries, 34
San Francisco Mercantile Library Association, CA, 34
San Jose State College Library, CA, 564
San Mateo County Library, CA, 130
San Quentin Prison Library, 568
Sanders, Minerva, 917
Sandusky Library Association, OH, 300
Sandusky Lyceum, OH, 300
Santa Cruz Public Library, CA, 135
Santa Fe Public Library, NM, 834
Sarah Hull Hallock Free Library, NY, 1021
Saturday Review of Literature, 820
Savannah Public Library, GA, 161
Sayville Library, NY, 1037
Scheuber, Jennie S., 868
Scheuber, Mrs. Charles, 349
Schomburg, Arthur A., 869
Schomburg Collection, New York Public Library, 239, 715, 869
School district libraries, 43, 70
School librarians, 644, 658
School libraries, 117, 123, 635-682, 840, 849, 872, 1129, 1140, 1167
Schuylkill College Library, PA, 524
Schwab, John C., 428
Science collections, 401
Scoggin, Margaret C., 1153
Scotland County Library, MO, 976
Scott, Carrie E., 176
Scott, Samuel P., 573
Seaford Public Library, NY, 1050
Secondary information services, 951
Security, 1165
Selden Public Library, NY, 1065
Sequin Guadalupe County Public Library, TX, 351
Serials cataloging, 712, 714
Shandelle, Henry, 431
Sharp, Katharine L., 444-446, 719, 870
Sheehan, Helen, 412
Shelter Rock Public Library, NY, 1057
Shera, Jesse H., 107, 871

Sherman Public Library, TX, 1091
Shores, Louis, 412
Shortess, Lois F., 660, 872
Sibley, Ruth, 170
Silas Bronson Library, CT, 147
Sill, Edward R., 280
Sillers, Dan, 412
Silver Springs Public Library, MD, 201
Sing Sing Prison Library, NY, 568
Sioux City Public Library, IA, 184
Skinner, Eliza J., 559
Sloan, Earl L., 265
Smith, Carleton S., 792, 948
Smith, G. Donald, 554
Smith, Miss Clyde, 245
Smithsonian Institution Library, DC, 401
Smithtown Library, NY, 1007
Social libraries, 6, 10, 36-37, 45, 47-48, 50-54, 56, 63-65, 67-69, 84
Social Responsibilities Round Table, 1132
Social Sciences Citation Index, 921
Social work, 922, 949
Society of American Archivists, 947
Society of California Pioneers Library, 584
Society of the Four Arts Library, FL, 633
Sociology literature, 892
Solon Public Library, OH, 293
Sonneck, Oscar G.T., 873, 948
Sound recordings, 383
South, antebellum, 4, 14, 69
South Bend Public Library, IN, 181
South Carolina, 9, 64, 69, 337, 403, 538, 670, 810
South Carolina, University of, Library, 403
South Dakota, 338
South Dakota State University Library, 338
South Dakota, University of, Library, 338
South Huntington Public Library, NY, 1062
Southern Association of Colleges and Secondary Schools, 123, 676
Southern Connecticut State College Library, 427
Southern Methodist University Library, TX, 542
Southern University Library, LA, 385
Southwestern Baptist Theological Seminary Library, TX, 827

Subject Index

Southwestern Library Association, 794, 838
Southwestern Louisiana Institute Library, 456, 872
Spain, Frances L., 764
Special Libraries, 898
Special Libraries Association, 742, 795
Spelling Reform Association, 823
Spenser, Gwladys, 107
Spivacke, Harold, 948
Spofford, Ainsworth R., 787, 874-877
Springfield Circulating Library, MA, 202
Springfield Library Company, MA, 203
Springfield Public Library, MA, 203, 208, 818
St. Edward's University Library, TX, 830
St. John's College Library, MD, 463
St. John's University Library, MN, 477
St. Joseph College Library, CT, 423
St. Louis, MO, early libraries, 2
St. Louis Public Library, MO, 809, 861, 980, 983
St. Paul, MN, 634
St. Thomas College Library, MN, 474
St. Vincent Archabbey Libraries, PA, 531
St. Vincent DePaul Seminary Library, FL, 1097
Stanford University Library, CA, 402, 564
Stanton, Madeline E., 878
Starges, William, 512
State university libraries, 403
Statesboro Regional Library, GA, 163
Steig, Lewis, 107
Steiner, Bernard, 197
Steiner, Lewis, 197
Stenson Memorial Library, NY, 987
Sterling, John, 96
Stetson, Willis K., 145
Stevens, Henry, 473
Stevenson, Burton E., 778
Stillwell, Margaret B., 537
Storage libraries, 392
Storytelling, 175, 231, 635, 803, 820
Stow Public Library, OH, 1084
Stuckert, Beatrice S., 1154
Submarine Force Library, CT, 1113

Subscription Books Committee, ALA, 775
Suffolk County Community College Library, NY, 1102
Sunday school libraries, 44
Supreme Court of the United States Library, DC, 605, 608
Survey of Libraries in the U.S. (1926), 113
Surveys, 382
Sweet, May, 310
Swingle, Walter T., 607
Syosset Public Library, NY, 1069

Taft, Robert A., 284
Talbot County Free Library, MA, 205
Taylor, Henry A., 142
Taylor Memorial Library, OH, 1072
Teachers College Library, NY, 486
Teaneck Free Library, NJ, 224
Teenage Library Association of Texas, 799
Temple University Library, PA, 835
Temple University, Medical School Library, PA, 579
Tennessee, 45, 339-344, 385, 403, 539-540, 614, 671, 705, 796-797
Tennessee Library Association, 796-797
Tennessee State Library, 705
Tennessee State University Library, 385
Tennessee Valley Authority, 614
Tennessee, University of, Library, 403
Texas, 51, 77, 345-360, 385, 541-549, 672-677, 706-707, 758-759, 795, 798-800, 813, 827, 830, 832-834, 837-838, 840, 843, 857, 862, 865, 868, 879, 884, 920, 1086-1092, 1127
Texas A & M University, Library, 865
Texas Christian University Library, 813
Texas College of Arts and Industries Library, 544
Texas Library Association, 798, 800, 833-834, 838, 862, 868, 884
Texas Library Journal, 920
Texas Southern University Library, 546
Texas State Library, 706-707, 862, 865, 884
Texas Technical College Library, 884
Texas, University of, Library, 541, 545, 547, 549, 833-834, 865
Theater libraries, 1020, 1112
Theological seminary libraries, 388-389, 395
Thomas Hughes Free Public Library, TN, 340

Subject Index 465

Thomas, Isaiah, 532
Thoreau, Henry D., 22
Ticknor, George, 96, 204, 880
Tilton, Edward L., 105
Titcomb, Mary, 226
Toledo Public Library, OH, 257, 277, 294
Tompkins, Julia, 150
Torrey, Jesse, 43
Training for Library Service (1923), 886
Transylvania University Library, KY, 41, 455
Traveling Libraries, 83, 226
Trenton Free Public Library, NJ, 223
Trinity College Library, CT, 427
Trinity College Library, DC, 430
Troup-Harris-Coweta Regional Library, GA, 972
Troy Public Library, OH, 1075
Trumbull, I. Hammond, 685
Tucker, St. George, 5
Tyler, Alice S., 764, 881

Union Library Company, CT, 36
Union Library Company, PA, 62
Union List of Serials, 720
Union Seminary Library, PA, 524
Union Theological Seminary Library, NY, 489
Unions, 81, 91, 212, 957
United Nations Library, NY, 622, 850
United States Air Force Library Service, 616
United States Atomic Energy Commission, 951
United States Congress, 24, 734
United States Department of Justice Library, DC, 600
United States Department of Labor Library, DC, 564
United States, Department of State, Division of Cultural Relations, 771
United States Department of the Interior Library, DC, 606
United States Geological Survey Library, CA, 617
United States Information Agency Libraries, 1110
United States Military Academy Library, NY, 1103
United States Naval Academy Library, MD, 465
United States Tariff Commission Library, DC, 613
United States Weather Bureau Library, MD, 604

University Microforms, 397
Urban public library, 86
Urban research library, 484
Urbana Free Library, IL, 169
Ursinus College Library, PA, 529
Ursuline College Library, OH, 518
Utah, 1093

Vail, R.W.G., 592
Valley Stream Public Library, NY, 988
Van Name, Addison, 428, 786
Vanderbilt University Library, TN, 71
Vassar College Library, NY, 485
Vermont, 678
Virginia, 5, 18, 20-21, 25, 47, 361-363, 391, 403, 408, 550-553, 581, 679-680, 728
Virginia Gazette, 18
Virginia, University of Library, 403, 581, 728
Vormelker, Rose L., 312, 883, 1155

Wagnall's Memorial, OH, 273
Wagnalls, Adam W., 273
Wagnalls-Jones, Mabel, 273
Wagner College Library, NY, 1101
Waitman Barbe Public Library, WV, 371
Wake Forest College Library, NC, 502
Wall, Alexander, 592
Walla Walla Public Library, WA, 366
Walter Hampden Memorial Library, NY, 1022
Waples, Douglas, 959
War and libraries, 778, 943, 955
Warder, Benjamin, 255
Warder Public Library, OH, 255
Warren, Althea H., 764
Warren Public Library, OH, 1073
Warren Public Library, PA, 331
Washington, 364-370, 554-556, 564, 681
Washington Academy, TN, 339
Washington and Lee University, VA, 47
Washington County Free Library, MD, 200

Subject Index 467

Washington State Library, 368
Washington State University Library, 554-555
Washington, University of, Library, 556, 564
Watch and Ward Society, 77
Waterman, Minerva, 135
Waterson, George, 734
Watkins, David, 474
Wayland, Francis, 96, 336, 536
Wayne County Public Library, OH, 1078
Webster, Caroline, 778
Webster City Public Library, IA, 184
Welland, James, 107
Welliston Public Library, OH, 296
Wellman, Hiller C., 208
Wells, Philip P., 422
Wesley, John, 496
Wesleyan University Library, CT, 379
West Division Book Society, West Hartford, CT, 144
West Grove Library, PA, 332
West Hartford Library Association, CT, 144
West Hartford Public Library, CT, 144
West Islip Public Library, NY, 1012
West Plain Library, CT, 148
West Virginia, 371-372, 557-560, 1142
West Virginia Library Association, 372
West Virginia Library Commission, 1142
West Virginia University Library, 559
West Virginia Wesleyan College Library, 558
West, Elizabeth H., 884
Westbury Memorial Public Library, NY, 1051
Westchester Library System, NY, 236
Western Maryland College Library, 461
Western Reserve Historical Society Library, OH, 594
Western Reserve, OH, early libraries, 66, 278
Western Reserve University Library, OH, 507-508
Western Reserve University, Library School, OH, 754, 881
Westhampton Free Library, NY, 1010
Wheeler, Joseph L., 105, 142, 197
Whig Society Library, NJ, 480
White, John G., 885
White Oak District Library, CT, 148

White Plains Public Library, NY, 986
White, William A., 452, 640
Whitman County, WA, 370
Whitney, James L., 765
Whittlessey Academy of Arts and Sciences, OH, 302
William Allen White Book Award, 640
William Allen White Memorial Library, KS, 452
William and Mary College Library, VA, 391, 408, 552
William L. Clements Library, MI, 473
Williams College Library, MA, 379, 846
Williams, Edward C., 432
Williams, George P., 472
Williamsburg Free Public Library, NC, 1070
Williamson, Charles C., 488, 638, 740, 749, 886
Williamson, Hugh, 24
Williston Park Public Library, NY, 990
Willoughby Public Library, OH, 289
Wilson Library Bulletin, 890
Wilson, Louis R., 433, 496, 700, 772
Wilson, Martha, 662
Winchell, Constance M., 1156
Windsor Book Club, CT, 36
Windsor Congregational Church Library, CT, 36
Windsor, Phineas L., 444, 446, 545, 738
Windsor Public Library, CT, 36
Winkler, Ernest W., 545
Winship, George P., 473
Winslow, Amy, 261
Winsor, Justin, 765, 773, 887, 917
Winston-Salem Public Library, NC, 247
Winthrop, James, 532
Wisconsin, 373-378, 561-562, 564, 584, 589, 639, 682, 760
Wisconsin Free Library Commission, 373, 760
Wisconsin Historical Society Library, 584, 589
Wisconsin Library Association, 373
Wisconsin State College Library, 561
Wisconsin, University of, Library, 564
Wisconsin, University of, Library School, 760
Women, 56, 99, 637, 764, 949-950, 952, 964, 1174
Women's Christian Temperance Union, 56
Women's Reading Club of Walla Walla, WA, 366

SUBJECT INDEX

Woodruff, William 128
Woodstock College Library, MD, 459
Worcester Public Library, MA, 836
Working class, 107
Works Progress Administration, 252
World War I, 778, 955
World War II, 943
Worthington Public Library, OH, 1081
Wright, Ethel C., 294
Wyche, Benjamin, 545
Wyer, Malcolm G., 450, 684, 888

Yakima Valley Regional Library, WA, 369
Yale University Library, CT, 379-380, 391, 408, 422, 427-428, 564, 612, 726, 878
Yenching Library, MA, 471
Yonkers Public Library, Crestwood Branch, NY, 1014
Young adult service, 78, 1153
Young Men's Christian Association, 60
Young Men's Christian Association Historical Library, NY, 1125
Young Men's Mercantile Library Association of Cincinnati, OH, 39
Young, R.L., 481
Youngstown Library Association, OH, 295
Youngstown Public Library, OH, 257
Youngstown University Library, OH, 517
Yust, William F., 235

AUG 2 3 1990